A MODERN HISTORY OF JAMMU AND KASHMIR

VOLUME TWO

The Karan Singh Years (1949-1967)

HARBANS SINGH

SPEAKING TIGER

SPEAKING TIGER BOOKS LLP
125A, Ground Floor, Shahpur Jat, near Asiad Village,
New Delhi 110049

First published as *Karan Singh: Jammu & Kashmir (1949-1967)* in 2018
This revised edition published by Speaking Tiger in 2023

ISBN: 978-93-5447-515-3
eISBN: 978-93-5447-509-2

10 9 8 7 6 5 4 3 2 1

Typeset in Minion Pro by SŪRYA, New Delhi
Printed at Chaman Enterprises, New Delhi

Harbans Singh was born in Samba, in the Jammu region of Jammu and Kashmir. He began his career as a college professor before moving on to journalism and occasional writing. Over the years, he has worked as a reporter for the *Observer of Business and Politics*; been a book critic and reviewer for *The Tribune*, Chandigarh for over twenty years; and was a regular columnist for *Dainik Bhaskar*.

As a bilingual, Singh has authored books in both Hindi and English. His primary area of interest is Jammu and Kashmir. He is the author of *Sufi Satta aur Samaj*, written in Hindi, which examines the impact of Sufism on Jammu and Kashmir and the overall Indian society. His books in English include a trilogy on the history of Jammu and Kashmir that spans from 1925 to contemporary times.

Contents

Foreword by Karan Singh *vii*
Preface *xi*

1. 24th November 1952 1
2. The Early Winds 8
3. Prelude to Article 370 19
4. The Making of Article 370 33
5. A Document of Change 53
6. The Land Reforms 68
7. The Regent Settles Down 81
8. The Response 88
9. Finally, the Constituent Assembly 106
10. Setting the Agenda 117
11. The March of History 131
12. The Crisis 146
13. The Die is Cast 167
14. The Fall 187
15. Period of Consolidation 201
16. The Clash of the Titans 222
17. The Chapter Closes 239

18. Holy Relic and its Aftermath 250
19. A New Era 271
20. Renewed Battle for Control 283
21. The Onward Journey 294
Appendix 1: Jammu Agitation I 309
Appendix 2: Jammu Agitation II 311
Appendix 3: Letter to Sheikh Abdullah 313

Acknowledgements 320
Notes 321
Bibliography 338
Index 341

Foreword

Harbans Singh has emerged as a significant re-interpreter of Dogra history, specifically dealing with the period that begins with the reign of Maharaja Hari Singh. This volume is the second part of a trilogy—*A Modern History of Jammu and Kashmir*—about the contemporary political history of Jammu and Kashmir.

The first volume of the trilogy deals with the events during my father's reign. The author holds that it is unfortunate that Maharaja Hari Singh is remembered only for the accession of the State, which had come under very severe pressure due to the tribal invasion from Pakistan. He points out that from when my father ascended the *Gaddi* (throne) in 1925, all the way to 1946, he undertook a series of far-reaching and progressive measures, including throwing all temples doors open to the Harijans (Dalits); abolishing the obnoxious Forced Labour System of *begar*; paying attention to girl's education, which was far ahead of the situation in most of the rest of India; setting up first-class hospitals and colleges both in Srinagar and Jammu; beautifying the Dal Lake by constructing a boulevard; and so on. His first statement, after assuming the high office in 1925, was 'justice is my religion'. In a memorable speech at the Round Table Conference on Indian Constitutional Reforms held in London in 1930-1931, he had stated, 'As Indians and loyal to the land of our birth, we stand as solidly as the rest of our countrymen for our enjoyment of a position of honour and equality in the British Commonwealth.' All these seem to have been forgotten and his rule has been overshadowed by the accession imbroglio, which is grossly unfair. Sheikh Abdullah, who was bitterly anti-Dogra, had launched a protracted movement against the Maharaja way back in 1931, which fructified in the crisis of 1947. Abdullah had seized the opportunity during Partition and had come to oust Maharaja Hari Singh and assumed power himself with the blessings of Pandit Nehru. All of this led to my father virtually going into exile in Bombay (Mumbai) in 1949. It was only his ashes that I brought back to Jammu after he passed away in April 1961.

From the vantage point of hindsight, it may be easy to say that the Maharaja could have handled the entire crisis better but, in my *Autobiography*, I have recounted in some detail the events that took place during those tumultuous times, the difficulties my father faced during the political crises of Partition and also my ideological divergence from his views. Regretfully, he has received a lot of negative press and, therefore, I am glad that this first volume not only puts the Maharaja in the right focus but also highlights the valiant role of the Jammu and Kashmir State Forces that historians have generally ignored. Readers will, no doubt, judge my father more fairly than contemporary historians have done.

The next volume, *The Karan Singh Years (1949-1967)* covers the events of the eighteen years that I was the Head of State under three different appellations—first as Regent, then as Sadar-i-Riyasat and finally as the Governor. This period also saw the ten-year rule of Bakshi Ghulam Mohammad and also the advent of G.M. Sadiq, who drastically moved towards further integrating the State into the Indian Union. The Presidential Order was welcomed in 1964 and the nomenclature of the Sardar-i-Riyasat and Prime Minister was changed to Governor and Chief Minister respectively, in line with the other States of the Union. Harbans Singh brings out the fact that right from the beginning, in my correspondence with Pandit Jawaharlal Nehru, I constantly put forward the importance of Jammu and Ladakh, which were generally neglected due to the Delhi Kashmiri-centrism. This period also covers the arrest and prolonged exile of Sheikh Abdullah for over ten years, until he finally returned as Chief Minister in 1965 after an accord with Indira Gandhi. The second volume takes the story up to March 1967 when I resigned as Governor and joined Indira Gandhi's Cabinet as Minister for Tourism and Civil Aviation.

The third and final volume in this trilogy traverses the period of the history of the State from 1975 to contemporary times. This covers the beginning of aggressive militancy in 1988, which resulted, among other disasters, in the mass exodus of the highly talented Kashmiri-Pandit community from the Valley. The volume also studies the drastic and dramatic events of 5th August 2019 whereby the State was bifurcated for the second time, with Ladakh and Jammu and Kashmir becoming Union Territories. Harbans Singh has evidently studied this whole period closely and his trilogy will surely become essential for all those interested in the history of Jammu and Kashmir. The series is a welcome opportunity to understand the Dogra point of view and set right the blatant anti-Dogra distortions by some historians.

I commend Harbans Singh for performing such a valuable service and congratulate him for his detailed research, which, I am sure, will be widely read and appreciated.

KARAN SINGH
March 2023

Preface

A few more letters from the select correspondence of Karan Singh with Jawaharlal Nehru and Indira Gandhi, have been included in this new edition. Hopefully, they will help in the better appreciation of the contemporary events and contribute to a better critical evaluation of the role of the leading protagonists of that era. It is my earnest hope that these new additions will help in appreciating the hopes and fears of the past and in evaluating the direction that was taken later. Not much has been changed from the earlier edition (*Karan Singh: Jammu & Kashmir (1949-1967)*), except giving proper context to the new letters.

This second volume of the *A Modern History of Jammu and Kashmir* trilogy is, in a way, a sequel to the author's earlier book, *A Modern History of Jammu and Kashmir, Volume One: The Troubled Years of Maharaja Hari Singh (1925-1949)*. The earlier book examined the events and the forces that heralded an era of communal, confrontational and separatist politics in the erstwhile Princely State of Jammu and Kashmir, which saw the Ruler ranged against the emerging forces of the time—Sheikh Abdullah, Jawaharlal Nehru and Mohammad Ali Jinnah. This volume examines the politics of a period that followed the exit of Maharaja Hari Singh from the State. This period incrementally failed to come to terms with a State that was created by the genius of Maharaja Gulab Singh in the nineteenth century. As a result, the Jammu region and the Dogras were forced to launch a stir, the repercussions of which continue to reverberate even today.

During this period, the role of Dr Karan Singh, first as an eighteen-year-old Regent and then as the Sadar-i-Riyasat (Head of State), was pivotal. His presence, in Jammu and Srinagar with every Durbar move, ensured continuity and acknowledged the centrality of Jammu and the Dogras to the State. However, it was up to those who were wielding the real power, to maintain equitable power sharing between Jammu, Kashmir and Ladakh—the three remaining provinces left in State's control. The successive governments, particularly the one under Sheikh Abdullah, alienated Jammu and the Dogras to an unimaginable extent. Very early in his career, Yuvraj Karan Singh had raised the issue of Ladakh and the need to give it autonomy, to preserve its distinct culture. When the Jammu-based Praja Parishad agitation rocked the State and the country, the Yuvraj never lost an occasion to plead with Prime Minister Nehru to conduct a dialogue and take corrective steps.

The truth is that while numerous books have been written on the 'Kashmir problem', another issue of equal significance that should have been addressed by the policy makers and the historians, was the 'Jammu problem'. Dr Karan Singh repeatedly raised this issue, but in vain. He pleaded for the inclusion of Jammu and Kashmir in the North Zone of States Council; he suggested the inclusion of the State in the scheme of reorganization of the States, when Punjab was to be reorganized as Punjab, Haryana and Himachal Pradesh; and, he went to the extent of articulating the need to treat the State as any other Indian State and reorganize it in conformity with the lingual and cultural reality.

Failure to have these problems redressed was somewhat balanced by the judicious use of the provisions of Article 370 of the Indian Constitution to integrate the State with the Union to a larger extent. It was not without reason that the then Home Minister, Gulzarilal Nanda, claimed in the Lok Sabha that only a shell of Article 370 had remained; the rest of its contents had been emptied. The credit for this needs be given to Bakshi Ghulam Mohammad and Ghulam Mohammad Sadiq, the two former Prime Ministers of the State. Bakshi and Sadiq, along with Dr Karan Singh, are the ones responsible for writing the story of the integration of the State with the rest of the country, after a stormy relationship under the reign of Sheikh Abdullah. It was the combination of Dr Karan Singh and Ghulam Mohammad Sadiq that piloted the process of changing the nomenclature of the Head of the State and the Executive Head from Prime Minister to Chief Minister and Sadar-i-Riyasat to Governor respectively. This single act alone went a long way in breaking the psychological barrier between the State and the rest of the country.

Dr Karan Singh acted as the Executive Head of State for eighteen years and never, during those long years, did he step outside its constitutional boundaries. Though always correct, reticent and measured in his public conduct, his voluminous correspondence with Prime Minister Nehru and Indira Gandhi reveal that he was never short of words while expressing his dissent, contrary views or suggestions. Honest and patriotic to the core, he always kept the interests of the nation, the Dogras and the State in his mind. But eighteen years in a constitutional role seems like a lifetime, and therefore, by the end, he was yearning to play a more active role in politics. Although, he was called to participate more actively in the State politics from time to time, during those eighteen years, he had evolved as an individual and politician, and had begun to feel restless within the confines of the State. He aspired to fly in the vast sky but was told twice to stay put because of his indispensability to the State. However, the opportunity arose when he was invited by Indira Gandhi to join her Cabinet in 1967. At the age of thirty-six, Dr Karan Singh finally moved on to the bigger stage in New Delhi.

1

24th November 1952

He felt a knot in his stomach as the plane took off from Srinagar. No, it was not a fear of flying, but the anxiety of what he might face on landing in Jammu. He was aware of the outrage that the events of the past months had caused, and had also been told that the Jammu-based right-wing political party, the Praja Parishad had threatened a black flag demonstration on his arrival in Jammu. To his utter dismay, the threat had been carried out! He heard derisive and hostile slogans from people lined up on both sides of the road from the airport near Satwari to the palace gates. Bakshi Ghulam Mohammad, the Deputy Prime Minister of the State was accompanying him in an open jeep, and Bakshi and the National Conference had worked hard to bring the people to accord him a warm reception. But, they were actually swarmed by those holding and angrily waving black flags. Yuvraj Karan Singh had apprehended a protest, but the scale and intensity of it shook him. The hostility of the Dogras had spilled on to the roads. The bonds of the past appeared to have vanished and it did not matter to the people that he was the scion of the Dogra dynasty.

They were the same people who had given him a tumultuous welcome only a few years ago on his return from a long sojourn in the USA, when the chartered DC-3 had touched down at Jammu. Though the people knew that his right hip would remain stiff forever, they had been happy that he was walking on his own. He too had exulted in the unrestrained happiness of the people. After the difficult times that his father and the family had been witness to, the people had found an occasion to cheer and to demonstrate their loyalty and affection for the Dogra ruling family.[1] They had then turned out in unprecedented numbers. No one remembered having seen so many people thronging the roads of Jammu in the history of the State. It took close to three hours to reach the palace after paying obeisance at the Raghunath Temple. That tumultuous reception was replicated when Karan Singh had brought his bride home to Jammu for the first time after their marriage. The joy of the people had been contagious, and they had celebrated for long on the streets of Jammu.

However, this time, it was not unrestrained happiness but anger that greeted the Yuvraj. The black flags clearly did not belong to only a small section of the populace. The much vaunted crowd-mobilization skills of Bakshi Ghulam Mohammad had, for once, been found wanting. There were only a handful of nervous and timid people to welcome him as their first and elected Sadar-i-Riyasat. They seemed like they wanted to be anywhere but there, pitted against the jeering and hostile crowd. It was obvious that the battle in the State was not just between Maharaja Hari Singh, the representative of the feudal order, and Sheikh Mohammad Abdullah, the perceived representative of all the people of the State. It was rather between Sheikh Abdullah's claim that he and his National Conference represented all the people of the State, including the Dogras, and the Dogras, who vehemently refuted his claims. Caught between the two, Yuvraj Karan Singh had the difficult task of not only surviving, but also playing a meaningful role in building a new future. Now looking at the sea of people shouting hostile slogans, he did feel demoralized, but knew that there was no turning back. He had made a choice, and he had to live with it. He loved and respected his father, and was aware and proud of the glorious history of his ancestors. But young as he was, he knew that the times and the rules of the game had changed. The game itself had been transformed by the winds of change, and it was futile to cling to ideas that were being swept aside by the forces of history.

He made a conscious effort to present a brave face and smiled. It was then that he noticed that even as people were vigorously waving their black flags and raising angry slogans, many among them paused for a moment or two when they thought they had caught his eye to wave back at him! There was hope, yet![2] He would renew his relationship, build bridges of mutual trust, and cement his bond with them, he thought.

***

It had all begun in that oppressively hot June of 1949. The preceding year had been excruciatingly difficult for all those who were dealing with the fortunes of the State and the country. Maharaja Hari Singh had made his unhappiness, agony, and unease known to Sardar Patel in his letter dated 30th January 1948. He was unhappy because of the extremely slow progress made by the Indian Army in getting the borderland territories back from the invader. In fact, he was agonized by the thought that even greater chunks of the State had fallen into the aggressor's hands after accession to India and the arrival of the Indian Army. He did not articulate it but it could not have been missed that while the siege of Skardu was still on, the Indian Army had not made any effort to send relief to the beleaguered but gallant soldiers of the State Forces.

In addition, the fact that the invasion of the State was mentioned to the United Nations had brought in extraneous issues to the Accession of the State, and had really made the Instrument of Accession superfluous. It was in this context that Maharaja Hari Singh had written a letter to Sardar Patel expressing his exasperation and his serious contemplation of withdrawing the Accession. He had argued that by doing so, the reference of the conflict to the Security Council would become redundant.[3] Obviously, the Maharaja was frustrated by the lack of progress on the military front and the possibility of losing hundreds of State Forces men due to the inability or unwillingness of the Indian Army to send help to Skardu and the Gilgit regions.

In response, Sardar Patel had cautioned him against despair. Sardar Patel had also informed Prime Minister Jawaharlal Nehru of the direction of the thoughts of the Maharaja and the counsel that he had offered. Never appreciative of the Maharaja, the Prime

Minister had responded with a note of criticism and justification of his own stand. He wrote back to Sardar Patel on 9th February 1948:

> Thank you for your letter of 9 February sending me a copy of the Maharaja of Kashmir's letter.
>
> It seems to me that the wisest policy he can pursue at the present moment is to do nothing at all. Certainly the idea of his canceling the accession is completely wrong. That will only lead to trouble for him and for us. As for his going out of Kashmir for a while, this might be feasible, but I rather think that he should just stay on for the present. You will have noticed the repeated references made in the Security Council about the so-called autocratic rule of the Maharaja. The system of Indian States finds little favour in foreign countries, and [Sir Mohd] Zafrullah [Khan, President of the United Nations General Assembly] has tried to make the most of this.

As for his advice that the Indian Dominion should carry on operations more effectively, certainly we have not desired to tone down our operations in any way. Indeed, we have done our utmost to push them on and have given these directions to our military commanders. If something has come in our way, it is not the fault of the Government. Our recent success in the Naushera [*sic*] region is an important one and should have considerable results in that region.

The Prime Minister of India was certainly not appreciative of the concerns expressed by Maharaja Hari Singh. While success in Nowshera was offered as evidence of the keenness of the Indian government to push the aggressor back, there was still no reference to Skardu and the vast region of Gilgit-Baltistan; though, the Srinagar Brigade of the Indian Army had asked the State Forces to muster whatever strength they had available in the Badami Bagh cantonment and send it to help the besieged Skardu forces. Dutifully, a rag-tag force was raised and sent through forty feet snow, across the Zoji La Pass. Significantly, the Prime Minister had not commented on the legality of rescinding the Accession by the Maharaja, though he had admitted that it would only lead to 'trouble for him and for us'. Moreover, Prime Minster Nehru had yielded ground to the Pakistani accusation, by conceding the existence of the issue of the Maharaja's 'autocratic rule'.

While the months following the appointment of Sheikh Abdullah as Head of the Emergency Administration had been a period of drift in military matters, it had witnessed accelerated constitutional changes, mainly the Proclamation appointing Sheikh Abdullah as the Prime Minister with the specific task of taking steps to convene a Constituent Assembly. But the period was also marked by the newly appointed Prime Minister's sustained aggression on the personal honour, dignity and the powers of the Maharaja. It was with this as the background, where the Indian Prime Minister was already wondering about the feasibility of the Maharaja going out of the State, that Sardar Patel had invited Maharaja Hari Singh, on whose authority India had accepted the accession of the State—albeit conditionally—and had sent its troops to defend the State from the invaders.

The Maharaja had been accompanied by the Maharani and the young Yuvraj on that fateful journey. Events after that dinner at Sardar Patel's home had moved rapidly and it is obvious that they had been carefully choreographed by Prime Minister Jawaharlal Nehru and Sardar Patel. Apart from Sardar Patel convincing Maharaja Hari Singh of the need to make the sacrifice, both the statesmen's ultimate goal had been to prepare the young Yuvraj for his upcoming constitutional role,[4] which, in their judgment, was important not only for retaining the character of the State of Jammu and Kashmir, but also to mollify the injured feelings of the Dogra people. However, although their goals were the same, their approach slightly different—while Jawaharlal Nehru would often indulge in monologues that focused on the broader context of Indian nationalism, Sardar Patel was more precise and pragmatic, admitting that even though injustice was being done to his father, the compulsion to have Sheikh Abdullah in good humour had left India with few options.[5]

Karan Singh had barely turned eighteen then. Because of his prolonged absence from the country for his medical treatment, he had lost out on formal education. Nevertheless, he did his best to absorb as much as possible of the new ideas to which he was being exposed. He remembered that as a school-going child, he had often dreamt of becoming a perfect ruler, a ruler who brought about substantial changes in the lives of his people. But he was quick to adjust to the reality that such an opportunity was never going to come his way, since the era of rulers had faded into history. Nonetheless, he recognized that two of the greatest leaders and influencers of his times were asking him to seize the chance to be a part of the change, and also act as a bridge between the two worlds. He was being exhorted by both Nehru and Patel to prepare himself for a significant role in the broader national interest. He was not willing to give up this opportunity.

He remembered the tension-filled days at the Imperial Hotel where the three members of the royal family were grappling with the emerging situation. His father was quick to recover from the shock of being asked by none other than Sardar Patel to not return to the State, and appoint the Yuvraj as his Regent. He was, however, totally opposed to the idea of abdication. Once he had reconciled to Sardar Patel's proposals, he was determined to safeguard his own and his dynasty's interests, since Nehru and Patel had paid scant respect to the sacrifices that he had made for the sake of India. He would often bitterly recall the contrasting treatment meted out even to the Nizam of Hyderabad, whose opposition to accession to India had resulted in armed intervention by India to secure it.

But in his case, all the aces were in the hands of Sheikh Abdullah, and Nehru and Patel had no option but to keep him in good humour. On his part, Sheikh Abdullah was systematically destroying the Maharaja's reputation by tarnishing his secular credentials, as well as spreading canards about his commitment to the wellbeing of the people.

Maharani Tara Devi had found adjusting to the changing circumstances even more painstaking. She loathed the idea that she and the Maharaja were not to return to Jammu. But once it became clear that the proposal was no nightmarish illusion, she was excruciatingly torn between her loyalty to her husband and her son. At that point of time, she had not comprehended that the Government of India, concurring with the wishes of Sheikh Abdullah, had said that she too was not to live in Jammu. The Maharaja's plea, that the Yuvraj was young and needed the presence of at least one of his parents and that it was unnatural, cruel and unjust to deprive a mother the proximity of her only son, had failed to move Sardar Patel and the Government of India. She had finally decided to shift to Kasauli, not only because of its cool climate, but also because it was closer to Jammu and her parental home in Kangra.

Yuvraj Karan Singh, on the other hand, while recognizing that all his childhood landmarks had vanished, was excited about the future. Often his excitement annoyed his father. In one such petulant mood, the Maharaja tried to dampen the Yuvraj's enthusiasm by darkly prophesying during lunch that since Sheikh Abdullah was determined to humiliate the Dogra dynasty and the Dogras, even if the Yuvraj was going to Kashmir as the Regent, soon enough Sheikh Abdullah would unceremoniously throw him out in disgrace. Karan Singh had not liked what his father had said. His mother too had been visibly irritated by the comment.[6]

On 20th June 1949, when his father had left for the railway station to board an early morning train to Bombay and his mother had left for Kasauli, he had sat in the hotel room, contemplating the future. However hard he tried, his father's remarks refused to leave his mind. Three years had passed since that day, but they continued to evoke mixed feelings.

Later that day, after a brief stopover at Jammu due to weather conditions at the Srinagar airport, his plane had finally flown over the clouds and the Banihal Pass. It was a clear day with a blue sky, and the Valley looked resplendent with the bounties that nature had blessed it with, and yet torn under centuries of strife and turmoil. As Yuvraj Karan Singh looked at the majestic Himalayas, the valley below, and the snaking Jhelum, he was even more determined to play a role in the new India that the leaders in Delhi were dedicated to creating.

The memory of that day was still fresh, as was the determination to be part of the change that was taking place not only in the State, but also the entire country. The Yuvraj wanted to make the Dogras an integral part of the national consciousness along with the people of the Valley.

2

The Early Winds

Yuvraj Karan Singh's arrival in Jammu and Kashmir alone in the summer of 1949 as the Regent was to mark a monumental change, the kind that Jammu had not witnessed since its creation in 1846. If 1846 had marked the pinnacle of the State's glory under the Dogras, 1949 marked the beginning of an era of uncertainty, lack of trust and physical danger to the contours of what was once one of the greatest Princely States of the Indian subcontinent. For the vast majority of people in the Kashmir Valley, the year marked the exertion of power to fulfil the promises that had been made by Sheikh Abdullah and the National Conference. The banishment of the Maharaja had demonstrated, beyond doubt, the ability of Sheikh Abdullah to deliver on his promises. The people could now hope for the beginning of the promised era of prosperity and empowerment. But as far as the State was concerned, between the third week of October 1947 and 1st January 1949, it had lost more than one-third of its geographical area. This was the period when the Accession had taken place and decisions regarding the defence of the State were being taken by the Generals of the Indian Army and the Government of India. The interim period after the Proclamation of 5th March 1948, had witnessed a radical change in the political climate, which had, though, been in the process much before that. The most important change had taken place in 1938, when the metamorphosis of the Muslim Conference into the National Conference occurred under the leadership of Sheikh Abdullah. Most observers believe that this change happened under the influence of the leaders of the Indian National Congress, but in no small measure, it was also the influence of the leftists that had furthered it. There were also those who believed it to be a tactical move on the part of the National Conference as it gained considerable moral support from the leaders of the national movement. Whatever the motives, this was to create deep divisions in the State that blurred the distinctions between regionalism and communalism.

On the face of it, by doing so, the National Conference committed itself to a united and democratic India. It was a significant development at a time when resurgent Islam and the struggle for giving Muslims a political role disproportionate to their strength was making ground outside the State. Such a movement was lent respectability by Sir Muhammad Iqbal, famously known as Allama Iqbal, the nationalist of yesteryears, who had chosen to champion the cause of Muslims of not only India, but also of Xinjiang, Palestine and Kashmir. For a short time Iqbal was elected the President of the Lahore-based Kashmir Committee that had aided and abetted the movement against the Dogra Rule. Later, he inspired the Muslims from India to form the All India Kashmir Committee to help bring unity of thought and objectives among the Muslims of the Valley.[7] But the interests of the Ahamadiyas in the Valley and their consequent conflict with mainstream Muslims had only resulted in deep divisions within the Kashmiri-Muslim community.[8]

It must also be recognized that before Partition, it was presumed that not only would the autonomous political identities of all the States be preserved, but it would also be mainly based on the reconciliation of communal balances. The Act of 1935 was to be the basis of the reorganization of what was British India. Partition, however, changed everything by destroying the basis of Indian unity. It is possible that the nationalist protestations of the National Conference leaders were genuine before the partition of the country, but the communal divide later swept aside all earlier arrangements. These were put under immense strain after Pakistan was created. The partition of Punjab and Bengal, the resultant displacement of millions, and the horror of the subsequent events, had questioned the ability of the Indian leaders to maintain communal harmony and provide security to the minorities. In the State, the shoe was on the other foot now. After all, the National Conference was dominated by Muslim leaders and had a Muslim following. It could not be ignored that in a democracy, the power structure would shift in favour of the majority Muslims in the State, and it would be they who would be under scrutiny regarding the rights of the minority Hindus, Sikhs and Buddhists. The fact that the party had been known as the Muslim Conference before it assumed a new identity gave reason to fear that under pressure, it could revert back to its communal politics.

Even after the northern regions of Jammu and Kashmir, along with the Mirpur-Muzzafarabad region, had been occupied by Pakistan, the State was still an overwhelmingly Muslim-majority State. This fact notwithstanding, even the secular constitution of the country did not allay the fears of Sheikh Abdullah. They felt that if they needed to protect the Muslim identity of Jammu and Kashmir, the State could not be brought within the political organization of India, which was predominantly Hindu. They also rejected the existing arrangements regarding Jammu and Kashmir's constitutional organization and relations with India, between the Maharaja and the Government of India.[9] According to the National Conference, any constitutional and federal relationship between the State and India should be an arrangement between the State's interim government and the Indian government.

Thus, while treating the stipulations of the Instrument of Accession that brought the State within the jurisdiction of the Dominion of India, as irrelevant, the National Conference refused to accept the secular integration of the State within the quasi-federal organization of India. This challenged the very basis of the Indian Constitution and could not have been acceptable to the national leaders and the Government of India. This view of the National Conference was first made known soon after the ceasefire had come into force and the fighting had been suspended.

Barely two days had passed after the ceasefire, when on 3rd January 1949, the Interim Government sent a long memorandum to the Minister of States of the Government of India, Sardar Patel. The memorandum was signed by all the members of the Interim

Government, including Girdhari Lal Dogra and Sham Lal Saraf, the two representatives of the National Conference from the Dogra region.[10] The Interim Government informed Patel that since the National Conference would be required to approach the people of the State to seek their support for India in the impending plebiscite, it would be necessary for the National Conference to explain its stand to the people regarding the future constitutional organization of the State and its position in the proposed federal structure of India. It needs to be pointed out that the Interim Government of Jammu and Kashmir was, in reality, a National Conference Government, since no other groups and interests were co-opted in it. Although on the face of it, Girdhari Lal Dogra and Sham Lal Saraf represented the Jammu region, everyone knew that the National Conference had hardly any presence in Jammu. Even the memorandum made no bones about the government being a National Conference Government. In contrast to the charade of a responsible government played by the National Conference and the Central leaders, the government appointed by the Maharaja after 1944had been more representative of the people and regions of the State. However, it had been sabotaged by the National Conference.

The memorandum was used by the National Conference leaders to inject an extraneous factor that made Pakistan a stakeholder in the future events. It argued that Pakistan had launched a severe campaign against Maharaja Hari Singh because that the Maharaja represented an autocratic Hindu rule, and affirmed that the Muslims in the State distrusted the Maharaja and considered the Dogra rule as the symbol of their subjection. Whether by design or unwittingly, the memorandum lent credence to the Pakistani argument for intervening in the Poonch region on the grounds that the 'suppression' of Muslims and the consequent 'uprising' necessitated the intervention of fellow Muslims from across the border.[11]There is no doubt that the Interim Government was not aware of the real purpose behind the accusations made by Pakistan within the State and at Lake Success. However, unmindfully, they made the bizarre proposal that in order to counteract the propaganda unleashed by Pakistan, it would be proper to remove Maharaja Hari Singh, banish him as well as the Maharani from the State, and assure the Muslims in the State that the future of the Dogra rule would be determined by the Constituent Assembly of the State when it was convened.

The latent ambition and real intentions of the National Conference were revealed when it wrote that Pakistan had offered the Muslims of the State complete independence in their internal affairs and the freedom to frame a Constitution for the government of the State without any interference from the State of Pakistan. The memorandum further pointed out that Pakistan had gone so far as to offer to vest in the State Government powers vis-a-vis the State Army and communications, and assume only such powers as were transferred to it with regard to defence and foreign affairs. For students of history, it would not go unnoticed that the offer of Pakistan was also known to the Prime Minister of India, since he referred to it in his letter to the Maharaja's Prime Minister Mehr Chand Mahajan.[12] A similar approach had earlier been made to the Maharaja as well, who had not only rejected it, but had also not used it as a bargaining counter with India.

It was a blatant bid to play India against Pakistan and a very unprincipled way of gaining advantage. But, unabashedly, the memorandum went on to suggest that in order to neutralize the effect of the offer made by Pakistan, the Government of India should also issue a declaration, which assured the Muslims in the State of their internal independence. It also visualized that the future constitutional organization of the State would be framed by the Constituent Assembly of the State and that the accession of the State would be limited to three central subjects—foreign affairs, defence, and communications, as the Instrument of Accession said. It also emphasised the fact that the future of the State Army would be determined by agreement between the Interim Government and the Government of India, but till the agreement was reached, the control of the State Army would be vested with the Indian Army. Obviously, the National Conference leaders had no confidence in the Indian Constitution and its ability to safeguard the multi-cultural and multi-religious character of the country, and, therefore, saw no future for the State within it. Gallingly, the representatives from Jammu—all Hindus—had concurred.

Understandably, the proposals made by the Interim Government were received by the Indian leaders with considerable consternation.

Sardar Patel had rejected the proposals outright and informed the Interim Government that the proposals involved issues which were beyond the competence of the States Ministry, and, therefore, could not be considered by him.[13]

The National Conference leaders were peeved by the refusal of the States Ministry to entertain the proposals they had made. Thus placed, the National Conference set about doing what it had mastered in the short decades of its existence—create any situation that might further disintegrate the status of the Dogra dynasty. Sardar Patel was seen as a supporter of Maharaja Hari Singh, and, therefore, as supporting the perpetuation of the Dogra and Hindu rule in the State. From then on, he became a target of malicious propaganda and was subjected to widespread rumours that portrayed him as a right-wing Hindu leader who was planning the alienation of the Muslims of Kashmir and wanting the way paved for the eventual accession of the Kashmir Valley to Pakistan. It was a diabolical propaganda that was used as a tool of the extortionist policy that was to soon become the hallmark of Sheikh Abdullah's dealings with New Delhi.

The memorandum was soon followed by Sheikh Mohammad Abdullah's letter to Nehru with the warning that in case the proposals made by the Interim Government were not accepted, the National Conference would not be able to secure the support of the Muslims for the accession of the State to India. Meanwhile, inside the State, the National Conference leaders had launched a frontal attack on the Maharaja. Among the many other allegations, they accused him of interfering with the functioning of the Interim Government and obstructing political and economic reforms, which the Conference leaders proposed to introduce in the State, as well as his alleged role in the killings of the Muslims in Jammu.

The tirade unleashed by the Conference leaders against the Maharaja and the implied threats to the Government of India had unnerved the national leaders. A meeting of the Indian leaders, in which Nehru, Sardar Patel, Maulana Azad and Gopalaswami Ayyangar participated, was convened in Delhi in April 1949. It examined the issues the Conference leaders had raised, and a decision was reached to advise the Maharaja to leave the State temporarily, and entrust his powers to his son Yuvraj Karan Singh.

It was also decided that the future of the Dogra rule would be determined by the Constituent Assembly of the State after it was convened. It was a major victory for Sheikh Abdullah, one which set the State on a course that was to constantly lead it from one uncertainty and crisis to another.

On 16th April 1949, Nehru had a long meeting with Sheikh Mohammad Abdullah, in which many of the issues raised by the National Conference leaders were brought under discussion. Nehru apprised Sheikh Mohammad Abdullah of the decisions he and his colleagues had arrived at, regarding the temporary removal of the Maharaja, the Constitution of the State, and future relations between the State and India.[14] It is said that he also expressed his disapproval of the wild accusations made against the Maharaja by the Conference leaders, but there is no evidence that the remonstrance had any effect on Sheikh Abdullah, for the concessions now being granted by Nehru and his colleagues proved that the tactics had worked.

Sheikh Abdullah had grown in confidence in dealing with the Government of India as a result of this success. But he had also grown in arrogance. Nehru informed Patel on 17th April in a resume of his discussions with Sheikh Mohammad Abdullah:

> We know that Sheikh Abdullah and some of his colleagues have been very unwise in their public remarks and they have improperly criticized the Maharaja and asked for his removal. I had a long talk with Abdullah last night and again pointed out to him very forcefully how unfortunate and wrong his attitude was in this particular matter, and how it was creating difficulties not only for us, but for himself. He repeated his old complaints, which included the very facts that our intelligence officer has stated. He promised that he would say nothing about the Maharaja in future, but he was very unhappy about it.[15]

Nehru, however, went on to write to Patel that it would no longer be advisable to allow the drift to continue, and proposed the removal of the Maharaja from the State. He suggested to Patel to ask Maharaja Hari Singh to come to Delhi and advise him to leave the State for sometime. The Prime Minister wrote:

> The consequences are undoubtedly bad and I feel that it is no longer safe for us to allow matters to drift. You will remember that we discussed this matter fully sometime ago in your house. Gopalaswami Ayangar [*sic*] and others were present. Ultimately we came to the conclusion that the proper course to adopt was for us to take the attitude that it was for the people of Kashmir in the Constituent Assembly to decide about the future of the Maharaja. But even now it was highly desirable that the Maharaja should take some time of leave and not remain in Kashmir. It was proposed to put this matter to the Maharaja and to ask him to come to Delhi for the purpose. As he has not been here since then, I suppose nothing has been done. Meanwhile, the situation deteriorates and an open conflict is going on in the State between the adherents of the Maharaja and the adherents of Sheikh Abdullah.[16]

While the Indian leaders were trying frantically to find a solution for the problems in the State and the subsequent removal of the Maharaja, Sheikh Mohammad Abdullah threw a bombshell in their midst. In a press interview, first published in *The Scotsman* and later in the influential English newspaper, *The Observer*, Sheikh Abdullah spoke to foreign correspondents Michael Davidson and Ward Price, and pleaded for the independence of the State. 'Accession to either side cannot bring peace,' Abdullah stated. 'We want to live in friendship with both Dominions. Perhaps a middle path between them, with economic co-operation with each, will be the only way of doing it. But an independent Kashmir must be guaranteed not only by India and Pakistan but also by Britain, the United States, and other members of the United Nations.' He further added, 'During the communal riots in Punjab after partition, we tried, in our humble way, to stem the wave of fanaticism. That is why I urged we should wait before deciding our affiliation. I pleaded with both Dominions to help us first to win internal emancipation before asking us to choose. India replied by refusing to make a standstill agreement with the Maharaja; Pakistan did so. When, during the crisis India accepted the Maharaja's accession, Pandit Nehru insisted that it was only provisional, and that people must decide later.'[17]

The Indian leaders received a rude jolt by the statements that Sheikh Mohammad Abdullah made. Patel wrote to Gopalaswami Ayyangar:

> You have probably seen the interview by Sheikh Sahib to Michael Davidson, which was published in the *Scotsman* of April 14, 1949. A vehement exponent of accession to India seems to have been converted to an "independent Kashmir". He wants absentee landlords, most of whom have gone to Pakistan, to be expropriated. At the same time he has got, according to the information brought here by Sethi of the Agricultural Ministry, large tracts of valuable irrigated lands vacant, lest non-Muslims should settle down on them, and this is at a time when elsewhere we are asking for every inch of land to be cultivated.[18]

Ayyangar asked Dwarka Nath Kachru, Nehru's personal secretary, to visit Srinagar and instructed him to convey to Sheikh Mohammad Abdullah his disapproval of the statement he had made. Ayyangar further asked Kachru to inform Abdullah that Ayyangar condemned the Sheikh's statement and considered it to be the first step in the plan to set up an independent State of Jammu and Kashmir. Ayyangar wrote to Sardar Patel:

> My attention was drawn to the contents of this interview earlier in the day. It is a more astonishing [*sic*] performance. Kachru, who is going to Kashmir tomorrow, has just been to see me, and I am sending a message through him to Sheikh Abdullah. I have asked him to tell the latter that I condemn the Sheikh's action and that I feel that what he has told Michael Davidson and what the latter has published will have the most serious and mischievous consequences, both in India and abroad. I have asked him to inform the Sheikh that, reading between the lines, I suspect a plan, the first step of which is this blessing by the Premier of Kashmir of the idea of an independent Kashmir and this public expression of his conviction that accession to India will not bring peace, and the first step of which may well be perhaps one of the greatest betrayals in history.[19]

It was, indeed, the greatest betrayal in history, and the later events proved that. As the scope of the Security Council intervention in the dispute widened, the National Conference rapidly drew closer to the idea of independence. Meanwhile the Indian leaders, too far committed in allowing Sheikh Abdullah to dictate the decisions about the State, were left fumbling for an adequate response and chose to turn a blind eye at several occasions as far as the public appearance was concerned.

Sheikh Mohammad Abdullah treated Kachru with scant respect and told him that he had never meant all that he had said in his press statement. All that he had done was some 'loud thinking'. Ayyangar had instructed Kachru to advise Sheikh Mohammad Abdullah to contradict the press statement he had given. When Kachru asked Abdullah to recant his statement, the latter refused to do so. It is not known as to how the Indian leaders chose to analyze the development despite it having become clear as daylight that Sheikh Abdullah had returned home from Lake Success a changed man. He was no longer the man who had made a solemn assurance to Maharaja Hari Singh about his loyalty to him and his family, and a resolve to lead the State under the Maharaja's guidance on to the path of glory and happiness.

The circumstances being such, and with Sheikh Abdullah's threats looming, the Indian leaders chose to sacrifice Maharaja Hari Singh. To the credit of Sardar Patel, he acknowledged that the country was demanding a huge sacrifice from the Maharaja. In a letter dated 23rd May 1949, Sardar Patel, while expressing his regret at having to ask of the Maharaja what he did, wrote,

> No one can be more cognizant than myself of the attitude which Your Highness has adopted ever since you signed the Instrument of Accession. I am grateful to Your Highness for the spirit of co-operation and understanding which you have always extended to me…I know full well the personal sacrifice involved in it, but, I am sure, along with so many other changes to which Your Highness has accustomed yourself, you will undertake this step also with the same sense of duty to your country and in the spirit of calm resignation to the superior dictates of events.[20]

That summer saw the last of Maharaja Hari Singh in his beloved State. Posterity alone will judge the Indian leaders for their decision to remove the Maharaja to keep the Conference leaders on their side. The Maharaja never asked Patel whether India would win the plebiscite after he had left. It is hard to imagine what the answer would have been, but the episode and the manner in which the design was carried out did not enhance the reputation of either Nehru or Patel. The only one to emerge with his dignity intact was Maharaja Hari Singh. Vilified by his opponents in the State, exposed to indignities by those whom he trusted, and forced to retreat from one position to another in the name of the country, he was the victim of a timid and vacillating Indian leadership's inability to come to terms with the communal question in what was a secular India in the making.

Patel assured the Maharaja that his stay outside the State would be 'a temporary phase' and that he would return to the State after a settlement, once the plebiscite in the State had been finalized. Of the Congress leaders, Maharaja Hari Singh trusted only Patel, and he had put his ship in Patel's hands. Patel drove him straight to the reefs. As events unfolded, the plebiscite never took place and only the ashes of the exiled ruler returned to Jammu.

3

Prelude to Article 370

Yuvraj Karan Singh had comfortably taken over the role of Regent. In fact, he was happy to be back in the Karan Mahal where he had spent much of his childhood. He also felt relieved having escaped the heat of Delhi but knew that there was serious business ahead. Prime Minister Jawaharlal Nehru had specifically asked him to work in harmony with Sheikh Abdullah. With the fate of the State in the hands of the Security Council of the United Nations, and Sheikh Abdullah having become indispensable for Nehru, the Yuvraj's role was to allay the emerging insecurities of the Dogras and to keep Sheikh Abdullah on the right side of the national leaders so that he could influence the plebiscite in favour of India.

Before the Yuvraj was called upon to assume the role of Regent, he had remained outside the country for a considerable period for reasons of health. However, this notwithstanding, he was fully aware of the disturbing events of the past and was mentally prepared to forget their baggage, and work for the future. In his own reserved manner, his father had kept him abreast with the events as they had emerged at home, and, in one of his letters, the Maharaja had prophetically written, 'I have no idea of how the new Constitution of India is going to affect us beyond the fact that before very long the rulers will disappear even in name.'[21] This prophecy apart, his father had loathed the manner in which the changes had taken place and how he was pushed from one agreed position to another. Because of this background, it required utmost tact, patience and ability to put the past behind to embark on a new journey.

For a short while, Prime Minister Sheikh Abdullah too appeared to be keen on establishing a relationship unencumbered by the past. Thus, in the balmy summer of 1949, Yuvraj Karan Singh, the Regent, was received at the airport of Srinagar by Sheikh Abdullah and his entire Cabinet, including his Deputy Prime Minister, Bakshi Ghulam Mohammad. Soon Sheikh Abdullah would make it a point to visit Yuvraj Karan Singh and enter into long monologues about the political situation. He took care not to ever mention Maharaja Hari Singh during these interactions. Perhaps, like Jawaharlal Nehru, he too hoped that being young, the Yuvraj's mind could be easily moulded and prepared along the lines of their worldview of a democratic world to which India and the State was committed.

Soon, however, a seemingly innocuous event occurred that was to 'pre-shadow the tensions that lay ahead.'[22] The Kashmiri Pandits had approached the Yuvraj and expressed their keenness to have him visit the shrine dedicated to Kheer Bhawani.[23] Their keenness was probably triggered by the sense of uncertainty that the Pandits felt despite the secular protestations of Sheikh Abdullah and the National Conference. It was obvious that many Pandits did not have faith in the professed secularism of a party that had till the other day borne the name of 'Muslim Conference' and which, on that fateful day in July 1931, had vent its communal anger on the Pandit shopkeepers of Srinagar. Yuvraj Karan Singh readily agreed to the invitation, but was in for a shock. No sooner had his visit to Kheer Bhawani been announced, than he got a message from Sheikh Abdullah advising him not to go.

The Yuvraj was in a dilemma. He had made a commitment, and in his judgment, not living up to it was not only dishonourable but also a betrayal to the minority community in the State. He was convinced that his visit would assure the minority community of being equal partners in the new era. So he decided to ignore the advice of his Prime Minister and went to the shrine. His reception at the shrine was not only moving but also tumultuous as thousands from the Kashmiri-Pandit community had gathered for the occasion. Among the warm slogans the one that resounded the most was '*Dogra Raj Zindabad*'. The event and the adulatory sloganeering greatly upset Sheikh Abdullah, bringing to the fore the fragile nature of his confidence when pitted against the Dogra scion. It was amazing that a leader who thought of himself as the undisputed leader of the people of not only Kashmir, but the State of Jammu and Kashmir, was so insecure that the adoration of a minority group for the heir of a vanishing order had shaken his confidence.

Soon thereafter, on 29th October 1949, the Yuvraj met with a car accident that confined him again to his bed. This time when he returned to the State from Bombay in the spring of the following year, he came with his bride. In the glow of the happiness shared by the people of the State, it appeared that the relationship of the Regent with the Prime Minister of the State had returned to normal. On behalf of the State, Sheikh Abdullah presented him with a diamond-studded *sarpech* (an ornament for the turban). But the Yuvraj knew that he had a difficult task ahead, with the leaders in Delhi remaining obsessed with perceptions and their inability to make a distinction between the heterogeneity of the State and the usurping of the whole space by the National Conference. Delhi also soon realized that the virtual exile of the Maharaja had only whetted Sheikh Abdullah's appetite for power. After having a formidable hurdle removed it did not take him long to unfold the next plan of action. As time passed, his tune kept changing, with each succeeding note becoming shriller, enigmatic and often threatening.

Meanwhile, the process of drafting a new Constitution and the complete integration of the Princely States was on its way in Delhi. The Princely States had, after initial hesitation, fallen into the pattern. There were a few hiccups but they had all ceded powers to the people. The manner in which they were made to fall in line differed from state to state, but sooner or later, all of them submitted to the greater idea of a united India under one Constitution. While plebiscite had worked in Junagarh, which had opted for Pakistan, police action had been required in Hyderabad, where the armed, vigilante Razakars had been used by the Nizam to terrorize the general populace and declare his independent status.

Deep in the south, on the southwestern coast of the country, Travancore too had declared its intention to be independent. It had made its intentions known even before the meeting of the Chamber of Princes on 25th July 1947. Travancore believed that it would be out of place for it to be part of India since it was much too advanced on socio-economic parametres compared to other states, both Princely and British Indian. It argued that becoming part of India would set the state back.

Indeed, Travancore was a progressive State. It was the first to introduce universal primary education. Like the Maharaja of Jammu and Kashmir, it had opened the doors of temples for the Dalits in 1930. It was rich in minerals and had thorium deposits used in the production of nuclear energy, and was already manufacturing aluminium and sea vessels. The Maharaja of Travancore ruled through a competent, but all powerful, Prime Minister, Sir C.P. Ramaswamy Iyer, who was so loyal to him that he feared that accession would only be the first step towards the elimination of his master. Travancore had, at that time, already entered into negotiations with a British company to exploit the thorium deposits, and the Princely State's Prime Minister also approached the American Consul in Madras, perhaps with some encouragement from the British, in an effort to seek American recognition for its independent status. However, the Secretary of States had forbidden the Consul to entertain such a request, and was thus shot down no sooner had the topic been broached. How Travancore was ultimately brought around to see daylight is best described by Narinder Singh Sarila in his book in the following words:

> The viceroy [Lord Mountbatten] reported: "He, Sir C.P., sought to prove that Mahatma Gandhi...was a most dangerous semi-repressed sex maniac...And that if he insisted on backing the unstable Nehru against the realistic Patel it would break up the Congress Party within two years...And said he was not prepared to ally himself with so unreliable a dominion. When arguments did not seem to work, I told him that it was reported that Seth [R.K.] Dalmia [the richest industrialist in India at that time and a supporter of the Congress Party] had that morning paid Rs 5 lakhs into the Travancore Congress Party funds in anticipation of starting internal trouble in the State after 15th August." The viceroy subsequently reported: "Shortly after his return to his State [from Delhi] at the end of July he [Sir C.P.]

> was assaulted with a bill-hook and very nearly killed. The State People's Organization turned the heat full on and Travancore immediately gave in. The Maharaja telegraphed his acceptance of the Instrument of Accession to me personally and Sir C.P. Ramaswamy Iyer's friends asked Sardar Patel to call off the State People's movement.

This was illustrative of the will of the Union in general, and Sardar Patel in particular, in getting the states on board.

The only state to have resisted Lord Mountbatten's charm and Sardar Patel's iron hand had been Jammu and Kashmir, where geography, culture, demography and religion inhibited an instant decision. The Pakistan backed forces attempted to forcibly occupy the State but the decision of the Maharaja to accede to India had put the legal stamp on the situation though the subsequent reference to the Security Council had complicated the issue. Now with the Yuvraj as the Regent, Nehru believed that it would be easy to deal with Sheikh Abdullah and make him a partner in the making of a new India—a new India to which, as a first step, the Constituent Assembly of India was to commit itself by adopting a Constitution for the Republic of India.

The States Department of the Government of India had adopted various modalities to assimilate the Princely States. Many of the princes had quietly adapted themselves to the changed circumstances; the prominent among them had been made the constitutional heads of their State. In some cases, the smaller States had been merged into bigger States and the leading prince among them recognized as the Rajpramukh. However, there was also the Mysore model, where the representative of the people was the administrative head, but the King, working with the assistance of a Dewan, remained the constitutional head and exercised all power in Reserved subjects such as finance, defence, land revenue etc.

The Mysore model was considered best for the State of Jammu and Kashmir and for a while it appeared that it would function effectively, especially after Sheikh Abdullah had written a letter after his release from jail, swearing allegiance to Maharaja Hari Singh.[24] He had made a solemn pledge that under the guidance of the ruler, the State would be led towards an era of peace and prosperity. It appeared that the rancour of the past had been forgotten and both the Maharaja and Sheikh Abdullah had resolved to open a new chapter in their relationship. This euphoria lasted only for a while, ending on a note of bitterness when the Maharaja realized that he stood isolated as even Sardar Patel had betrayed and abandoned him. Left with no choice, he had appointed Yuvraj Karan Singh as the Regent before leaving for Bombay. The ground had been carefully prepared for the Maharaja's exit when Prime Minister Nehru, Sardar Patel and a few of their colleagues met Sheikh Abdullah on 15th-16th May 1949 at Sardar Patel's residence to discuss the future of Jammu and Kashmir. Among the subjects that were discussed were: '(i) the framing of the constitution for the State; (ii) the subjects in respect of which the State should accede to the Union of India; (iii) the monarchical form of government in the State; (iv) the control of the State Forces, and (v) the rights of the citizens of the State to equality of opportunity for service in the Indian Army.'[25]

Prime Minister Nehru also reiterated these points of convergence when he wrote to Sheikh Abdullah on 18th May 1949:

> As regards (i) and (iii), it has been the settled policy of the Government of India, which on many occasions has been stated by Sardar Patel and me, that the constitution of Jammu and Kashmir State is a matter for determination by the people of the State represented in a Constituent Assembly convened for the purpose...the Government of India have no objection to the Constituent Assembly of the State considering the question of the continuance of the association of the State with a constitutional monarchy.
>
> With regard to (ii), [the] Jammu and Kashmir State now stands acceded to the Indian Union in respect of three subjects, namely, Foreign Affairs, Defence and Communications. It will be for the Constituent Assembly of the State, when convened, to determine in respect of what other subjects the State may accede.

According to the letter, the matter of the State Forces too had been settled with the administrative and operational control exercised by the Indian Army. It was assured that the draft of the new Constitution under consideration of the National Constituent

Assembly had already recognized that equality of opportunity for employment under the state, including employment in the Indian Army, was a fundamental right of all the citizens of India. With these clarifications, the national leaders believed that the path to complete assimilation of the State had been paved, and therefore, representatives of the State in the Constituent Assembly would take their due place.

Unlike other Princely States, Sheikh Abdullah's Jammu and Kashmir had dragged its feet in nominating members to its allotted seats in the National Constituent Assembly even by 27th May 1949, and a concern over it was being expressed by the Assembly members during the debates. This had also begun to create speculation about the nature of accession of the State. Therefore, N. Gopalaswami Ayyangar was forced to state in the Assembly during the debate on the Revision of Rules for Admission of J&K's Representatives to the Constituent Assembly on 27th May 1949:'But I think that a few words have to be said about one or two observations that were made by my honourable friend, Maulana Hasrat Mohani. He doubted whether the Prime Minister's description of this accession as being complete is altogether correct. I maintain that it is perfectly correct…It is an absolutely unconditional offer…The accession was offered by the Maharaja and it was accepted by the Governor General of the time…But my honourable Friend referred to what has happened since and I know my other honourable Friend Prof. Shah also seemed to imply what the Maulana contended. Now the correct position is this. The accession is complete. No doubt we have offered to have a plebiscite taken when the conditions are created for the holding of a proper, fair and impartial plebiscite…In this connection, I should also like to draw the attention of the House to the Provisions of the Indian Independence Act under which, when a state accedes and subsequently wished to get out of the act of accession, thus separating itself from the main Dominion, it cannot do so except with the consent of the Dominion. Our commitment is simply this, that if and when a plebiscite comes to be taken and if the verdict of that plebiscite is against India, then we shall not stand in the way of the wishes of the people of Kashmir being given effect to, if they want to go away from us…'[26]

Gopalaswami Ayyangar was more forthright and emphatic on the question of the need to bring in representatives of the State at such a late stage. He said, 'We are not bringing them into this House for the purpose of placing their seal on the act of accession. We are giving them an opportunity for the exercise of the rights which they obtained by virtue of the fact that the accession has already taken place. We are making a new constitution which affects not merely the Union as a whole, but affects the units of the Union, and Kashmir, on account of the fact of accession, is at present a unit of that Union.'[27] But the fact was that quite a few members questioned the complete accession since they knew that even though the Maharaja had unconditionally acceded to India, Lord Mountbatten, the Governor-General, had added a rider to the acceptance. It was this that made the members question the nature of accession.

In addition, a few members had not taken kindly to the State being referred to as 'Kashmir' and Gopalaswami Ayyangar was hard pressed to explain the technicality of having to accept the nomenclature at that point of time. But it was a comment made by Prof. K.T. Shah from the General Constituency of Bihar that had particularly aroused the ire of Prime Minister Jawaharlal Nehru. Discussing the representation in the National Constituent Assembly, Prof. Shah had said: 'It has been the declaration of the highest authority in India also that the accession of the State made by the Maharaja, who was the complete constitutional head on the day that accession was agreed to, was subject to confirmation by the result of the plebiscite.'[28]

Jawaharlal Nehru had impatiently interjected: 'That is absolutely incorrect—cent per cent incorrect. I am amazed, surprised and astounded that such a statement is made by Professor Shah.'[29] Of course, Prof. Shah was referring to the conditional acceptance of the Instrument of Accession by Lord Mountbatten, Governor-General of India. The Indian Cabinet had then concurred. But now Nehru had vehemently termed that as absolutely incorrect. He was probably making a subtle distinction between commitment to plebiscite and the endorsement of accession by the people of the State. But it is surprising that Prof. Shah did not refer to the letter of acceptance. It is left to our imagination to search for a possible reaction if it had been read on the floor of the Assembly. Somewhat later, while on the same subject, the President of the Assembly, Dr Rajendra Prasad, said that as far as he was aware, all the states, which had acceded, had already come to the Constituent Assembly, except Bhopal and Kashmir. Then he added, 'As far as Hyderabad is concerned, I do not know in what stage of accession it is, but so far as the other states, about whose accession there is no doubt, are concerned, they have all come in except Kashmir and Bhopal, and steps are being taken today to bring in Kashmir.'[30]

However, when H.V. Kamath, a member from Bidar, also brought up the issue of incomplete accession, Nehru got irritated again. He said, 'The honourable member is a master of irrelevancy. He does not quite understand what has happened. Nearly all the states which have acceded are represented here except Kashmir.'[31]

It was obvious that there were certain facts about the events of Jammu and Kashmir that sent Prime Minister Nehru into a state of denial, and even mentioning them, riled him. Eighteen months had elapsed since Maharaja Hari Singh signed the Instrument of Accession, and more than fourteen months had passed since the Proclamation of 5th March that appointed Sheikh Abdullah as the Prime Minister. The Proclamation was considered to be the first step towards a full responsible government and election on the basis of universal adult suffrage. Yet there was no sign of the State moving towards republican goals, though considerable efforts were made to dismantle the Dogra symbols. How it was being done is another subject. Suffice it to say that the media in Delhi had got some inkling of what was happening though not fully understanding its import.

This finds an inadvertent reference in H.V. Kamath's speech on the subject of representation of Jammu and Kashmir in the National Constituent Assembly. Making his point, Kamath said, 'The last point is this. In yesterday's issue of an important Daily of this city, there was a report that the Maharaja of Kashmir was going on a short holiday and somebody else would act as Regent. I hope, Sir, that this resolution which we are going to pass today will be implemented by the Ruler of Kashmir on the advice of his Prime Minister before he leaves the State on a short holiday.'[32]

Those who now know this with the advantage of hindsight fully understand the implication and can wonder at the deceit, deception and lies that were being resorted to by Delhi in dealing with Maharaja Hari Singh. Even the Constituent Assembly was being fed with half truths and coloured facts. Now, a member of the Constituent Assembly had come to know through a newspaper that the Maharaja was about to go on leave (permanent and not short, as reported) and that a Regent was to be appointed. The concern of the said member was not why there was the need to appoint a Regent, but that the representatives from the State should bear the authority of the very same Maharaja under whose patriotic signatures the State had legitimately acceded to India, and whose authority had set in motion the devolution of powers to the people. It is no coincidence that soon after the Maharaja had left the State after appointing a Regent, Sheikh Abdullah appointed Mirza Mohammad Afzal Beg, Maulana Mohammad Syed Masoodi, Moti Ram Bagda and himself as the four nominees of the State to the National Constituent Assembly. But as the constitutional debates and controversies reveal, the aim seemed to be to keep the integration pot boiling rather than making any genuine effort to be partners in the inclusive growth of the country to which the State had acceded and which had saved it from falling into the ravishing hands of Pakistan.

In the tug of war that followed between the National Conference and the national leaders, the authority of the Proclamation of 5th March 1948 was repeatedly invoked. Whenever Sheikh Abdullah found himself cornered by the national leaders over the issue of falling in line with the rest of the states, he would resort to using the ruse of the plebiscite and the authority of the Proclamation to wriggle out of it. Never for a moment had he paused to remember that the very same Proclamation had made provision for a Dewan who was to act on behalf of the ruler and be part of the Cabinet, and that the subjects in the Reserved list were the exclusive preserve of the ruler. He created such conditions for the Dewan, Mehr Chand Mahajan, a confidant of both the Maharaja and Sardar Patel that Mahajan gave up the job in disgust as he accused the National Conference of ruling like the Nazis of Hitler's Germany. The express purpose of the Proclamation was to take steps towards convening a Constituent Assembly of representatives elected on the basis of universal adult franchise. None of these steps had been taken even at the time when the State's representatives to the National Constituent Assembly were nominated in May 1949.

The Proclamation read:

> My Council of Ministers shall consist of the Prime Minister and such other Ministers as may be appointed on the advice of the Prime Minister. I have by Royal Warrant appointed Sheikh Mohammad Abdullah as the Prime Minister with effect from today.
>
> The Prime Minister and other Ministers shall function as a Cabinet and act on the principle of joint responsibility. A Dewan appointed by me shall also be a member of the Cabinet.

The Proclamation also visualized a speedy transition to a democratically elected Assembly that would draft a new Constitution. The Maharaja had proclaimed, '…I have, from time to time, provided for increasing association of my people with the administration of the State with the object of realizing the goal of full Responsible Government at as early a date as possible…' At that point of time the Maharaja had already appointed Sheikh Abdullah as the Head of the Emergency Administration and therefore, it was added, 'It is now my desire to replace the Emergency Administration by a Popular Interim Government and to provide for its powers, duties and functions, pending the formation of a fully democratic Constitution…My Council of Ministers shall take appropriate steps, as soon as restoration of normal conditions has been completed, to convene a National Assembly based on adult suffrage…'

The clause of 'as soon as restoration of normal conditions has been completed' was effectively used by Sheikh Abdullah to continue exercising the executive, legislative and, to a fair degree, judicial powers till his hand was forced by the Regent and the Government of India.

Riding on the wave of popularity in the Valley and having increasingly become indispensable to the schemes of Delhi, Sheikh Abdullah was no longer content with limited powers. It has never been adequately explained as to how the transformation of Sheikh Abdullah, from one who had expressed his loyalty as a subject of

Maharaja Hari Singh to the Maharaja's most implacable and avowed enemy, took place. But soon, in the name of the people, Sheikh Abdullah wanted all power to be vested in him, and to achieve this end, he had systematically launched an assault on the reputation of Maharaja Hari Singh. The Maharaja was not only reviled as a person who had left the people of the Valley to the mercy of the marauding invaders but also persistently accused of being instrumental in the purge and killings of Muslims in the Jammu region. The aggressive tenor of the Sheikh's outbursts might have been helpful in consolidating his hold on the people of the Valley, but it created an environment of bitterness in the Jammu region. Among other symbols of the Dogra rule, the Jammu and Kashmir State Forces were particularly and repeatedly targeted by him.

The definition and administration of the Reserved subjects and especially those related to the J&K State Forces had earlier brought the rift between the Maharaja and his Prime Minister into the open. Failing to obtain control over the Forces, Sheikh Abdullah indulged in besmirching the personal honour of Maharaja Hari Singh in his speeches in the State, and went on to reiterate the charge of the Maharaja abandoning the State in his speech to the United Nations Security Council. Aggravating the rift, the said speech had been distributed by the State government as a pamphlet under the heading of, 'Kashmir: Appeal to World Conscience'. Since the Maharaja was not prepared to let this matter go unchallenged, the relationship between the two had worsened till that fateful dinner at Sardar Patel's house where the Maharaja was virtually told that he was 'exiled' from the State. The fate of the State Forces was, however, to remain undecided for quite some time in the future, and it was left for the Yuvraj to play a role in the ultimate destiny of the Forces that had such a glorious and historical past.

Politically, however, the period after April 1949 was hectic. Apologists for the never-ending demands of the leaders from Kashmir do not tire of harping on the Delhi Agreement, 1952 between Pandit Jawaharlal Nehru and Sheikh Abdullah, which laid down the terms and conditions between Delhi and the State. They argue that the document outlined the relationship between the State and the Centre, and that the non-fulfilment of the agreed-upon contours has been at the root of Kashmiri discontent. The people of the Valley were betrayed, they claim. These arguments suggest that they believe that the modern history of the State's uneasy relationship with the rest of the country began in 1952 and thereafter. In the din of such claims, what is often forgotten is that the legitimacy to powers that Sheikh Abdullah began to exercise were given to him under the Proclamation signed by Maharaja Hari Singh on 5th March 1948. At that time, the Maharaja was recognized as the only legal entity who could have entered into any agreement with the Government of India or any other power. Any decision taken by the Government of India with regard to the State was because of the agreement between the Maharaja and the Government of India under the clauses of the Instrument of Accession. Logically, therefore, any analysis of the turbulent relationship between the State and the Centre ought to begin with the Instrument of Accession and thereafter the Proclamation, since Sheikh Abdullah came into the frame subsequent to both. All later events, natural and contrived, follow them.

Like in other Princely States, the Proclamation was the first step towards the constitutional integration of all such States with the rest of the country. However, the formalities of a few states, including Jammu and Kashmir were slightly different from the others. In fact, the Jammu and Kashmir model was based on that of Mysore, where the ruler had appointed a popular leader as the executive to head the administration consisting of a Cabinet. The ruler was to also appoint his Dewan who would represent him in the Cabinet; moreover, quite a few subjects were reserved for the ruler. Even a casual perusal of the Proclamation is elucidation enough of this point.

After becoming the Prime Minister, Sheikh Abdullah used the Pakistani occupation of one-third of the State and the inability of the United Nations to restore 'normal conditions', as an excuse to exercise all his powers without taking any step to convene the Constituent Assembly of the State. His ambition, too, had begun to alienate the Indian leadership. Much before the minor discord over the manner in which land reforms* were to be implemented, Delhi

* See Chapter 6 for more details.

had come to realize that he was pursuing agendas that were often at variance with the national needs. However, when similar doubts were expressed by Professor K.T. Shah, a member of the general constituency of Bihar, Prime Minister Jawaharlal Nehru was roused to respond rather vehemently, 'That is absolutely incorrect—cent per cent incorrect. I am amazed, surprised and astounded that such a statement is made by Professor Shah.'[33]

The point of controversy and the source of Sheikh Abdullah's power was not the conditional nature of the offer of accession or whether India was obliged to let the State go if the result of the plebiscite was not in its favour. It was the fact that the Government of India had, in its wisdom or under the unwarranted influence of its British Governor-General Lord Louis Mountbatten, accepted it on the condition that it would be subject to approval by the people of the State. Both Gopalaswami Ayyangar and Prime Minister Nehru had skirted the issue, with the former taking refuge behind the technicality of the provision dealing with the non-feasibility of the accession by a State and the subsequent desire to secede, the latter expressing outrage even at a suggestion that, in fact, was his own making.

Ayyangar had then asked and answered the question: 'Why should the representatives be brought in at this stage? We are not bringing them into the House for the purpose of placing their seal on the act of accession. We are giving them an opportunity for the exercise of the rights which they have obtained by virtue of the fact that accession has already taken place.'[34] This was correct since the question of accession had been settled by the Maharaja and now the purpose of bringing in representatives from the State was to give them an opportunity to contribute to the process of framing the Constitution.

May is not a very pleasant month in the plains, especially when the hot winds force one to stay indoors. In Delhi, where the black roads shimmer and the heat drains out energy from the body, the month borders on oppression. Yet, there was urgent business at hand in the Constitution Hall in New Delhi in May 1949. The members of the Constituent Assembly were, on 27th May 1949 earnestly debating how Jammu and Kashmir could be given representation in that august house.

4

The Making of Article 370

Looking back at those momentous years, one cannot but feel the irony of the subject of the debate of the National Constituent Assembly that day in May 1949. During the course of his speech, Gopalaswami Ayyangar justified the nomination of the Jammu and Kashmir representatives by the ruler on the advice of the Prime Minister of the State, on the pretext that the Praja Sabha—the Legislative Assembly of the State—though elected in December 1946, was 'dead' and had become a 'rump' body. Little did he know that the elected Constituent Assembly of the State would have seventy-three unopposed representatives out of seventy-five, as the main opposition party in Jammu, the Praja Parishad, had boycott the election. Moreover, the nomination of those aspiring to contest in the Valley had their candidatures rejected by the returning officers at the behest of Sheikh Abdullah and his National Conference. On such an ominous note began the tryst of the State with Republicanism.

It is only of academic interest today to wonder if the Praja Sabha of Jammu and Kashmir was really a 'dead' and 'rump' body. It is true that the constitutional progress in the State was never revolutionary, however, as a result of the demand made by the people and the conviction of the State's ruler, small steps were taken towards shouldering the responsibility of making a responsible government. In this, the Jammu and Kashmir Constitution Act, 1939* was significant and relatively far ahead of its times. This

* On 7 September 1939, the Jammu and Kashmir Constitution Act, 1939 was promulgated with the goal of consolidation and amendment of laws related to the Government of Jammu and Kashmir.

Constitution gives the lie to all those who accused Maharaja Hari Singh of autocracy, for even in as important a matter as appeal in civil and criminal matters, he did not take arbitrary decisions. He had a Board of Judicial Advisors who expressed their opinion on all cases, and the Maharaja would accept their advice. In the matter of legislature, there was a provision for constituting a Praja Sabha consisting of seventy-five members. It included forty elected and thirty-five nominated members, including the ex-officio members, who were not to exceed eight. They were nominated by the Maharaja.[35] As it was in the rest of the country, the franchise was limited. The Praja Sabha's term was three years from its first meeting. However, the ruler could dissolve the Praja Sabha before the expiry of the term, and *he could also extend the term, if in special circumstances he thought it fit.*[36]

Although in matters of constitutional reforms the State of Cochin was far ahead, it cannot be denied that Jammu and Kashmir was not too far behind. Justice A.S. Anand notes in his book, that in the Nizam's 'Hyderabad a Legislative Assembly was set up in 1946 but the Muslim members had by official orders, a majority of 10 over the Hindus in a House of 132, though the population was 85% Hindu.

'Scindia of Gwalior only announced his intention of granting responsible government in December 1946, and in May 1947 he summoned an interim government of popular representatives as well as the Constitution-making body.

'In Jaipur, the first Legislative Assembly was established only in 1944.'[37]

By no stretch of the imagination can it be claimed that the Constitution of 1939 measured up to the democratic values that later came to be the pre-condition of a civil society. However, it has to be conceded that it was, in many ways, far ahead of many big and influential states. It is also unclear how and why the Maharaja did not exercise his power of extending the life of the Praja Sabha in 1947, considering the fact that India had suffered a similar fate in losing some members to the fallout of Partition. In India, the reduced number of the Constituent Assembly members—those who had migrated to Pakistan—had not deterred it from going ahead to finalize the Constitution of India. But in Jammu and Kashmir, a similar body had been declared 'rump' and 'dead'. Nevertheless, this statement went uncontested in the Constituent Assembly and was accepted by everyone in the Assembly.

Meanwhile, the Constituent Assembly of India was grappling with the challenge of giving the people a Constitution that reflected the aspirations of the people, guaranteed them fundamental rights, became a tool that would bring socio-economic justice, and help the country take a respectable place among the comity of nations. For the leaders of the National Conference, there was a different kind of challenge. With the Valley having been cleared of invaders, the issue of accession referred to the United Nations, the eagerness of the Central leaders to keep Sheikh Abdullah appeased, and with the unwavering support of Prime Minister Nehru, favourable conditions evolved for Sheikh Abdullah to pursue his goal step-by-step.

Soon after the removal of Maharaja Hari Singh from the scene, the National Conference leaders, who had by now assumed complete control over the government of the State, began to extricate themselves from the agreement reached by Sheikh Abdullah with the Central leaders in Delhi in May 1949. Hectic activity marked this period, and the agreement was subjected to intense debates. Soon this style was to become the hallmark of the National Conference. Not used to double speak and prevarication, it was also to exasperate a leader like Sardar Patel.

This period also put under the scanner the role of the Hindu and the Sikh leaders of the State who were deliberately excluded by their Muslim counterparts in the deliberations that took place. The fact that these meetings were organized secretly was proof enough of the sinister design. During this critical period, leaders like Girdhari Lal Dogra and Sham Lal Saraf from the Jammu region were guilty of acquiescing to the treachery of the Muslim leaders of the party. Most of the Hindu leaders with the National Conference, like Girdhari Lal Dogra, Balraj Puri and Ram Piara Saraf, were part of the left or left of the centre politics. They can perhaps be excused for their presence in the National Conference because of the party's stated commitment to the socio-economic ideology that included 'land to the tiller' policy. But they could not have remained completely unaware of the consequences of the malignant moves that were afoot. It would not be wrong, then, to suggest that the presence of the Hindu leaders in the National Conference was ceremonial and a result of the planning of Sheikh Abdullah and his advisors in order to identify willing collaborators among the minority community.

This was not all. The seeds of converting the State into a playground for extraneous forces that created fifth columns were also laid during this period. According to the scholarly Mohan Krishen Teng, prominent and influential Muslims who opposed the accession of the State to India and senior Muslim officers of the State government who were opposed to the National Conference when it seemed to be supporting the accession, were believed to be specially invited to attend these meetings. Reports suggested that many among them were in clandestine contact with the so-called 'Azad Kashmir' authorities on the other side of the ceasefire line.[38] They were also suspected of working for the intelligence agencies of Pakistan, which had developed a wide network in the State as a result of the apparent official patronage. These meetings were productive and the general consensus that emerged was then conscientiously implemented.

Initially, Sheikh Abdullah vehemently opposed the idea of plebiscite since he was convinced that he represented the will of the people and his word was enough for the people to accept the State's accession to India. But soon he realized the political value of the proposal. It was because of this that the important decision of not opposing the plebiscite was taken by Mirza Afzal Beg and Bakshi Ghulam Mohammad, among others from the National Conference. The plebiscite was made the fulcrum of all their programmes; its acceptance meant that they had a handy tool to argue the need to keep the State out of the territorial jurisdiction as well as the constitutional organization of India. Ironically, Alastair Lamb believes that if the plebiscite had taken place in 1948-1949, the outcome would have been in India's favour. He writes, 'in the early stages of the Kashmir problem, when the memory of the horrors of the tribal invasion of October 1947 was still fresh in the minds of the local population, and the prestige of Sheikh Abdullah (who was still perceived as Jawaharlal Nehru's man) at least among the inhabitants of the Vale, at its height, thoughtful Pakistani leaders cannot have been entirely convinced that the vote would in fact go in their favour.'[39] However, this was not to be. As a consequence of the altered strategy, for a number of years, winning the plebiscite for India was the weapon with which Sheikh Abdullah succeeded in extracting concessions from the timid Central leaders. The opinion of some legal experts and Pakistan apart, the fact was that the law recognized the accession of the State as perfectly legal. In view of this, there should have been no room for the plebiscite and even less for India to have ceded any part of the State's territory to anyone since the provisions of the Instrument of Accession did not contain any clause for ceding of a part of the territory or the secession of the State.

Justice A.S. Anand, in his monumental book, *Constitutional History of Jammu & Kashmir*, is categorical in rejecting the suggestion that the clause wherein the State's accession was to be settled 'by a reference to the people', added in a separate letter by Lord Mountbatten while accepting the Instrument of Accession signed by Maharaja Hari Singh, is an integral part of the acceptance of the Instrument of Accession. He argues[40] that since there was no provision for conditional acceptance of the accession in the Government of India, it could not form a part of the Accession documents.

The National Conference, including the Dogra leaders of the party, also raised the phantom of majoritarianism and the deliberations focused on the fact that India was a predominantly Hindu-majority nation. While expressing faith in the secular credentials of Prime Minister Nehru, the National Conference began to wonder if India's commitment to secularism would retain its intensity in the future too. It feared that if the proposals of the constitutional organization of India were to be accepted by the State then there would be the possibility of it losing its identity in a set up where the Hindus would always exercise dominance. The main concern then became to evolve a constitutional guarantee that would maintain, at all costs, the Muslim-majority character of the State. But for the National Conference, another way of not impairing this character and providing safeguard to protect it would be to keep the State out of the constitutional organization of India.[41]

Significantly, it was also agreed that no urgency needed to be shown in convening the Constituent Assembly as enjoined by the Proclamation of March 1948. Had its convocation taken place before a final decision regarding the accession of the State was reached, it would not only have been premature from the point of view of the National Conference, but also a step in ending the 'rule without accountability' of Sheikh Abdullah and his party. However, to give a loftier reason, it was said that such a convocation should not take place till those areas of the State that had been occupied by Pakistan were reunited with the mainland. In the meantime, to justify its actions and lend constitutionality to decisions, it was agreed that the Interim Government should work under the provisions of the Proclamation of 5th March 1948.

The National Conference leaders, including Sheikh Mohammad Abdullah, Mirza Afzal Beg and Maulana Masoodi, who negotiated the agreement that exiled Maharaja Hari Singh, with the Central leaders at Delhi in May 1949, had also agreed to nominate four members from the State to the Constituent Assembly in Delhi.[42] They also agreed with the view that the relations between the State and the Union of India should be strictly based on the terms, which the Instrument of Accession specified for the accession of the State to India. Thus, Sheikh Abdullah, who had been appointed by the Proclamation of 5th March 1948 as the Prime Minister of the State, began to exercise all executive, legislative and judicial powers that had hitherto been vested in the Maharaja's person under the Jammu and Kashmir Constitution Act, 1939.

With such vast powers in one person, the first confrontation with the Centre occurred soon after a list of amendments concerning the States was circulated for discussions by the drafting committee of the Constituent Assembly in late September 1949. The confrontation that followed was the first attempt to undo the accession. The National Conference leaders also began to take steps to repudiate the agreement reached with the Central leaders in May.

The National Constituent Assembly circulated a draft regarding a temporary provision with respect to the State of Jammu and

Kashmir. In response, the National Conference came up with a new set of proposals on which, they claimed, the constitutional relations between the State and the Union of India would be based. The proposals were to convince the Central leaders to agree that the State would not be brought within the territorial jurisdiction of the proposed Union of India or its constitutional organization, and that the terms and conditions of the first Instrument of Accession would strictly apply in determining the relationship of the State with India. Even more significant was the decision regarding the State Forces. It was decided that the Central leaders would be asked to restore the administrative control of those Forces to the State after they were reorganized and the State was in a position to undertake their operational control.[43]

The National Conference went a step further and also wanted a constitutional guarantee that no instruments, including the Constituent Assembly of Jammu and Kashmir, would be vested with any constituent power to change and modify the existing constitutional relationship between the State and India. The Constituent Assembly of the State would be vested with the power to draw up the Constitution of the State, which would deal with the quality of judicial review, fundamental rights, the quantum of individual freedom and the related legal safeguards, principles of the State policy, and election to the representative bodies in the State. Clearly, the National Conference leadership wanted to put the State beyond the scope of the Constitution of India even on fundamental issues. In effect, they wanted double insurance for the goals they had set for themselves.

The outcome of this planning was sprung upon the Central leadership at an opportune time. It would never be adequately explained as to why these leaders wanted to keep their demands a great secret from the Central leaders till the draft provisions of the Constitution of India were drawn up and sent to them for their approval. Perhaps they had rightly judged that the Central leaders would be flustered, and in the ensuing confusion the National Conference would succeed in extracting maximum concessions for their designs. The bitterness that was to follow could have been avoided by open discussions and exchange of views. The National Conference leaders could not have been unaware that their demands would come as a shock to those who had, against their better judgment, backed them in their tussle with Maharaja Hari Singh for the control of the State's destiny. But this is what they did, and when they disclosed their intent, Gopalaswami Ayyangar was among those left shocked and perplexed. The draft provisions were based on the agreement concluded between the Conference leaders and the Central leaders. The draft provisions were enshrined in the draft Article 306-A of the Constitution of India. The Article stipulated:

> Notwithstanding anything contained in this Constitution, until on the recommendations of the Constituent Assembly constituted for the purpose of framing the Constitution of Jammu and Kashmir State (hereinafter referred to as State in this Article) the President may, by public notification, alter, modify or mend this Article,
>
> a) Only such provisions of this Constitution shall apply in relation to the State as are declared by the President, in consultation with the Government of the State, to relate directly to the matters specified in the Instrument of Accession governing the accession of the State to the Dominion of India;
>
> b) The power of Parliament to make the laws for the State shall be limited to:
>
> Those matters in the Union List and the Concurrent List which are declared by the President, in consultation with the Government of the State, to correspond to matters specified in the Instrument of Accession governing the accession of the State to the Dominion of India as the matters with respect to which the Dominion Legislature may make laws for the State,
>
> Explanation:
>
> The Government of the State in this Article means the person for the time being recognized as the Maharaja of the State by the Union acting on the advice of the Council of Ministers as at present constituted and not acting in his discretion or in his individual judgment.[44]

Thereafter, the Working Committee of the National Conference held a series of meetings to deliberate that draft and, to the utter astonishment of the Central leaders, refused to approve it. It could not accept the stipulations of Article 306-A as a basis for constitutional relations between the State and the Union of India and was deeply resentful of the preamble to Article 306-A, which stipulated that the provisions of the Article would be of a transitional nature and would be subject to modification by the Constituent Assembly of the State. The acceptance would have meant that the National Conference, in principle, agreed to the fact that this was not the final document to determine the relationship of the State with India. In addition, the Working Committee also disapproved of the application of any provisions of the Constitution of India to the State, except the provisions which corresponded to the terms of the Instrument of Accession. The Working Committee expressed their fears that the application of the provisions of the Constitution of India with regard to citizenship, fundamental rights and the related constitutional legal guarantees would prejudice the domiciliary State subjects rules in force in the State.

Significantly, almost all the Muslim members of the Working Committee of the National Conference now denounced the very same settlement, which its leaders had reached with the Central leaders in May 1949 in Delhi. They now insisted on its retraction. But in the larger context, the disturbing aspect was that the Hindu and Sikh members of the Committee watched the proceedings with helpless indignation. There is nothing on record to show that they protested against this volte face of their Party. There were only sullen mumblings expressing mild disagreement with the decisions of the Working Committee. Understandably, these muted expressions were from the Jammu region as they were acutely aware that the people of Jammu would never support the move to keep the State out of the constitutional organization of India, and any attempt to do so would not only alienate them, but would also evoke severe resistance from them. The very fact, which made the National Conference leaders argue for the need to keep the State beyond the pale of the Indian Constitution, argued for it being part of the provisions of the Indian Constitution from the point of Jammu's Hindu-majority population.

Armed with the resolve of the Working Committee, on 12th

October 1949, Sheikh Abdullah communicated the decisions to Gopalaswami Ayyangar and informed him that the Working Committee disapproved of the draft constitutional provisions embodied in Article 306-A. He informed Ayyangar that the Committee had refused to accept the fact that the constitutional provisions with regard to the State would be transitional in nature and would be subject to modification by the Constituent Assembly of the State. Ayyangar was aghast to hear that the Working Committee had disapproved of the application of the Constitution of India to the State, except in respect of those of its provisions, which corresponded to the terms of the Instrument of Accession. Ayyangar heard in disbelief as Abdullah informed him that the application of the provisions of the Constitution of India pertaining to the Indian citizenship, the fundamental rights and the Directive Principles of State Policy would prejudice the domiciliary State subject rules. Then, Sheikh Abdullah sent an alternative draft to Gopalaswami Ayyangar, which stipulated the application of only such provisions of the Constitution of India to the State, which corresponded to the stipulations of the Instrument of Accession. Sheikh Mohammad Abdullah added an explanation to his draft, which defined the State Government as 'the Ruler of the State acting on the advice of the Council of Ministers appointed under the proclamation of the Maharaja dated March 5, 1948.' This significant addition was to add more drama and anxiety to the already exasperating situation.

Ayyangar, who desperately tried to fit into the role of a person knowing Kashmir and its leaders well due to his stint as Prime Minister of the State, received a jolt when the communication of the Conference was delivered to him. Desperate to break the deadlock, on 14th October 1949, he had a long meeting with Sheikh Mohammad Abdullah and Mirza Afzal Beg and tried to persuade the National Conference leaders to accept the draft provisions of Article 306-A. Ayyangar explained to them that the State would reserve the right to frame a Constitution for its government and would be vested with all powers of the government except those, which had been transferred to the Dominion Government by the Instrument of Accession. However, he told the Conference leaders that the accession of the State underlined that the State would be brought within the broad structure of the imperatives of the Constitution of India. The Conference leaders stuck to their stand and told Ayyangar bluntly that the State had acceded to India regarding only three subjects: foreign affairs, defence and communications, and that it retained its independence in all other aspects. They were adamant that it was on that understanding that the people of the State had supported the accession and since the National Conference owed a duty to the people of Kashmir, they would not be able to accept these provisions.

Ayyangar was left fuming and exasperated for he did not possess the acumen to deal with the National Conference leaders. He was cast in the role with the belief that he knew the State well, but he had only dealt with the administration of the State when he had the Maharaja's full authority behind his back. On his own, he turned out to be a non-entity who could be easily manipulated and brow-beaten into coming around to the National Conference's point of view. He had neither the stature of Sardar Patel nor his will and determination. He was capable of doing only what he thought Nehru would want him to do, and now Nehru being away in USA at the time only added to his anxiety and woes. Overwhelmed by the experience at the Security Council, Ayyangar dreaded to antagonize the Conference leaders. Cowed by the situation, he redrafted the provisions of Article 306-A, restricting the application of the Constitution of India to the State to Article 1—which defined the territories of the Union and the provisions pertaining to Indian citizenship—and making the fateful omission of deleting the provisions with regard to the fundamental rights and the related constitutional safeguards. He wrote to Sheikh Mohammed Abdullah:

> Our discussion this morning, as I indicated to you, left me even more distressed than I have been since I received your last letter from Srinagar.
>
> But this personal reaction of mine is irrelevant when I feel weighed with the responsibility of finding a solution for the difficulties that after Panditji left for America and within the last few days have been created, from my point of view, without an adequate excuse.

> In spite of this personal feeling, I am anxiously keen now as ever I have been to see that you are not given any cause for genuine or even imagined grievance in regard to the policy that the Government of India are following, in relation to Kashmir. I have therefore, since you left me this morning, tried to find a way out of the present situation in regard to Article 306-A.
>
> I enclose a draft of Article 306-A with the language of it readjusted so as to meet practically all your points.
>
> I do not wish to write a thesis on the changes that I have made. You will be able to recognize them easily. If you wish to have any further elucidation in the matter I would request you to come over and discuss it frankly with me.
>
> I do hope you will appreciate the gesture I am making. If you are agreeable to this new draft being substituted for the one of which the Drafting Committee had already given notice, I shall ask the Drafting Committee to give notice of this draft in substitution of the other one. Personally, I should like you to move this draft yourself in the House. We shall be there to support you, and I hope the debate would be maintained at such a high level that a report on it, when cabled to America will have an effect on the discussions of the Kashmir problem, that may there be going on which will be of the maximum help to Panditji.
>
> I am looking forward to your rising to the occasion.[45]

The tone and tenor of the letter almost suggests that it was the work of a timid person who dreaded the failure of reaching a settlement—a state of mind hardly conducive for resolving as complex an issue as had arisen. It was also apparent that Ayyangar had learnt no lessons. Otherwise he would not have called upon the Kashmir delegation to initiate the debate on the special constitutional provisions for the State. By doing that, he had unilaterally handed over the veto power to the National Conference leaders in deciding the fate of the State. It was also uncertain what level of discussion he had expected Sheikh Abdullah to maintain that would let Nehru take advantage of it in America. If Ayyangar sought to please Nehru, he should have realized that no fair-minded person would have applauded him for having framed the draft provisions of Article 306-A and having condemned the people of the State, particularly the Hindus, Sikhs and Buddhist minorities, to permanent servitude and suffering. Ironically, Ayyangar had served the State as the Prime Minister to Maharaja Hari Singh for more than six years and he ought to have been aware of the intricate balances of community demands, regional pressures and class interests, which characterized the political sociology of the State. Yet he failed to put his knowledge to good use. Ayyangar, along with Nehru, experienced the ruthless severity with which the National Conference leaders had sought to reorganize these balances and establish fresh alignments, which ensured political precedence for the Muslims in the State. It was apparent that both Nehru and Ayyangar were failing the non-Kashmiri population of the State and putting India in a difficult situation. Now fearful of the consequences of his timidity, he hoped to obtain Patel's authority for this act of perfidy by writing to him:

> Sheikh Abdullah and two colleagues of his had a talk with me for about an hour and a half this morning. It was a long drawn out argument, and, as I told you this morning, there was no substance at all in the objections that they put forward to our draft. At the end of it all, I told them that I had not expected that, after having agreed to the substance of our draft both at your house and at the party meeting, they would let me and Pandit Ji down in the manner they were attempting to do. In answer, Sheikh Abdullah said that he felt very grieved that I should think so but that in the discharge of his duty to his own people, he found it impossible to accept our draft as it was. I told him thereafter to go back and think over all that I had told them and hoped that he would come back to me in a better frame of mind in the course of the day or tomorrow.
>
> I have since thought over the matter further and dictated a draft, which, without giving up the essential stand we have taken in our original draft, readjusts it in minor particulars, in a way which I am hoping Sheikh Abdullah would agree to.[46]

Patel, apparently, had had enough of the National Conference leaders and naturally did not favour the modifications Ayyangar had made in Article 306-A. He did not approve of the deletion of the fundamental rights and the Directive Principles of State Policy from the provisions of the Constitution of India, which would apply to the State. Perhaps, Patel visualized the consequences to which such a course of action would inevitably lead. He wrote to Ayyangar:

> I find there are some substantial changes over the original draft, particularly in regard to the applicability of fundamental rights and Directive Principles of State Policy. You can yourself realize the anomaly of the State becoming a part of India, and at the same time not recognizing any of the provisions.
>
> I do not at all like any change after our party had approved of the whole arrangement in the presence of Sheikh Sahib himself. Whenever Sheikh Sahib wishes to back out, he always confronts us with his duty to the people. Of course, he owes no duty to India or to the Indian Government, or even on a personal basis, to you and the Prime Minister who have gone all out to accommodate him.
>
> In these circumstances, any question of my approval does not arise. If you feel it the right thing to do, you can go ahead with it.[47]

Sardar Patel had washed his hands, since he must have known that the Nehru-Ayyangar combine did not have it in them to call off the bluff of the National Conference leaders.

Ayyangar's discomfiture did not end there. Even the revised draft of Article 306-A was rejected by the National Conference leaders. Sheikh Mohammad Abdullah wrote to Ayyangar that it was not possible for him and his colleagues to accept the revised draft as well. He sent an alternative draft to Ayyangar, which stressed that the provisions of the Constitution of India, which corresponded to the terms of the Instrument of Accession would apply to the State, and the other provisions would apply only with the approval of the Interim Government. Abdullah wrote to Ayyangar that the alternate draft 'went far beyond the sphere in aspect of which we had acceded to India.' Apparently, the National Conference had attained a state of mind where it had begun to believe that it was the National Conference that had signed the Instrument of Accession. Amnesia had struck the party regarding the situation that existed when Pakistan-supported raiders had crossed the Kohala bridge and marched towards Baramulla to subject it to the barbaric acts of rape, plunder and arson. It pretended as if the arrival of the Indian Forces was an exigency that could be put aside after the threat had passed. It also forgot that the Instrument of Accession, from which it drew its arguments, was signed by the Maharaja and had, on occasions, been rejected by the National Conference precisely for that reason.

The events that followed this confrontation gave birth to manufactured controversy and debate regarding the adoption of Article 306-A by the Constituent Assembly. The fact was that, unable to reach a consensus, Afzal Beg had given the Constituent Assembly the notice of an amendment in Article 306-A, which sought to restrict the application of the Constitution of India to the terms of the Instrument of Accession.

A desperate Ayyangar met the National Conference leaders once again and tried to persuade them to accept the revised draft. However, they did not relent. Finally, Ayyangar drew up a fresh draft in consultation with Afzal Beg, who was deputed by Sheikh Mohammad Abdullah, to negotiate a settlement. Abdullah remained behind the scenes. The revised draft, as suggested by the National Conference, stipulated:

> Article I would apply to the State, and the State would be included in the territories of the Union of India;
>
> No other provision of the Constitution of India would be applied to the State, except with the approval of the Interim Government of the State;
>
> The division of powers between the Union and the State would be determined in accordance with the terms of the Instrument of Accession;
>
> The President of India would be empowered to terminate or modify the operation of the Constitutional provisions with regard to the State on the recommendation of the Constituent Assembly of the State;
>
> The State Government would be construed to mean the Maharaja acting on the advice of the Council of Ministers appointed under his proclamation dated 5 March, 1948.

Apparently, Ayyangar failed to convince the National Conference leaders on the definition of 'government'.

The revised draft of Article 306-A was circulated in the Constituent Assembly on 16th October 1949. It came up for the consideration of the Assembly the next day. Many of the members of the Constituent Assembly objected to the explanation defining the Government of the State and pointed out to Ayyangar that the explanation vested the powers of the government with the 'Council of Ministers appointed under the Maharaja's Proclamation dated 5 March, 1948', and, in perpetuity and in effect, excluded all subsequent governments of the State from the purview of the Constitution of India. Ayyangar, not sure as to what extent Nehru wanted him to accommodate the National Conference, and perhaps too eager on his own to reach an agreement, wanted the matter to be closed as soon as possible. But it is more likely that, in his opinion, this was what Prime Minister Nehru would have wanted him to do. Under pressure, Ayyangar modified the explanation in so far as the Government of the State would be construed to mean the 'person for the time recognized by the President as the Maharaja of Jammu and Kashmir acting on the advice of the Council of Ministers for the time being in office under the Maharaja's Proclamation dated the fifth day of March, 1948.' Ayyangar informed the Conference leaders about the modifications he had made in the explanation on the morning of 17th October 1949. Having tasted minor victories, the Conference leaders refused to approve the modification Ayyangar had made. Ayyangar, along with Maulana Abul Kalam Azad, assured the Conference leaders that the modification in the explanation was deemed necessary to avoid the discrepancy in Article 306-A, which implied a perpetual Interim Government. The Conference leaders, however, did not approve of the amendment and told Ayyangar and Azad that if the modifications to the explanation were not withdrawn, the National Conference leaders would move the amendment of which they had given notice to the Assembly before the draft was revised by Ayyangar and Beg.

Unable to convince the Conference leaders to accept the changes he had brought about in the draft provisions, Ayyangar presented the draft Article 306-A to the Constituent Assembly for its consideration. This was the forum for open debates and it had discussed every possible contentious issue before it. Many amendments were moved by various individuals and groups, and not all of them were adopted. But all of them were discussed before they were voted out. Thus, it was the most appropriate forum where the National Conference leaders could express their views in public for their peers to listen and debate. It would also give them an opportunity to know publicly what the rest of the country thought of their proposals. But they had become accustomed to the style of the conspirators who avoided openness and public debates. They were more used to discussing across the table to win some concessions. Hence they sulked and did not join the debate on the provisions. In fact, they joined the deliberations of the Assembly after Ayyangar had already delivered a part of his speech. The Conference leaders had watched the proceedings in grim silence as 'the President of the Assembly waited for a minute or two for members to rise for making speeches before he put the draft article to the House', as Ayyangar later explained to Sheikh Abdullah.[48] Since the Conference leaders did not rise to speak and did not move any amendment to the draft, it was adopted by the Assembly without any dissent.

The democratic credentials of the Conference leaders are best judged by the fact that after getting the opportunity of explaining to the country as to why they had a different view on the subject, they gave vent to their bitterness outside the forum after the Assembly had adopted the draft. Sheikh Mohammad Abdullah wrote a sharp rejoinder to Ayyangar asking him to reconsider the decision the Constituent Assembly had taken on Article 306-A. He was virtually hoping to exercise the power of veto. He wrote to Ayyangar saying if this was not done, he would resign from the Constituent Assembly along with the other representatives of Jammu and Kashmir. 'As I have told you before, I and my colleagues have been extremely pained by the manner in which the thing has been done, and, after careful consideration of the matter, we have [arrived] at the conclusion that it is not possible for us to let the matter rest here. As I am genuinely anxious that no unpleasant situation should arise, I would request you to see if even now something could be done to rectify the position. In case I fail to hear from you within a reasonable time, I regret to say that no course is left open for us but to tender our resignation from the Constituent Assembly,' Sheikh Abdullah wrote.[49]

On the other hand, Ayyangar too was feeling let down and disappointed in the National Conference's leadership. He felt aggrieved that he had not been treated with any consideration by the National Conference leaders. Indeed, he had gone to the farthest limits to accommodate their views. He could not retrieve the ground he had lost, but it was evident that he could not go any further to appease the State leaders. He wrote back to Abdullah: 'It is true that after having unsuccessfully attempted along with Maulana Azad, to persuade you to agree willingly to substitution of the words "for the time being" for the word "appointed", I did move the Article with the amendment after obtaining the permission of the President to do so. The whole House accepted this. I am sorry that you could not move any amendment of your own against the one I moved. There was, however, nothing to prevent you or any of your colleagues from opposing the amendment that I did move, and as a matter of fact, we were looking forward to your making a speech on the whole of the article, and believe the President waited for a minute or two for members to rise for making speeches before he put the draft article to the House.'[50]

Ayyangar also added that if Sheikh Abdullah and his colleagues felt aggrieved then they could take such steps as the rules of the House allowed for any rectification. He forewarned Abdullah that the resignation of the National Conference members from the Constituent Assembly would have serious repercussions, in Kashmir and outside. He wrote: 'I do not consider, therefore, that there is any justification for your entertaining any idea of resignation from the Constituent Assembly. The step, if taken, would produce the most unwelcome and serious repercussions in Kashmir, India and the world, and I must ask you to communicate with the Prime Minister before you decide on anything like it. For myself, I shall pass on to him your letter and this reply of mine to it.'[51]

In his eagerness to mollify Abdullah, in the same letter of 18th October 1949, Ayyangar tried to justify the use of the phrase 'for the time being in office' in the following words: 'The words appearing in the Article as passed yesterday are "the Council of Ministers for the time being in office under the Maharaja's Proclamation dated March 5, 1948." Under the Article, the Council of Ministers has to be consulted on certain matters and its concurrence has to be obtained in other matters. It is obvious that members of this Council appointed under the Maharaja's Proclamation cannot give their advice or concurrence unless they happen to be functioning, that is, in office, at the time when such advice or concurrence has to be given.'[52]

Sardar Patel also recorded the differences in his letter to Pandit Jawaharlal Nehru on 3rd November1949 and was more forthright on the subject of the alteration of the phrase 'for the time being in office'. He wrote: 'There was some difficulty about the provision relating to Kashmir. Sheikh Sahib went back on the agreement which he had reached with you in regard to the provisions relating to Kashmir. He insisted on certain fundamental character which would exclude in their application to Kashmir the provisions relating to citizenship and fundamental rights, and make it necessary in all these matters as well as others not covered by the accession to three subjects to seek the concurrence of the State Government which is sought to define as the Maharaja acting on the advice of the Council of Ministers appointed under the proclamation of 5 March, 1948. After a great deal of discussion, I could persuade the party to accept all the changes, except the last one, which was modified so as to cover not merely the first Ministry so appointed, but any subsequent Ministries which may be appointed under that proclamation. Sheikh Sahib has not reconciled himself to this change, but we could not accommodate him in this matter and the provision was passed through the House as we had modified.'[53]

At the revision stage, Article 306-A was renamed Article 370. On 25th November 1949, the Regent of the State, Karan Singh, by a Proclamation, ordered that the relations between the State and the Union of India be governed by the Constitution of India. According to the Proclamation, the Constitution of India superseded and abrogated all other constitutional provisions inconsistent with it which were in force in the State. On 26th January1950, the Constitution of India came into force. But in the process, once again, Sheikh Abdullah invoked the authority of the 5th March 1948 Proclamation to achieve his political goal. He wanted the world to believe that his appointment as Prime Minister by the Maharaja was in perpetuity and that only he and he alone had been made the voice of the State that needed to be recognized by the Government of India and the rest of the world. It did not occur to him that if he were not there at the scene, the Maharaja had the authority to appoint a new Prime Minister who would then be recognized as the Head of State by the Government, and on whose advice the Maharaja would act. 'The King is dead, long live the King' is an old axiom but the same is true of Prime Ministers in a parliamentary democracy.

When Yuvraj Karan Singh, the Regent of Jammu and Kashmir, issued a Proclamation accepting the New Constitution of India as drafted by the Constituent Assembly on 25th November 1949, he concluded the proclamation by saying:

> I now hereby declare and direct:-
>
> That the Constitution of India shortly to be adopted by the Constituent Assembly of India shall, in so far it is applicable to the State of Jammu and Kashmir, govern the constitutional relationship between this State and the contemplated Union of India and shall be enforced in this State by me, my heirs and successors in accordance with the tenor of its provisions;
>
> That the provisions of the said Constitution shall, as from the date of its commencement, supersede and abrogate all other constitutional provisions inconsistent therewith which are at present in force in this State.

The confrontation over Article 370 between Sheikh Abdullah and the leaders of India established the fact that even though Sheikh Abdullah and his colleagues were neither elected representatives, nor were they accountable to any legislative institution, they arrogated to themselves the right to speak on behalf of all the regions of the State. In theory, Prime Minister Sheikh Abdullah was accountable to the Maharaja who appointed him, but in practice, he did not recognize the authority of the Maharaja as bringing him under his ambit. With the absence of any legislature, there was no way any other authority could hold him responsible for his acts. The recurring theme that became his central point was that he owed a responsibility to his people and that Pandit Jawaharlal Nehru had made certain promises that were not being honoured. Never, as Sardar Patel pointed out in his letter to Gopalaswami Ayyangar, did he once mention either his responsibility towards India or to any promise and assurance that he might have made to Nehru.

5

A Document of Change

Article 370 was to leave the ultra nationalists as well as the leaders of Kashmir deeply dissatisfied. While the mainstream national leaders were convinced that it was the best arrangement under the circumstances, there was a section who believed that it queried the complete integration of the State to India. The transitory character of the Article had both sides feeling like the business had been left unfinished. The fact that the State was brought under the Indian Constitution, in whatever manner, was lost on ultra-nationalists, while the Kashmiri leaders felt that they had been deprived of their cherished goal.

Smarting at not being allowed to make a fool-proof arrangement of keeping the Indian State and Constitution out of Jammu and Kashmir, Prime Minister Sheikh Abdullah made a dramatic announcement on 13th July 1950, which triggered a course of action that was to irretrievably alienate large sections of the population and drive a wedge between him and the Dogras. Except for the adherents of the National Conference, the day was remembered for the unfortunate events that occurred in 1931 when the first communal riot had taken place in Srinagar after some Hindu shopkeepers were attacked.[54] It had led to a series of events that ultimately resulted in firing by the Dogra police and the death of several Kashmiris. The day was therefore celebrated, much to the chagrin of the Dogras, as 'Martyrs' Day' by the National Conference.

In 1950, Sheikh Abdullah was very close to the pinnacle of his popularity, but he had also begun to demonstrate all the traits of a dictator. He was charming and charismatic when he wanted to be; of brilliant mind that brimmed with self-confidence and independent thoughts. But like most dictators, he periodically needed to make grand gestures that enhanced his reputation to bring about revolutionary changes. So, to gain more political mileage, he sent two proposals regarding the abolition of the *Jagirdari* system of land tenancy and of landlordism without any compensation, a month before the Martyrs' Day, to the Regent. The proposals were obviously progressive, but the finer details needed to be worked on. Moreover, it needed to be reconsidered as these were to affect large sections of the population that were non-Muslim. Thus, Yuvraj Karan Singh referred the matter to Vishnu Sahay, Secretary for Kashmir Affairs to the Government of India, to guide him about the implications of the proposal.[55] When Sheikh Abdullah was told of this, he was furious and roundly castigated the Regent in a memorandum:

> It appears that the obvious limitations of the Constitutional head of the State have escaped the attention of Shri Yuvraj. The action taken by Shri Yuvraj is entirely opposed to the spirit of the Proclamation dated 5th March 1948 under which the present government was set up. It has all along been understood that the Ruler or his Regent will strictly act as [the] Constitutional head of the State and it is on this distinct understanding that the present government hold their office...It is also clear that the subjects in regard to which the submissions were made did not relate to a matter in which the State had acceded to the Dominion of India and, therefore, in the existing constitutional set up the Government of India has no jurisdiction in this matter.[56]

After consultations with New Delhi, the Yuvraj wrote to his Prime Minister on 12th July 1950:

> I appreciate the Constitutional position under the Proclamation of 5th March, 1948. Nonetheless it seems to me that these very far-reaching proposals, which will drastically affect the economy of very large sections of the population and for the sanctioning of which there is no properly functioning legislature at present, should, in the existing delicate political situation, be first examined in concert with the Government of India, and that we should not rush this legislation without satisfying...[57]

Not to be thwarted in his designs, even though he was aware that the Government of India had asked him to further discuss the matter in New Delhi and was informed that these measures were not legal without the signature of Yuvraj Karan Singh, Sheikh Abdullah went ahead and made the announcements the next day.

Sheikh Abdullah's action jolted New Delhi. For the first time, it got an inkling of the Sheikh's dictatorial traits and the extent to which he was willing to go to make his point. This was also the first time New Delhi realized that the Indian Government and the Prime Minister of Kashmir not only had differences of opinion but also had a different approach to dealing with challenges of development. This was also the first time Yuvraj Karan Singh, the Constitutional Head, and his Prime Minister, Sheikh Abdullah, differed on a matter of policy. It was obvious that while the Yuvraj was conscious of the fact that his role in the peculiar circumstances was to safeguard the national interest in the State, his Prime Minister was determined to treat the State as his fiefdom, where the Constitutional Head was a mere rubber stamp to the Prime Minister's decisions. It had also not occurred to Sheikh Abdullah that the Proclamation that he invoked to justify his decision was made a good two years ago, and that the purpose of that Proclamation was to facilitate the transition to a responsible government elected through a democratic election based on universal adult franchise. The changes relevant to development and transformation to a welfare State were to follow after the elected set up had been put in place. While there was no sign of any steps being taken to elect a Constituent Assembly that would ultimately lead to that goal, the Proclamation was being used to perpetuate the autocratic and arbitrary rule of Sheikh Abdullah and his political party, and take decisions that would have ramifications within and outside the State.

The proposal, as announced by Sheikh Abdullah, expectedly roused the Dogra people of the Jammu region who could not be blamed for interpreting it as yet another step to humiliate them so soon after the Maharaja had been forced to leave the State. Apart from the humiliation, the proposal was to vitally affect the economy and the social relationship between various sections of the society. It was also aimed at alienating Jammu from Kashmir.

The proposal therefore had a dual purpose, both contradictory, but integral to Sheikh Abdullah's scheme of things. The price to be paid was not much in Sheikh Abdullah's estimation. This was preceded by the short but eventful history of the uneasy relationship regarding the devolution of power between Prime Minister Sheikh Abdullah and the Maharaja. However, the political conditions, evolving out of the conflict, and the internationalization of the matter had given unbridled powers to Sheikh Abdullah and the National Conference, and later, the ruse to relegate the convocation of the Constituent Assembly into the background. Thus, for more than two years, Sheikh Abdullah had exercised arbitrary and dictatorial powers to implement the agenda of the National Conference without being accountable to any authority but himself.

The National Conference had begun to propagate and argue at every available forum that the Instrument of Accession did not mean that the political integration of the State had automatically followed it. It repeatedly questioned the validity of the Treaty of Amritsar* and refused to accept the integration of Kashmir into the State of Jammu and Kashmir. Consequently, it ignored the fact that this very argument disqualified the National Conference from claiming to speak on behalf of the State created after the Treaty, which had merged Kashmir with the parent State of Jammu, Ladakh and the Gilgit-Baltistan region. The National Conference either had to accept the Instrument of Accession as it was and refrain from precluding the whole State from the political jurisdiction of the Indian Dominion or had to confine itself to articulating only on behalf of Kashmir. If the making of the State was based on what it derisively called a 'sale deed' that had no validity, and if the Valley was to enjoy the right to self-determination, then the other regions had the same right.

---

* The Treaty, entered into by the East India Company and Raja Gulab Singh of Jammu, handed over Kashmir to Gulab Singh after seizing it from the Sikh empire, which had failed to pay the war indemnity that was imposed by the Company on the Sikhs. Gulab Singh agreed to pay the stipulated amount and hence incorporated Kashmir into his kingdom.

It has been seen how, after much cajoling, four representatives of the State were nominated to the Constituent Assembly of India. Of the four, three represented Kashmir, only a non-entity was nominated to represent Jammu, and Ladakh had no representation. As a result, the full force of the intransigence of the National Conference was on display during the tension-filled behind-the-scenes parleys before Article 370 was adopted. The discussions and the exchange of letters where both, the Congress and the National Conference, accused each other of betrayal, clearly indicated that the National Conference was hesitant to recognize any obligations, which emanated from the accession of the State to India, including the obligations that involved the delegation of powers to the Dominion Government. By not nominating representatives to the Constituent Assembly, the National Conference had hoped to legally keep itself out of the ambit of the Indian Constitution. But having once nominated the representatives, it now had a duty to participate in the parleys rather than sulk and bargain behind the scenes.

It was too late in the day when Sardar Patel reminded Sheikh Abdullah that without Maharaja Hari Singh's signature, neither India and its army nor the National Conference would have been where they found themselves in the State. The National Conference leaders presumed, like a few other Princes had tried to argue, that with the lapse of the British Paramountcy all conditions that governed the relations of that State to that of India automatically stood terminated. In this, after assuming power, they were on the same page with the mischievous stipulations of the Cabinet Mission Plan, which had envisaged the restoration of sovereignty to the States after Paramountcy was withdrawn. This, undoubtedly, would have led to the balkanization of the subcontinent and the creation of numerous small and mutually-agnostic nation-states, and would have suited the geostrategic and post-colonial, imperialistic designs of the British who still vainly clung to the image of an empire where the sun never sets.

The British world view certainly did not satisfy the vision that the leaders of the Indian Freedom Movement nourished. However, that concept also suited the myopic ambitions of some of the rulers who continued to believe in the ability of the British Empire to protect their independence. Ironically, the National Conference also joined their ranks. The difference though was that Sardar Patel had found dealing with the recalcitrant States easier because the matter had been considered internal. In the matter of Jammu and Kashmir, however, there were extraneous circumstances that had given it a different dimension.

After his sullen participation in the making of the Indian Constitution, Prime Minister Sheikh Abdullah had turned his attention to dismantling the symbols of Dogra Rule. In this, a document that came to be known as 'Naya Kashmir' became a handy tool, since it expressed a progressive ideology and lent respectability to the strategy. All this was part of a carefully executed image makeover. The National Conference had risen from the Reading Room in Srinagar[58] and had passed through various phases of transition—from being an avowedly communal party known as the Muslim Conference, to assuming secular credentials as the National Conference. In the process it had also formulated its socio-economic and political goals.

The 1930s was a period when all the left-leaning thinkers and activists began to organize themselves. Even the literati had come together under the banner of the Progressive Writers' Movement, and a few among them were committed to one political movement or another. The fact that the Russian Revolution had succeeded in overthrowing an order that had been entrenched since centuries, had given hope to many among them. As a result, many progressive intellectuals had begun to take a keen interest in the affairs of Jammu and Kashmir. The National Conference was only too keen to enlist their support. Consequently, the evolution of young, educated Muslims—from the Reading Room gatherings in Srinagar to a secular and socialist party—was a result of an evolutionary process.

The earlier avatar of the National Conference as the Muslim Conference had taken roots in the Valley as well as in the Poonch-Mirpur areas, where British Punjab exerted considerable influence. In the Jammu region, although it had a tall leader in Chaudhary Ghulam Abbas, it failed to garner the same support as it had done in the Valley. Abbas was nevertheless a very important ally of Sheikh Abdullah. During the course of their political activities, the

Muslim Conference and Sheikh Abdullah came in close contact with national leaders like Mahatma Gandhi, Jawaharlal Nehru, Abdul Ghaffar Khan, Mohammad Ali Jinnah,[59] and many others. In the process, it either realized on its own or had been persuaded by the national leaders to become a part of the greater movement for socio-economic equality and political freedom that had already taken root in the country. It was in these circumstances that the Muslim Conference, under the influence of Sheikh Abdullah, chose to rechristen itself as the National Conference in 1939, and open its doors to people of all religions and walks of life. However, in the process, Chaudhary Ghulam Abbas and a few others who disagreed were forced to walk out of the new party to resurrect the communal ideology under the old name with closer ties with Mohammad Ali Jinnah's Muslim League.

The period immediately after the Second World War days was of lull, though the freedom movement in the rest of the country gathered momentum even as British India was dragged into the World War. The Indian National Congress, after the bitter experience it had during First World War when cooperating in the war effort on the promise that self-rule would be conceded after the conclusion of the war, was in no mood to trust the British again. The Princely States of India, understandably, contributed their utmost to the war effort. But, strangely, during this period, when the Quit India Movement was launched by Mahatma Gandhi and the Congress, Sheikh Abdullah and the National Conference chose to maintain a low profile. It was only when the war was drawing to a close that the National Conference came into action and presented its demands to Maharaja Hari Singh.

The manner in which the demands were presented was dramatic. Maharaja Hari Singh was a member of the Imperial War Cabinet and had gone to Britain to participate in its deliberations in April 1944. On his return, the citizens of Kashmir lined the roads to welcome him. As his cavalcade (consisting of a flotilla of boats on the river Jehlum) approached Mujahid Manzil, the headquarters of the National Conference, Sheikh Mohammed Abdullah, along with his party members, garlanded the Maharaja with flowers. Bouquets were given to him. Then the Sheikh submitted a memorandum demanding far-reaching democratic reforms that would lead to the establishment of Jammu and Kashmir as a constitutional, democratic and welfare State, with the Maharaja as the nominal constitutional head. This was the memorandum that became famous as the 'Naya Kashmir' document. Attached with this document was an economic plan projecting a humanistic view of development, which progressive people endorsed and lauded as far ahead of its time.

It was not surprising, since the making of the document was the collaborative effort of avowed communists, based in Lahore and with strong links to Kashmir. Sheikh Abdullah, in his memoir *Aatish e Chinar* (*Flames of the Chinar*), writes that the job of drafting the Naya Kashmir was given to his friend B.P.L. Bedi. Bedi's wife Freda, typed the manuscript. Marxist historian, K.M.Ashraf, Urdu poets, Mohammad Din Taseer[60] and Ehsan Danish, and advocate, Danyal Lateefi had assisted in its drafting. Other sources mention the name of Pandit Jia Lal Kilam and celebrated poet, Hafeez Jullundhri, but Sheikh Abdullah does not acknowledge their roles. All those involved had communist leanings; it is said that the document had the support of all the progressive elements and the leading communists of the region.

Naya Kashmir was the outline of a plan to convert Jammu and Kashmir from an absolute monarchy to a constitutional democracy, with the Maharaja remaining the Head of the State, just as the Monarch is in Britain. It was subsequently adopted by the National Conference as its manifesto and translated into Urdu so that the majority of the people of the State could understand it. It also envisaged all aspects that affected the life of a citizen and defined citizenship, its basic rights and obligations, in the following words:

> A single State Citizenship is hereby established for all citizens of Jammu, Kashmir, Ladakh and the Frontier Regions, including the Poonch and Chinani [Chenani] illaqas. The equality of the rights of all citizens, irrespective of their nationality, religion, race, or birth, in all spheres of national life—economic, political, cultural, and social shall…be an irrevocable law. Any direct or indirect restriction of these rights, or conversely the establishment of direct or indirect privileges for any citizens or class of citizens on account of nationality, religion, race or birth, as well as the

> propagation of national, racial or religious exceptionalism or hatred and contempt shall be punished by law.[61]

On the subject of the defence of the State, the document was unequivocal in stating:

> The defence of the Motherland is the supreme and sacred duty of all citizens. Treason to the Motherland, violation of oath, desertion to enemies of the Motherland, impairing the military power of the State, espionage shall be punishable with the full severity of the Law as the gravest crime in pursuance of this sacred task every citizen is obliged to arm himself to use and shall be ensured the right to bear arms.[62]

In retrospect, it is hard to say if this was motivated, but it must have been directed at the Maharaja to assure him that the National Conference was not antagonistic to the army of the State and that it was prepared to put all its weight behind it. The Dogras, particularly the Rajputs, famously possessed firearms and other conventional weapons, and this clause could have been added to appease them. But it is more likely that, like the Second Amendment of the American Constitution, which also gave Americans the right to keep and bear Arms, this was meant for the Kashmiri populace who had hitherto been outside the pale of martial attributes. However, when the hour of trial arrived, it became obvious that Sheikh Abdullah respected neither the State Forces nor the Dogras. He was in the forefront of those unleashing a calumnious attack on the integrity of the State Forces and the Dogra people, even when those forces were locked in threatening battles to defend the territories and integrity of the State.

Significantly, Naya Kashmir was one of the earliest documents to speak of the right to work, food and security in old age through social insurance. In an early warning of things to come, it also said:

> The right of personal property of [the] citizens, as well as the right of inheritance of personal property of [the] citizens, is protected by law within the limits of the planned economy of the State.

It is obvious that the subject and the need of a planned economy was inspired by the Soviet model that was also to be adopted by

India after it gained independence. Nevertheless, it was a very progressive document.

On the subject of constituting the National Assembly of the State, it read:

> The highest legislature of the State, the National Assembly, is elected by citizens of the State by electoral districts on the basis of one deputy per 40,000 populations for a period of five years.

It also categorically stated that,

> Subject to the general control of H.H. the Maharaja Bahadur the jurisdiction of the National Assembly shall include: representation of the State in exterior relations; conclusion and ratification of treaties with other States; approval of alterations of the boundaries of the States; organization of the defence of the State and the direction of its armed forces; foreign trade upon the basis of State monopoly; protection of State security; establishment of the National Economic Plan of the State; approval of the State Budget; administration of banks, industrial and agricultural establishments…[63]

It also contained a clause on the role of the Maharaja of the State and said:

> The ruler of Jammu and Kashmir shall:
>
> convene sessions of the National Assembly twice a year; shall convene extraordinary sessions of the Assembly at his own wish or at the request of the speaker of the Assembly; and dissolve the National Assembly and fix new elections; conduct a referendum upon his own initiative or upon the demand of the majority of the legislators; declare general or partial mobilization; ratify international treaties after they have been approved by the National Assembly. Summon the leader of the largest single party in the National Assembly to form the Ministry.[64]

In the matter of the electoral process, it had some unusual points to make:

> Deputies to the National Assembly as well as to the People's Panchayats are selected by the electors upon the basis of universal equal direct suffrage by secret ballot. Franchise shall be universal:

> all citizens of the State who have reached the age of eighteen years, irrespective of race and sex, nationality or religion, educational qualifications, residential qualifications, social origin, property, status, or past activity shall have the right to participate in the elections of deputies and to be elected with the exception of insane persons and those deprived of electoral rights by court sentence. Franchise shall be equal: every citizen takes part in elections upon an equal basis. Every citizen shall have one vote, provided that, during the transitional period, Sikhs, Kashmiri Pandits and Harijans shall be provided with two reserved seats each, and for this purpose they shall exercise the right of a second vote. Women shall have the right to elect and to be elected upon equal terms with men in all institutions of the State.
>
> Citizens serving in the armed forces shall have the right to elect and be elected on equal terms with all citizens.
>
> Candidates shall be put forward for election according to electoral districts. Any one hundred electors residing in an electoral district may sponsor a candidate. No other precondition, whether money security or otherwise, shall be required of a candidate.[65]

This document, that was to assume the form of a manifesto, had, long before India amended its law, made eighteen years olds eligible for voting. It also visualized dual vote for the minority communities of Sikhs, Kashmiri Pandits and Harijans, and allowed even the serving personnel of the State Forces to contest in election while making the support of 100 voters essential for the nomination as a candidate for the election.

On the subject of the judiciary, Naya Kashmir had an extremely radical take and is justifiably accused of blindly following the communist model of the Soviet system that makes all institutions subservient to the Party:

> Justice is administered by the High Court of Jammu and Kashmir, and by the District and Tehsil People's Courts. In all courts, cases shall be tried with the participation of the people's Judges with the exception of cases specially provided for by law…The High Court of Jammu and Kashmir is elected by the National Assembly for a period of five years. The lower courts are appointed by the

> High Court for a period of five years, with the exception of the People's Courts which are elected by the People's Panchayats for a period of five years.[66]

Naya Kashmir was extremely articulate on the subject of local administration, the level where the reputation of a government is made and unmade:

> The organs of State power in District of the Tehsils, Cities and Villages, shall be the People's Panchayats. The People's Panchayats direct the activities of the organs of administration subordinate to them, ensure the maintenance of State order observance of laws and the protection of the rights of citizens, direct local, economic and cultural development in fulfillment of the National Plan, organize civil defence, and draw up the local budget. The People's Panchayats adopt decisions and issue orders within the limits of the powers vested in them by law. The executive and administrative organs of the People's Panchayats are the Executive Committees elected by them, composed of a Chairman, Vice Chairman, Secretary and Members.
>
> The Executive Committee of the People's Panchayats are directly responsible to the People's Panchayats which elected them and are also subject to the Council of Ministers of the States.
>
> The People's Panchayats are elected by the people of their area of jurisdiction for a period of five years.
>
> The ratio of representation in the People's Panchayats shall be determined by law.[67]

This again was a model adopted from the communist mode of governance that was followed in the USSR. However, the success of this model had been questioned even at that point of time. Additionally, it also depended heavily on the widespread presence of the cadre of workers at the village and local level. It can be conceded that the National Conference had the presence of sufficient numbers in the Valley, but the same was far from true in Jammu, Ladakh, Poonch and the Gilgit-Baltistan region. This situation carried the seeds of resentment in the majority who did not support the National Conference and believed that it was undemocratic and blatantly unjust. But, if the provisions regarding the functioning of the local administration as well as the judiciary, and the role of the elected nominees were to be selectively implemented, then it had the seeds of debilitating corruption and oppression.

The reality was that the Government of Sheikh Abdullah had begun to function as a full-fledged government under the 5th March 1948 Proclamation with the Naya Kashmir document as its Constitution, but it had taken no steps to initiate the process of holding elections to convene the Constituent Assembly to frame a proper Constitution. As a result the workers of the National Conference had already begun to function in the capacity of the elected representatives of the Panchayats and had bullied the administration to run their writ.

The consequences of party workers being appointed to government positions and their meddling in the administration have been critically commented upon by Balraj Puri in his book *Kashmir: Insurgency and After*,[68] since people with dubious credentials got themselves appointed to important positions. This was more pronounced in the Jammu region, where the National Conference had minimal presence, hence the party and by extension the administration, came to be manned by people in whom even the National Conference did not have faith.

On the important subject of economy, Naya Kashmir had a separate clause, but confined itself to saying:

> The economic life of the State shall be determined and directed by the National Economic Plan for the purpose of increasing public wealth, of ensuring a steady rise in the material and cultural level of working men and women, and consolidating the defence capacity of the State.[69]

Thus, much was known of the revolutionary socio-administrative philosophy, but there was no inkling of the land reforms that Sheikh Abdullah was determined to push through.

The Naya Kashmir plan, was soon translated into Urdu for the common man and proved to be immensely popular in Kashmir as it must be said that the blueprint for a welfare state was far in advance of its times. But it would have been unrealistic to expect Maharaja Hari Singh to accept these demands though he was favourably inclined to a number of them. He, by his own admission, was willing to assume the role of a constitutional head but to expect of him to concede certain other demands, particularly regarding judiciary and local administration, was expecting too much. In fact, even the sympathizers of the National Conference in India were not too keen to go to the extent that Naya Kashmir had gone. As for the land reforms, the Maharaja had initiated the process of radical reforms on becoming the ruler of the State. Apart from bestowing proprietary rights upon the tenants and distributing village lands, he had freed the peasantry from the clutches of usury. He could be expected to accept a few reasonable reforms, but certainly not the kind of sweeping reforms that the National Conference envisaged.

That Maharaja Hari Singh was not averse to the document in its totality is clear from the assertion in his Memorandum to the President of India,[70] where he says that he had absolutely no hesitation in accepting the role of a constitutional monarch, and that he was himself in the process of drawing up a new constitution for the State. But he had hoped that a more representative process would be carried out that not only made him a constitutional monarch but also envisaged a central legislature that gave representation to the regions of Jammu, Kashmir, Ladakh and the northern regions and feudatories of Gilgit, Baltistan, Chitral etc, while at the same time let all these regions have their own autonomous legislative bodies.[71]

On the face of it, the Naya Kashmir vision was a significant improvement in the stance towards the State. Historically, the anti-Dogra movement of first the Muslim Conference and then the National Conference had consistently claimed that the Dogra rule in Kashmir was a product of a document that was nothing more than a 'sale deed', and as such, did not have the authority to subjugate the people of one region to another. Thus the implied meaning of the National Conference movement had been that it did not recognize the 'State of Jammu and Kashmir' as created by the Dogras. Having thus argued in the past and without retracting the stated philosophy and the fact that the demands presented to the Maharaja in 1944 bore the title of 'Naya Kashmir', it was obvious that the manifesto thus created was primarily for the people of Kashmir and that the other regions of the State were only at the peripheral vision of the movement. The unstated purpose was of pushing them into subordinate roles.

Protestations regarding the separate identity of the Kashmiri people apart, in reality, neither Sheikh Abdullah nor the National Conference were willing to let go of the region of either Jammu or Ladakh from their clutches once they assumed power. They had little interest in the Northern regions of Gilgit, Baltistan, Hunza, Rondu and other smaller feudatories, since it was in the interests of neither; the regions had expressed their hostility towards both India and a separate identity and expressly desired to be part of Pakistan.

The inexplicable halt of the Indian Army in its march towards Muzaffarabad and the reluctance to commit its troops in the Gilgit-Baltistan region came as a blessing to the National Conference. Many since then have suspected that to be a deliberate move in order to pave a smooth way for Sheikh Abdullah after the cessation of hostilities. But Jammu was a prize worth having since it was this region that was desperate to hold on to the nomenclature of 'Jammu and Kashmir'—having been its creator.

By the time the power was transferred to Sheikh Abdullah, first as the Head of the Administration and then as Prime Minister under the 5th March 1948 Proclamation, the National Conference had in its ranks leaders like Girdhari Lal Dogra, Ram Piara Saraf, Bhagat Chhajju Ram, Masha Nahar Singh, Balraj Puri, and a few more. All of them at that early stage appeared to be standing left of centre even if not being communists, and were enthusiastically working for the rights of the downtrodden. Maharaja Hari Singh's efforts notwithstanding, the society in Jammu remained feudal and afflicted by all the ills of the Hindu society. There was thus, definitely, a strong case for a socio-economic transformation.

6

The Land Reforms

Another year elapsed before the election for constituting an Assembly—the avowed goal of the 5th March 1948 Proclamation—was called. Thus, for more than three years, Sheikh Abdullah wielded absolute powers that did not brook either dissent or accountability or fair play. He used this period to consolidate his power, diminish and hound the dissenters in his party, and demonstrate a mean and vindictive streak in dealing with the Dogras in general and the dynasty in particular. His will became law and his interpretation of the National Conference's manifesto, the Constitution. In the process, he tested the patience of the Central leaders and a flash point reached, forcing Sardar Patel to write to him after he made nasty allegations against the Maharaja: 'You do not seem to realize that both you and we ourselves owe the technical correctness of our position in regard to Kashmir to the Maharaja's signing the accession and calling upon you to form the ministry. Without that, neither we nor you would have been where we are.'[72]

This admonishment had no effect on a person who had become too arrogant and conceited to be reasonable. However, soon his hand was to be forced by Delhi's insistence that he could not be allowed to pass laws and implement policies that did not have the sanction of the will of the people. Momentous changes can be ushered only by the will of the people and no interim arrangement can be allowed to stretch indefinitely as was happening in Jammu and Kashmir.

His apologists might argue that his proposal for radical land reforms, involving distribution of land to tillers without paying any compensation to the owners, had caused anxiety in the entrenched vested interest. But it cannot be ignored that such reforms needed to be carried out by elected representatives and not by an autocratic and arbitrary use of power. Thus, only when he realized that even Prime Minister Nehru had had enough of his histrionics that Sheikh Abdullah decided to have a Proclamation issued for convening a Constituent Assembly. But before that, Delhi was to see more of the tactics of the National Conference leaders in an effort to carve a special niche for the State in the Indian Constitution.

Like all mass leaders, Sheikh Abdullah periodically needed to make grand and populist gestures that gave people hope and renewed their faith in the great leader. He also needed to reinvent the critical moments of history. The commemoration of Martyrs' Day was the perfect occasion for him in 1950 and he decided to back the gesture with the declaration of a strong intent that ushered in a new era for the deprived classes. Defying propriety, without the authority of the Regent or of a duly constituted legislature, and in the face of the Centre's urging to exercise caution, he declared his intention to introduce radical land reforms without showing any urgency for convening the Constituent Assembly, which alone could have given him the legal authority for so momentous a reform.

The announcement of land reforms was also intended to proverbially kill two birds with one stone. In initiating a war of nerves with the Central leaders over the issue, he also reiterated the National Conference's views relating to the integration of the State and the intention of keeping it out of the purview of the Indian State and Constitution. It would also allow him to wean away the Scheduled Caste population of the Jammu region from the influential sections of the society, thereby gaining some support in the region. This class was engaged in tilling the land and lived on land tenancy and worked as landless labourers. In addition, they were often the victims of the oppressive *begar* system of labour and other vagaries of the feudal order that Sheikh Abdullah challenged and wanted dismantled. Technically they these stood abolished during the early years of Maharaja Hari Singh's rule, but in practice, they continued in the countryside.

Sheikh Abdullah, like most populist leaders and dictators wanted to make a dramatic gesture on a day that had become the rallying point for Kashmiris. But it was also a day that caused discomfort to the Dogras. For the first time, the Kashmiris had rioted during the Dogra regime and the State authorities had to use force to control the mobs. Therefore, as 13th July drew near in 1950, Sheikh Abdullah seized the opportunity to declare his intention to introduce radical land reforms that encompassed not only the abolition of the *Jagirdari* system but also imposed a ceiling on land holding and redistribution of appropriated land to the tenants and the landless labourers.

Understandably this did not register well either with those who were to suffer or those who championed the cause of propriety. Sheikh Abdullah was appointed by the Proclamation of Maharaja Hari Singh as the Prime Minister and was specifically tasked by the same Proclamation to take steps to constitute and convene a Constituent Assembly that would frame the Constitution for the State. Major changes in governance could be brought about only by a government that was a product of that new Constitution. But Sheikh Abdullah vigorously pursued the powers vested in the office of the Prime Minister without being accountable to an Assembly or the person of the ruler who appointed him to the office. However, the legality notwithstanding, the fact remains that one could argue that there was dire need to usher in radical changes and ownership of land, and that, land reform was a reasonable tool to achieve that goal.

The agrarian system in the State, like in the rest of the country, was basically feudal in nature and the cultivators suffered greatly due to heavy taxation, levy on the land and the disproportionate share that had to be given to the landlord by the tenant. Only those who served the State to the satisfaction of the kings were bestowed with land in the form of *jagirs** or *muafis*†. Some of the leading officials of the administration also got some land as privilege and came to be known as *chakdars*. The main demand of the National

* Grants of public revenues of a district given to a person.

† Lands which were mostly given to religious people.

Conference movement, which was launched in 1931, was the transfer of ownership rights on land from the Maharaja to the peasants. This just demand was partially conceded by Maharaja Hari Singh and lakhs of petty cultivators, who were till then tenants at will, got ownership over the land. Later when the National Conference Government came to power in March 1948, it gave priority to the reorganization of agriculture, presumably on a modern and rational basis, much like the communists, through the abolition of landlordism, securing the land to the tillers and the formation of cooperative associations. Consequently it was in this context that the Big Landed Estates Abolition Act 1950 was to be introduced.

The main features of this legislation were:

(i) Fixation of a ceiling on the holding of the proprietor at 22.75 acres (182 *kanals* [unit of area equalling 1/8 acre]) of land, excluding orchards, fuel and fodder reserves and cultivable wasteland.

(ii) Transfer of surplus land to the tillers cultivating the land without any payment.

(iii) Fixation of ceiling (at 160 *kanals*) on land including what was owned, and had been leased out.

(iv) Surplus lands which were not in the cultivating possession of any person, were acquired by the State.

The Jammu and Kashmir Big Landed Estates Abolition Act, 2007 (1950 A.D.) Act No. XVII of 2007 was promulgated by the Yuvraj exercising powers vested in the Maharaja (exercisable by the Yuvraj, the Regent, during the absence of Maharaja Hari Singh) under Section 5 of the Jammu and Kashmir Constitution Act, 1939.

It is pertinent to note that not only was The Jammu and Kashmir Landed Estate Abolition Act, 2007 (1950 A.D.) promulgated under the provision of the Jammu and Kashmir Constitution Act of 1939, the Proclamation appointing Sheikh Abdullah as the Prime Minister was also made under the said Constitution. However, it should also be noted that the Constitution was considered relevant only to the extent that it served the purpose of the new rulers. The Constitution vested in the Maharaja the power to extend the life of the Praja

Sabha. But it was not exercised when the need arose to ratify the State's accession and integration to India. On the contrary, it was dumped as being a 'rump' body so that the same power could be exercised by the new government appointed by the Maharaja under the Proclamation of 5th March 1948. This power was exercised, as it was done in the case of the Big Landed Estates Abolition Act, by the Prime Minister and the Maharaja or his Regent were obliged to carry out that advice.

The 1939 Constitution was promulgated by Maharaja Hari Singh on 7th September 1939 by his Proclamation. Since all the powers were vested and inherent in the Maharaja, he drew up the Constitution, which despite shortcomings was progressive in the context of the times.

Section 5 of the Constitution reads:

> Notwithstanding anything contained in this or any other Act, all powers, legislative, executive and judicial, in relation to the State and its Government are hereby declared to be and to have always been inherent in and possessed and retained by His Highness…

In 1949 when the Maharaja was made to leave the State, he issued a proclamation on 20th June 1949 declaring that all the powers vested in him shall be exercisable by Yuvraj Karan Singh Bahadur, his Regent, during his absence. In other words, it is argued that since the order passed by the Maharaja could not be challenged, therefore, the Regent, who was obliged to exercise powers that had been vested in him under the Proclamation of the Maharaja on the advice of his Prime Minister, and his order too could not be challenged. The same Constitution, however, made elaborate provisions to ensure that there was no miscarriage of justice. The High Court heard all appeals, civil and criminal, that had a certain value. An appeal against the order of a single Judge of the High Court lay in a Bench consisting of two other Judges. However, the High Court was not the final interpreter of the Constitution. Section 75 of the Jammu and Kashmir Constitution Act, 1939 Part IV provided:

> If any dispute arises as to the interpretation or carrying out of any of the provisions of this Act or the rules made there under, the decision of the Council, subject to the provisions of Section 5 [relating to the inherent powers of His Highness], shall be final.

The Council was actually known as the Board of Judicial Advisors and was akin to the Privy Council of the King of England. All appeals when made to the Maharaja were referred to this Board for advice and the Maharaja was not known to have ever overruled the advice rendered to him. However, in the matter of the Big Landed Estates Abolition Act, 1950 a peculiar situation arose since Prime Minister Sheikh Abdullah convinced everyone that under the Proclamation of 5th March 1948, the Maharaja, and in the present case the Regent, was bound by the advice given by the Prime Minister. Hence, despite reservations, the Regent had to exercise the powers delegated to him by the Maharaja and sign the said Act. It is argued that since it was promulgated in the name of the Maharaja, who was the ultimate repository of all powers, the Act could not be challenged or appealed against in any forum. Thus, there was an example of a technically correct (mis)use of powers that were arbitrary and autocratic.

The irony was that the Maharaja, who was repeatedly accused of being an absolutist and despotic, had never exercised powers in such a manner. But those exercising power in the name of the people had no qualms in being unaccountable and arbitrary. As a result of the enforcement of the Big Landed Estates Abolition Act, 1950, as many as 9,000 odd landowners were dispossessed of 4.5 lakh acres of land held in excess of the ceiling. Out of this, 2.31 lakh acres of land were transferred with ownership rights to cultivating peasants free of any encumbrances. With all the flaws of propriety and legality, the reforms were a trail blazer in the country since many other states had grappled with the same problem without any success. In a number of states, the tenants had been struggling to get proprietary rights to the lands they tilled not only under the leadership of the Communists but also the Congress. The headwind that the movement ran into was the reason for Vinoba Bhave to launch his 'Bhoodan' movement, which attempted to persuade wealthy landlords to give up a percentage of their land to the landless.

In Jammu and Kashmir, the process of land reforms continued for many decades. The Government of Jammu and Kashmir in 1963 set up a Land Commission to find various discrepancies, which had crept in over the years in the land tenure pattern. The recommendations of this Commission formed, by and large, the basis of the Jammu and Kashmir Agrarian Reform Act, 1972. It was further amended as the Jammu and Kashmir Agrarian Reform Act, 1976 with a ceiling of 12.5 standard acres including orchards with certain conditions.

As intended, the manner in which these land reforms were announced and then implemented in 1950, once again brought the Central government into confrontation with Sheikh Abdullah. Tracing the events of that fateful summer, Prithvi Nath Kaul Bamzai writes, 'In April 1949, the government appointed a Land Reforms Committee to prepare a plan to abolish big landed estates and transfer of land to tillers...But before the Land Reforms Committee prepared and submitted its report, Sheikh Abdullah announced drastic and sweeping land reforms in a speech [on Martyrs' Day, 1950] from the National Conference platform. The assent of the Maharaja, the Head of the State, was not obtained...'[73]

At that point in history, Sheikh Abdullah was not a person who was amenable to either reason or caution. He began to demonstrate resentment whenever New Delhi appeared to thwart his designs. Thus, the more it appeared that the Centre cautioned him, the more determined he became to implement any scheme that he and his party thought was needed for Kashmir. Therefore, while the rest of the country adopted the democratic process of discussing and debating the land reforms in legislatures and other forums, Sheikh Abdullah decided to give his constituency a gift on the occasion of Martyrs' Day.

When first announced under controversial circumstances, several problems arose because of the Act, not the least political, that drove the Hindus of Jammu region towards the Praja Parishad—it being the only political forum that dared to have a dissenting voice and champion the cause of the Dogras. Much of the land in the Jammu region, except that of Ranbirsinghpura in Jammu and a small patch in Kathua, mainly the Chandgraon region that bordered Punjab, was rain fed and difficult to cultivate. The Act was unjust to these regions and the general perception was that the Hindus of the region were being punished for being Dogras and for their loyalty towards the Dogra ruler. Consequently, the Act generated more hostility since even those who were marginal land holders identified themselves with those who were deprived of their holdings because it became the symbol of the assault that had been launched by Kashmiris on the Dogras. In addition, the land that was appropriated from the land holders and distributed to the tenants and landless was not sufficient to sustain a family on the land for the whole year. Thus, without providing for adequate sustainability, the National Conference had created a hostile environment in the villages. This suited the National Conference since the new constituency by nature had to be in opposition to the old order.

In the Valley, the situation was no different. Daniel Thorner, professor at the University in Pennsylvania in Philadelphia had visited Jammu and Kashmir in April 1953[74] to study the impact of these land reforms. Not surprisingly, he was told that if he wanted to see the real land reforms in India, he should go to Kashmir. The leaders of the freedom movement in India had for long been seized by the problem arising out of the *Zamindari* system and had grappled with it to find a solution that did not create a schism in the rural society. Thus, though the Congress too was eager for their reforms to be carried out speedily and in a just manner, it was also conscious of the presence of a strong pro-*Zamindari* lobby within and was wary of dividing the society soon after achieving Independence. This caution and the desire to carry out reforms rather than start a revolution in land ownership pattern slowed the process in the country. Sheikh Abdullah, however, was not inclined towards such a slow pace since those about to be deprived were in any case not part of his political constituency. On account of political and personal necessities, he adamantly pushed the reforms even without an Assembly or any sort of legislature to give him the sanction for such a radical reform.

After his visit to the Valley to study the efficacy of the reforms, Thorner wrote in the *The Economic Weekly*, 'Jagirs and similar special grants had been abolished. Debt conciliation boards had been set up and were operating so vigorously…that they amounted to debt cancellation boards. Rents were lowered. Security of tenure was provided for the tillers. A ceiling on all land holdings was set at

22.75 acres. All arable land above that figure was taken away from the owners and redistributed.'

Obviously the reforms were carried out vigorously, but Thorner wanted to see everything for himself. So, along with a young friend, he set out for a reality check. In a village close to Srinagar, he was told by some villagers that of a population of 1,800, there were only ten families with enough land to grow the food necessary for sustenance throughout the year. The rest were forced to go elsewhere to look for odd jobs to sustain life. The redistribution of land in the village could be categorized. One set was of former tenants of the land who got the same land they had earlier tilled. But the other category was much larger and less fortunate. It consisted of those landless farm labourers who were distributed land in patches of one quarter to one-half of an acre and a maximum of two acres. This land too required considerable investment and labour to make it fertile since much of it was reclaimed after the flooding. No peasant in that village at that time had cultivated or held 22.75 acres of land whether as *marusi* (ancestral), as a tenant of the absentee landlord, or as a combination of both.

At another village, Professor Thorner found the *Halqa* (area) President of the National Conference in the company of the *Patwari*, the official who kept records of land ownership. The administration had by then been overtaken by the National Conference, the administrative machinery had become a tool in its hands, often with both the *Haqla* President and the *Patwari* conniving to further mutual interests. On close questioning, the *Halqa* President confessed that the land had been unfairly distributed among the more-affluent tenants of the absentee landlords and the landless labourers. Among the beneficiaries in the village was a contractor, a brick kiln owner and a trader. All of them held more than the land ceiling.

In another village Thorner discovered that of 200 families, only twenty were able to support their members on their land income and about twenty-five families found that it was exceedingly difficult to pay land revenue to the government. Since the short fall had to be covered somehow, the *Halqa* President either paid them from his own reserves or more often would lend money on interest to the suffering farmer. Thus the inequitable and irrational distribution of land created a system where the marginal farmers were forced into a debt trap.

In the same village, a young office bearer of the National Conference admitted that the distribution policy was deeply flawed. A peasant who already had thirteen acres of his *marusi* land should not have obtained an additional six acres of the dispossessed landlords land simply because he was a tenant. The same land could have been more justly and fruitfully allotted to a landless farmer who would have found sustenance in it. Analyzing the reasons for the failure to make the land reforms just and meaningful, the young leader admitted to Professor Thorner that the reforms were carried out without the formation of a Peasants' Committee at the village level. They were carried out by the administrative machinery, controlled by the vested interest of the National Conference, which was already accused of corruption and insensitivity. They had thus created a system where such officials, as they are prone, simply did the bidding of their new masters. It was a classic case of triumph of corruption and favouritism.

In addition, the young man pointed to Professor Daniel Thorner the flawed procurement policy of the government. As a rule the government took 40-50 per cent of the paddy, depending on the size of the area at the rate of Rs 9 per *khirwar*—two *maunds* and three *seers* or 170 pounds. This was then sold by the government from the ration shops at controlled prices. If the farmer did not have enough left for his family's sustenance, then he was obliged to buy from the free market at a higher rate. Unfortunately for him the produce that had been procured from him at the rate of Rs 9 per *khirwar* had to be bought from the free market at the rate of Rs 20 to Rs 32 per *khirwar*.

This was nothing short of extortion. There is no recorded evidence to show if the National Conference leadership was aware of this, but if it was not, then it points to a serious flaw in its governance and the system it was evolving. What, however, is on evidence is that the government never shied away from claiming credit for ushering in a new era of socio-economic justice and used the figures to show the success of the policy. However,

Professor Daniel Thorner writes, 'Mere statistics of so and so many hundred of thousand acres taken away from the landlords can be quite misleading. India's most publicized land reforms cannot be said to have succeeded in improving the lot of the Kashmiri peasant. Whether the legislation was well conceived for this purpose remains debatable. In practice any beneficial results have been more than balanced by the government's food procurement policy, the cooperative reign of extortion, the implementation of redistribution through the old bureaucracy, and the sole political party's setting itself up as yet another privileged rural hierarchy.'[75]

Analyzing the impact of the Land Reforms, Prithvi Nath Kaul Bamzai, further observes in his book that, 'Without formulating a regular plan and enacting a law, the leaders announced the outline of the scheme from public platforms to gain minor political advantages. When it became known that the landlord had to surrender their estates above 182 *kanals*, there was a scramble among the more influential peasants for the would-be expropriated land and the *patwaris* entered into negotiations with tenants and other villagers on the method of sharing it. Ultimately, when the law came into force, it was found that most of the distributable land had already been allotted to non-deserving people. In many cases a tenant who shared in the distribution of the landlord's extra land was himself the owner of a much larger area.'[76]

Meanwhile, even when the National Conference basked in the success of depriving landlords of their lands without compensation, a crisis had been brewing in the State. The crops failed for two successive years, 1949-50 and 1950-51, which led to a grave situation that could only be retrieved by the timely intervention of the Government of India. But, to quote Bamzai again, 'the distributing agency—the Food Control Department—fell into the hands of some unscrupulous and greedy people who sold a sizeable portion of the grain into the black market.'[77] Reiterating, what Professor Thorner had found in the Valley, Bamzai adds, 'The food procurement drive added to the misery of the peasants who were forced to part with their stock of grains at nominal rates, while they had to purchase grain at exorbitant prices to pay the *Mujawaza* [land tax in kind]. The people's patience was exhausted and when the

Food Minister, Mirza Afzal Beg, rose to address a meeting of the National Conference workers, he was heckled and made to leave the Conference room.'[78]

The distribution of land, and the outcome, demonstrated the flaws in the proposals as mentioned in the Naya Kashmir document regarding the functioning of the local government. The fact that the system was soon to deteriorate into a corrupt and extortionist system in the Valley, where everyone believed the National Conference had undisputed presence, only warned the wise of the danger that lay ahead in the State, particularly Jammu where, according to noted political and social worker Balraj Puri, the National Conference leaders were appointing and dismissing party officials whimsically since, with no base of the party, no one was sure about the credentials of anyone.[79] This disconnect with the people was to prove disastrous for the State in the years to come.

The reason for this is not hard to discern. There is no doubt that the National Conference boasted of the massive presence of its workers in the Valley, but the same was not true of the Jammu region. In the Valley, the National Conference was well placed into packing all the administrative posts at the ground level with party loyalists; it was also in a position to create a cadre that oversaw the working at all levels of governance as visualized by its philosophy, but the same was not possible in Jammu. This explains Balraj Puri's observation that officials and party office bearers were as arbitrarily appointed as they were removed. With no genuine party apparatus that was functional, it was hard to trust any appointee and hence the turmoil in appointments. This reinforces the perception that the purpose of the land reforms was less to ameliorate the lot of the peasants, increase food production and eliminate inequalities, and more to make the Dogras realize that they had not only been deprived of the political power under the new regime but also the ownership of the lands. The forcible deprivation not only hurt the self-esteem of the Dogras but also raised primordial fears and insecurities. If in Kashmir, the situation was what had been observed by Professor Thorner, then in Jammu it was worse because most of the land holdings were in the difficult and dry hill terrain and were therefore even less productive. Those who were allotted land—up to two acres—naturally found themselves burdened with the responsibility of earning enough to pay the rent.

If the purpose of the land reforms was to demonstrate the helplessness of the Dogras then Sheikh Abdullah and the National Conference had achieved a remarkable success. Like pathological dictators before him, Abdullah too needed to reassure himself of the powers that he could wield. Hence, the more the saner voices cautioned against steps that were arbitrary and unlawful, the more determined he became to prove to them that he was not only a law unto himself but also beyond the reach of New Delhi and the rest of the country. One can be charitable to Jawaharlal Nehru and Sardar Patel for giving him a long rope in the matter of his conduct towards Maharaja Hari Singh by rationalizing it as a necessity in the given circumstances of Accession and the reference of the issue to the UN Security Council. Forced to choose between the Maharaja and Sheikh Abdullah, Sardar Patel had opted for the latter, even at the risk of being accused by future historians of betraying the person under whose signature India had the authority to send the army to push back the invaders. One can attribute bad judgment and bias in favour of Sheikh Abdullah by Jawaharlal Nehru with some justification in the context of the manner in which Sheikh Abdullah prevailed upon national leaders to deal with the Maharaja. But that episode and the manner in which Sheikh Abdullah had already begun to retract on his words and promises to Jawaharlal Nehru when the Constituent Assembly of India had debated the matter of Article 370 should have aroused suspicions in New Delhi. Inability to prevail over the collective will of the Constituent Assembly had only steeled Sheikh Abdullah's resolve to strike his independent note. His well-meaning friends outside the State must have noticed the irony of a leader professing democratic credentials continuing to exercise executive powers without being responsible to either any legislative body or person.

7

The Regent Settles Down

Putting his run-ins with Sheikh Abdullah over the visit to Kheer Bhawani, and proposals regarding the land reforms and the abolition of *jagirdari* system behind him, Yuvraj Karan Singh immersed himself in his new role. Even at that young age, he remained focused not only on his official duties but also his personal development. Acutely conscious of the fact that he had missed out on his formal education, first because of medical problems and then because of the onerous responsibility that he had to bear, he found himself wanting to catch up with his academic studies and individual development. In this, he had the good fortune of finding a soulmate in his wife Yasho Rajya Lakshmi, from the illustrious Rana family of Nepal. The formal studies of both had been disrupted but now they wished to make up for lost opportunities.

Of the two, Yuvrani Yasho Rajya Lakshmi had a more conservative upbringing and it deprived her of learning English. Now, as the Yuvraj proposed to continue his formal studies and prepare for his Bachelor's degree, the Yuvrani too devoted the morning hours to formally learn English and Hindi from tutors. In addition, she was fond of the fine arts and began learning to paint. This was a happy reprieve from the high-pressure politics where treachery and deception were at the turn of every corner. In between, the young couple enjoyed an active and rewarding social life. Twice or thrice a week, they hosted lunch at a table for sixteen. The guests at times would consist of visiting dignitaries, ambassadors, United Nations personnel and local gentry. Since the

Yuvrani was still not comfortable conversing in English, it fell on Yuvraj Karan Singh to carry the conversation on behalf of both. As time passed, the Yuvraj realized that perhaps these were the most productive sessions since the guests were intelligent and the conversation stimulating. It aroused the desire to know more since it was apparent that there was so much more to learn than what his immediate life offered.[80]

This period made formal education important for Yuvraj Karan Singh, and wanting to make some contribution in that field, he had the brilliant idea of donating Gulab Bhavan, the main palace of the Dogra dynasty, to house the newly established Jammu and Kashmir University.[81] Serving the cause of education was not new to the Dogra dynasty. It contributed liberally towards the establishment of the Banaras Hindu University when Pandit Madan Mohan Malviya undertook the mission. The State had always patronized learning and a treasure trove of ancient manuscripts, including the world famous Gilgit manuscripts, were preserved in the State Museum, Srinagar and in the Raghunath Temple, Jammu. The dynasty provided for modern education in the State when a college each was established in Srinagar and Jammu, and had also provisioned compulsory primary education in the cities. High schools were spread all over the State with hostel facilities so as to cover most of the vast geographical area and most importantly, liberal scholarships and stipends were provided to the Muslim students and special provisions made for the students from the far flung areas of Gilgit and Baltistan. The Dogra rule also provided scholarships for higher studies and those who wished to study in universities.[82]

Hitherto, the colleges in the State were affiliated to Punjab University, Lahore when the country was undivided, and then to Panjab University, Shimla. Evidently the idea of donating Gulab Bhavan was not only to be a great contribution to the cause of education in the State but also a gesture that would have gone down well with the people of Kashmir. Thoroughly excited and eager to see his idea implemented, the Yuvraj mentioned his proposal to Pandit Jawaharlal Nehru[83] and Gopalaswami Ayyangar. Both were expectedly pleased by the young prince's generosity and Nehru responded: 'I am very glad to learn that you intend donating the

Gulab Mahal Palace to the University of Jammu and Kashmir. That is the very best use you can put the building to and I am sure it will be greatly appreciated by the public.'[84]

However, cold water was thrown over Yuvraj Karan Singh's keenness because of miscommunication. While he had shared his intent with Prime Minister Nehru and Ayyangar, he had also asked his father's advisor to inform the Maharaja of it. But Maharaja Hari Singh got to know of the proposal only when Ayyangar wrote to him to urge him to allow the Yuvraj to make the donation. The Maharaja was furious at the suggestion since it appeared that the advice regarding what he should do with his private property seemed to emanate from the very same quarters that had connived to humiliate him. Evidently, after being so shabbily treated by the new dispensation, bitterness had got the better of him. It was left for the Yuvraj to explain the reasons for making the suggestion of that gift. He wrote: 'Considering all these factors—a fast deteriorating building which is ideally suited to be a University and which is lying neglected and unused, and the fact that our University urgently requires a suitable building and that education is as noble and worthy a cause as can be possibly found—I sincerely feel that it would be a magnificent gesture on your part if you were to donate the building. The effect of such an act on the public would, I am convinced, be electrifying.'[85]

But having been propelled from one stand to another and finally discarded, Maharaja Hari Singh was in no mood to do any more favours to the new rulers. He wrote: 'The Jammu and Kashmir Government have gone out of their way to harass me personally and to humiliate the dynasty in the eyes of the public…I hope that you will realize that the gift in present circumstances with however lofty ideals behind it would be misconstrued as one more instance of the ruler being proved a nonentity and of no consequence.'[86]

Obviously nothing could have been done after that and there the matter rested. But the idea touched the core of the Yuvraj's heart and after a few years he donated the hundred acres of Amar Singh Bagh, an orchard near Hazaratbal named after his grandfather, for the premises of the new university. Thus, the State University came to have its own sprawling campus. Later, the Yuvraj was to appear for his BA examination from the same university. Much before that, he became its Chancellor. Many found this amusing since Yuvraj Karan Singh was the youngest Chancellor of a University. This finds mention in a letter written by Pandit Jawaharlal Nehru to the Yuvraj on 11th September 1949. He wrote: 'Sheikh Saheb arrived here this evening and gave me a copy of the speech you intend [on] delivering as Chancellor of the University…I find it very interesting. Surely you must be by far the youngest Chancellor that a University has had.'[87]

The letter was delivered to Yuvraj Karan Singh by Indira Gandhi, who had reached Srinagar to recuperate after a bout of ill health. He responded on 15th September 1949 and the letter demonstrates the ease and confidence with which he reacted to the mild humour of the Indian Prime Minister. He wrote: 'I am enclosing a revised copy of the address which I will deliver on the 24th. The previous copy contained quite a lot of what I thought was superfluous and over-flowery. I went over it and cut it here and there, thereby, I think, improving it. Yes! I suppose I am the youngest Chancellor a University has ever had. It will be a great privilege for me to address such a distinguished audience.'[88]

The first convocation of the Jammu and Kashmir University was addressed by Pandit Jawaharlal Nehru and Yuvraj Karan Singh, on 24th September 1949, in Srinagar in an open park under chinar trees. After congratulating the students, the youngest Chancellor exhorted them to continue following the traditions of Jammu and Kashmir and to be the ambassadors of unity.

As for Gulab Bhavan, in 1956, it was to be converted into a prestigious hotel that accommodated world class tourists to the Valley and made them feel like royalty during their stay. With it began a new phase in world tourism in India, as more and more palaces, fortresses and havelis were converted into hotels.

The two power centres in the State thus evolved as entirely different persons. The young Yuvraj, eager to play a meaningful role in the State created by his ancestors but where the conditions had radically changed, tried to play the constitutional role to the best of his abilities, without compromising on the issue of post-accession challenges. Among the people of Jammu, he evoked emotions that were tinged with regret and helplessness over the treatment meted out to their beloved Maharaja and also of hope because of the Yuvraj's presence. The old guard resented the Yuvraj's playing a subsidiary role to Sheikh Abdullah, but simultaneously his presence among them was reassuring and also acted as an anchor and a beacon for the future. He was acutely aware of these responses but was confident that the Dogras would soon realize that life could not be the same and that following his example, they too should work hard to adjust to the new order and then occupy the place that their talent warranted. On a personal level, the Yuvraj was also exploring his inherent talent to learn more about the world he lived in. A life that was also occupied by social engagements was being put to good use in the company of people who helped to satisfy his curiosity by exchanging ideas and experiences. Over a period of time this was to engage him more passionately.

Sheikh Abdullah, on the other hand, turned out to be authoritarian, vindictive and capricious in his treatment of those who disagreed with him. In part, this was a product of the peculiar history of the State and the composition of its society. The homogeneity of the Valley's population and the siege mentality that it suffered because of historical factors, ever since its annexation by the Mughal emperor Akbar, was ideal for creating authoritarian leaders. Balraj Puri explains: 'The consensual nature of its society, and the lack of a strong middle class favoured the emergence of a powerful, charismatic leader...He symbolized not only their political aspirations but also their socio-cultural make up...As life president of the *Auqaf** trust he controlled most of the mosques and *ziarats*† in Kashmir. The sacred shrine of Hazratbal in Srinagar from where he launched his offensive against the Muslim League and its theory of two nations became the political, religious and emotional centre of Kashmiri life. One-leader [Abdullah], one-party [National Conference] and one-manifesto [party manifesto of Naya Kashmir] were the basic slogans.'[89]

* An Arabic word meaning assets donated to be held in perpetual trust for specific charitable causes.

† A shrine of a saint.

In this environment, there was hardly any room for dissent. Gradually Kashmir moved towards an Orwellian State with the society becoming monolithic and the leader intolerant of any dissent. Balraj Puri, who was part of the new establishment, further observes that when the Maharaja appointed Sheikh Abdullah as the Head of the Emergency Administration, the twenty-three-member Emergency Council was first packed with the workers of the party. Then they were appointed to the administrative posts. 'Many government officials held positions in the party,' Puri writes. He adds, 'The Abdullah administration functioned arbitrarily and without any defined constitutional powers—party workers assumed the de facto authority to arrest and punish whoever they held guilty. With unchecked political power and a tightly-controlled administration, Abdullah was able to further regiment all aspects of Kashmiri life.'[90]

Balraj Puri claimed in his book that as a member of the National Conference he had raised the issue of separating the party from the administration, but his demand was rejected by Sheikh Abdullah on the plea that he was not prepared to repeat an experiment that had been undertaken in the rest of the country. Presumably, he was under the influence of the communists and also because the control of all aspects of administration helped him to push an agenda that lacked propriety. But determined to push the demand to its logical end, Puri drew the attention of Prime Minister Nehru and for illustration, showed him the copy of a letter of the *Wazir Wazarat* (Deputy Commissioner) of the Doda district. The said officer was also the president of the district unit of the National Conference. Puri writes, 'He had after visiting Kishtwar, ordered the expulsion of the office-bearers of the local National Conference [vide order No. HC 989, dated 24th November 1948] allegedly "for their anti-government and anti-national activities" and appointed new office-bearers in their place. Copies of the order were sent to the prime minister of the state and general secretary of the party.'[91]

It was a blatant attempt to take advantage of the special circumstances that had partially evolved but largely manufactured to impose a monolithic political system on the regions of Jammu and Ladakh. This was deeply resented by the two regions and not surprisingly, very soon the leaders from the Valley were faced with stiff resistance. The National Conference was ill-equipped to deal with these regions as it refused to give space to their ideological aspirations, and the more the party cadre misused power and the tool of administration, the more these regions became alienated. Clearly Sheikh Abdullah was getting carried away by the adulation he received in the Valley and as a result, lost perspective of the State.

At the same time, he was also becoming a huge disappointment for the leaders in Delhi. With him as Prime Minister of the State, the leaders in Delhi had thought that the home front was taken care of. But his utterances kept alive the issue of the integration of the State. He was fortunate that he had the unfailing support of Prime Minister Nehru because not only did Sardar Patel distrust him but Yuvraj Karan Singh was to learn soon that this distrust was shared by Dr Rajendra Prasad as well.[92] Leaders like Ayyangar and Kailash Nath Katju, who succeeded Sardar Patel after his death, were more prone to act in a manner they thought would be approved by Prime Minister Nehru. As for Prime Minister Nehru, he was also not happy because of the trouble that India faced in the United Nations. This he also acknowledged in the letter that he wrote to the Yuvraj on 11th September 1949. He observed, 'The United Nations Commission has given us a lot of trouble and taken a great deal of my time. I understand two of them are coming here tomorrow.'[93] This was not a happy situation but nothing could be done. In fact, there were unmistakable signs of Sheikh Abdullah getting entangled with the forces that were inimical to the Indian interest. He was unquestionably drifting away from his friends in Delhi and in the process was also driving a deep wedge between the various regions of the State. Lauded and feted by the Western diplomats, he began to suffer from the same malaise that had, in the past, cut short the careers of ambitious governors and rulers of the Valley.

Not drawing any lesson from the past, Sheikh Abdullah chose to strike back by deciding to use the constitutional tool of convening the Constituent Assembly to frame new laws. Unfortunately, the undemocratic and dictatorial manner in which he proceeded to achieve his goal only added proverbial fuel to the fire.

8

The Response

The controversial land reforms were announced and pushed even after it was pointed out to Sheikh Abdullah that such a radical reform needed the sanction of an elected body. In fact, he had been enjoined by the Proclamation of 5th March 1948 to convene a Constituent Assembly. Even the Constitution of India had visualized a Constituent Assembly for the State in October 1949. Yet, no effort was made to convene it.

In the prevailing circumstances, the inaction probably suited Sheikh Abdullah. In the name of the 'people' he was free to launch a tirade against the Maharaja, whimsically run his administration through the workers of the National Conference and yet not be accountable to any democratic set up. The result was that in a short period of time the State came to be governed by people whose only qualification was that they were a member of the National Conference. The dangers of such an arrangement were pointed out by the veteran freedom fighter, writer-journalist and social worker BalrajPuri, but to no avail.[94]

Adding to the woes of the Centre, the issue of Jammu and Kashmir stood unresolved in the Security Council of the United Nations. In a misplaced trust of fair play and just disposal of conflict in the emerging world order after the Second World War, India had also agreed to a plebiscite. This commitment was used by Sheikh Abdullah as leverage to force India to dance to his tune. Thus, even after exhaustive consultations between representatives of the Government of India and the State leaders led by Sheikh

Abdullah, and an unequivocal assurance by the Central leaders that the State would have the right to convene a Constituent Assembly that would not only frame a constitution but also decide the fate of the hereditary Headship of the State in April 1949, no further progress was made.

The first six months of 1950 passed with Sheikh Abdullah planning and then plotting the execution of the proposal for abolishing the *jagirdari* system and appropriating lands of the owners beyond a specified limit without compensation. All this while he chafed under the constitutional constraints that he was reminded of by the Regent and the Central leaders. The Regent also drew his attention to the wider ramifications of the proposal on the economy of the State.[95] The objections raised involved the issue of his not having the support of any elected body of the people. The proposal had finally roused the leaders in Delhi to take notice of the manner in which Sheikh Abdullah had exercised his authority to subvert democratic principles. This was radically different from the inclusive path that leaders of young India had adopted. It had recognized the desirability of beginning its new history on a note of conciliation, even with the British. The bitterness of the freedom struggle and the anger at the exploitation that the land resources and people had been subjected to by the imperial power was given a decent burial. The continuation of Lord Mountbatten in India represented the spirit of confidence that can even forgive and accommodate the symbol of the oppressor. The same generous spirit was demonstrated in dealing with the numerous princes, some of them, undoubtedly recalcitrant. The Nizam of Hyderabad had gone to the extent of transferring huge quantities of bullion to bail Pakistan out of a financial crisis. This was used by it to fight the Indian Army in Jammu and Kashmir. The Maharaja of Jodhpur had to be literally arm-twisted by Sardar Patel to sign the Instrument of Accession and even the Nawab of Bhopal took a long time to realize the folly of believing that he could carve an independent State for himself. But they were all very generously accommodated in the Republic.[96]

There is no doubt that these Princely States suffered from all the flaws that were inherent to feudalism. But the States administered by the British shared with them the peculiar socio-economic challenges that could have encouraged many impetuous leaders to opt for popular and radical reforms that signalled the coming of a revolutionary era. Leading Congressmen were avowedly left of centre and socialists by conviction, and many among them had led the struggle of the tenants and landless labourers for their rights. But they had come to accept the need for gradual and inclusive change so that there was no rupture in the social fabric. During those momentous years, with Mahatma Gandhi's restraining hand removed from the scene by the bullets of an assassin, no one would have faulted these leaders if they opted for revolutionary land reforms. In fact, none could even have faulted, after the Mahatma, if they had declared India a Hindu Rashtra. After all, the country was partitioned on the basis of communal principles and, in a manner, Partition had institutionalized communalism in the subcontinent. But India had opted to undo the madness of the preceding years by choosing a different, and in the view of the many, the right path of secularism.

The import of all this was apparently lost on Sheikh Abdullah and he continued to be driven by motives that were decidedly less noble than what he professed. He also could not appreciate the fact that the representatives of Jammu and Kashmir in the National Constituent Assembly were among the few who did not represent any communal constituency. The election that took place for the Assembly in 1946 was on the basis of a communal electorate consisting of Muslims and general seats. A large-number from the Muslim constituencies, none belonging to the Congress, had gone to Pakistan, leaving India's Constituent Assembly with members from the general constituency. Many of them were part of the communal-based elections. Yet, all of them buried the rancour and bitterness of Partition and the betrayal of the idea of India by their Muslim comrades to come together to draft a constitution that made secularism the cornerstone of new India. Thus while originally, the Provinces were to elect 292 members and the Indian States were allotted a minimum of ninety-three seats, the membership of the House was reduced to 299, of whom 284 were actually present to append their signatures to the Constitution that was finally adopted.[97]

The ideals that drove the members of the National Constituent Assembly to rise above the passions of the times and look forward were evidently not useful to the leaders of the Valley. Sheikh Abdullah, insensitive to the aspirations of the country and driven by the passion of his heart, resorted to the rhetoric of the promise made to his 'people' to usher in a revolution, the centrality of which was the destruction of the remnants of the Dogra legacy. The proposed land reforms were part of that grand design. Yuvraj Karan Singh, after careful deliberation, reminded his Prime Minister that the proposal would affect a large section of the population and 'for the sanctioning of which there is no properly functioning legislature at present.'[98]

Sheikh Abdullah's inability to convince the Central leaders not to object to the manner he was wielding power made him embark upon a course that would usher in radical change. The political and the socio-economic advantages were tempting for him. In a single stroke, Sheikh Abdullah would succeed in dismantling the Dogra legacy in a constitutional manner. He hoped that he would also win over a new constituency of farmers who were bereft of any proprietary rights to the lands they tilled. He was sure that this would provide him with a political toehold in the Jammu region.

His relentless drive against Maharaja Hari Singh had already succeeded in exiling the Maharaja from the State. It had buoyed him, and Sheikh Abdullah unleashed the next phase of his plan against the Dogras by focusing on the formal abolition of the ruling dynasty. This, he realized, could not be done without the genuine backing of a democratic set up. Thus, he was now prepared for the Constituent Assembly, having learnt from his experience after having a brief but bitter run-in with Yuvraj, and consequently to grudgingly accept some of the amendments to land reforms that he had made in consultation with New Delhi.

In the meantime, unknown to New Delhi or even some of his own colleagues, Sheikh Abdullah is believed to have already begun to toy with the idea that was so close to the heart of Maharaja Hari Singh, and which, in the face of the reality around him, the latter had been quick to jettison. Following his trip to the US to attend the Security Council meeting, Abdullah was a changed man. 'After returning from Lake Success in 1949, Abdullah began distancing himself from Kashmiri communists, who had played a key role in the anti-Maharajah movement and helped the National Conference draft its New Kashmir Program of land to the tillers, workers' rights, and women's rights. Discussions began to take place among Abdullah loyalists within the National Conference on a "third way" to the resolution of the Kashmir "problem". In an editorial on July 13, 1950, the National Conference's own newspaper, *Khidmat*, wrote: "We could easily arrive at a settlement with the Americans but for the communists." [cited in Raina 1988:210] A full one-year campaign that sought to purge progressive elements within the National Conference followed. This witch hunt was one of the factors that killed the democratic core of the National Conference movement and strengthened communalist and opportunist elements in the party.'[99]

Balraj Puri concurs with this assessment. He wrote, 'The first fissures in the monolithic politics of Kashmir and the leadership of the regimented National Conference occurred when Ghulam Mohiuddin Karra parted company with Sheikh Abdullah in 1948. Karra…was generally acknowledged as the number two leader of the party. But in order to cut him to size, Abdullah offered the number two position of deputy prime minister and vice president of the party to Bakshi Ghulam Mohammad…In view of the importance of Karra's personality and well-known secular convictions, I pleaded with Nehru that his loyalty to the country need not be routed through Abdullah and that his democratic right to oppose the state government should be recognized. Nehru agreed to the theoretical soundness of my arguments but maintained that India's Kashmir policy revolved around the personality of Abdullah and, therefore, nothing should be done to weaken him.'[100]

Karra's parting was to signal the beginning of the direct role and influence that Pakistan exerted in the domestic politics of the State. This was also to reverberate for long with disastrous consequences. Karra was the only person who could measure up to Sheikh Abdullah and hence the latter was apprehensive of having his position and influence subverted. Such a person, when left out of the Cabinet for no meritorious reason, walked out of the National Conference in anger.

A few years after this event, under the influence of Pakistan, Karra formed the Kashmir Political Conference, which advocated outright accession to Pakistan. This was the beginning of Pakistan's covert actions, and in the words of B.N. Mullik, 'Pakistan switched on to internal subversion and sabotage and developed contacts with various anti-Indian groups and individuals and financed several mushroom organizations, Karra's Political Conference being one of them.'[101] It is obvious that in his arrogance Sheikh Abdullah was oblivious to the threat that his brand of politics was posing to the stability and security of not only the State but the country as well.

Soon after, Sheikh Abdullah represented the Indian position from Kashmir's point of view at the Security Council meeting in Lake Success. Upon his return it was noticed that his attitude towards India and his friends in Delhi began to change. It is also widely believed by many analysts that when USA's Ambassador to India, Loy Henderson met Sheikh Abdullah in September 1950, he brought up the idea of an independent Kashmir. These analysts saw a marked change precipitating in the attitude of the Western press towards Sheikh Abdullah. *The Daily Telegraph*, *The Washington Post*, *The Manchester Guardian* (later *The Guardian*), and *The New York Times* all began showering praises on Abdullah's leadership. But there were a few who saw through him. When the Constituent Assembly of Jammu and Kashmir was convened on 5th November 1951, Michael James reported in *The New York Times*: 'The ambitious and unprincipled Sheikh Mohammed Abdullah—a communalist in the early 1930s and a vacillating supporter of unity with a progressive India in the 1940s—fell in the 1950s to the temptation of an independent Kashmir supported by the United States.'

Meanwhile, a new dimension was added to the problem when India reposed faith in the United Nations Security Council. By offering a plebiscite on the condition that Pakistan withdraw its forces from the State, India reduced its policy options and, according to Dr Ashok Kapur in his book *India's Strategic Problems*, 'it gave up the option and the right to escalate the fight in Kashmir and to take it to Pakistan, and it passed on the issue to UNSC which was dominated by Western powers.' The debates in the Security Council began to needle the democratic sensibilities of the Indian leaders, and Sheikh Abdullah took advantage to push for the changes that he thought would convince the world of a democratic set up in the State. He argued that Pakistan was using example of the Hindu monarchical rule to convince the world of the sufferings of the majority Muslims in a Hindu-ruled State. Therefore, India needed to make a material and substantial gesture to ensure that the sensibilities of the Muslims were appropriately satisfied.

It was in this context that New Delhi discovered that the concept of the Constituent Assembly could be used as a broader political strategy to render the plebiscite redundant.[102] This strategy emerged from the fact that though India was committed to the plebiscite in Jammu and Kashmir, the conditions were such that no plebiscite could be held. Pakistan was still in occupation of the State territories, and showed no signs of withdrawing its forces. Therefore by not adhering to the primary condition set by the Security Council, there was no possibility of a plebiscite. It was partly this condition that forced India to incorporate Article 370 to its Constitution where it was specified that the sanction of the Constituent Assembly of the State was required for any future changes in the relationship between the State and Union. In this context, States' Minister Gopalaswami Ayyangar, told the Constituent Assembly that were the outcome of the plebiscite not in favour of India, it would not hesitate giving up its claims on the State.[103] But with the indefinite uncertainty over the holding of the plebiscite, it was also becoming clear that India's commitment to the United Nations notwithstanding, the idea of the Constituent Assembly did meet and reaffirm the State's accession to India. Certainly when a Constituent Assembly, made of representatives chosen in a free and fair election, ratified the State's accession to India, it would have an impact on the world opinion in favour of India!

Soon, the All Jammu and Kashmir National Conference passed a resolution on convening a Constituent Assembly for the State on 27th October 1950. It read:

> This meeting of the General Council of the All Jammu & Kashmir National Conference views with great concern the repeated failure of the UN to redress the wrongs of aggression of which the people

> of the State continue to be victims. This failure in its opinion is due to the continued concessions given to Pakistan by placing a premium on its intransigence.
>
> The indecision and unrealistic procedure adopted so far has condemned the people of the State to a life of agonizing uncertainty. The All Jammu & Kashmir National Conference is gravely concerned and cannot any longer afford to ignore the perpetuation of these conditions of doubt and frustration. In the opinion of the General Council, the time has come when the initiative must be regained by the people to put an end to this indeterminate state of drift and indecision.
>
> The General Council recommends to the Supreme National Executive of the people to take immediate steps for convening a Constituent Assembly based on adult suffrage and embracing all sections of the people and all the Constituents of the State for the purpose of determining the future shape and affiliations of the State of Jammu and Kashmir. In this sovereign Assembly embodying the supreme will of the people of the State, we shall give ourselves and our children a constitution worthy of the traditions of our freedom struggle and in accordance with the principles of New Kashmir.[104]

Nowhere did the resolution mention that the recommendation for convening the Constituent Assembly was being made in pursuit of the Maharaja's Proclamation of 5th March 1948, which enjoined the Prime Minister to convene an Assembly to give the people of the State a Constitution of its own. Instead of giving any credit to the Maharaja, the resolution appropriated all credit of seizing the initiative to put an end to the 'indeterminate state of drift and indecision', and determine 'the future shape and affiliations of the State of Jammu and Kashmir.'

The convening of the Constituent Assembly suited both New Delhi and Sheikh Abdullah. India could resolve the Kashmir dispute or so the leaders in Delhi thought, and Sheikh Abdullah, who was eager to use it to strike the final blow at the Dogra dynasty, would get an opportunity to realize his dream. However, there was a snag to it. No Assembly of the kind could come into existence without the approval of Yuvraj Karan Singh, who, by himself, could not take such a momentous decision because he was nominated only as the Regent of the Maharaja who had not abdicated, and legally, was still the ruler of the State. The reluctance of the Yuvraj to sign the Proclamation was understandable. But this was deeply resented by Sheikh Abdullah, who responded by launching a personal and obnoxious attack on the former that needed the intervention of Prime Minister Nehru. Meanwhile, the Government of India entered into consultations with Maharaja Hari Singh over the convening of the Assembly. In November 1950, Vishnu Sahay, Secretary for Kashmir Affairs, wrote to the Maharaja enclosing a draft proclamation to be issued by Yuvraj Karan Singh asking for his comments.

Maharaja Hari Singh had still not fully reconciled to the manner in which he was pushed from one stand to another, used by the Government of India and then cast away as a used and now unwanted tool. In a tragic misreading of the circumstances, he saw in the emerging situation a chance to play some role, make a substantial contribution and reclaim some of the relevance that was taken away. After all, he was the one who had toyed with the idea of a responsible government and constitutional monarchy in the State!

On 10th December 1950, Maharaja Hari Singh wrote to Sardar Patel and expressed his views on the subject. While agreeing wholeheartedly with the object of the Proclamation for convening the Constituent Assembly, he was of the opinion that such a Proclamation should be issued by him as the ruler and not his Regent. He also thought that the powers and functions of the Assembly should be well defined and should exclude from its purview, matters not expressly entrusted to it. The Assembly should report to the person who constituted it, i.e. the ruler who would then seek the advice of the Parliament of India. In a separate letter to Yuvraj Karan Singh, he told the Yuvraj that he was taking up the matter with the Government of India and that the Yuvraj should not sign the Proclamation till the Maharaja had clarified the matter.[105]

There is little doubt that the treatment meted out to Maharaja Hari Singh by the Government of India in general, and Prime Minister Nehru in particular, had left a lacerated heart. He had been relentlessly pushed from one position to another till he was forced to leave the State and appoint a Regent. He had been asked to attribute his absence from the State to reasons of health, and when he protested that it would be ironical that while people came to Kashmir for reasons of recuperating from ill health he was being asked to leave the State, he had virtually been told to find his own explanations. He had then asked to be given any assignment on behalf of the Government of India as a face-saving measure but his suggestion was curtly turned down.[106] Finally, he was resigned to his fate but now it appeared that he once again sensed an opportunity to play an active role in the affairs of the State.

In the past there were many opportunities to play his hand for the coveted stakes but he had missed them. Often he was torn between his loyalty to the country as an Indian and as the ruler of Jammu and Kashmir. By the time he realized that he was being gradually marginalized, it was too late. On all occasions, he found himself on the wrong side of the ascendant historical forces. In the past, he distrusted the British and detested the communal politics of Mohammad Ali Jinnah. He also found himself pitched against the rising power of Nehru and Abdullah. Yet when he tried to adjust to the changed equations, his efforts endeared him to neither the one nor the other. He missed out on the opportunity to introduce responsible government and constitutional monarchy in the past. Perhaps now he was trying to make up for the lost opportunities? What would he have done if he had been allowed to play the role that was legitimately his? The answer is in the realm of conjecture, even though in the past, once a law had been formulated, he had always followed it to the last letter. Even when he was the fountainhead of all power, he had never overturned the recommendations of his Ministers, Prime Ministers, and more importantly, the Board of Judicial Advisors in the matter of justice. Unfortunately, the issue now was the assertion of Sheikh Abdullah's will in alliance with Nehru.

There is no way of knowing how Sardar Patel would have handled the matter for unfortunately, he died on 15thDecember 1950. A different set of people were entrusted to deal with the subject. So, soon after, Vishnu Sahay enclosed a copy of the proclamation with his letter and suggested to Yuvraj Karan Singh that when he received a 'submission' in that regard from Sheikh

Abdullah, he should sign it. On 27th January1951, the 'submission' was duly made by the Prime Minister of the State in which he stated that the Proclamation to convene the Constituent Assembly be made and that clauses 4 to 6 of the Proclamation of 5th March1948, superseded, as they did not meet the present requirements. He also stressed that both the State Government and the Government of India had agreed on the draft that was being sent to Yuvraj Karan Singh to sign as the Regent.[107]

It was a piquant situation for the young Yuvraj, for on the one hand was the express direction of his father and the ruler of the State not to affix his signature to the Proclamation, and on the other hand, he found that having agreed on a common draft, both the Government of India and Sheikh Abdullah were asking him to sign it at the earliest. Unable to take a reasoned decision, Yuvraj Karan Singh flew to New Delhi for consultation with Gopalaswami Ayyangar, who had taken over as Minister for States after the death of Sardar Patel. On his return the Yuvraj wrote a note on the submission of Sheikh Abdullah:

> Prime Minister,
>
> As you are aware, I derive my powers from His Highness' proclamation dated June 20, 1949, appointing me Regent.
>
> The draft proclamation which you have now put before me is a very important document, involving, as it does, far-reaching consequences to the future of the State. The Ministry of States had sent a draft proclamation to His Highness for his comments. His Highness sent his comments thereon to the then Hon'ble Minister of States [the late Sardar Patel], and at the same time directed me not to append my signature on any proclamation on the subject without his express approval.
>
> You will, therefore, appreciate that as I have received no such approval from him yet, I am at this stage precluded from signing the document you have submitted to me. I therefore suggest that you ask the Government of India to pursue this matter with His Highness.
>
> Karan Singh
> Regent
> January 30, 1951[108]

Sheikh Abdullah considered the delay as an act of defiance that gave another reason to add Yuvraj Karan Singh to his list of targets. But, when he launched a tirade against the Yuvraj it came as a surprise and a shock. The bitter personal attack came on 9th April 1951, six months after the National Conference had passed the resolution for the convening of the Constituent Assembly. The Sheikh had obviously been simmering with resentment by the delay and now, no longer used to defiance, he made an unprovoked and intemperate attack that betrayed his pathological dislike of the dynasty. It also demonstrated his newly acquired arrogance of power. He chose the venue for the attack very carefully to demonstrate the reach of the power he exercised and the inability of the Dogra dynasty to respond.

During a public meeting held at Panthal, a few miles near Jammu, he launched a bitter and personal attack on both Maharaja Hari Singh and Yuvraj Karan Singh. He accused the Yuvraj of 'frequently conferring with the reactionary communal leaders who are plotting to bring back the Maharaja.' He added: 'I still hope the young Prince will listen to better counsels. But if he persists in seeking the advice of the reactionaries and the communalists, I can tell him, for the time has come for plain speaking that his future will not be far different from that of his father. Let the Yuvraj realize that the days of the rajas and nawabs are past. Even in those places where monarchy is still tolerated, it is only subject to the will of the people which is supreme.'[109] Sheikh Abdullah also used the oft-repeated malicious allegation that the Maharaja and the Maharani were responsible for instigating communal riots against the Muslims in Jammu. During his earlier confrontation with Maharaja Hari Singh over the State Forces he proceeded to hold the State Forces responsible for the killing of Muslims in the Jammu region after it was made clear to him by the Maharaja that the State Forces could not be put under his control. Now impatient with the delay in signing the Proclamation he included Yuvraj Karan Singh as a legitimate target of his attack.

The unprovoked attack, made in the heartland of Jammu, came as a shock to the Yuvraj. Probably it was an attempt to intimidate the Yuvraj into signing the Proclamation. Taken aback by the vehemence of the tirade, the Yuvraj immediately sent to Prime Minister Nehru cuttings of the news reports as carried out in *The Tribune* and *The Hindustan Times* along with a covering letter, expressing his hurt over the factually incorrect and misleading accusations, as also the copy of the letter he wrote to Sheikh Abdullah.[110]

Nehru was prompt in his reply regretting that Sheikh Abdullah had made a personal reference to Yuvraj Karan Singh but expressed satisfaction that the Yuvraj had chosen to immediately communicate with Sheikh Sahib. However, he also tried to explain away the unsavoury incident by writing: 'The position in regard to Jammu and Kashmir is, as you know, a very difficult one and we are up against great powers. This fact does not seem to be realized by many people. Oddly enough, those who are more opposed than any others to Pakistan's intrusion in the State, often act in a manner to help Pakistan.'[111]

The situation is best appreciated by recalling some of the events that preceded this unpleasant incident. Soon after becoming the Prime Minister, Sheikh Abdullah had started encroaching upon the rights of the Maharaja, not only as the Head of the State but also as the Trustee of the Dharmarth Trust.[112] The Trust funds, which were accumulated by personal donation from successive rulers of the Dogra dynasty, could be rightfully used by the Maharaja for any charitable cause. However, Sheikh Abdullah had vehemently objected to Hari Singh's use of the funds to provide relief to the Hindu and Sikh refugees from Pakistan and the border villages. This had not gone down well with the Maharaja. Could anyone blame then him for relating those objections to the communal character of the National Conference, when earlier it was known as the Muslim Conference—a decidedly communal organization? Could anyone deny the fact that the incident that was now commemorated as Martyrs' Day was actually provoked by an attack by Muslim hordes on Hindu shopkeepers? Even the background to that attack was steeped in communalism. As a result, all subsequent steps of marginalizing the Dogras and exiling the Maharaja had only hardened the positions.

The consequence was that the Dogras were convinced of the

communal agenda of Sheikh Abdullah and the National Conference and they felt that it should have been obvious to Pandit Nehru that in this undesirable confrontation with the Dogras, the agent provocateurs were the National Conference in general and Sheikh Abdullah in particular. Moreover, the kind of campaign launched by Sheikh Abdullah against the Dogra dynasty was not being matched by the enthusiasm for the State's commitment to India. He was clamouring for more arbitrary powers but was not prepared to be a part of India as the rest of the States were. His ambivalence on the subject of complete integration was giving rise to uncertainty and encouraging those who could play mischief. Not for a moment did Sheikh Abdullah introspect and understand why each of his utterances against the Dogra dynasty was only alienating the Jammu region from the people in power.

With the exception of very few pockets of influence, the rest of Jammu was hostile to Sheikh Abdullah and the exile of the Maharaja had only hardened the stands of the Dogras. The platform for protest and resistance had been offered by the Praja Parishad, and the Dogras, seething as they were, seized it. It did not matter to them that the Praja Parishad was a regional variant of the newly formed political party, Bharatiya Jana Sangh. Since the Dogras suffered at the hands of Sheikh Abdullah and his vindictive policies, they had, of necessity, veered towards the only organized platform. In response, Sheikh Abdullah dubbed the Dogras as reactionaries, knowing full well that by branding them as such he would deprive them of any communication link with Pandit Nehru. The Prime Minister of India was mindful of any action taken by the majority community of the country that could create uncertainties and insecurities among the Muslims. It was to these 'reactionary' forces to which Sheikh Abdullah was referring to in his speech when 'warning' Yuvraj Karan Singh.

In the circumstances, Yuvraj Karan Singh had no alternative but to quietly follow Pandit Nehru's advice. Perhaps by now, after Sardar Patel's death, Sheikh Abdullah had realized that Pandit Nehru had become a victim of his own idealism and that he needed Sheikh Abdullah more than the other way around. So, instead of expressing any regret over the outburst during his speech of 9th

April, he responded to Yuvraj's letter with a letter running into five pages. He made it known to the Yuvraj that he was expected to behave as a virtual prisoner of his government and that even the public appearances made by him must first seek the approval of Sheikh Abdullah! The letter, in fact, made his pathological hatred for the Dogra dynasty clear and in the light of Pandit Nehru's advice to Yuvraj Karan Singh, little could be done to contain him as he rode the crest of the wave.[113]

There is no record that could certifiably point out to the person, persons or groups to whom Nehru was alluding and one can only surmise that he was referring to the rising tempo of the anti-Sheikh Abdullah and anti-National Conference sentiments in Jammu that was led by the Praja Parishad, and which had become an anathema to Nehru since he accused it of communalism and therefore the enemy of secular India. The letter, however, was sufficient to assuage the feelings of the young Yuvraj who was obviously keen at that early stage to play a significant role in the new India that was emerging. In this he was constantly being guided by the Prime Minister of India who somewhat later in June of the same year wrote to him saying: 'I think that it is exceedingly important that your contacts with Sheikh Sahib should be almost continuous or, at any rate, very frequent. I think that you should have a good talk with him regularly once a week and, if necessary, oftener. This will keep you in touch with what is happening and to take Sheikh Saheb's advice on many matters...I have mentioned this matter to Sheikh Saheb also and he fully agreed...Apart from these direct contacts, there should be indirect but satisfactory contacts also. This can take place most conveniently by your having a Secretary of high standing and experience, who can continually act as a liaison between you and Sheikh Saheb...He should, of course, be one who has your confidence...And he should have Sheikh Saheb's confidence.'[114]

Pandit Nehru went on to assure him that it was a normal practice to have such an arrangement by the Head of the State and that the President of India too had such Secretaries to liaison with him in New Delhi. Undoubtedly Pandit Nehru's advice was sound and practical. Only that kind of an arrangement allows for a smooth functioning between the Head of the State and his Prime Minister.

However, he failed to see the essential difference between the kind of functional relationship forged between him and President Dr Rajendra Prasad and the one between Sheikh Abdullah and a scion of the Dogra dynasty. Pandit Nehru and Dr Rajendra Prasad were comrades in arm during the long freedom struggle and despite their ideological differences had developed a healthy respect for each other. Moreover, both of them were driven by the motivation to leave behind democratic traditions that would stand the test of time. In addition, Pandit Jawaharlal Nehru had succeeded in setting a precedent in New Delhi of having established a healthy relationship with the first Governor-General Lord Mountbatten even though he was the symbol of all that British imperialism stood for. He had left the prejudices and confrontations of the past behind and encouraged everyone to begin with a clean slate.

The Maharaja, in the meantime, had taken the opinion of legal experts who agreed that such a Proclamation for setting up the Constituent Assembly could only be signed by the ruler. This opinion ignored the stark fact that what Maharaja Hari Singh was up against was not the legality of a situation but the hard and cruel realities of power politics. Soon he was to find out that once again he had played the wrong cards. V.P. Menon visited Bombay for talks with the Maharaja and reported back to Ayyangar. The Minister of States wrote a blunt letter that informed the Maharaja of the Central government's intention to go ahead with the convening of the Constituent Assembly with or without his signature.

Ayyangar wrote, '...The Government of India [is] committed to the convening of a Constituent Assembly, the preparations for which are in active progress in the State. That Assembly will be held whether the formal Proclamation issues or not. In the view of the Government of India it must be convened, if both their commitments to the people of Kashmir and their stand at Lake Success are to be implemented, in spirit and in letter...No purpose will, therefore, be served by any act of Your Highness which holds up the signing and issue of this Proclamation by Shri Yuvraj.'[115]

Significantly, Ayyangar went on to add, 'On neither of the two matters about which I can understand your entertaining apprehensions, namely, the continuance of the accession of the Jammu and Kashmir State or of part thereof to India and the connection of the Headship of the State with your dynasty, no final decision should be taken by the Constituent Assembly to be convened. They are essentially matters which could be decided only as a matter of agreement between the Government of India and Parliament on the one side and the Government of Jammu and Kashmir and the State Constituent Assembly or legislature on the other. The Government of India will, no doubt, at the proper time take the decision on these matters, which I need hardly assure you, would be essentially just from the standpoint both of your dynasty and the people of the State. You have obviously to put your trust in the people of the State and the Government of India in respect of this matter. I hope, therefore, you will immediately lift the ban which you have placed on Shri Yuvraj affixing his signature to the agreed Proclamation and which naturally has placed him in great embarrassment...'[116]

Ayyangar's ultimatum undoubtedly with the consent of Jawaharlal Nehru, was enough to persuade the ruler to lift the ban imposed on the Yuvraj and also left the whole matter to the Yuvraj's discretion. He made it amply clear that in the matter of the hereditary, Headship of the State by the dynasty, was no longer a subject to be decided by the Maharaja or his family. Henceforth, it was to be decided by the Government of India and the Parliament on one side and the Government of Jammu and Kashmir and the State Constituent Assembly on the other. The Government of India was, indeed, in a hurry to draw the curtain on the ruling family of the State even as other rulers were to continue to be Heads of States till the Reorganization of States in 1956.

Finally, after the usual jostling and jockeying, the Proclamation for convening the Constituent Assembly was made on 1st May 1951 by Yuvraj Karan Singh, the Regent.

> Whereas it is the general desire of the people of the State of Jammu and Kashmir that a Constituent Assembly should be brought into being for the purpose of framing a Constitution for the State;
>
> Whereas it is commonly felt that the convening of the Assembly can no longer be delayed without detriment to the future well-being of the State;

> And whereas terms of the proclamation of the Maharaja dated March 5, 1948 in regard to the convening of a National Assembly as contained in clauses 4 to 6 of the operative part thereof do not meet the requirements of the present situation;
>
> I, Yuvraj Karan Singh, do hereby direct as follows:
>
> A Constituent Assembly consisting of representatives of the people, elected on the basis of adult franchise shall be constituted forthwith for the purpose of framing a constitution for the State of Jammu and Kashmir;
>
> For the purpose of the said elections the State shall be divided into a number of territorial constituencies each containing a population of 40,000 or as near thereto as possible and each electing one member. A delimitation Committee shall be set up by the Government to make recommendations as to the number of constituencies and the limits of each constituency;
>
> Elections to the Constituent Assembly shall be on the basis of adult franchise, that is to say, every person who is a State subject of any class, is not less than twenty-one years of age on the first day of March, has been a resident in the constituency for such period as may be prescribed by the rules, shall be entitled to register in the electoral rolls of that constituency, provided that any person who is of unsound mind or has been so declared by a competent court, shall be disqualified for registration;
>
> The vote at the election shall be direct and by secret ballot;
>
> The Constituent Assembly shall have power to act notwithstanding any vacancy of the Membership thereof;
>
> The Constituent Assembly shall frame its own agenda and make rules for the governing of its procedure and the conduct of its business;
>
> The Government shall make such rules and issue such instructions and orders as may be necessary to give effect to the terms of this proclamation.

The process of convening the Constituent Assembly, as envisaged in the Proclamation of 5th March 1948, had finally begun.

9

Finally, the Constituent Assembly

The Proclamation for convening the Constituent Assembly was followed by an election of the members. Of the seventy-five members, seventy-two were elected unopposed—all belonging to the National Conference. In the Valley, the aspiring candidates belonging to other political outfits were either physically stopped from reaching the designated venue to file their nomination papers or were rejected on one pretext or another. In Jammu, the Praja Parishad initially contested twenty-eight out of thirty seats allocated to Jammu. But after the nomination papers of thirteen of its candidates were rejected on the grounds of technicalities, it sensed that the elections were being hijacked by the ruling National Conference. They announced a boycott shortly before the polling. Consequently, all the National Conference candidates were declared as winners from the Jammu province. Thus, the end result was that the Constituent Assembly that was to draw up the Constitution was not represented by anyone who opposed the National Conference. Even Pandit Prem Nath Dogra, a widely respected person from the Jammu region did not make it to that august House. It was truly an ominous start!

By now Sheikh Abdullah had assumed such an Orwellian image of himself as a leader that he could ignore the normal courtesy that is extended to the person under whose signature the Assembly is convened. Yuvraj Karan Singh, the Regent therefore was not invited for the opening address. Sheikh Abdullah took it upon himself to inaugurate the Assembly and in a 'pompous' address drew upon the authority of various great men, including Thomas Aquinas.

We the people of Jammu and Kashmir, Ladakh and the Frontier regions, including Poonch and Chenani Illaqas commonly known as Jammu and Kashmir State, in order to perfect our union in the fullest equality and self-determination to raise ourselves and our children forever from the abyss of oppression and poverty, degradation and superstition, from medieval darkness and ignorance, into the sunlit valleys of plenty, ruled by freedom, science and honest toil, in worthy participation of the historic resurgence of the peoples of East, and the working masses of the world, and in determination to make this our country a dazzling gem on the snowy bosom of Asia, propose and propound the following constitution of our State.

This was the resolution passed at the 1944 session of the National Conference in Srinagar. After seven years of that resolution, and more than three years of unfettered rule by Sheikh Abdullah, an Assembly was finally convened so that the pledges made in the past could be redeemed. Addressing the Constituent Assembly, Sheikh Abdullah recalled the National Conference's resolution of 1944 in his opening address to the Constituent Assembly:

> Today, in 1951, embodying aspirations, men and women from the four corners of the State in this Constituent Assembly have become the repository of its sovereign authority. This Assembly, invested with the authority of a constituent body, will be the fountain-head of basic laws laying the foundation of a just social order and safeguarding the democratic rights of all the citizens of the State.[117]

Then he went on to spell out the goals and objectives that it had to achieve:

> One great task before this Assembly will be to devise a Constitution for the future governance of the country…Another issue of vital import to the nation involves the future of the royal dynasty… The third major issue awaiting your deliberations arises out of the land reforms which the government carried out with vigour and determination. Our "land to the tiller" policy brought light into the dark homes of the peasantry; but, side by side, it has given rise to the problem of the landowners' demand for compensation. The nation being the ultimate custodian of all wealth and resources,

> the representatives of the nation are truly the best jury for giving a just and final verdict on such claims. So in your hands lies the power of this decision.
>
> Finally, this Assembly will after full consideration of the three alternatives that I shall state later, declare its reasoned conclusion regarding accession. This will help us to channelize our energies resolutely and with greater zeal in directions in which we have already started moving for the social and economic advancement of our country…
>
> You are no doubt aware of the scope of our present constitutional ties with India. We are proud to have our bonds with India, the goodwill of those people and government is available to us in unstinted and abundant measure. The Constitution of India has provided for a federal union and in the distribution of sovereign powers has treated us differently from other constituent units. With the exception of the items grouped under Defence, Foreign Affairs and Communications in the Instrument of Accession, we have complete freedom to frame our Constitution in the manner we like. In order to live and prosper as good partners in a common endeavour for the advancement of our peoples, I would advise that, while safeguarding our autonomy to the fullest extent so as to enable us to have the liberty to build our country according to the best traditions and genius of our people, we may also by suitable constitutional arrangements with the Union establish our right to seek and compel federal cooperation and assistance in this great task, as well as offer our fullest cooperation and assistance to the union.[118]

Then while reiterating the need to work for social and economic justice for all the people of the State, Sheikh Abdullah was back to his favourite obsession:

> …the Constituent Assembly will now re-examine and decide on the future of the present ruling dynasty, in respect of its authority.
>
> It is clear that this dynasty can no longer exercise authority on the basis of an old *discredited* [emphasis added] Treaty. During my trial for sedition in the "Quit Kashmir" movement, I had clarified the attitude of my party when I said: "The future constitutional set-up in the State of Jammu & Kashmir cannot derive authority from the old source of relationship which was expiring and was bound to end soon. The set-up could only rest

> on the active will of the people of the State, conferring on the head of the State the title and authority drawn from the true and abiding source of sovereignty that is the people."
>
> So far as my Party is concerned, we are convinced that the institution of monarchy is incompatible with the spirit and needs of modern times, which demand an egalitarian relationship between one citizen and another. The supreme test of a democracy is the measure of equality of opportunity that it affords to its citizens to rise to the highest point of authority and position. In consequence monarchies are fast disappearing from the world picture, as something in the nature of feudal anachronisms. In India, too, where before the partition, six hundred and odd Princes exercised rights and privileges of rulership, the process of democratization has been taken up and at present hardly ten of them exercise the limited authority of constitutional heads of States.
>
> After the attainment of complete power by the people, it would have been an appropriate gesture of good will to recognize Maharaja Hari Singh as the first constitutional Head of the State. But I must say with regret that he has completely forfeited the confidence of every section of the people. His incapacity to adjust himself to changed conditions and his antiquated views on vital problems constitute positive disqualifications for him to hold the high office of a democratic Head of the State. Moreover, his past actions as a ruler have proved that he is not capable of conducting himself with dignity, responsibility and impartiality. The people still remember with pain and regret his failure to stand by them in times of crisis, and his incapacity to afford protection to a section of his people in Jammu.[119]

Three years of autocratic and arbitrary rule, when none of the lofty principles that he enunciated so pompously before the Assembly were upheld, had transformed Sheikh Abdullah into a person who began to believe in the falsehoods that he uttered and see virtue in what was otherwise, blatant politics of vendetta unleashed by him. While acknowledging that there were still some rulers in India who enjoyed the privileges of constitutional heads, including the Nizam of Hyderabad[120] who had loaned Rs 21 crore to Pakistan and which might have been used during the war efforts in Kashmir, he resorted to amnesia and complete falsehoods in laying charges against

Maharaja Hari Singh even on that solemn occasion. Knowing full well that he was asked to retract and correct the statements made against the Maharaja, he thumbed his nose not only at the decency and dignity of the occasion but also the leaders in Delhi who went out of their way to support his cause.

His lie about the Maharaja not protecting a section of the populace in Jammu is nailed by the report of General Scott, the commander-in-chief of the State Forces, who was a British national serving in the State but had sought retirement on realizing that Maharaja Hari Singh was not inclined to accede to Pakistan. General Scott's report read: 'The State troops escorted one lakh Muslims through Jammu territory on their way to Pakistan and an equal number of Sikhs and Hindus going the other way.'[121]

It was plain to everyone that even though the Maharaja was in exile and was reconciled to the fact that he had been made a spectator, he had maintained his dignity even in the face of serious provocation. But the new ruler, in contrast, had continued to demonstrate his pettiness. Never during those years of his exile had the Maharaja made any public statement, for he knew that it would greatly embarrass the Government of India. He protested to Sardar Patel about the falsehoods spread by Sheikh Abdullah and his National Conference in several letters but had never gone public to speak against his Prime Minister and ministers. It is hard to recall an occasion when he failed to act in a manner appropriate to his position. However, now the person accusing him of undignified behaviour had chosen a solemn occasion to display his hostility towards the Maharaja. In one breath, he became the accuser, prosecutor and judge. He accused him of nursing 'antiquated views' choosing to ignore the fact that the Maharaja's deeds had proven that he was the most progressive of Indian rulers and had been a pioneer in political, social, economic and land reforms. But the most preposterous charge was that the Maharaja was 'not capable of conducting himself with dignity, responsibility and impartiality' because it was personal dignity and a sense of deep responsibility towards India that had made him seal his lips regarding many controversies.

At this juncture, when Sheikh Abdullah seemed to be completely alienating the Dogras, in total contradiction to his expected behaviour, he offered an olive branch and said, 'I am sure none of us is interested in a personal controversy with the Maharaja's family. In the conduct of public affairs, it is necessary that an impartial view of every individual's deeds should be taken. Our judgment should not be warped by ill-will or personal rancour. During our association with Yuvraj Karan Singh these last few years, my colleagues and I in the government have been impressed by his intelligence, broad outlook and keen desire to serve the country. These qualities of the Yuvraj single him out as a fit choice for the honour of being chosen the first Head of the State. There is no doubt that Yuvraj Karan Singh in his capacity as a citizen of the State, will prove a fitting symbol of the transition to a democratic system in which the ruler of yesterday becomes the first servant of the people, functioning under their authority, and on their behalf.'[122]

Commenting on this offer, Yuvraj Karan Singh writes, 'Clearly this had been the compromise worked out during the long discussions conducted with Jawaharlal and other representatives of the Government of India. This was a shrewd move, on the one hand to avoid offending the Dogras irretrievably and on the other of retaining in a subtle way the constitutional authority of our family. After all, the legal and constitutional validity of Jammu and Kashmir's accession to the Indian Union rested on the Instrument of Accession signed by my father, and now that very person was being unceremoniously pushed out by an Assembly which was convened through a proclamation signed by me as his son and Regent!'[123] Not unlike Robespierre of the French Revolution, who had framed a law that was used to declare him guilty and hence sent to the guillotine, the Yuvraj too had become the instrument for drawing up a law that would bring the dynasty to an end.

Sheikh Abdullah went on to address the more substantial question of the solution to what had come to be known as the 'Kashmir problem'. He put before the Assembly the issue:

> The problem may be posed in this way. Firstly, was Pakistan's action in invading Kashmir in 1947 morally and legally correct, judged by any norm of international behaviour? Sir Owen Dixon's

> verdict on this issue is perfectly plain. In unambiguous terms he declared Pakistan an aggressor. Secondly, was the Maharaja's accession to India legally valid or not? The legality of the accession has not been seriously questioned by any responsible or independent person or authority.[124]
>
> These two answers are obviously correct. Then where is the justification of treating India and Pakistan at par in matters pertaining to Kashmir? In fact, the force of logic dictates the conclusion that the aggressor should withdraw his armed forces, and the United Nations should see that Pakistan gets out of the State.
>
> In that event, India herself, anxious to give the people of the State a chance to express their will freely, would willingly cooperate with any sound plan of demilitarization. They would withdraw their forces, only garrisoning enough posts to ensure against any repetition of that earlier treacherous attack from Pakistan…
>
> We as a government are keen to let our people decide the future of our land in accordance with their own wishes. If these three preliminary processes were accomplished, we should be happy to have the assistance of international observers to ensure fair play and the requisite conditions for a free choice by the people.
>
> Instead invader and defender have been put on the same plane.[125]

After thus succinctly expressing the problem, Sheikh Abdullah went on to enumerate the alternatives that were offered for solving the problem. He claimed that the Cabinet Mission Plan[126]had offered three alternatives—accession to India, accession to Pakistan and claiming the right to remain independent, though the third choice was categorically rejected by the Congress. He went on to analyze the various options presented to the people of the State and did so as a 'realist'. 'I am conscious that nothing is all black or all white, and there are many facts to each of the propositions before us. I shall first speak on the merits and demerits of the State's accession to India. In the final analysis, as I understand it, it is the kinship of ideals which determines the strength of ties between two States. The Indian National Congress has consistently supported the cause of the State's people's freedom. The autocratic rule of the Princes has been done away with and representative governments have been entrusted with the administration. Steps towards democratization have been taken and these have raised the people's standard of living, brought about much-needed social reconstruction, and above all built up their very independence of spirit. Naturally, if we accede to India there is no danger of a revival of feudalism and autocracy. Moreover, during the last four years the Government of India has never tried to interfere in our internal autonomy. This experience has strengthened our confidence in them as a democratic State.'[127]

Sheikh Abdullah found an even more positive reason to accede to India in the Indian Constitution. 'The Indian Constitution has set before the country the goal of secular democracy based on justice, freedom and equality for all without distinction. This is the bedrock of modern democracy. This should meet the argument that the Muslims of Kashmir cannot have security in India, where the large majority of the population is Hindu.'[128] He dismissed the religious divide that led to Partition as the handiwork of imperialism, and asserted that no modern State can afford to encourage artificial division if it is to achieve progress and prosperity. He found reason to rejoice in noting that the Indian Constitution had repudiated the concept of a religious State by guaranteeing the equality of rights of all citizens irrespective of their religion, colour, caste and class. He claimed that the national movement of the State naturally gravitated towards these principles of secular democracy. Sheikh Abdullah also urged the Assembly to consider this affinity in political principles, past association and the common path of suffering in the cause of freedom, properly while deciding the future of the State.

Even more emphatically, Sheikh Abdullah enunciated the concern for the economic wellbeing of the people of the State. 'As I said before', he continued while referring to constitution-building, 'political ideals are often meaningless unless linked with economic plans. As a State, we are concerned mainly with agriculture and trade. As you know, and I have detailed before, we have been able to put through our "land to the tiller" legislation and make of it a practical success. Land and all it means is an inestimable blessing to our peasants who have dragged along in servitude to the landlord and his allies for centuries without number. We have been able under present conditions to carry these reforms through…We have already heard that news of our land reforms has travelled to the peasants of the enemy-occupied area of our State, who vainly desire like status, and like benefits. In the second place, our economic welfare is bound up with our arts and crafts. The traditional markets for these precious goods for which we are justly known all over the world, have been centred in India. The volume of our trade, in spite of the dislocation of the last few years, shows this. Industry is also highly important to us. Potentially we are rich in minerals, and in the raw materials of industry; we need help to develop our resources. India, being more highly industrialized than Pakistan, can give us equipment, technical services and materials. She can help us too in marketing.'[129]

He also addressed the alleged disadvantages of accession to India and after going through the geographical and logistic compulsions that inhibited Maharaja Hari Singh from taking a quick decision and conceding that these could be overcome with the availability of advanced engineering technology, he came to the substantial apprehension of the fear of the religious fanaticism not only raising its head but asserting itself in India. '*Certain tendencies have been asserting themselves in India which may in the future convert it into a religious State wherein the interests of Muslims will be jeopardized. This would happen if a communal organization had a dominant hand in the government, and [the] Congress ideals of the equality of all communities were made to give way to religious intolerance.* [Emphasis added] The continued accession of Kashmir to India should, however, help in defeating this tendency. From my experience of the last four years, it is my considered judgment that the presence of Kashmir in the Union of India has been the major factor in establishing relations between the Hindus and Muslims of India. Gandhiji was not wrong when he uttered [the] words before his death which paraphrase, "I lift up mine eyes into the hills, from whence cometh my help".'[130]

Following this, Sheikh Abdullah explored the arguments in favour of acceding to Pakistan and was very categorical in its rejection. He said, 'The most powerful argument which can be advanced in her favour is that Pakistan is a Muslim State, and, a big majority of our people being Muslims the State must accede to Pakistan. This claim of being a Muslim State is of course only a camouflage. It is a screen to dupe the common man, so that he may not see clearly that Pakistan is a feudal State in which a clique is trying by these methods to maintain itself in power. In addition to this, the appeal to religion constitutes a sentimental and a wrong approach to the question. Sentiment has its own place in life but often it leads to irrational action. Some argue, as a supposedly natural corollary to this, that on our acceding to Pakistan our annihilation or survival depends. Facts have disproved this, right-thinking men would point out that Pakistan is not an organic unity of all the Muslims in this subcontinent. It has on the contrary, caused the dispersion of the Indian Muslims for whose benefit it was claimed to have been created. There are two Pakistans, at least a thousand miles apart from each other. The total population of Western Pakistan which is contiguous to our State, is hardly 15 million. While the total number of Muslims, resident in India is as many as 40 million. As one Muslim is as good as another, the Kashmiri Muslims if they are worried by such considerations should choose the forty millions living in India.'[131]

Significantly, he also did not shy away from having a hard look at the right of self-determination and declared that it could not be given up. 'Our national movement in the State considers this right of self-determination inalienable, and no advantage, however great, will persuade our people to forego it,' he said and then brought up the issue of the third option. 'The third course open to us has still to be discussed. We have to consider the alternative of making ourselves an Eastern Switzerland, of keeping aloof from both States but having friendly relations with them. This might seem attractive in that it would appear to pave the way out of the present deadlock. To us, as a tourist country, it could also have certain obvious advantages, but in considering independence, we must not ignore practical considerations. Firstly, it is not easy to protect sovereignty and independence in a small country which has not sufficient strength to defend itself on our long and difficult frontiers bordering so many countries. Secondly, we must have the goodwill of all our neighbours. Can we find powerful guarantors among them to pull together always in assuring us freedom from aggression? I would like to remind you that from August 15 to October 22, 1947 our State was independent and the result was that our weakness was exploited by the neighbour with invasion. What is the guarantee that in future too we may not be victims of a singular aggression?'[132]

Thus, while exhorting the members of the Assembly to see the positives of acceding to India as it gave better opportunities of socio-economic growth, freedom from feudalism, secular character and importantly non-interference in internal affairs and decisions, he had also reiterated the right to self-determination. This was significant as Sheikh Abdullah also put before the Assembly the alternative of independence and found that it was not feasible in the absence of powerful guarantors of independence and security. What if some powerful nations, like the USA and UK, or an international forum like the United Nations provided that guarantee? Would then the people of Kashmir invoke their right to self-determination, which Sheikh Abdullah claimed to be the inalienable right of the people of the State and a right over which no compromise could be made?

10

Setting the Agenda

In unambiguous words Sheikh Abdullah had set the task before the Constituent Assembly. Deciding the premeditated future of the ruling family and passing a verdict on the land-owners' claim to compensation following the abolition of big-landed estates were objectives that were to be undertaken before anything else was decided. The significance of the urgency attached to these two objectives was not lost on anyone.

The second objective was clearly juxtaposed with the first and thus, along with the ruling family, the Dogras in general were targeted even when in every other Princely State, the rulers had been accommodated in the process of change. With the land reforms, which Sheikh Abdullah admitted in his opening remarks were already 'carried out with vigour and determination', the only question left was whether compensation to the land owners was to be paid or not. But the last and the most consequential of them all, after deciding the future of the dynasty, was the issue of the State's accession on which hinged the fate of the whole State.

The State of Jammu and Kashmir was not the only one to be dealing with the future of a ruling dynasty. All the Princely States had to grapple with this challenge, and in each one of them the States Department was successful in applying closure by integrating the princes in the process of assimilation. In a few cases, Sardar Patel had to resort to threats and arm-twisting but in most cases his persuasive skills were put to good use. Thus, he had set in motion a process that was inclusive of all the aspects that governed their relationship with India and resulted in their gradual integration.

We know that in the rest of the country, the integration of the Princely States had begun, even as the Constitution drafting progressed and the idea of forming a Republic took concrete shape.Many among them, particularly those falling in the 'Part C' category, barely pretended to be independent states. It was not difficult to convince them to surrender their powers in lieu of attractive privy purses and other privileges. As a general rule, it was decided that all the Princely and covenanting States would merge with the Indian Republic and all the Maharajas would be provided with a privy purse and privileges as enjoyed by them, on 15thAugust 1947 by constitutional guarantees. Besides it was also decided that the Maharaja of Mysore, Jammu and Kashmir, the Nizam of Hyderabad and the Rajpramukhs of the covenanting states would continue to be the constitutional heads of their respective states. By 26th October 1949, as the Constituent Assembly finalized a new Constitution for India, all the acceding Indian states and the covenanting states merged their kingdom and covenanting state respectively with the new Republic of India. These agreements were entered into before 26th January 1950 so as to bring them within the ambit of Article 363 of the Indian Constitution*. On 26th January 1950 India became a republic.

The new Constitution created four types of administrative divisions in India. Nine 'Part A' states, which were the former British provinces, were ruled by an elected government and state legislature. Eight 'Part B' states, which were former Princely States or groups of covenanting states, were governed by a Rajpramukh. Ten 'Part C' states that included both former Princely States and provinces, were governed by a chief commissioner and a union territory was ruled by a governor appointed by the Indian President. It was a Herculean effort undertaken by Patel's iron will and the indefatigable energy of K.P.S Menon. Both succeeded in producing treaties that were designed to be attractive to rulers of the Princely States and to discourage them from pursuing a path

* According to Article 363 of the Indian Constitution, all treaties and agreements entered into between erstwhile rulers and the Government of India were taken out of the purview of the courts.

of confrontation. As a result, two key documents were produced. The first was the Standstill Agreement, which confirmed that the agreements and administrative practices that existed between the Princely State in question and the British would be continued by India. The second was the Instrument of Accession, by which the ruler of the Princely State in question agreed to the accession of his kingdom to independent India and to granting India control over specified subject matters.

In discussions, Lord Mountbatten reinforced the statements of Patel and Menon by emphasizing that the documents gave the princes all the 'practical independence' they needed. During his address to the Chamber of Princes, Mountbatten categorically told the princes that if they did not accept the terms put to them, then, they would subsequently have to accede on substantially less favourable terms. He highlighted that in any case, the three powers—foreign affairs, defence and communications—that they had to surrender were never exercised by them.[133] Patel and Menon also issued a similar threat couched in advice. However, the Standstill Agreement was used as a negotiating tool, as the States Department *categorically ruled out signing a Standstill Agreement with the Princely States that did not sign an Instrument of Accession.*

It is clear that, to begin with, all Instruments of Accession were limited; transferring control of only three matters to India, and would by themselves have produced a rather loose federation, with significant differences in administration and governance across the various states. Full political integration, in contrast, would require a process whereby the political actors in the various states were 'persuaded to shift their loyalties, expectations, and political activities towards a new centre', namely, the Republic of India. When Maharaja Hari Singh signed the Instrument of Accession, he did so in the belief that, like many other rulers of the Part B states, he was surrendering only limited control to the Government of India. He genuinely believed that the Government of India controlled only the defence, external affairs and the communications of the State and that he was free to exercise powers in other subjects. It was only gradually that the Ministry of States and the personal influence of Sardar Patel were able to persuade him to follow Delhi's instructions in clearing the way for such constitutional changes that were not required in other Part B states.

Sheikh Abdullah inherited this legacy from the Maharaja but had an additional advantage. The Pakistani aggression, followed by the reference of the matter to the Security Council and then the commitment to hold a plebiscite over the accession, gave him a grip. In the process, a monstrous constitutional arrangement evolved in the State and a quiet coup was carried out. It ousted the Maharaja who was routinely called an autocrat by his critics and vested executive, legislative and judicial powers in the hands of Sheikh Abdullah, which were infinitely more than what the Jammu and Kashmir Constitution Act, 1939 had vested in the Maharaja.

With the Government of India dependent on Abdullah for winning the Kashmir battle in the international forum, he became more possessive of the vast and unlimited powers that he came to wield. For close to three years he pretended to be the Prime Minister of a sovereign State and in this, Article 370 played a significant part. It set him on a course where any attempt to bring in uniform laws was seen as an assault on the constitutional safeguard provided to the State. In this, he was aided and abetted by his colleagues who pushed him into shifting his stands even after he and they would have agreed to some arrangement with the Government of India regarding the Maharaja or the Constitution.

All his efforts were directed at achieving the twin goal of humiliating the ruling dynasty and sending a message to New Delhi that the State was free to act independently of it. In order to humiliate the Maharaja, Sheikh Abdullah chose to record the blatant lies that he had been spreading about the Maharaja. If this was not sufficient proof of the vendetta that he had unleashed, then the third objective of the Constituent Assembly made it amply clear. There is no knowing how long Sheikh Abdullah would have continued in power without a legislative body if the Regent had not raised the question of propriety and the Centre had not reminded him that momentous changes like appropriation of land without compensation and ceiling on land holdings ought not to be implemented without the authority of a democratically elected legislative body. But, he still carried out land reforms by exercising the powers under the Jammu and Kashmir Constitution Act, 1939, which according to the Maharaja's critics vested all powers in his person.

However, the final issue was the question of accession that has been historically of great significance. Sheikh Abdullah claimed that there were three alternatives before the State. He did not mention that the so-called three alternatives that he referred to were before the ruler of the State and not the Constituent Assembly. What Sheikh Abdullah also did not say in the opening address was that even when the Cabinet Mission Plan was unfolding, the Congress working committee had categorically rejected the third alternative of independence. Jawaharlal Nehru had said that it was not acceptable because the plan was an obvious attempt to divide the country into smaller and weaker states. Thus though the Plan might have suited the geostrategic and political aspirations of the UK, it was suicidal for India to accept it. In fact, throughout the period when the Princely States were being integrated, the princes were impressed upon the fact that there was no third alternative. Even Lord Mountbatten had impressed upon Maharaja Hari Singh that independence was not an option and that it was advisable that before the British got out of the State, the Maharaja should choose to be part of one of the Constituent Assemblies.[134] Thus the necessity for Sheikh Abdullah to address the Assembly on a settled issue is a matter of conjecture. What is of deeper significance is that Sheikh Abdullah's speech does not take into consideration the fact that lawfully only Maharaja Hari Singh could have taken a decision regarding the accession. In fact, he ignored the right of the Maharaja and pretended to appropriate the right of the decision to accede to himself and the National Conference.[135]

Even if it was conceded that the Maharaja ought to have taken into account the opinion of the people of the State, as suggested by the then Congress President J.B. Kripalani and Mahatma Gandhi during their visit to Srinagar, no one could have presumed that Sheikh Abdullah and the National Conference represented the whole State. The opinion was deeply divided, particularly with the Gilgit-Baltistan region and Jammu region unequivocally wanting a merger, respectively with Pakistan and India.[136] By his address, Sheikh

Abdullah seemed to be reopening a debate about the accession, though after having raised this question, he unambiguously told the Constituent Assembly that the 'legality of the accession has not been seriously questioned by any responsible or independent person or authority.' In other words, in his own opinion the subject was settled.

The debate should have rested there. However, after injecting a new lease of life to the issue and appropriating the right to decide the issue of accession on himself, Sheikh Abdullah proceeded to lucidly examine the 'three' alternatives before the State. On very pragmatic grounds he ruled out the feasibility of the third alternative of 'independence'. He made a reference to the short-lived independent and sovereign status of the State before Pakistan attempted to capture it, but he forgot to mention the historical past when many ambitious Governors, Generals and Subedars had tried to carve a kingdom for themselves in this region with limited success. In a heart-warming manner, he enumerated the advantages of hitching the fate of the State with that of India. He was also frank enough to acknowledge the communal angle in deciding the issue of accession in favour of Pakistan, but rejected it on the practical aspect of India having a much larger Muslim population bordering West Pakistan, and the danger to the future of the farmers, artisans and craftsmen of the State by aligning with the feudal forces of Pakistan. It was this argument that gladdened the hearts of the secular leaders in India and probably, it weighed heavily on Pandit Nehru's mind whenever he saw the Praja Parishad movement gaining ground in Jammu. The Indian Muslims who had rejected communalism in polity and had decided to stay in India too must have felt vindicated.

This euphoria was short-lived, and there would be an eternal debate about the reasons of Sheikh Abdullah's drift away from the lofty pronouncements that were periodically made by him earlier. The irony was that the good that he intended to do was far outweighed by the harm that he eventually did to the regional and communal balance because of the evil motives behind these changes. It carried the seeds of strife in which the tools of the battle became nastier and sinister. With the passage of time, the resolve to succeed became stronger, and with it, the means became uglier. After having secured the banishment of the Maharaja, a statesman would have taken steps to ensure winning back the support of the class that was most affected and alienated because of it. However, brimming with confidence by the significant success, Sheikh Abdullah decided that the Maharaja's support base should also be punished by depriving them of their lands without paying any compensation. It was well known that many Indian leaders, including Sardar Patel, were vehement opponents of taking over of private land without compensation and considered it as 'theft'. Yet, Sheikh Abdullah was secure in the knowledge that the circumstances did not permit the Indian leaders to rein him in and, therefore, he was even more adamant to not only implement the land reforms but also abolish the dynasty.

It was in this background that the Praja Parishad movement drew its strength, and out of the cumulative frustration, resentment and anger of the Dogras against the rule of Sheikh Abdullah, a people's movement was born. Just as the Muslim Conference took birth to further the cause of the Muslims of the State, the All Jammu and Kashmir Rajya Hindu Sabha too had developed roots in the State soon after. One of its leading members was Pandit Prem Nath Dogra. However, confident that the interests of the community were safe in the hands of the Maharaja, the activities of the Sabha, unlike that of the Conference, were mindful of not taking an action that could be detrimental to the Maharaja's interests. Such was the confidence of the Sabha in the ability of the Maharaja to safeguard the interests of the community and the State, that during the critical period of 1947, it decided to support any decision taken by the Maharaja regarding the accession.

By 1942, the Rashtriya Swayamsevak Sangh (RSS) too had established its first *shakha* (wing) in Jammu, and later in the Valley, under the leadership of Balraj Madhok. Both the Sabha as well as the RSS gained ground after the events of the invasion of Pakistan and the arrival of the refugees. The National Conference government also contributed to their growth by its mistreatment of the Jammu region and the refugees who had arrived not only from Punjab but also from within the State after its parts were occupied by Pakistan. In the wake of these events, in November 1947, the Sabha decided to reorganize itself as a political outfit; the Praja Parishad was born. Pandit Prem Nath Dogra was elected its first President.

In early 1949, the Praja Parishad organized its first democratic protest against the policies of the National Conference Government. It was dealt with a heavy hand and 294 party workers, including the leaders, were arrested. The crude and dictatorial manner in which the protest was handled shocked even the Central leaders who had spent a lifetime protesting against the policies of incumbent governments and suffered to such an extent that they intervened to secure the release of the protesters.

This intervention of the Central leaders was resented by Sheikh Abdullah and probably firmed his resolve to be even more vindictive. Therefore, unmindful of adding insult to injury, he lost no opportunity to publicly gloat over the changes that he was bringing in those emotionally charged and turbulent times. Add to it the other factors like the separate constitution, flag and the head of the State, and it was a perfect recipe for a period of turmoil. The last proverbial straw on the camel's back was the first general election that elected representatives for the State Constituent Assembly. It sowed the seeds of discord in the Valley and of confrontation in Jammu. In the Valley, the workers of the National Conference had not allowed anyone else to file nominations for the elections, and hence, all seats from the Valley had given the National Conference a cake-walk into the Assembly. In Jammu, where the Praja Parishad candidates were expected to give a tough democratic challenge, the Parishad had decided to contest twenty-eight seats out of thirty. But when thirteen candidatures of its members were rejected, it boycotted the elections. Such were the first steps of democracy in the State under the self-styled people's leader! As a result, the composition of the Constituent Assembly was that, of the seventy-five Assembly seats, the National Conference having cornered seventy-two seats.

Finally, the situation exploded when an apparently minor incident ignited it. Jyoti Bhushan Das Gupta describes the situation thus: 'The simmering disaffection found an outlet in 1951-52 again with the conclusion of the first general election in Kashmir since independence. The dubious methods adopted by the National

Conference in eliminating the opposition of the Jammu Hindus at the polls had already made things hot…A minor incident, however, touched off the conflagration. On January 15, 1952, Sheikh Abdullah was to speak at an official function in the premises of Government Gandhi Memorial College, formerly Prince of Wales College, in Jammu where the flags of the National Conference were hoisted alongside the Indian Union Flag. A few students staged a demonstration and registered a protest against the flag of the National Conference, for which they were penalized. On 8th February a big procession was out to demonstrate sympathy with the victimized students, but the violent nature of the agitation necessitated the intervention of the military and imposition of 72 hours curfew in the town. Oddly enough, the students were released but the leaders of the Praja Parishad, who had taken no part in the agitation, were arrested with their President Prem Nath Dogra.'[137] Their release was secured only when Gopalaswami Ayyangar intervened on their behalf, but the intervention aroused Sheikh Abdullah's ire further against the Dogras as well as the Centre that interceded on their behalf. Ayyangar's intervention was interpreted as another attempt by the Centre to curb the freedom of the State to act.

The incident demonstrated the depth of Sheikh Abdullah's antipathy to the Dogras. His arrogant insistence to have the party flag fly alongside the national flag in a place where the party had a negligible presence, was also a blatant attempt to equate the party with the State. It showed that Sheikh Abdullah had developed preconceived notions about the Dogras and the leaders of the Praja Parishad. The fact that he had become a changed man after his return from Lake Success was not lost on anyone. By then, he had already begun to toy with the idea of the third option, and after his interview with the two foreign press correspondents in 1949, it became public knowledge. Now he was busy finding reasons to rationalize his change of heart and in this the resentment of the Dogras came in handy, as it was a proof, which was also good enough for Prime Minister Nehru, that soon after the partition communal politics had begun to rear its ugly head. Both were convinced that the Jammu resentment was the outcome of the coming together of the reactionary and communal elements. Moreover, 'Sheikh Abdullah was not only vindictive in his treatment of the Praja Parishad and the people of Jammu but also had the guts and audacity to ask Mr. Nehru to take action against the organization.'[138]

Resentment against Sheikh Abdullah's politics began to take many shapes and also drew a variety of fringe elements. Notwithstanding the fact that despite the presence of largely Hindu members, the National Constituent Assembly had chosen a secular Constitution for India, it could not be ignored that in exercise of the new-found freedom, the reactionary forces were active in the garb of nationalism. Thus, disparate elements like Swami Karapatri, whose sole agenda was to seek a constitutional ban on cow slaughter, joined hands with democratic leaders like Dr Shyama Prasad Mukherjee. Myron Weiner, the celebrated American political scientist, wrote: 'Circumstance developed which brought the Hindu Mahasabha, Jana Sangh and Ram Rajya Parishad even closer together. At that time an organization called the Jammu and Kashmir Praja Parishad launched an agitation in Jammu...The Praja Parishad advocated full and unconditional accession of the State of Jammu and Kashmir to India...The three organizations agreed to meet to consider what steps could be taken to aid the movement in Jammu.

'Greater unity between the three seemed to be evolving. In late February they took part in a four-day conference inaugurated by Swami Karapatri, leader of the Ram Rajya Parishad, demanding a government ban on cow slaughter. A few weeks later the three organizations jointly launched a satyagraha in support of the four-month-old Jammu Parishad agitation.'[139]

After Independence, this was the first occasion when religious and political agenda had converged. In these circumstances, it is easy to lay all the blame on the reactionary forces that were primarily Hindu, but the truth is, as we have seen in earlier chapters, the process of the break between Sheikh Abdullah and India began much earlier. However, it got aggravated when 'G.M. Ashai Registrar of Kashmir University had gone on a tour of India and on his return reported to Sheikh in June 1949 that Muslims in India were treated as second class citizens and that they had no future in India. His clamour and insistence on securing constitutional safeguards for the State began after this.'[140] It is not known what evidence was presented by Ashai to convince Sheikh Abdullah about the second-class citizenship of the Indian Muslims, but whatever it was, it had to be strong enough to convince him, unless he had already harboured such thoughts, which were only waiting to be articulated by a second source. But that evidence was never made public, much less, scrutinized. The seeds thus sown had with the passage of time grown into a poisonous tree that was watered by the Jammu agitation. Never suspecting the folly of his own righteousness, Sheikh Abdullah was convinced that the Jammu agitation was the result of the Hindu conspiracy to subjugate the Muslims in the Hindu-majority India. Hence, he was even more determined to secure constitutional guarantees for the separate identity of the State.

On the other hand, the Jammu province was equally suspicious of Sheikh Abdullah and hence insisted on the full integration of the State on the basis of one constitution, one flag and one president. In this, they were given enough reasons to be suspicious. They were still smarting under the humiliation of having their Maharaja exiled and to top it, they had also suffered due to the land reforms that confiscated their lands without compensation. An additional reason for their anger was the unfair treatment of refugees who were displaced from Occupied Kashmir. On the specious plea that the fate of the region that was occupied by Pakistan was to be decided by the plebiscite, Sheikh Abdullah linked relief to them with the final outcome, whereas those who suffered heavy losses due to displacement, needed urgent rehabilitation. This was not forthcoming. This problem was not faced by the Valley since no Muslim refugees had come to Kashmir and those who came were all Sikhs and had not been allowed to settle in the Valley. Consequently, not only had the refugees from the Poonch-Mirpur region come to Jammu but also those Sikhs and a few Hindus who were displaced from the Muzaffarabad area. Convinced of the Hindu conspiracy to swamp the State with Hindu agenda, Sheikh Abdullah dealt with the Praja Parishad with a heavy hand. Often the state response was brutal and this only steeled the resolve of the agitators who grew in strength; the stronger the agitation grew, the more brutal became the state response.

A similar agitation was also launched in Delhi by the Jana Sangh under the leadership of Shyama Prasad Mukherjee, and the Delhi administration too had responded strongly. Day after day the protestors had to be dispersed after a lathi-charge. These agitations made Sheikh Abdullah bitter and 'categorized this as Hindu revivalism which was trying to swamp the Muslims of Kashmir and the Muslim-majority areas of Jammu. [Before this, as an administrative measure the Muslim-majority areas of Doda and Kishtwar were formed into a separate district detaching them from Udhampur, which had an overall Hindu majority.] The Sheikh took this opportunity to give vent to hostile feelings against the Dogra community of Jammu, which he naturally linked with the Hindu community of Punjab and the rest of North India. He treated the Jana Sangh agitation as symptomatic of the general Hindu mentality and this he expressed in bitter language which added further grist to the mill of [the] Jana Sangh propaganda.'[141]

Ironically, while Sheikh Abdullah was accusing the Hindus of carrying out a communal agenda, he himself had found a Todarmal* in Mirza Afzal Beg, who vigorously carried out the National Conference's communal agenda by carving out new districts, in a manner that would create Muslim-majority districts, and in the process, reduce the Hindu-majority areas. As for the Hindus of the Jammu region, it was very easy for them to smell the communal rat in the whole exercise since they still associated the National Conference with the Muslim Conference that had triggered the first communal violence in Srinagar in 1931. Sheikh Abdullah responded with a speech in Ranbirsinghpura, near Jammu that was read as threatening by the Dogras and which rattled the Prime Minister of India and other leaders of the Congress. Sheikh Abdullah said, 'Many Kashmiris are apprehensive as to what will happen to them and their position, for instance, if something happens to Pandit Nehru.'

As a result of the intransigence shown by both sides, 'Nehru was worried about the impact of these developments on the Muslim minds in Kashmir. In principle he agreed with the demand of the Jana Sangh that the State should be completely integrated with

* Todarmal had been Mughal emperor Akbar's revenue expert.

the rest of the country but he insisted that because of peculiar circumstances this was being done gradually. Referring to the Jana Sangh demand that at least Jammu be fully integrated, he said that this would amount to subscribing to the two-nation theory and would destroy the raison-d'etre of India's existence in the valley. He was shocked by the Jana Sangh agitation and for the first time was doubtful of Kashmir's future.'[142]

Shocked as he was by the agitation of the Jana Sangh, Nehru felt exasperated by the fact that as a majority community, the Hindus were not setting higher standards in public life. What he failed to recognize was that, in no small measure, Sheikh Abdullah was responsible for provoking the Hindus of Jammu, and by extension the rest of the country, by his daily statements that were aimed at the Dogras in general and their Maharaja in particular.

If Nehru ever admonished Abdullah for his false accusations, then it certainly had no effect on him. Thus, in the words of B.N. Mullik, he continued to make 'violent accusations against the Dogras of Jammu in general and ex-ruler and the Praja Parishad in particular and spoke contemptuously of the RSS and the Jana Sangh. He repeated for my benefit the lurid details of the alleged atrocities that had occurred in [the] Jammu province and compared the Dogras with wild animals bereft of any human feelings.'[143]

Nehru failed to see the essential difference between the Hindus of Jammu and Kashmir and the rest of the country. They were part of the majority community in the country, but in the State, they were a minority who were being further targeted by the National Conference Government as the reorganization of Udhampur district had demonstrated. When the Praja Parishad agitation had Nehru extremely worried, he sent B.N. Mullik, his intelligence chief to the State to diffuse the situation. According to Mullik, in spite of his best efforts, he 'could not persuade him to desist from indulging in his theme of hatred against the Dogras and giving expression to his great contempt for them. He himself would have probably liked the entire Dogra community to migrate to India and make over the lands to persons of his choice.'[144]

Sheikh Abdullah's hatred of the Dogras assumed pathological dimensions and unless something was done urgently, it was bound to affect not only the State but also the country. No one realized this better than Prime Minister Nehru though it has never been explained why he was not able to exert his influence on Sheikh Abdullah to make him see the folly and futility of pursuing a negative policy as a leader of the people. Even when he was openly speaking against India, between the years 1951-1953, the personal relations between the two remained cordial and normal. All this while, Nehru periodically rendered advice to Yuvraj Karan Singh about how to conduct himself in office. But there is no evidence of him ever having given any advice to Sheikh Abdullah in the art of statesmanship. In fact, all senior Congress leaders were known to be extremely liberal in giving advice to one another on all subjects they considered important in any given circumstance. In Kashmir, somehow Nehru felt inhibited.

As a consequence, the Praja Parishad agitation crippled Jammu, and in the process, the attitudes of all concerned hardened.

11

The March of History

The inaugural address of the Constituent Assembly made it clear that Sheikh Abdullah was not prepared to offer even a titular role to the Maharaja whose signature and proclamation had put him in the position he was in. However, he was amenable to the idea of having his son, the Yuvraj, as the elected Head of the State, as a gesture of continuity and a mark of concession to the Dogras. He found Yuvraj Karan Singh a likeable person and perhaps hoped that it would be easy to influence and manipulate him because of his youthfulness and inexperience of the world and politics. Yuvraj had just turned twenty-one, but ever since he was eighteen, he had not only been put in the midst of choppy seas but also exposed to some of the most influential personalities of the time. All of them, in some degree, had an influence on the lives of people. On a personal level, for the second time in less than four years, Yuvraj Karan Singh was forced by history to take a decision that would leave a lasting impact on his relationship with his father. It was to remain frosty for a few years.

He had just turned eighteen when Sardar Patel proposed his name as Regent to Maharaja Hari Singh. Shocked as he was, his father had not explicitly asked him to turn down the suggestion but was worried about the fate that awaited his son after his own experience with the Indian leaders, including Sardar Patel who had pushed him from one position to another. He was apprehensive that the next installment of humiliation to the dynasty would be served when the young Yuvraj too would suffer the ignominy of being unceremoniously banished from the State by the ever-vindictive Sheikh Abdullah. At least on one occasion, he had mentioned this apprehension to his son.[145] In addition, the old loyalists of the Maharaja too were in opposition to his becoming the Regent and had exerted subtle pressure on him to decline the proposal, notwithstanding the fact he was being appointed as such by the Maharaja. Understandably they could not imagine a son taking the father's place under duress of extraneous factors. It is true that the founder of the dynasty, Maharaja Gulab Singh had abdicated in favour of his son Maharaja Ranbir Singh on health grounds. But this situation did not even remotely resemble that one. It had not been easy for an eighteen year old to defy the traditional mind-set and advice, and recognize that if he did not submit to the forces of change then not only he but his family and people too would be swept away by such forces. If the dilemma was excruciating then, it was doubly so now when it was expected of him to be persuaded to become the elected Sadar-i-Riyasat and preside over the dissolution and total 'elimination of [his] father from the political scene'.[146]

The question of whether Yuvraj Karan Singh should accept becoming the elected Head of State, elected by the same people who had humiliated his father and forced him into exile, raged as a controversy, particularly in Jammu. The people were outraged by the fact that while a person like the Nizam of Hyderabad, who had worked against India's interests and who had declared himself independent and resisted the Indian Army, had been treated so magnanimously as to designate him as the Rajpramukh, Maharaja Hari Singh, who had made numerous sacrifices in the name of the motherland's interests, had not only been shabbily treated and banished from his State, but whose dynasty too was now being abolished. Adding insult to injury were the speeches of Sheikh Abdullah and his colleagues, which were not only against the dignity of the Maharaja but also spewed poison against the Dogras as they publicly gloated at the National Conference's success. Unlike in other states, the abolition of 'monarchy' was being made out as a drama by the National Conference. The people of Jammu found this extremely galling. Because of this they were convinced that the Yuvraj was to become a 'puppet Head of the State', who had betrayed his family and people. Even the Maharaja was furious at the suggestion for he saw the whole idea in a sequence of events that had first begun as appeals to his sense of duty towards India and then gradually pushed him from one position to another till he was left with no space in his State. Now as a coup de grace, he was being totally eliminated in absentia.

It was not easy for Yuvraj Karan Singh to take a rational and thoughtful view of the situation. He was convinced of the futility of resistance to change and remembered very well the letter that Gopalaswami Ayyangar wrote to his father to convince him to lift the embargo that he had placed on the Regent to sign the Proclamation to convene the Constituent Assembly. Maharaja Hari Singh had then sensed an opportunity to play a role in the drafting of the new Constitution and therefore tried to assert his legal right. He had forgotten that at the cusp of change, history often does not recognize either legality or what is morally and ethically right. In no uncertain words, Ayyangar had told his father that it was futile to stand in the way of the process to convene the Assembly because the Government of India and that of the State was determined to convene such an assembly with or without his consent. Recalling that episode, which ended in another setback for his father, Yuvraj Karan Singh was aware that the process of abolishing the monarchy and electing a Head of the State was bound to be pursued, with or without his being on board. He was convinced that if he declined to be the Head of the State, the National Conference would go ahead and elect a person of its choice.[147] After all, the election was to be made by the members of an Assembly that had seventy-five members of which seventy-two were from the National Conference. As it is, the name of a Dalit leader, Masha Nahar Singh had already begun to do the rounds. Apart from this fact, out of a sense of loyalty to his family, if he were to decline the post, particularly at a time when tempers were frayed in Jammu, the decision would have pushed Jammu towards a situation that would have been disastrous for communal harmony. His mere presence in Jammu was reassuring regarding the continuity and constitutionality of the situation. His declining would have also spelt his banishment from the State since his presence would have become the symbol of Dogra discontent and resistance against the rule of Sheikh Abdullah. The outcome of this confrontation would have been uncertain.

But there was more to the subject than the wishes of his father and his advisors. The affairs of the State were not just a family matter or even an internal affair of the State. It also affected the whole country and hence it was imperative for as strong a symbol as the scion of the Dogra dynasty to be active in the State to reassure the people there and build strong links of unity and oneness in the country. It was very clear to the Yuvraj that even Nehru wanted him to be in the State in a new capacity, as a mark of the Centre's representation, apart from that of the Dogras. Thus, for the second time in three years, he was forced to make a choice between the advices given to him by his father and Prime Minister Nehru. Many members from his father's staff and quite a few Dogra leaders tried to influence him into refusing the new position. 'It was pointed out that if I accepted the office it would be tantamount to selling the Dogras out to Kashmiris; that I would go down in history as a traitor to the dynasty founded by Maharaja Gulab Singh; that if I defied my father I might well be disinherited and lose my patrimony worth many crores of rupees.'[148]

Yuvraj Karan Singh was also warned of the possibility of a well-laid-out trap by Sheikh Abdullah. His pathological hatred for his family was well known. Therefore, it could not be ruled out that after having secured the elimination of the dynasty with the connivance of Yuvraj Karan Singh, Abdullah would not turn against the Yuvraj and force him out of office. They reminded him that only a few months ago, Sheikh Abdullah had threatened him in the heart of Jammu with banishment and that the Government of India was too weak to either restrain him or change his mind. The recent history was proof of the single-minded pursuit of his goal of banishing, and belittling the Maharaja and the Dogras respectively, and in that the Government of India too was compelled to resile from the commitments that it made to his father. There was nothing to stop him from going back on whatever promises he might make to him or the Government of India.

The pressure notwithstanding, the young Yuvraj was convinced that the proposed changes were in the offing and they would take place whether he was on board or not. He just could not erase the memory of the manner in which his father's erstwhile Prime Minister and now Minister for Kashmir Affairs in the Government of India had brusquely written to his father about the futility of delaying the process of convening the Constituent Assembly. All that he could do in the circumstances was to delay taking a decision and for this he had a very good excuse. He knew that the State Government was in consultation with the Government of India regarding certain constitutional provisions that covered not only the headship of the State but also other important matters like citizenship, fundamental rights, the Supreme Court, financial integration, the flag, the powers of reprieve of the President and other allied subjects. Thus, in defiance of the pressure being exerted on him, the Yuvraj chose to plough his furrow—the one which looked lonely at the time.

In the meantime, Yuvraj Karan Singh finally addressed the Constituent Assembly on 5th May 1952. Sheikh Abdullah and his colleagues on the other hand, continued to pressurize the Government of India to ensure that the State was left out of the ambit of the Indian Constitution as much as possible. Sheikh Abdullah's apologists would say that his attitude had changed towards India because of the changed politics of the country. They would like to lay all the blame on those rightist political parties that came together to demand not only complete administrative integration of the State with India but also mix cultural and religious demands into the agenda. This, it is argued, frightened Sheikh Abdullah into stridently demanding constitutional guarantees for continued autonomy of the State within the parameters of the Instrument of Accession. However, many outsiders along with the Dogras viewed him with suspicion and were convinced that posturing apart, the National Conference had remained the Muslim Conference and Kashmiri in spirit and soul.

In these circumstances, the Government of India reached an agreement regarding the constitutional arrangements between India and Jammu and Kashmir. The agreement, announced on 24thJuly 1952, is known as the 'Delhi Agreement'. Prime Minister Nehru informed the Parliament about it and also disclosed its salient features. It was agreed that (i) the Head of the State of Jammu and Kashmir would be a person recommended by the state legislature and recognized by the President of India; (ii) the Indian flag would have the same status in Jammu and Kashmir as in any other part of India, but the Jammu and Kashmir State flag would be retained; (iii) citizenship would be common in two parts of the country but the state legislature would have power to define and regulate the rights and privileges of permanent residents in Jammu and Kashmir; (iv) the fundamental rights as laid down in the Indian Constitution would be extended to the State, but these would not come in the way of the State's programme of land reforms; (v) power to reprieve or commute death sentences would belong to the President of India; (vi) the Indian President's power to declare a state of emergency in case of external danger or internal disturbances would be extended to the State, but in regard to external danger or internal disturbances it would be used only at the request of the State government; (vii) residuary powers would be retained by the State but the State could transfer more rights to the Union; (viii) the Supreme Court could adjudicate regarding disputes between the State and the Central and other provincial governments and on fundamental rights agreed to by the State; and (ix) the details of the financial arrangements would be further considered.

That day the Prime Minister not only informed the Parliament of the agreement that was reached but also the historical background of the events that led to it. The agreement had not been easy to reach, the Prime Minister confessed to Yuvraj Karan Singh, since it involved 'complicated' aspects of the legal, constitutional and 'other aspects which were at least, if not more, important'.[149] The Prime Minister sounded satisfied with the agreement and wrote in the same letter, 'The best part of this agreement was this psychological atmosphere of friendship and cooperation. Many things were decided by this agreement which knit the Jammu and Kashmir State closer to India and which make our Constitution applicable in greater measure to the State. At the same time, we recognized the special position of the State and gave it greater autonomy in many matters than our other States of Indian Union possess.'[150]

All this was known to the Yuvraj since it was part of the

statement that the Prime Minister made in Parliament and was widely reported. He was more interested in finding out about the arrangement that was to be made about the Head of the State. His personal life and relationship with his father were to be deeply affected by it. So, in the same letter, Nehru focused on it in considerable detail and did his best to prepare Yuvraj Karan Singh for the new role. He began by recalling that during the Yuvraj's earlier visit to Delhi, Nehru had impressed upon him the inevitability of change. 'Circumstances had so developed and they could not be denied without causing injury to all concerned and the cause we have at heart.'[151] What he did not acknowledge is that the major change that took place was that Sheikh Abdullah had become too intransigent and that Nehru had committed himself to Abdullah to such an extent that he did not know how to retract without suffering deep embarrassment and loss of face not only at home but also abroad. Basically, he did not know how to deal with his friend and the fall-out of a situation where he refused to endorse the Indian cause. For too long, the Government of India had given in to the ever-changing demands of Sheikh Abdullah. Now Nehru thought that unlike the earlier occasions, this one was to be the final deal. In the process, after the Maharaja, now his son too was being asked to make an appropriate sacrifice and adjustment.

Very persuasively Nehru went on to write, 'Whatever law or Constitution might say, in the last analysis, we have to pay heed to the wishes of the people. That indeed had often been declared by us regarding the Jammu and Kashmir State. But really the principle applies everywhere in India. When this question was raised positively, in the manner it had been raised, it became impossible to bypass it or to postpone it for long. It was better to face it and to come to a decision than to leave a feeling of uncertainty and doubt in people's minds and thus not even have the great advantage of a settlement by agreement with all the psychological consequences of friendly feeling that this produced.'[152] Obviously, the Prime Minister was very pleased with himself at having reached an agreement with the entire friendly psychological consequences attendant to it. It also meant that he believed that the opinion that was to be expressed by the Constituent Assembly truly represented the people of not only Kashmir but Jammu too. It also meant that he believed that the opposition, building up in Jammu, was not really representative of the will of the people, or was the handiwork of a handful of disgruntled people.

Nehru also informed the Yuvraj that the proposal was to suggest his name for the elected Head of the State and his term was to be for five years. Although in all likelihood, the Yuvraj would be re-elected for another term, Nehru added that if any attempt was made to force the National Conference leaders to announce a longer term, then that would be counter-productive. Then the Prime Minister went on to remind the Yuvraj that the world was changing at a fast pace and monarchies all over the world were crumbling, with King Farouk of Egypt having been recently forced to abdicate. In the circumstances, Nehru argued that five years was a long period in politics. He added, 'For any of us to think in static terms of continuing things as they are, is to misunderstand this changing and dynamic world. We have to understand this world and adapt ourselves to it.

'I am sure you will appreciate what I am writing. I need not tell you that now and later, you will be in my mind and you can always come to me for advice or any help that I can give you. The best advice is to accept cheerfully and willingly the changes suggested and thereby to put yourself in the forefront of them, instead of appearing as if you unwillingly agreed to something that you disliked. If we have to do something, we should do it gracefully and thereby gain the goodwill and respect of others.'[153]

Probably in a very subtle manner Prime Minister Nehru tried to tell the Yuvraj that the fate that his father suffered was entirely brought upon by himself, since he did not acknowledge the fact that the world around him was changing at a rapid pace, and therefore, failed to gracefully acknowledge the changes. In a gentle way, Nehru was telling the Yuvraj to fall in line or else he too would be swept away by the forces of history. Yuvraj Karan Singh would not have failed to see that almost the same message was delivered, but far more bluntly and crudely, by Ayyangar to his father almost a year ago, and now it was being repeated to him in a more sophisticated and and gentler way by the Prime Minister.

Yuvraj Karan Singh knew that the advice of the Prime Minister was sound and pragmatic. He did not suffer from the infirmity that is characteristic of most of those raised in a feudal atmosphere and knew well that the days of monarchy and absolute power were gone. But that did not mean that he did not have his doubts regarding the system that was to replace the old order. The Constituent Assembly had been convened and tasked with the responsibility of framing a Constitution. It was for the Constitution to define the terms, conditions and responsibilities of not only the Head of the State but also other organs of the State. But in an act of vindictiveness and perversity, Sheikh Abdullah was determined to first abolish the dynasty and elect a Head of the State, and then draw up other provisions of the Constitution. In this, the Government of India conceded fair ground to him, and consequently, the Yuvraj was being pressed to take a decision regarding the acceptance of the Headship of the State, even before the Constitution was finalized.

After giving the subject a thought, Yuvraj Karan Singh wrote to Prime Minister Nehru on 3rd August 1952 that though it was his ambition to serve his country in whatever manner and in any position that he was asked to do, in the present circumstance, 'I feel that it is not possible for me to come to any decision until the new Constitution for Kashmir emerges in its final shape from the Constituent Assembly and receives the approval of the Government of India. I am sure you will appreciate that it is hardly possible for me to accept a position without knowing exactly and clearly the duties and functions which attach to it, the responsibilities which I will have to shoulder and the conditions under which I will have to work.

'If the Indian Constitution was going to be accepted in toto by Kashmir, the position would have been quite clear. But as you said in your speech the situation in Kashmir differs from that which obtains in other States of the Union, and Kashmir Consembly [Constituent Assembly] may draft a Constitution along lines which may differ from the Indian...As Head of State I will have important responsibilities to fulfill and, as Sheikh Sahib is reported to have reiterated in some of his recent speeches, if I fail to fulfill them satisfactorily, I will even be liable to impeachment.'[154] Sheikh

Abdullah had indeed been making such speeches, probably only to impress upon his audiences of the power that the people of the State were going to wield. Even the possibility of the scion of the Dogra dynasty being impeached and punished gave him satisfaction though when the provisions regarding the Head of the State were finally passed, the impeachment clause was not added.

In addition to the absence of any clarity regarding a well-defined role, powers and responsibilities of the Head of the State, the Yuvraj also had reservations about the term of the office of the Head of State. The National Conference leaders had proposed, and the Government of India concurred, with the idea of a five-year term. This was not unusual but considering the circumstances under which the constitutional changes were taking place and the constraint of having Yuvraj Karan Singh as the Head of the State, in a subtle way, it was a message to the people that the changes were accepted by the ruling dynasty and that the new constitutional arrangement was a mark of legitimacy and continuity. But there was also the possibility that the announcement that Yuvraj Karan Singh would be elected Head of the State for only a five-year term could send wrong signals to the Dogras. As it was, the frustration and anger of the Dogras was manifesting itself in the ever-increasing support for the fledgling Praja Parishad, which had made known its opposition to the abolition of the dynasty, let alone a five-year term for the Yuvraj. It is apparent from the correspondence of the Yuvraj with Pandit Nehru that his plea to prevail upon Sheikh Abdullah to change his mind regarding the decision about the Head of the State before the Constitution was finalized was futile because the latter was determined in his resolve to put an end to the dynasty before anything else.

As a result of this, Sheikh Abdullah had led a constitutional negotiating team consisting of himself, Mirza Afzal Beg, D.P. Dhar and his constitutional advisor, M.A. Shahmiri. It is not without significance that this team did not consist of a single representative from the Jammu region, and the only Hindu member of the team was a left of centre politician from Kashmir. This team had evidently taken a very rigid stand, as the Yuvraj discovered when he too visited Delhi to personally discuss the matter with Pandit

Nehru, Maulana Azad and Gopalaswami Ayyangar. He later wrote in his *Autobiography* that 'for the first time I noticed a slight hint of displeasure in Jawaharlal's remarks about Sheikh Abdullah. Although he did not say so in so many words, I gathered the distinct impression that he wanted me to be on the scene so that I could be of help if some difficulty arose in the future.'[155]

In fact, before the Yuvraj's visit to Delhi, Pandit Nehru's letter dated 8th August 1952 was a kind of oblique confession about some of the decisions that ought not to have been taken. He also mentioned the visit of the constitutional negotiating team of the State and the consultations that took place. Apparently D.P. Dhar had been deputed by the team to hold talks with Pandit Nehru and had shown some drafts, which were not approved by the Prime Minister, who suggested a few changes. In that letter, Nehru also wrote, 'I can very well understand your anxieties and difficulties in this matter. To a large extent, I share them with you, and have not liked much that has happened...I quite agree with you that this business of hustling through a part of the Constitution is neither normal nor ordinarily desirable...But this matter was discussed by us at very great length when the Kashmir delegation was here and ultimately we came to the conclusion which were embodied in the points of agreement...Much has been done which cannot be undone at the present stage and any attempt to do so would only produce further complications. Therefore, we have to accept the present position as it is. That is to say that a part of the Constitution dealing with the Head of the State, in the form agreed upon, should be adopted first.' Aware of the negativity of the agreement, he went on to write, 'You will have noticed that several other important matters were agreed to between us. The whole picture has to be seen together. Some of these other points bring Jammu and Kashmir State closer to India and to our Constitution. If all this is given effect to, then the other remaining provisions need not make much difference.'[156]

In July 1952, all representatives of Part B States had held a conference in Srinagar and urged the Government of India to abolish the system of lifelong Rajpramukhs. Nehru thus found another argument for the Yuvraj to accept the offer of Head of State, whenever it was made. He further wrote in that three-page letter, 'I have thought about this matter not only from your personal point of view but also from the larger point of view of the State. Grave decisions are being taken which will naturally affect the future of the State. I think from this larger point of view, it is highly desirable that you should undertake this responsibility. For you not to do so now would create grave difficulties for the State.'[157]

Nehru also addressed the issue of tenure and re-election of the Head of the State and the finalization of the new Constitution. He wrote, 'As for the tenure and re-election, re-election there can always be and I am told this is the present intention. But in the nature of things it is hardly possible for any person to guarantee it. I told you when you were here that the next five years would very probably see the end of the present system of Rajpramukhship for life. Indeed, I think a change is likely to occur long before those five years are over. Already people are beginning to talk about it and press for it.'[158] It was in the context of these exchanges that Yuvraj Karan Singh had gone to Delhi and found that for the first time Nehru appeared annoyed by Sheikh Abdullah's attitude. It was during this visit that Yuvraj Karan Singh succeeded in softening the attitude of the Prime Minister towards the Praja Parishad leaders. For the first time Nehru realized that there was need to explain to the Jammu leaders the rationale and need for the changes that were in the offing and agreed to Yuvraj's suggestion that they be invited by him, either in Jammu or Srinagar, for consultations. 'This itself was a major shift in view of his well known allergy to the Praja Parishad, and reflected the fact that he appreciated my difficulty,' Karan Singh wrote in his autobiography.

This exercise began on the wrong foot when among the many groups and individuals invited, Girdharilal Anand, the President of Commerce of Jammu, refused the Yuvraj's invitation to meet him in Srinagar on the plea that 'the present Kashmir Government as well as the Constituent Assembly have by their action shown scant regard for the opinion of the Jammu people'. This was splashed in the newspapers and when brought to the attention of Prime Minister Nehru, he was outraged and livid with anger at the discourtesy. He declared that he was not only out of the 'pale' but also wanted to be excluded from any future meetings. Yuvraj Karan Singh too concurred with this but he continued to meet all other shades of people from Jammu. With Pandit Prem Nath Dogra he had several rounds of talks. But Jammu was seething with anger and too far gone in opposition of Sheikh Abdullah that there was no common ground. Yuvraj Karan Singh understood this well and explained to Prime Minister Nehru in his letter dated 8th September 1952: 'The Jammu people do, however, feel distressed and injured for several reasons. They say that they have neither any voice in the State Assembly [which they boycotted under protest, and which contains representatives of only one party], nor in the State Government and nor again in the Indian Parliament, because the members from our State were nominated and not elected…The proposed ending of the ruling dynasty has upset them immensely, not because of sentimental attachment alone but because they feel that this step will break the only link which bound them to Kashmir, and that unless it is followed by complete accession to India their position will be even more precarious than it has been for the last five years.'[159]

In the same letter, the Yuvraj strongly pleaded for making a genuine effort to appreciate Jammu's point of view. He requested Pandit Nehru to go to such an extent as to receive a delegation of the Praja Parishad and set up a group to look into their grievances. He wrote, 'I feel that everything possible should be done to redress the legitimate grievances of the Jammu people, because this internal discord and disharmony is to my mind most unfortunate. It is rather a tragic irony, I think, that those who want complete accession to India should be proving a source of embarrassment to India and should feel unhappy and oppressed…I feel that the Jammu situation has not been handled as well as it might have been. My sincere desire is that this unfortunate state of affairs should be ameliorated, and, if the State is to remain as a single unit, the maximum amount of cooperation and goodwill should be sought from all sections.'[160]

As these letters were being exchanged, word spread that Maharaja Hari Singh had sent a Memorandum to the President, Dr Rajendra Prasad, which concluded with the demand for holding a referendum in the State to put to rest the debate regarding the abolition or retaining of the monarchy. Cheekily, Yuvraj Karan

Singh mentioned this in the same letter to Nehru. He wrote, 'I wonder what your view about this is. If it is possible to have a referendum—and I do not see why it should not be—I feel it would be a good thing, as it would give the people of the State a fully democratic method of expressing their decision as to whether they would like a member of the dynasty to be their Constitutional Head or would prefer to elect someone periodically. Thus no section or group will feel its views have been ignored in coming to a decision on this important question. I must add that from indications both in Jammu and in the valley I feel that the result of such a referendum is by no means a foregone conclusion.'[161]The Yuvraj was not privy to the memorandum and hence was not aware of the actual demand, which was holding of a referendum between him and Sheikh Abdullah to ascertain the claim of the latter that the Maharaja had lost the confidence of the people of the State.

Bypassing the main issue, Prime Minister Nehru acknowledged that the Maharaja had sent a memorandum but dismissed it as 'an angry and tendentious document. Your father does not seem to realize at all that the world has changed and is changing rather rapidly.' Then he went on to add, 'I am rather surprised at your reference to the referendum. This is not at all possible either from the local or from the international point of view. We have been talking about the plebiscite over other issues and even this cannot come off because there is no agreement. If the question of a referendum on a limited issue was raised, this would immediately lead to all kinds of international complications and the demand for a plebiscite immediately over a wider area. Even this referendum, it would be said, if held at all, should be over the wider area, including that part which is held by Pakistan. Within the present boundaries of the State under our control the referendum issue would, naturally lead to bitterness and controversy and in effect tend to split up the State, regardless of the final issue. Indeed, I think that such a proposal is completely out of court in the present circumstances.'[162]

Nehru did not see the contexts in which that demand was made. It was that limited area that had elected representatives to the Constituent Assembly, and it was they who were deciding the fate of the dynasty and drafting a Constitution for the State. By his logic, they should not have been drafting the Constitution till the time the whole State was represented in the Assembly.

Meanwhile, riding high on the wave of success, Sheikh Abdullah began to display signs of impatience and, to exert pressure from the National Conference workers, had begun to circulate the name of Masha Nahar Singh as their alternate candidate for headship. It was in this situation that the Yuvraj noticed a perceptible change of attitude towards Sheikh Abdullah, which was finally made to yield to the force of the circumstances and the cajoling of Prime Minister Nehru. But before taking the plunge, he made another trip to Delhi. Nehru once again impressed upon him the national implications of his decision and the need for the Yuvraj to be present on the 'scene to be able to help if some problems arose in the future. It was this final aspect that clinched the issue as far as I was concerned.'[163]

On 15th November 1952, the Constituent Assembly met to elect Yuvraj Karan Singh as the Head of the State with the designation of 'Sadar-i-Riyasat'. He had turned twenty-one only in the month of March and therefore the Assembly lowered the statutory age of thirty-five to twenty-one years. On 17th November 1952, Yuvraj Karan Singh drove to the Rajgarh Palace on the Jhelum and there, in the old palaces of the Dogra rulers, he was sworn-in as the first Sadar-i-Riyasat of the State by Chief Justice, Wazir Janki Nath.

12

The Crisis

Yuvraj Karan Singh knew of the furore that his acceptance of the elected Headship of the State would cause in Jammu, but he had not anticipated the intensity and magnitude of the resentment and anger. The hostile reception that Jammu gave him on 24th January 1952, rattled him. He tried to put on a brave face and waved at the crowd. It was then that he noticed that a few, who caught his eye, reciprocated even amidst the bedlam of hostile and angry sloganeering. That was a sign of hope for it signified that the anger of the people was actually a measure of solidarity for his father.[164]

A few days before Yuvraj Karan Singh was to be sworn in as Sadar-i-Riyasat, the Praja Parishad had launched a state-wide agitation on 14th November 1952 with the demand of '*Ek vidhan, ek nishan ek pradhan*'—'one constitution, one flag, one president'. The pent up anger of the Dogras against the loss of prestige, their beloved Maharaja, lands and their subjugation to Sheikh Abdullah, united one and all. This was aggravated by the fact that Sheikh Abdullah not only made no attempt to mollify and win them over, but went out of his way to express his hostility and aggression towards them. This attitude was visibly demonstrated by him when, in accordance with the resolution of the Constituent Assembly, the new State flag was to be hoisted at the Jammu Secretariat. It was decided by the State that the new State flag would be flown on all occasions while the national flag was to be flown only on formal occasions. The seeds of discord were thus sown right at the beginning. Obviously the old State flag was to be hauled down and this caused considerable hurt. The Yuvraj suspected as much, and therefore, advised the government that, along with the new flag, the national flag should also be hoisted. The advice was rudely declined by Sheikh Abdullah forcing the Yuvraj to also decline the invitation to hoist the new State flag.[165] The new chapter in the State's history began on such a sour and confrontational note.

The next crisis was also not too far ahead. Sheikh Abdullah, uneasy with the presence of a strong and popular number two, had already got rid of Ghulam Mohiuddin Karra. Therefore, there was a struggle within the National Conference to occupy that position. In a bid to keep Bakshi Ghulam Mohammad out of contention, Ghulam Mohammad Sadiq, Mirza Afzal Beg and Girdhari Lal Dogra joined forces; but their success was short-lived since Bakshi Ghulam Mohammad made up with Sheikh Abdullah to gain that position. Meanwhile, the Constituent Assembly appointed a Basic Principles Committee, which produced a final draft in March, 1953. This created considerable debate and dissension within the Cabinet that was to turn into a poisonous tree, which succeeding generations failed to uproot.

It soon became obvious that the Cabinet was divided among those who wanted a fair degree of integration with the rest of the country and those who were adamant on claiming total autonomy in all affairs except those which fell under the Instrument of Accession. The former group consisted of Bakshi Ghulam Mohammad, G.M. Sadiq, D.P. Dhar, Girdhari Lal Dogra and Sham Lal Saraf. This tug of war began even before the State plunged into the crisis, even before Yuvraj Karan Singh accepted the status of elected Head of the State.

In April 1952, Gopalaswami Ayyangar wanted to bring the State under the purview of the Comptroller General of India so as to initiate the process of financial integration. Sheikh Abdullah reacted violently to the proposal and accused the Government of India of wanting him to write a promissory note in favour of India. It was in this context that he had made the highly provocative and ominous speech at Ranbirsinghpura near Jammu, saying, 'Kashmir's accession to India will have to be of a restricted nature'. He had added that the full application of the Indian Constitution to Kashmir was 'unrealistic, childish and savouring of lunacy'. Soon after this speech he made another speech saying, 'It would be better to die than submit to the taunt that India was our bread-giver. Kashmir is not eager for India's aid.'[166] It was in the context of these differences that the necessity to have an agreement with the rest of the country about certain basic principles arose. Thus, the much-debated, much-quoted and invoked Delhi Agreement was signed.

Later, on 11th August 1952, Sheikh Abdullah commended the Delhi Agreement and made a statement in the State's Constituent Assembly. 'A satisfactory position has emerged and we are now able to assess the basic issues of our constitutional relationship with India in clearer terms. There has been a good deal of accommodation of our respective points of view. Both the representatives of the Government of India and the Kashmir Delegation have been impelled by the desire to strengthen further the existing relationship and to remove all obscurity and vagueness. We are convinced, as ever before, that we have the full support of the government and the people of India in the fulfilment of our democratic ideals and the realization of our objectives,' he said.[167]

However, before he had made this statement, it was a reluctant horse that was dragged to Delhi by his colleagues. He had, at first, refused to go to Delhi to discuss and defuse the situation but was prevailed upon by Bakshi and Sadiq who had the backing of the majority of the Constituent Assembly. Finally, accompanied by Bakshi, Beg, Lal Dogra and Dhar he went to Delhi and signed the Agreement. Unfortunately, his heart was not in it and that explains his arrogant and provocative refusal to hoist the national flag on the Jammu Secretariat building, even when he made the following statement in the Constituent Assembly regarding the agreement on the State flag: 'We agreed that in view of the clarifications issued by me in my public statements while interpreting the resolution of this House according to which the old State flag was substituted by a new one, it was obvious that the new State flag was in no sense a rival of the National flag. But for historical and other reasons connected with the freedom struggle in the State, the need for the continuance of this flag was recognized. The Union flag to which we continue our allegiance as a part of the Union will occupy the supremely distinctive place in the State.'[168] A few months later came his rejection of Sadar-i-Riyasat's suggestion to fly the national flag alongside the State flag.

The 'flag' incident was preceded by another disturbing development. Sheikh Abdullah and the National Conference made a studied attempt to ignore Ladakh and its people. Kushak Bakula, the Head Lama and their undisputed leader at that time, was denied his rightful place in the political set-up. All this while, Delhi, blinkered as it was, was unaware of this development. It was left to the Sadar-i-Riyasat to raise the red flag. He wrote to the Prime Minister on 25th August 1953 that 'I feel that at this stage a goodwill gesture to the people of Ladakh, who are bitter and resentful as a result of the treatment they received from the previous regime, will be of considerable value. I have discussed with Bakshi the idea of taking a Ladakhi Deputy Minister for Ladakh Affairs, a gesture which will not only be much appreciated by the Ladakhis but will also make the task of the administration vis-a-vis Ladakh much easier and smoother.'[169] The Yuvraj also visited Leh along with the Yuvrani, and the entire population of the surrounding area, led by Kushak Bakula, turned out to greet them. Ladakh was conquered during the 1830s by the intrepid General Zorawar Singh on behalf of Maharaja Gulab Singh. For quite some time the Ladakhis bore a grudge against the ruling Dogra family.

The Yuvraj and his wife had taken with them thousands of metres of cloth, which was enough to gift every person of Ladakh with enough cloth for a coat. It was very gratifying for the Yuvraj to learn that they received that piece of cloth with reverence and gratitude. Obviously, the Dogra rule must not have been tyrannical and oppressive for them to forget that they were conquered by the very same family to which he belonged.[170]

The couple stayed in Ladakh for three days and apart from visiting the monasteries of the Lamas and sightseeing, The Yuvraj had lengthy discussions with Kushak Bakula and his colleagues. He was surprised to find that it was Ladakh, even more than Jammu, which felt uneasy and restive under Sheikh Abdullah's new dispensation. They were a distinct cultural entity, which felt concerned about its future. It was ironical that while Sheikh Abdullah often wondered about the fate of Kashmiri Muslims in a dominant Hindu India, here in Ladakh, the situation was genuinely worrisome since the Ladakhis were not even on the fringe of the power structure. On the basis of their population they had only two members in the Assembly. With a weak voice in governance, they felt they were 'totally subordinate to the Kashmiris. They suggested that a Statutory Advisory Committee should be set up to which it should be obligatory for the State Legislature to refer all legislation vitally affecting Ladakh. They also urged that, instead of leaving them at the mercy of the Sheikh's Government, an administrator should be sent from the Centre.'[171]

On his return to Srinagar, Yuvraj Karan Singh informed Prime Minister Nehru of the situation prevailing in Ladakh. He brought into focus the fact that resource crunches and the step-motherly treatment had forced Ladakhis to hit the streets, and there was a series of agitations, demonstrations and violence. As a result, they were drifting away from the State and wanting the region be taken into the direct control of the Centre. Choosing their own course became the recurring theme there. Apart from making general comments about his visit and general impressions, the Yuvraj wrote a secret note to the Prime Minister on 24th September 1952. He informed him that the Ladakhis 'want a statutory Advisory Committee to be established in Ladakh [excluding Kargil which, it seems, is content to remain in the present position]. This Committee would be elected on the basis of full adult franchise, and would consist of five or seven members. It would be obligatory for the State Assembly to refer all legislation which vitally affects Ladakh to this Committee for its views and approval... Secondly, they feel that Zanskar district, which is at present with Kargil tehsil, should be joined with Leh. This district is predominantly (over 95% I believe) Buddhist, and is also economically linked with and geographically contiguous to Leh tehsil. The inhabitants of that district have suffered considerably during the last few years, and it is reported that they are almost on the point of migrating en masse if they are not joined with Leh...this can, if necessary be verified by sending a committee consisting of Kushak Bakula, the Kargil representative, Ibrahim Shah, and a third impartial person… The joining of that area with Leh will make the cultural group more homogeneous, and prove to be greatly helpful to the people of Zanskar.'[172]

The Yuvraj went on write, 'Ladakh is strategically very important, more so for India as a whole than for the State, and it will be a tragedy if for the lack of an accommodating spirit the people of Ladakh remain unhappy and discontented, and thus an easy prey to all sorts of exploitation, both communalist and communist. I would also add that if the Government of India decides to advise Sheikh Sahib to agree to these proposals of the Ladakhis, they should put them into effect as soon as possible, preferably before the winter sets in.' He ended his note by saying, 'when there is a situation which I feel needs remedying I consider it my duty to acquaint you with my views and what I feel is the true state of affairs. As a matter of fact, I feel that this is one of my more important functions, in addition to the purely formal duty of affixing my signature to official documents.'[173]

The Yuvraj was obviously conscious of the fact that largely he had a ceremonial role but he also possessed the courage of his convictions to express the view that had hitherto not been expressed. He was, thus, the first non-Ladakhi to point out the dangers of communalism and communism that lay ahead in Ladakh if Srinagar and Delhi continued to be insensitive to the aspirations of Ladakh. His views were confirmed by Nehru's intelligence point-man in the State, B.N. Mullik.[174]

Prime Minister Nehru always had more than one source of information, and regarding Jammu and Kashmir, he kept himself abreast with developments through the Yuvraj and Dhar apart from the intelligence network established by Mullik. Thus, when he spoke to Sheikh Abdullah on an issue of particular interest, he was fully aware of almost all the aspects. This would arouse the suspicion of Sheikh Abdullah regarding the source of his information. Usually, when put in an embarrassing situation, the Sheikh would suspect the Intelligence Bureau. Nehru's concern about Ladakh was particularly galling for him and he demanded the transfer of the officials posted there. He was so peeved that he also conveyed through his Deputy Prime Minister, Bakshi Ghulam Mohammad that in case his demand was not complied with, he would have the two officers arrested. He was so serious about his demand that Prime Minister Nehru sent Mullik to Srinagar to resolve the issue with a warning that in case Sheikh Abdullah refused to move then the Bureau should be prepared to yield ground in the country's larger interest.

Mullik had long discussions with Bakshi and Dhar and was able to convince them that the Bureau was not involved in any activity that might be against the interests of the State. Importantly, he was able to make them appreciate the good work that the Bureau officers were doing for the security of the State against 'subversion by foreign agents', and that they had 'succeeded in unraveling several attempts at conspiracies initiated by Pakistan.' It was after much cajoling that Bakshi and Dhar too were convinced, and they, in turn, succeeded in convincing Sheikh Abdullah to withdraw his demand.[175]

Mullik visited Ladakh during this trip and on his return filed a report that confirmed what the Yuvraj had written in his secret note to Prime Minister Nehru. He also returned with a new worry. The information reaching him indicated that the British had connived in the early 1930s of the twentieth century to assist the so-called 'liberation movement' for the people of the Valley. The 'movement' was encouraged by the British because of their intense dislike of Maharaja Hari Singh for refusing to be subservient, and was headed by Sheikh Abdullah. The British had used the Punjab-based leaders of the Ahmadiyya community to fan unrest in the State. It also caused a rift between the Hindus and Muslims of the Valley. Because of unearthing this evidence, Mullik was convinced that Sheikh Abdullah had remained a communalist at heart.[176]

Outwardly, probably under the influence of his leftist colleagues like Sadiq, Sheikh Abdullah professed socialism and secularism. Consequently, there was a time when many people believed that he could be a worthy successor to Prime Minister Nehru. However, the combination of his own natural inclination towards communalism and the pressure that was being built upon him by the Praja Parishad movement proved to be too much for him to handle. The seeds of a drift away from India were always present but the combination of these two powerful influences led him to explore new possibilities. With the shadow of the emerging 'Cold War' situation engulfing the world, Sheikh Abdullah became an easy pawn to handle.

The resentment of Jammu against the National Conference in general and Sheikh Abdullah in particular was brewing ever since the efforts to marginalize and humiliate the Maharaja had been set afoot. His exile and eventual abolition of monarchy had hurt the people; it was accompanied by the land reforms that primarily targeted the Dogras; the shabby treatment extended to the Hindu and Sikh refugees was also an irritant,[177] and, on top of it all was the fact that not only was Sheikh Abdullah resisting all attempts to fully integrate the State with the rest of the country, but he left no stone unturned to ensure that there were constitutional guarantees for the special and separate status of the State. The accumulation of these grouses found a voice in the agitation launched by the Praja Parishad with the goal of '*ek vidhan, ek nishan, ek pradhan*', that is, 'one constitution, one flag, one president'.

The agitation was handled with brutal force by the government, and in turn, the people responded in greater numbers. The cycle of the growing number of agitators and reprisals by the government, soon became a routine. The State government claimed that the agitation was spearheaded by communalists from Jammu and was deriving strength and support from like-minded people from outside the State. Prime Minister Nehru too believed this, but both forgot that Jammu had maintained communal harmony even when riots were triggered by people led by Sheikh Abdullah in 1931. During the entire history of Dogra rule, Jammu had remained an example of communal amity and brotherhood despite each community rigidly maintaining its customs and lifestyle. In fact, the Centre, more than the State was responsible, first for not addressing the genuine grievances and apprehensions of Jammu, and then, letting the frustration of Jammu pass for an expression of the reactionary forces.

The trouble had begun to brew soon after Sheikh Abdullah

took charge. With the lop-sided representation in the government, the signs of his prejudiced approach to Jammu were there from the beginning. His vindictive targeting of the Maharaja had only aggravated the suspicion, and no one in Delhi realized that Jammu was being pushed into a corner, and that it would soon lash out to break the shackles. The signs of things to come were visible from early 1951 when, unable to get a sympathetic ear in Delhi, the Praja Parishad began to approach anyone who was inclined to lend it support. Thus, in April of that year, Pandit Prem Nath Dogra visited Delhi to meet various leaders and make them understand the ground realities of the State. Meeting Prof Balraj Madhok was natural since he had an old connection with the State. But Pandit Dogra also met others, including Jawaharlal Nehru and Dr Shyama Prasad Mukherjee. On 21st October 1951, when the Jana Sangh was formed, Dr Mukherjee made a statement regarding the situation in Jammu and Kashmir. The cause of Jammu also got support from Master Tara Singh and Akali Dal, and not surprisingly, the Akali Dal lent wholehearted support to the Praja Parishad when the agitation was launched.

Unable to distinguish between the frustration and anger of the Dogras and communalism, Nehru was apprehensive that the agitation would frighten the Muslims of Kashmir and thereby the cause of India in the Security Council would be adversely affected. In none of his correspondence with the Yuvraj did he demonstrate any understanding of the Dogra cause even though in numerous letters the latter had urged him to meet the leaders from Jammu. His inherent prejudice against Jammu was only strengthened by some of the deeds of Dogra leaders, who went out of their way to show disrespect even to Yuvraj Karan Singh.[178]

Not discouraged by the lack of a positive response from the Prime Minister, the Yuvraj nevertheless kept urging him to meet the Praja Parishad leaders. He himself kept communicating with them but with limited political success except that his sincere efforts were appreciated by the Dogra leaders. Pandit Nehru was not totally unaffected by his persistence and informed him in a letter dated 9th September 1952 about raising the issue of disparity among the regions of the State with Sheikh Abdullah.

He wrote, 'I have no doubt that the Jammu people have a number of grievances and feel rather frustrated. Some of these grievances have, I believe, justification. Indeed, both Sheikh Saheb and Bakshi Ghulam Mohammad mentioned to me some of the disabilities that Jammu Province was suffering from and their desire to remove them. At the same time they pointed out to me certain difficulties. Thus, for instance, the lack of water in Jammu is a very serious handicap.'[179]

Obviously, Nehru and the state government believed that the feelings of Jammu could be assuaged by solving their water problem! His next paragraph of the same letter brought out all the prejudices that he nursed against the Praja Parishad. He also gave vent to his anger against Pandit Prem Nath Dogra. 'The Praja Parishad people have largely to blame themselves for the plight they have landed themselves in. Others may also be to blame. But, consciously or unconsciously, the Praja Parishad in Jammu has acted in a manner which has been quite deplorable and excessively stupid. It is not that they have not had a chance of meeting other people and discussing affairs with them. They have met them. As you know, I met Pandit Prem Nath Dogra and had a fairly long talk with him. In the course of our talk he agreed almost entirely with what I told him. Soon after he made public statements exactly contrary to what he had said to me and embarrassed me greatly. I found him and his companions completely irresponsible.

'The kind of agitation they have been carrying on in the part of Delhi itself, apart from what they have done in Jammu, has been pernicious in the extreme. They have sided with the most communal elements in Delhi... If a person is known from his associations, then Praja Parishad's associations were the most undesirable in Delhi or the Punjab. Their activities did more harm to the Kashmir issue, from our point of view than anything else that has happened in recent years. As a result, they received the greatest publicity in Pakistan.'[180]

The letter also made it very clear that the influence of the Praja Parishad agitation on the rest of the nation was disruptive. 'The forces in India which we consider most harmful have been encouraged by the attitude of Praja Parishad of Jammu,' Nehru commented. But in the next sentence he also referred to the personal slight that he felt was inflicted upon him by the Praja Parishad. He said, 'I do not like being exploited and treated with discourtesy by anyone in my official capacity. The Praja Parishad people have done that and, normally, they would have scant courtesy from me'; then displaying magnanimity, he added, 'But I have no objection to meeting them should you so desire. I am sure Maulana Saheb would also be prepared to meet them. So also Dr Katju and Shri Gopalaswami Ayyangar.'[181]

Hardly had the Yuvraj placated Pandit Nehru when on 20th September 1952 the Praja Parishad threatened to launch a civil disobedience if their demands were not conceded. This riled Nehru in the extreme. Almost admonishing the Yuvraj for repeatedly advocating dialogue and discussions with the Praja Parishad, he wrote on 23rd September 1952, 'You write to me about [the] Jammu Parishad leaders. I read two days ago another statement by them. They have a peculiar knack of saying the wrong thing and saying even that in the wrong way. They are all the time issuing an ultimatum… [The] Praja Parishad leaders evidently have got such an idea of their high importance that they presume to speak as if they could dictate terms. I am not used to this manner of speaking or being addressed… But I confess that the more I learn about them, the less I like them.'[182]

It was easy for Pandit Nehru to hold strong views about the Praja Parishad but the situation thrust Yuvraj Karan Singh into the forefront for he belonged to the people who felt increasingly marginalized and frustrated. First, he was the representative of the Maharaja and later the elected Head of the State. The Dogras expected some action from him that gave them a hope for the future. Therefore, the option of being intimidated and silenced because of the strong views expressed by Nehru was not his. The Yuvraj persisted in his efforts to find a middle path and make Nehru understand that there was a genuine problem in Jammu that had nothing to do with communalism. Finally, he wrote a note on the situation in Jammu on 22nd December 1952. He categorically stated that it would be an inaccurate appreciation of the situation in Jammu and would be treated as the handiwork of a 'reactionary clique', and warned that the 'frustration has now begun to turn into desperation.' In an honest and pragmatic assessment of the situation, he emphasized the psychological and economic causes of the discontent. During the past five years, the people of Jammu were treated with scant respect and their sentiments trampled. The manner in which the ruling family and the State flag were handled had deeply scarred them. The much touted Delhi Agreement was used in a selective and discriminatory manner, and that left them frustrated and angry. Yuvraj Karan Singh's note said: 'The people feel that they have not only been treated with scant regard, but that consistent and vindictive efforts have been made to ruin them economically over the last five years and to outrage their deepest and most cherished sentiments, without giving them the compensatory satisfaction of becoming wholly integrated with India. They would not have minded the abolition of the old State Flag if they had seen the state government adopting the Indian national flag, and they would not have minded the abolition of hereditary rule if a system of Rajpramukh—as in the other Part B States—had been introduced. What has caused great resentment is that while their deeply cherished flag and rule have gone, in their place they have not been given what has been given to the rest of Part B States and that a new flag and a new kind of Head of the State has been foisted upon them against their will.'[183]

Yuvraj Karan Singh suggested that instead of the piecemeal approach to the finalization of the new Constitution, it should not only be hastened, but the Indian National flag should also be immediately hoisted, at least at the Secretariats in Jammu and Srinagar along with the State flag. He further pointed out that at that point in time, the National flag was not hoisted at a single place in the State. It was not only a mockery of the accession of the State but also of the recently concluded Delhi Agreement by which the State was allowed to have its own and new flag.

He brought up the issue of the highly emotive and unjust nature of the Big Landed Estates Abolition Act, which failed, probably deliberately, to see the difference between the productivity of the lands in the Valley and those in the arid hilly tracts of Jammu's dry and arid *Kandi* area. Most of those who suffered were from the

Rajput community, which was also affected by another decision of the government that disbanded three units of State Forces. Most of these soldiers were Rajputs and Brahmins and at one go 3,000 of them had been left without a job. The Yuvraj pointed out that counting their dependents, about 20,000 had been left without adequate means of support. These factors were not on the radar of Prime Minister Nehru, who continued to believe Sheikh Abdullah who told him that the major hardship that Jammu faced was that of drinking water!

The Yuvraj's frank and blunt appraisal was preceded by extremely unfortunate incidents. First in Samba and then in Sunderbani, police fired on the Praja Parishad demonstrators. This forced the Yuvraj to cut short his visit to his mother, the Maharani, in Kangra. In between, Nehru too took cognizance of the serious repercussions of the continued agitation. On 14th December 1952 he wrote to Sheikh Abdullah about it and said that the Praja Parishad had, 'for the moment got the sympathy of a large number of people. There does appear to be a widespread feeling of frustration in Jammu. Some of it may have legitimate causes, some may be wholly unreasonable. But there is a grave feeling of dissatisfaction and frustration. I get the impression that the Jammu people feel that all importance is attached to Kashmir in the State and they are ignored. Not only are they ignored but often condemned as a bad lot.'

In response, Sheikh Abdullah wrote on 23rd December 1952, justifying his government's stand on the Praja Parishad agitation. He described the whole Jammu problem as the work of communal organizations and characterized it as 'a violent reaction on the part of Jammu landlords and other upper classes'. He added, 'The real problems of Jammu do not relate to the completion of its association with India and Kashmir nor to the propriety of this or that symbol. These problems are colossal in magnitude and need the active participation of every man and woman so that the wretchedness, poverty and degeneration of the vast masses of Jammu people are vanished.'

The Prime Minister of the State was either too naïve or deliberately attributed causes to the agitation that he, like everyone else, knew were of serious concern to Pandit Nehru. In his letter dated 4th January 1953, Yuvraj Karan Singh referred to the explanation that Sheikh Abdullah had given and commented: 'But that letter contains only an analysis of the past developments, an analysis—I might add—which is not complete in all respects... It is now over a month and a half since the agitation began on the 14th November, but I am afraid that during this period nothing positive or concrete has been done by our government...there is another point which I would like to submit. Sheikh Sahib reiterates, and probably correctly, that the control and direction of this movement is from outside the State in India. If that is so then we should tackle those factors if we wish to solve the problem, and to end the present deadlock which in addition to the internal disruption in Jammu is having an unhappy effect upon Indian public opinion and also upon the Valley.

'The initiative in this respect can lie in your hands alone, and I would earnestly and sincerely request you, for the sake of the State and the tremendous stake India has in it, to make a decisive move to end this unhappy deadlock.'[184]

The Yuvraj's constant urgings were not bearing any immediate change of heart, but Nehru did take notice of them and was quick to respond, whenever possible, to lament the futility of holding talks with the Jana Sangh and its associates. Writing to Yuvraj Karan Singh on 14th February 1953, Nehru observed: 'The Jammu situation is very much before me and I am giving constant thought to it. As a matter of fact, it is no longer a Jammu situation, but an all India situation in which, unfortunately, several communal organizations in India are taking an important part...I am keeping in fairly close touch with Sheikh Abdullah by correspondence. I have had some correspondence also with Dr Syama Prasad Mookerjee [*sic*] and Mr N.C. Chatterjee. The letters they wrote to me were similarly unhelpful and to some extent rather irritating.'[185] The Prime Minister was referring to the coming together of the Jana Sangh, Hindu Mahasabha and Ram Rajya Parishad, the latter being solely obsessed with having a ban on cow slaughter enforced. The Prime Minister also seemed to be riled by Dr Mukherjee's ultimatum at a public meeting on 9th February 1953 to solve the Jammu situation within the next three weeks, failing which the agitation would spread to other parts of the country. But Nehru failed to see that the patience of these leaders was running out because of the brutal handling of the agitators. Chatterjee particularly mentioned the heavy handed and unprovoked arrests of protesters in Punjab.

Not deterred either by the Prime Minister's rigid attitude towards the agitation led by, in his opinion, reactionary forces, or the provocative statements of those spearheading the agitation, the Yuvraj continued to inform the Prime Minister about the manner in which the agitation was being handled. He also refused to shy away from suggesting what ought to be done in the given situation. Thus on 23rd February 1953 he reported the brutal and inhuman manner in which even the women, their homes and livestock were treated, and commented: 'Violence and hooliganism have, of course, to be dealt with, with a firm hand, but such unwarranted behaviour only spreads unnecessary resentment and bitterness and, while making a difficult situation all the more intractable, brings discredit upon the government.'[186] He also offered his opinion about the offer made by Dr Mukherjee in the Lok Sabha to withdraw the agitation, provided all the prisoners were released and the Praja Parishad leaders invited to hold comprehensive discussions on the whole issue. He found a silver lining in this offer and suggested that because of a lull in the agitation, it was an opportune time to hold talks. But he also mentioned that Sheikh Abdullah could turn out to be an insurmountable wall since 'in his conversations [he] lays great stress upon the "absolute impossibility" of his meeting or having anything to do with the leaders of the Praja Parishad.'

It is difficult to say if the Prime Minister developed a hard attitude because of Sheikh Abdullah's influence or was it vice versa? This approach was self-defeating and negative in the extreme in the opinion of the young Sadar-i-Riyasat, and he further wrote to Nehru, 'Although I can understand his basic sentiments, I confess I cannot quite appreciate this attitude of his. After all, if these leaders had been in the State Assembly…then Sheikh Sahib whether he liked it or not would have had to discuss matters with them on the floor of the House.' He also urged to initiate certain other steps to diffuse the situation to bring the State back on rails—the important one being the appointment of an impartial and independent committee to go into the various firings that took place in Jammu. He recalled that this was the practice during the Maharaja's rule too and eminent Englishmen and others drawn from British India were entrusted the task of enquiry to instil confidence among the people. He particularly mentioned that while the government claimed that only eleven people had lost their lives, the reports from Jammu suggested that at least thirty people had died during the agitations. To find the truth, the Yuvraj suggested that a committee of two retired judges, one from outside the State and the other from within, be constituted. He also urged the Prime Minister to prevail upon Sheikh Abdullah to have the National flag fly alongside the State flag.

The Prime Minister, however, had a deep-seated prejudice against that agitation and could not help but express it in his letter dated 22nd March 1953: 'You refer to police excesses. Probably there had been excesses and undoubtedly where such excesses take place, they should be dealt properly. On no account must there be any vindictiveness on the part of police. But the kind of reports that are circulated by [the] Praja Parishad are, on the face of it, so wildly exaggerated and often without foundation that hardly any credit can be attached to them. Many of these reports here emanate from the Pathankot office of the Praja Parishad.'[187] In the same letter, he dismissed Dr Mukherjee's offer to withdraw the agitation since he believed it to be a consequence of the internal dissension between the leaders and search for an excuse to withdraw the agitation and still adopt the posture of a peacemaker. His rigidity once again came to the fore, as he declared that though he was prepared to meet Dr Mukherjee as an MP, he would not give any encouragement to the Jana Sangh or the Praja Parishad.

The Yuvraj, however, did not let despair rule him and continued his efforts to make Prime Minister Nehru realize that whether he liked or not, the Praja Parishad represented the Dogra sentiments and that they had genuine grievances that needed to be addressed. In April 1953, he made it a point to hold detailed discussions during his visit to Delhi and appraise Pandit Nehru of not only how the Dogras were being treated but also the difficult position he found himself in due to his association with the government. He had accepted the headship of the State against the wishes of a large section of his people, and now, when the original grievances receded into the background because of the continued and increased atrocities of the police, they began to ask him about the futility of it all if he could not safeguard them from such brutalities. He also flagged the issue of implementing the Delhi Agreement by pointing out that Sheikh Abdullah intended to keep the provision of the Constitution of 1939 that provided for a Board of Judicial Advisors and rendered the Supreme Court of India superfluous. When these issues were brought up by the Yuvraj, Nehru was not inclined to make any substantive gesture regarding holding an independent and impartial enquiry or asking Sheikh Abdullah to honestly implement the Delhi Agreement. He continued to harp on the theme that India's case regarding the State hinged upon Sheikh Abdullah and hence not much could be done. However, he had no answer when the Yuvraj wondered what would happen to India's stand in case Sheikh Abdullah was 'no more'. The only saving grace was that during this meeting, Nehru did not flare up when pushed to appreciate the relevance of the Praja Parishad to the cause of the State.

By May 1953, Sheikh Abdullah had further drifted away. Yuvraj Karan Singh was in for a shock after a private meeting with Sheikh Abdullah in which the Sheikh made his intention to go back on the Delhi Agreement clear. Undeterred by the lack of response from Nehru, the Yuvraj continued to appraise him of the developments and his own opinion. Finally, during a meeting on 23rd May 1953, Nehru expressed his deep anguish and 'admitted that he had no answer when asked in Parliament or outside as to why the Delhi Agreement had not been implemented...he had written a long letter to the Sheikh pointing out that the matter had been greatly delayed... When I asked him what reply he had received he turned to me and said in an incredulous and hurt voice, "I received no reply at all." He added that the Sheikh was thoroughly confused and was avoiding meeting him.'[188]

After all that had happened, if it was to be followed by Sheikh

Abdullah going back on the Agreement, then it would have made the Yuvraj's position untenable, and he made that clear to the Prime Minister, who, for the first time pondered over the possibility of betrayal by his friend and protégé. According to Karan Singh, before the meeting ended, Nehru said, 'Look here, one point I quite agree on is that if our agreements are thrown overboard or something like that, your position becomes absolutely impossible.'[189] The picture, for the young Sadar-i-Riyasat, was becoming clearer, and when he remarked that 'unlimited power seems to have brought out the worst fascist and totalitarian tendencies in Sheikh', Nehru agreed!

By the time, the Durbar moved to Srinagar the situation in Jammu had further deteriorated. On 8th May 1953, Dr Mukherjee sent a telegram to Sheikh Abdullah informing him of his intention to come to the State. This was duly forwarded to the Prime Minister by the Sheikh. Dr Mukherjee, along with a few of his companions, was arrested on 11th May when he tried to cross the bridge on the river Ravi, from Madhopur in Punjab, to enter the State without the formal permission. He had insisted that since Jammu and Kashmir was an integral part of India, there was no need to obtain a 'permit' to enter a part of the country. Consequently, Jammu observed an absolute closure in protest.

At this point in time, there were parallel but related developments taking place in the State. The restiveness of Jammu was known to everyone but behind the scenes there was trouble brewing within the government and the National Conference. Sheikh Abdullah, after discussions with his colleagues, had entered into the Delhi Agreement and had made certain promises to Delhi. Now, he seemed determined to renege on them, and was supported in this by Mirza Afzal Beg. However, a larger group in the Cabinet and the party, led by Bakshi Ghulam Mohammad and Ghulam Mohammad Sadiq, was in favour of implementing the Agreement honestly. The Sadar-i-Riyasat sent a report to the Prime Minister who had gone to London for the coronation of the Queen Elizabeth. He wrote: 'The political situation in the valley continues to be extremely fluid. The division within the party is causing considerable tension. The pro-Indian faction continues to be determined, and claims to be strong and to have a majority both in the Working Committee and in the Assembly.

'I was shocked and astounded to gather from a private meeting with Sheikh Abdullah last week that he seems to have decided to go back upon the solemn agreements which he has concluded with India and upon his clear commitments. This cannot be allowed, as it would make our position absolutely impossible and be a grave blow to our national interests and naturally to our international position also.'[190]

Soon, the situation took an ugly turn when the shocking news about Dr Mukherjee's death broke. If he was ill then no one was informed. Sadar-i-Riyasat Karan Singh had no inkling and Dr B.C. Roy, the Chief Minister of West Bengal, who was also his family physician, too was kept in the dark. Karan Singh alleges that not only was he not informed of his illness or removal to hospital but that he came to know about his death from unofficial sources 'several hours after his body had been flown out of Srinagar'. In his letter of 26th June 1953 to the Prime Minister, he wrote, 'Apart from its grave political repercussions it came as a great shock, particularly as we were completely unaware that he had not been keeping good health for some time. I was not informed of his illness or his removal to hospital, and, most amazing of all, I learnt of his demise several hours after the body had been flown from Srinagar, and that too from unofficial sources. There is a widespread feeling and indeed there are strong reasons which indicate that in this whole unfortunate matter, the State Government, to say the least, acted in most questionable and incompetent manner.'[191] Later, he recalled in his autobiography that the reaction in Jammu was naturally furious. 'The circumstances in which he died in the custody of the state government were a cause of great resentment and suspicion. Jammu was furious because Dr. Mookerjee [*sic*] had been martyred while fighting for the Praja Parishad cause, and there was an open talk that his death had not been from natural causes.'[192] Dr Roy had angrily wired a telegram of protest and the whole country, particularly West Bengal, was outraged.

This also shook the Prime Minister. He realized that the Praja Parishad agitation and the vindictiveness of Sheikh Abdullah and his drift away from India were feeding on each other, and that, unless something was done to contain both, the harm to the country and its prestige would be incalculable. For the subsequent events, B.N. Mullik claims much of the credit for he says that he was called by Nehru and asked to proceed to Jammu and Kashmir and make both the antagonistic parties see some wisdom. Mullik claims that he was asked to convey to the Praja Parishad leaders that India agreed with the Jana Sangh and the Praja Parishad's view that the State should be fully integrated. But this could not happen at one go because extraneous factors like Pakistan and the UN Security Council too were involved in it. He also asked them to see reason regarding their demand of integrating Jammu if the whole State could not be done because that would destroy the legitimacy of India's stand in the Valley. Finally, Nehru asked Mullik to tell them that, 'the Jana Sangh agitation had given him a shock and for the first time in five years he had started feeling doubtful about the future of Kashmir.'[193]

The Prime Minister also asked Mullik to go to Jammu and visit all the hot spots of the agitation and the places where the firings had taken place or atrocities committed by the police, and persuade the Praja Parishad leaders to call off the agitation. They were to be convinced of the integration of the State and told that even the Constituent Assembly of the State would ratify it and put the issue beyond any debate. They were to be convinced that the special privileges were a temporary matter and would gradually disappear to make Jammu and Kashmir like any other state of the country. Mullik was also to meet Sheikh Abdullah and request him to desist from making communal and anti-Hindu speeches. Sometimes Sheikh Abdullah was provoked but usually his communal speeches were orated without provocation. He had acquired the habit of referring to the alleged atrocities by the Hindus on Muslims in Jammu during 1947 but he never made any reference to the similar atrocities, if not worse, committed on the Hindus in the areas occupied by Pakistan. Nehru asked Mullik to tell Sheikh Abdullah that these statements 'were creating a hostile atmosphere against him in India.'

Mullik claims that as a result of his efforts during this visit, the

Praja Parishad leaders were convinced and mollified to an extent. Soon thereafter, 'the intensity of the agitation dropped immediately and, after a short while, it petered out.'[194] Perhaps, he was right in claiming some credit for the softening of the Praja Parishad. After all, they were a nationalistic force and had a greater stake in the idea of India. Unfortunately, the same could not be said of Sheikh Abdullah and, therefore, more drama and events of far-reaching consequences were to follow.

13

The Die is Cast

For quite some time, Sheikh Abdullah had looked for an excuse to drift away from India. In retrospect, it is apparent that even the much-touted Delhi Agreement was little more than friendly sparring before the actual skirmish occurred. On his part, Prime Minister Nehru either failed or refused to appreciate the concerns of the Praja Parishad that the Delhi Agreement virtually conceded that the accession of the State was not complete, and even the power of the President of India to declare a state of emergency could only be exercised in the State 'at the request or with the concurrence of the Government of the State'. The fact that the State was to have its own flag and special provisions to elect the Head of the State, too, did not go down well with the Praja Parishad. The Agreement also conceded that the 'residuary powers' should be vested not in the Centre but the State.

Commenting on this, historian Alastair Lamb writes, 'Nehru had evidently persuaded himself that at the end of the day his old friend would come down firmly on the Indian side. In the meantime it might be as well to permit a measure of ambiguity to persist, if only to blunt the force of the United Nations' protests. It still seemed essential, moreover, to keep Sheikh Abdullah happy… Nehru was soon to discover, or be persuaded, that there were grave flaws in this line of reasoning.'[195] The Prime Minister also did not see that even if Sheikh Abdullah was the undisputed leader of the Valley at that point, he was far from drawing any credible following in Jammu or Ladakh. In fact, he had minimal knowledge or interest in the Ladakh region in particular. The simmering discontent of the otherwise peaceful and contented Buddhists of the region was pointed out, as early as 1952, by Yuvraj Karan Singh in his note to the Prime Minister after his visit there. Lamb made an incisive comment about the crisis in the State when he stated, 'Indeed, from the first days of Indian involvement after the accession crisis it was clear that one of the major problems arising from Nehru's dependence on Sheikh Abdullah was how to maintain the cohesion of the empire which Gulab Singh had built'.[196] Thus, when the Praja Parishad agitation began, Nehru failed to understand the sense of alarm that Jammu felt in the aftermath of the Delhi Agreement.

More often than not, liberal thinkers are inclined to blame the Praja Parishad and the Jana Sangh for alienating Sheikh Abdullah, ignoring ample evidence indicating that the drift began much before the Praja Parishad movement was even conceived. It is unreasonable to blame the Hindus alone for the drift that began. Sheikh Abdullah blamed the Maharaja and the Hindu communalists for the communal violence of 1947. But it is obvious that it was more because it suited his political agenda of maligning the Maharaja and consolidating his hold. Communal violence took place on a much larger scale in the Punjab and Bengal, and elsewhere too, but neither the Congress leaders nor the provincial and Central governments were blamed for it.

A close study of the rhetoric, context and politics of Sheikh Abdullah from his Reading Room days would reveal that it was based on communalism. It is true that, at a later stage, he tried to sublimate as a secularist but whenever under political stress, he would fall back on his communalism. There is no doubt that he drifted away from the nationalistic agenda because of his biases and his narrow regional ambitions. When did he actually begin to entertain the idea of a separate and independent guarantee? Probably 'during the initial discussions on Kashmir at the Security Council in 1948, the Argentinian delegate, Dr Jose Arce, said, "The Kashmiri people may well decide not to accede to India but to be independent". Later, in 1951, Dr Percival Spear, a Cambridge University historian who had once taught in India, suggested that the Valley be made an independent state guaranteed by the UN as well as India and Pakistan, and be policed by UN troops.'[197]

During his visit to New York, Sheikh Abdullah had an undisclosed meeting with Warren Austin, the US representative at the UN. After that meeting, Austin sent the following message, to the US Secretary of State, George Marshall on 28th January 1948, which was recorded in the State Department papers and subsequently made public: 'It is possible the principal purpose of Abdullah's visit was to make it clear to the US that there is a third alternative, namely independence. He was overtly anxious to get this point across... He did not want his people to be torn by dissensions between Pakistan and India. It would be much better if Kashmir was independent and could seek American and British aid for development of the country. I, of course, gave Abdullah no encouragement on this line and am confident that when he left he understood very well where we stand on this matter.'[198] The Cold War still a few years away, and at that time unhindered by the geo-political liabilities, the US was firmly in the corner of India.

If there was any ambiguity in any quarters among the US diplomats, it was soon removed by George Marshall himself in a telegram to the US Embassy in New Delhi on 4th March 1948: 'Re various proposals for Kashmir's independence, we had in the past, as you know, followed the line that princely states be incorporated in either India or Pakistan on the assumption that balkanization of the Indian subcontinent would jeopardize and complicate economic transition and create conditions of instability ultimately adverse to broad US interests [in] that area. One current thinking re Kashmir is influenced by these considerations subject to proviso that should concept of independence...be the basis of GOI-GOP [Indian and Pakistani governments'] peaceful settlement of Kashmir issue, we would probably not oppose such a solution but would certainly take no initiative in supporting it.'[199]

These diplomatic rebuffs do not seem to have discouraged Sheikh Abdullah who continued to sound out the Western diplomats about the third option. One of the more significant people he met was Loy Henderson, the US ambassador to India. He held two secret meetings with him, which were duly reported by the ambassador to the State Department. These meetings were held soon after he implemented his famed law, breaking up large estates without compensation. The word was out that he was a pro-communist politician and this stood in his way to establish a rapport with the US. Sheikh Abdullah was at pains to explain away his stand and vouch that he was not a communist or their sympathizer. But he also brooked the subject of independence for his state. Henderson reported to the State Department that Abdullah vigorously stated his opinion about the independence of Kashmir and asserted that a vast majority of the Kashmiri people wanted independence. He had reason to believe that even leaders of Kashmir under Pakistani occupation were willing to cooperate with the leaders of the National Conference, provided there was a reasonable chance of gaining independence. He argued that Kashmir had a distinct cultural background and even the Hindus of the Valley were vastly different from the Hindus of India and the Muslims from the Muslims of Pakistan. Henderson asked if independent Kashmir could remain stable in the absence of either India or Pakistan; Abdullah replied for that it would need US assistance, either directly or through the UN.

As time passed, Sheikh Abdullah too persisted with his idea of independence. Walter Crocker, then Australian High Commissioner in New Delhi wrote in his book, *Nehru: A Contemporary's Estimate* that Abdullah favoured independence during the meeting he had with him while on a visit to Srinagar in 1952. The meeting between Sheikh Abdullah and Adlai Stevenson II, the US ambassador to the UN, was a much publicized event because it was known that the latter was a presidential candidate in the forthcoming US election. In comparison, the meeting between Crocker and Abdullah was hardly noticed and thus remained largely secret.

Prime Minister Nehru, meanwhile, had remained blissfully oblivious of these developments. He was convinced that Sheikh Abdullah's perceived drift was a temporary phase, and that he was being pushed by the communalism within and outside the State. Nehru was not prepared, as we have seen in the earlier chapter, to attend to the pleadings of Yuvraj Karan Singh. In his prejudice, he did not see that Jammu never had a history of communal tensions and that if it raised its head then the reason for it had to be identified. On the other hand, there were developments in the rest of the country that gave Sheikh Abdullah an excuse to vent his anger and hatred against the Dogras in particular and Hindus in general. The election of Dr Rajendra Prasad was one such development. Undoubtedly he was a conservative and lacked Nehru's dynamism and liberalism, but to accuse him of harbouring communal feelings was far-fetched and unfair. The election of Purushottam Das Tandon as the Congress president against Nehru's express will was read as a sign of the emergence of a new and Hindu India. The apologists of Sheikh Abdullah offer these examples as the first nudges that gradually persuaded him to chart his own course.

By 1952, that worrisome strain had begun to find voice in his speeches. On 11th April 1952, Abdullah became so bold as to express his heartfelt feelings in a speech in Ranbirsinghpura, near Jammu. In effect, he was threatening the Dogras for their continued support to a cause, which in his opinion, was a ruse for communalism. He insisted that Kashmir's accession to India had to be restricted as long as communalism had a toehold in India. He described the application of the full Constitution of India to the State as 'unrealistic, childish and savouring of lunacy'. According to *The Hindu* of Madras his reasoning was: 'We want to join India without any kind of mental reservations. But how can we do so as long as we are not convinced about the complete elimination of communalism in India? We are prepared to welcome application of India's constitution to Kashmir in its entirety once we are satisfied that the grave of communalism has been finally dug in India. Of that we are not clear yet.

'It is very well for the people of India to think that communalism has been finally eliminated. But no one can deny that the communal spirit still exists in India. Many Kashmiris are apprehensive as to what will happen to them and their position, for instance, [if] something happens to Pandit Nehru. We do not know. As realists, we Kashmiris have to provide for all eventualities...

'I would like to warn those who talk lightly of Kashmir's complete accession to India in all subjects that they are fanning fires of conflict once again. For if there is no special status for Kashmir in the Indian Constitution, how can we go to the Muslims in Kashmir and convince them that India does not intend to interfere in the internal affairs of Kashmir? I am not saying that India will interfere in our internal affairs but there is something called sentiment which has to be recognized. We have accepted India in regard to defence, foreign affairs and communication and not in respect of other subjects because we wanted some kind of autonomy for ourselves in internal matters. Now some people here and in the Indian press are questioning our very fundamental right to shape our destiny in our own way. They do not tell us what will happen to Kashmir if there is a resurgence of communalism in India and how in those circumstances we are to convince the Muslims of Kashmir that India does not intend to swallow Kashmir.'

The phantom of communalism was enough to make Nehru refuse to see the widening gulf between the Dogras of Jammu and Buddhists of Ladakh on the one hand, and Kashmir on the other. The Delhi Agreement was thus a calculated risk on Nehru's part, and the result of the clever moves played out by Sheikh Abdullah. Nehru's desire to buy peace with him at any cost, with the belief that Abdullah would finally see reason and accept his point of view was to end in his disillusionment. Sheikh Abdullah's speech left little room for speculation; by referring to Nehru's departure and the ensuing weakening of the secular forces, he confirmed the suspicion of those who were convinced that he was threatening separation. This fear had always been at the centre of the plebiscite proposal and his insensitive and grossly exaggerated communalism of Hindus was offensive to India's reputation abroad.

Communalism, and for that matter all baser emotions, are never too far from the surface of any society. The onus of keeping them at lower and containable levels falls upon polity and the leaders. History, even of Kashmir, is replete with many periods when the benign and tolerant rulers were followed by those who have aggressively promoted their own religion and handled others with heavy and cruel hands. Sheikh Abdullah never grew tired of boasting of the homogeneous and distinct cultural identity of Kashmir. He would have others believe that actually there was no difference between the Kashmiri Hindus and Kashmiri Muslims. The truth, however, was that the successive pogroms initiated by many of the Muslim rulers of Kashmir and the all-pervading influence of the Rishis*, who were Muslims, had led to mass conversions in Kashmir, both forced and voluntary. The Kashmiri Hindus were reduced to such a minority group that they were hardly in any position to assert themselves. All they could do was to accept the living conditions imposed on them and watch the ever decreasing number of their community.

The Ranbirsinghpura speech upset everyone, including Nehru. Nevertheless, he continued to put all his eggs in Sheikh Abdullah's basket. The Indian Prime Minister wrote to Sheikh Abdullah on 16th April 1952: 'I have felt deeply about Kashmir because it represented to me many things and many principles. It has always been an axiom with me, quite apart from the constitutional position and the like, that the people of Kashmir must decide their own fate. For me the people of Kashmir were basically represented by you. If you feel as you do then the link that has bound us together necessarily weakens and I have little heart to discuss such a matter.'[200] The letter was from a person who had already given up and lost hope. Not surprisingly, the Delhi Agreement soon followed. It was a significant victory for Sheikh Abdullah and those who nursed separatist sentiments. It was a double insurance, Article 370 being the first. The nationalists in the Congress felt that the Agreement contained certain provisions that were designed to bring the State closer to the rest of the country if they were honestly implemented. But for Jammu, this was another step in a 'drift away in incorporation [of the State] into the Indian Union and towards the creation of what might almost be called a mini-Pakistan, an autonomous [if not fully independent] state which was in its essentials Islamic…it [Jammu] had been particularly perturbed by Sheikh Abdullah's land reforms; and, increasingly it came to see the ruling National Conference both as an Islamic communal party and as a cover for the extension of communist ideology.' The Delhi Agreement for them was another step in realizing Sheikh Abdullah's goals.[201]

* The Rishis belong to the Rishi order of the indigenous Sufism of Kashmir. They embody the region's ethnic, social and cultural consciousness. Nund Rishi or Sheikh Noor-ud-din Wali, along with Resh Mir Sahib are the most prominent Rishis.

Leaders in Delhi, other than Nehru, came to see a pattern in the dealings with Sheikh Abdullah. After extracting significant concessions he would go back to Srinagar and then write to them to alter some of the arrangements agreed to in the earlier agreement. He argued that his 'people' were not amenable to the earlier arrangement, or he would say that his colleagues were not satisfied with the terms. In the process, Delhi would yield even further. However, after the Delhi Agreement and securing the annihilation of the Dogra dynasty and bullying Delhi and the Yuvraj into accepting a five-year term as Sadar-i-Riyasat, Sheikh Abdullah embarked on a much more ambitious and dangerous path. He also changed his tactics. No longer did he write that his 'people' or colleagues were not satisfied with the terms of the agreement; he simply refused to keep his end of the bargain. In addition, his concern about the future relationship with the country was also constantly questioned in increasingly strident terms.

Nehru, if he was concerned at the new development, kept the worry to himself. He was under constant attack from all over the country, in parliament and outside it. The agitation launched by the Jana Sangh, Hindu Mahasabha and Ram Rajya Parishad in support of the Praja Parishad rattled him. But the more strident the attack, the more prone he was to blame the communal and reactionary forces for setting a dangerous trend. He was deeply concerned and expressed his views in his regular letters to the state chief ministers. On 4th December 1952, he wrote: 'The far-reaching land reforms in the State have naturally not pleased some of the old landlord elements and they have joined the agitation against the government there. In this they are being helped directly by some communal elements in other parts of India… In the name of a closer association with India, they are acting in a manner which might imperil that very association.'

He wrote again on the subject on 27th January 1953: 'The Jammu agitation, about which I have written to you [the start chief ministers] previously, is again a remarkable instance of folly or mischief. [It] plays into the hands of Pakistan. It is clear that the objective of these organizations is not confined to Jammu and they are aiming at bigger quarry. Their dislike of the Government of India and the secular policy it pursues is so great that, in order to injure it, they are prepared even to harm our relationship with Jammu and Kashmir State.'[202]

Not many sympathized with Sheikh Abdullah within the country but he was not lacking in support from the outside world, particularly the conservative Western press. The then English editor of Calcutta's *The Statesman,* Ian Stephens, was one of them. Ever eager to find fault with India, he found a readymade hero in Sheikh Abdullah. After having a three-hour long session with Abdullah, this is how he described him:

> The impression left on my mind after three hours in the poplar-bordered Srinagar garden with the Prime Minister of Indian-held Kashmir…was a courageous, forthright, vigorous man, intelligent, though without intellectual range, gifted with a strong personality and therefore probably an inspiring leader of the downtrodden.
>
> He was obviously non-communal, wholeheartedly so. He spoke with pride of a pleasant reality I had noticed: that in and around Srinagar, no doubt because of his administration's efforts. Hindus, Sikhs and Muslims mingled in cordiality. Pre-eminently he appeared to me a Kashmiri patriot full of zeal to impress his countrymen's plight, preoccupied with the vale, the centre and motive of his whole political life, but concerned with the rest of the subcontinent's affairs…
>
> Evidently, he thought now if not before, in many Hindu Congressmen, a façade of secular tolerance had an actual communalism as narrow as any in Pakistan, indeed perhaps worse, because of the caste system.[203]

Ian Stephens, for the record, was a strong supporter of Pakistan and often argued for the handing over of Jammu and Kashmir to it, not only on the basis of communal balance but because of geography. A notable contributor to the English press, he was one of the leading media personalities to peddle the mischievous report about the Muslim massacre in Jammu and Maharaja Hari Singh's involvement in it. The support lent by him to the cause of Sheikh Abdullah was symptomatic of a concerted effort by the Western media to gather support for his cause, and probably, encouraged him to chart a course that was contrary to the legality and morality of the situation. Thus, even after the Delhi Agreement there were sustained efforts by many Westerners to sabotage it by encouraging Sheikh Abdullah to adopt a defiant and anti-India posture.

The year 1953 began with Prime Minister Nehru and Sheikh Abdullah being on the same side on the issue of the Jammu agitation. The former was convinced that the Jammu movement was subversive, communal and fed by reactionary forces in and outside the State. Even in a letter to Dr Kailash Nath Katju, then Home Minister, Nehru described the agitation as an attempt of the most poisonous kind to unsettle the policy of the Government of India, and was convinced that Dr Mukherjee was playing a clever and dirty game. At this time, Yuvraj Karan Singh began to inform him of the atrocities unleashed by the police on the people of Jammu, but the Prime Minister seems to have either ignored him or tolerated his comments because of the necessity to have him on his side. He not only paid scant attention to them but also considered the actions of the Home Ministry inadequate to tackle the reactionary forces. He suspected many of the officials of being sympathetic to the communalists. What Nehru refused to take note of, some would say, was that his friend Sheikh Abdullah had drifted away. The fact, though, is that his politics had always been Kashmir-centric and he never understood the State that was created by the genius of the Dogra rulers. Even after becoming Prime Minister, he made no effort to broaden his outlook. Nehru and the Congress were tools in his armoury to further the cause of Kashmiris and having achieved that goal, and now in sight of new allies from the Western world, he began to distance himself from his former benefactor.

A few months after the Delhi Agreement, in early 1953, with his target of finishing of the dynasty secured, he began to express his reservations about not only the constitutional arrangement that was offered to him but also about the accession of the State to India. According to Sandeep Bamzai, 'He was of the opinion that Jammu would never reconcile with the Valley. In a confidential note to the prime minister after conversing with Sheikh Saheb, senior government officials claimed that he [Sheikh Abdullah] was convinced that Jammu wanted to separate with the help of India's external support.'[204] It was a preposterous charge but such was the state of Sheikh Abdullah's mind that he never thought of his own contribution towards the alienation of the Dogras. He would never recall his sustained efforts to hurt and humiliate the Dogras and expected of them a quiet subservience as subject to his master. Their refusal and defiance baffled him. But he used it to justify the whole Kashmir issue all over again.

As far as Nehru was concerned, he made feeble efforts to persuade Sheikh Abdullah into taking steps to assuage the hurt feelings of Jammu. In a letter written to the State Prime Minister on 30th January 1953, Nehru not only proposed that a commission be appointed, as suggested by Yuvraj Karan Singh, but also said, 'It is clear that a considerable section of the people in Jammu province have been unfortunately moved by this misconceived agitation. They have to be won over and not merely suppressed…I am very glad, therefore, that in your speeches you have made the right kind of appeal… The recent display of the union flag on Republic Day had a good effect in Jammu. It would be a good thing if the national flag is put up in one or two places together with the state flag.'[205]

Only a few days after this very optimistic letter, Nehru was constrained to appeal to Sheikh Abdullah for the full implementation of the Delhi Agreement. Yuvraj Karan Singh seemed to have finally prevailed upon Nehru and he saw the necessity of a substantial gesture to mollify the people of Jammu. By this time, the Yuvraj's views were being echoed by the Intelligence Bureau reports. Nehru must have realized that on different occasions and issues, including the alienation of Ladakh, the reports sent by the Yuvraj were almost repeated by the Bureau. Thus, on 10th February 1953, he wrote: 'It would help us greatly if some indication came from your government about the early implementation… That would partly disable any big agitation.'

Sandeep Bamzai has quoted in his book *Bonfire of Kashmiriyat* from the notes of his grandfather (K.N. Bamzai) regarding the dilemma Sheikh Abdullah faced. Even after making allowance for the element of subjectivity and the fact that those days many Kashmiri Hindus were firmly entrenched in the Abdullah camp for various reasons, including ideological, they have a bearing on the situation. Those notes say, 'Even the Delhi Agreement is not going to satisfy certain elements in India…I cannot continue to keep people in the Valley on tenterhooks. So far the people of the Valley have been silent because they know that I will not barter away their interests. Moreover, how can we have peace in the State if the solution which India and Kashmir adopt is not acceptable to Pakistan?… Sir Mirza Mohammad Ismail's plan should be considered dispassionately. If today Jammu has rebelled, it is not far when we will lose all sympathy in the Valley. In the circumstances, independence is best because Pakistan would never agree to a unilateral agreement and our borders will always be attacked by them. Tell Panditji to have a solution which will be honourable to all—Pakistan, India, Kashmir and to him… During the last five years, several solutions have been provided. To me plebiscite is out of the question. Keeping the Jammu people with us is not at all possible. War is ruled out. Let Panditji look at the probable solutions including that of Jammu and Ladakh [with river Chenab at places as boundary] completely merged with India and the Valley accede for three subjects only.'[206]

Elaborating the plan, Sandeep Bamzai claims that Jammu, Poonch, Rajouri, Bhadarwah, parts of Kishtwar and Reasi, and Ladakh, with Zojila as the boundary from the Valley side and joined from the Kulu-Manali side, be acceded fully to India; and that the Kashmir Valley, Uri, Titwal, Gurais, Zojila, Taragabal, and regions from Jammu and Ramban, including the Doda district, be a separate identity acceding only on the three subjects of the Instrument of Accession. The suggestion, if true was preposterous and made a mockery of not only the Constitution of India but also of Sheikh Abdullah's claim that he had struggled against the Dogra rule to free Kashmir that was brought in by Maharaja Gulab Singh through a 'sale deed'. He was, unmistakably injecting the element of communalism by dividing the State between the Muslim and Hindu majority areas. In hindsight, one can clearly discern that this plan was in the making soon after he took control of the state government and reorganized the district of Udhampur to create a Muslim-majority Doda district.

Throughout his political career, Sheikh Abdullah had raised the rhetorical levels to an unrealistic degree, and now he did not know how to get off the tiger's back. He fanned hatred against the Dogras in the Valley, and derided the family that had, in fact, *created* the State that he wanted to rule. It can be argued that the struggle of Jammu was because of the inability of that region to reconcile to the loss of power, privileges and preeminent position. But how does one explain the discontent among the Ladakhis? The truth was that Sheikh Abdullah did not understand the State as created by the Dogras, and wanted to draw a new Radcliffe Line in the composite State held together by the Dogras for a century, not just by an iron hand but with equitable participation of all the communities in the act of governance. One shudders to think what might have happened if the region of Gilgit-Baltistan had remained in the control of the State. For then, Sheikh Abdullah probably would have suggested the carving of another unit to create a Shia-dominated State comprising Gilgit-Baltistan and possibly, Gurais and parts of Kargil.

By this time, Sheikh Abdullah was convinced that the Western powers would support him in his desire to make a Switzerland out of Kashmir, and therefore, 'all his references to India were in hostile terms and contained strong criticism of any action of the Central or any State Government or any event anywhere in India which he could malign as communal in nature and he used all these instances to prove that India's profession of secularism was only on paper. He made several speeches with direct or indirect allegations on these lines and took advantage of the Friday gatherings at the Hazratbal Mosque to spread his poisonous propaganda.'[207]

Sadar-i-Riyasat Karan Singh, along with the young deputy minister in the state government D.P. Dhar and the Intelligence Bureau's Mullik, kept Nehru informed of all the developments indicating the change in Sheikh Abdullah. Nehru naturally felt betrayed and let down. Rarely had a politician backed someone against the better judgment of all his colleagues only to be let down by that person. Even at that late stage, Nehru sent several hints to Sheikh Abdullah to come to Delhi and discuss matters; but they were spurned. An open invitation was not responded to and Sheikh Abdullah is believed to have commented that the matter had been discussed between the two many times over and another meeting was not going to yield any result. But still, Nehru wanted to give the Agreement another chance, and in the words of Mullik, 'If Muhammad would not come to the mountain, then the mountain had to go to Muhammad!' So, the Prime Minister went to Srinagar in May 1953.

Nehru's visit coincided with the session of the National Conference between 16th and 21st May. Nehru used the occasion to invite all the leaders of the National Conference to his residence after the conclusion of the session to talk over the situation and warn them of the impending dangers and threats. But right through his stay, Sheikh Abdullah maintained his hostile and recalcitrant attitude towards India and refused to relent. The Prime Minister returned to Delhi a disillusioned man. Still he made another attempt at reconciliation by sending Maulana Azad to Srinagar. 'He [Maulana Azad] too utterly failed to convince the Sheikh about the folly of his ways. In fact, he could not engage the Sheikh in any useful talks. On the other hand, the Sheikh totally ignored him and even went to the length of insulting this highly respected leader at the Id meeting. The Maulana Sahib's advice to the Prime Minister on his return was to dismiss Sheikh Abdullah before he committed any more mischief,' writes B.N. Mullik.[208]

Dr Shyama Prasad Mukherjee suddenly passed away in the month of June, while Prime Minister Nehru was in London attending the coronation of Queen Elizabeth II. If he suffered from an ailment, no one was aware. Even his family physician, Dr B.C. Roy had not been informed and he appropriately expressed anger and protest. His co-detenue, Guru Dutt Vaid, alleged 'that proper medical care had not been provided to Mookerjee [*sic*] and this negligence of the state had hastened his death… The Jana Sangh demanded a high level impartial enquiry into the circumstances leading to Mookerjee's death. This demand was supported by various other leaders such as Purshottam Das Tandon and Jayaprakash Narayan.'[209]

The opposition was incensed by the manner in which Sheikh Abdullah treated the aftermath of Dr Mukherjee's death. He did not even express regret or send a reply to Dr. Roy's telegram of protest. His attitude to the tragedy was, in the words of Mullik, 'Mookerjee [*sic*] was the founder-leader of the Jana Sangh, which was helping his mortal enemy in Jammu, i.e. the Praja Parishad, and as Dr Mookerjee had broken the law in furtherance of the agitation for the complete integration of Jammu and Kashmir with India to which the Sheikh was opposed, he did not deserve any special consideration and had to meet the consequences of his actions. In any case, the Kashmir Government had not thrown him into jail but kept him under house arrest and had arranged for proper medical attendance.'[210] After a very insensitive and inhuman response when the rest of the country, particularly Bengal, erupted in protest, Sheikh Abdullah found, even in that, some evidence of the communal nature that India had acquired. He alleged that these protests were another way of denying an honourable place to Kashmir under the sun.

On return from his foreign tour, Nehru made yet another bid to make Sheikh Abdullah see reason. On 28th June 1953, he wrote him a letter warning of the possible consequences of the Sheikh's actions and also appealed for mutual understanding. He reiterated his open invitation and suggested that Sheikh Abdullah bring along his hard-line colleague and advisor Beg and also his Deputy Prime Minister Bakshi to observe: 'Recent developments have, however, led me to think that you have either changed your mind completely or are not clear about your thinking… You told me that there were only two courses open for Kashmir: either full integration or full autonomy, whatever that might mean. I did not agree with you on this, nor do I agree with you even now because there are many other middle courses…

'We have argued enough and must accept each other's present conclusions and then discuss the future on that basis. If that unhappily leads to divergence with all its consequences we fashion our respective courses accordingly… Thus far, I have proceeded on the basis of friendship and confidence in you and have been vain enough to expect the same approach from you. Whether that is justified or not that is for you to say. Individual relations should not count in national affairs and yet they count and make a difference.

'To me it has been a major surprise that a settlement arrived between us should be bypassed or repudiated, regardless of the merits. That strikes at the root of all confidence, personal or international. No treaty would be worth the paper it is written on if it is to be repudiated soon after. So far as I am concerned, no power in the world would make me go back on the pledge I gave in that Agreement. If my Parliament or my people in India repudiate that, they repudiate me... My honour is bound up with my word... It is always painful to part company after long years of comradeship, but if our conscience so tells us, or in our view an overriding national interest requires, then there can be no help for it...'[211]

The warning of the impending events was loud and clear for any person who wanted to hear, but by now Sheikh Abdullah's ego had become so inflated that he did not listen to the warning that his friend of many years had sounded. Nehru went on to do some plain speaking too in that letter and seemed to be replying to Sheikh Abdullah's oft repeated charge that India was only wearing a thin veil of secularism. The Prime Minister further wrote, 'My government has stood, as you have so consistently stood, for a secular democracy. I do not know what your feelings are on this subject now. But I fear the tendency in Kashmir is to keep away from it. Unfortunately that will have its reactions in India as such tendencies in India have their reactions in Kashmir.' He concluded by forewarning Abdullah about the future, 'What I have felt lately has been that your government is very far from harmonious and in fact pulls in different directions, that your organization is also disintegrating in the same way. If this process continues, I have no doubt that Kashmir would relapse into utter backwardness, so far as political life is concerned.' He was, of course referring to the growing differences between the majority in the Government and the National Conference, consisting of those desiring more integration, and the minority, led by Sheikh Abdullah and Beg, wanting total autonomy.

Sheikh Abdullah, of course refuted the allegations. In a letter dated 3rd July, he wrote: 'I have not been able to understand how you have the impression that I was lacking in this clarity. It is possible that some people may consider a particular line of thought to be the only clear one while others may hold a different line and similarly believe that to be more clear [*sic*]. I have now been in intimate touch with Kashmir and its people for the last 22 years. I have never been hazy in regard to this objective and therefore there is no confusion in my mind.

'Objectively, the State is subject to pulls from India and Pakistan. The external pressure naturally creates internal reactions to terms of divided loyalties. In order to neutralize these reactions, we had devised a formula and considered a restricted relationship with India as a suitable course conducive to internal consolidation. We believe that the accession of the State to India on the terms of the Instrument of Accession would provide the necessary opportunities of allaying the fears of various sections of the people of the State.

'...The fact of transfer of three vital subjects, *viz* [emphasis added] defence, communications and foreign affairs, to the Union is a sufficient guarantee to the minorities of the state that their interests would not be jeopardized in any way. The presence of Indian defence forces, for instance, should have afforded the necessary sense of security to the minorities. Similarly, in the case of the majority community, we felt that it was necessary that they should not be haunted by the fear of being swamped by the majority community in India, even in the normal course of administration. To this end, we thought it necessary to secure a certain amount of autonomy within which the majority community would have adequate safeguards and opportunities of exercising their rights.'[212]

Then Sheikh Abdullah went on to list his grievances and the alleged going back of the Government of India on the sub-themes of the Agreement—the foremost being Article 370. He forgot that even in the Constitution of India, accepted by Sheikh Abdullah and the National Conference, the Article was visualized as a transitory provision. He wrote, 'When Article 370 was devised, we felt assured by Sardar Patel's statement that the Instrument of Accession would be the final basis of the Indo-Kashmir relationship. Subsequently, when the Delhi Agreement came up before the Council of State on August 5, 1952, Shri Gopalaswami Ayyangar stated that Article 370 was not a permanent feature of the Indian Constitution and "when the time was ripe", this provision would be removed from the Constitution... This clearly shows that even though assurances were given to us in regard to the restricted application of the Indian Constitution to this State, such assurances came with a good deal of mental reservations.'

Then the Sheikh went on to find fault even with the manner in which the State was made to suffer regarding the three subjects acceded to under the Instrument of Accession. He accused the Government of India of not recruiting Kashmiri youth in the Armed Forces even though the State Forces were under the administrative control of the Centre. In the other two subjects, he found fault on the same basis and accused India of not employing enough educated youth from Kashmir in the other services. He also refuted Nehru's comment regarding dissension within the State Government and the Party. 'I…assure you that so far as the basic principles are concerned, there is no difference of opinion among us in Kashmir. There can be, of course, variations in the points of view or in the respective approaches, [b]ut these variations are normal and helpful for the democratic functioning of all institutions and governments… I wish to add that there is perfect unanimity among us as far as these conclusions are concerned… But, all the same, I feel greatly hurt and grieved when even friends like you start doubting and misunderstanding me. My conviction in the principle I have upheld all along has not faltered even when I had to face heavy odds. I may remind you it was a difficult decision to take when I proposed conversion of the Muslim Conference to [the] National Conference. Even when we were faced with what seemed almost an inevitable fate in 1947, I did not turn my face on these principles but fought [for] them. My idea about secular democracy is not cramped or narrow minded. I believe in justice for all sections of the people and my attitude is conditioned by realities and by wishful thinking. I agree that the personal relationship between individuals should not be a consideration where larger national interests are involved.'[213]

The die had, by now, been cast. Both, Nehru and Sheikh Abdullah seem to have made up their minds by the time this exchange of letters took place. Sheikh Abdullah was, obviously, oblivious to the gathering clouds. As subsequent events proved, he was not even aware of what was happening within his government and the Party. He was unaware that one of his emissaries to Delhi, Deputy Prime Minister Bakshi Ghulam Mohammad, had been updating the Indian Prime Minister of the growing discontent. Evidently, he had so isolated himself from reality that even his own intelligence department was not providing him with the information about the growing disenchantment with his leadership and the parleys that the dissidents were holding.

However, there was one person who still hoped to make him change his mind. Indian independent activist and politician, Mridula Sarabhai, a close associate of Prime Minister Nehru and also a very good friend of Sheikh Abdullah, made a final attempt at reconciliation. Her letter, after having met the Sheikh in Srinagar, as reproduced in *Bonfire of Kashmiriyat*, gives an insight of the manner in which the events were being shaped. She wrote on 17th July 1953:

> Soon, after reaching Delhi, I handed over your letters to Jawaharlalji, Rafi [Ahmed Kidwai] Saheb and Maulana Saheb. To know that they carried your feelings that no useful purpose can be achieved by carrying on oft talked subjects and hence you had decided not to come to Delhi—really, if I may say so, has come as a shock—which during recent years was a first.
>
> I had gone to Srinagar to understand you—not that I did not know about it—but the fact is that I wanted to personally know as to what was the best way you consider and what is called from persons like me who have a strong belief in the cause that Jawaharlalji and you have stood for till now; and who also believes—may hold strong conviction that—whatever the evolution of the relationship between the two states' destiny can be best moulded with mutual cooperation and confidence between Jawaharlalji and yourself.
>
> I thought I had understood you and wanted to facilitate the way, but I find that I was mistaken. In the morning talk you were good enough to explain to me the basic issues and emphasis. Both Jawaharlalji and you should understand the need of the hour and only then can a way be found. If the doors are closed between the two of you, then what is the way out? I have taken the liberty of conveying my feelings to you and urge you again to reconsider my appeal to you and Jawaharlalji—that for Kashmir and India—for humanity and its confidence in both of you—please understand each other and find a way out. For such a national problem, talk and exchange of views, even though they might be "futile" can never be useless.[214]

Meanwhile, Rafi Ahmed Kidwai too had been roped in to break the deadlock and was shocked by the rude manner in which Sheikh Abdullah began to rebuff all efforts at reconciliation. He wrote a letter to Sheikh Abdullah, offering to come to Srinagar for that purpose, but was curtly told that it would be futile. He rang to that effect and was similarly snubbed.

Finally, the crisis arrived and the ensuing confrontation marked the end of a chapter and the beginning of another.

14

The Fall

Rafi Ahmed Kidwai too, after his futile effort to help resolve the issue, advised Prime Minister Nehru to remove Sheikh Abdullah before a crisis of greater magnitude was created. The director of the Intelligence Bureau, B.N. Mullik records in his book that the Prime Minister was distraught at the development of events. The action suggested by his colleagues was not only going to terminate a long association but also a period of personal friendship marked by shared values and strengthened by the step-by-step realization of the goals set by them. But he was also aware that the removal of Sheikh Abdullah was going to throw Kashmir into turmoil with no certainty of the end results. Nehru was certain that the people of the Valley would rise in protest. He was also certain that Pakistan would take advantage of the situation and make the position awkward for India in the United Nations. But he also knew that letting matters drift would make it worse.

Sheikh Abdullah, as was obvious from his speeches, had made up his mind. He was not going to take the State to Pakistan, as Mullik had rightly read him; he knew that his identity there would be submerged under the greater Islamic identity of Pakistan. He wanted to be in a place where he remained the king of the jungle. According to Mullik, 'He was evidently angling for a special status—just short of independence. He knew he would have no position in Pakistan: but a semi-independent status for the Valley would give him all that he desired—security from foreign invaders, economic prosperity due to the influx of tourists and munificence of India and yet no subservience to the Central government which according to him was Hindu-dominated.'[215]

The Sheikh had reached a stage where he decided that even the finalization of the Constitution of the State could be put on hold till this primary issue was resolved. Blinded by his own ambition, he failed to see that in the process he had antagonized many of his old comrades. Bakshi Ghulam Mohammad and G.M. Sadiq were two of his early supporters. While the former provided him with all the strength that the streets of Srinagar possessed, the latter added luster with his intellect and ideological moorings. Sheikh Abdullah also failed to see that most of the Hindu leaders within his party had begun to feel uneasy because of his increasing Islamic rhetoric and anti-Hindu fulminations. Both, Sham Lal Saraf and Girdhari Lal Dogra were pushed beyond the margins. Both of them could not be accused of being sympathizers of the Praja Parishad. On the contrary, they continued to suffer the odium of being Abdullah's followers and be derided by the society in Jammu.

Instead of introspecting, the Sheikh chose to be suspicious. Never doubting his own righteousness, he sensed treachery even in his long-time friend and benefactor, Prime Minister Nehru. His autobiography refers to this while recounting how Bakshi and Sadiq turned against him when he writes about Nehru's final visit in May 1953, before the showdown. 'I noticed that Jawaharlal was not the same man; clearly his confidence was shaken. I was amazed to see him speaking quietly to Bakshi Ghulam Mohammad and his friends. Whispering in corners had started.'[216] Sheikh Abdullah blamed the long Praja Parishad agitation and its demand for full merger for making Nehru succumb to the demands of 'communalists', and found that 'Nehru and Maulana Azad were interested in the proposition, but did not agree with the strategy.' Azad was evidently in favour of the immediate removal of Sheikh Abdullah, whereas Nehru hesitated. He feared it would strengthen Pakistan's psychological war against India.

As far as Sadar-i-Riyasat Karan Singh was concerned, he had made his view abundantly clear by 1st May 1953, when he sent a note to Prime Minister Nehru on the political situation in the State, terming it as 'extremely fluid'. He had found that the pro-Indian faction within the government was determined and was claiming a majority in the Working Committee and the Assembly. 'The minority community in the Valley, including even those who have been intimately connected with Sheikh Abdullah, is feeling most apprehensive and distressed at the way things are moving here, and there is great panic and despair among them.'[217]

Sheikh Abdullah remained oblivious to even that component of the Kashmiri culture, which had supported him despite the history of the Valley where periodically concerted efforts of the ideological Islamists had reduced the Hindus to a small minority. He was even willing to take the risk of their total purge or annihilation to achieve his own goals. Maulana Azad caught the drift of his mind accurately, and therefore, fearful of the events to come, wrote to him: 'What I am telling you now is as a personal friend. There is only one way of safeguarding the future wellbeing of the people of Kashmir and that is the way we laid down in 1949 and which you accepted. Hold steadfast on this way and be assured that you will never have to regret it.'[218]

All advice fell on deaf ears. Sheikh Abdullah had parted company with his friends in Delhi. In the State, he was to discover that he had lost the confidence of many of his colleagues. The showdown happened during a Working Committee meeting. To his anger and dismay, Sheikh Abhdullah found that he had the support of only Afzal Beg and Mohammad Shafi Qureshi, whereas Bakshi, Sadiq, Masoodi, Mir Qasim, Saraf, Lal Dogra and Dhar were all ranged against him. By now, Sheikh Abdullah had identified Bakshi as the leader of the dissidents and therefore, to cut him to size, he forced an organizational election in Srinagar. It was Bakshi's stronghold and the Sheikh drew all his strength from the streets of the city. If Bakshi suffered a defeat he would automatically lose his preeminent place. But Bakshi proved too wily and turned the tables with his faction emerging victorious by a thumping majority. Even this electoral defeat did not deter Sheikh Abdullah and he continued the battle in the Working Committee and the Assembly.

At this point in time, Kidwai was looking after the Kashmir affairs. He not only kept a close watch on the developments but also sent his own representative to Srinagar to keep updated of every move that was being played out. It is evident from Sheikh Abdullah's autobiography, *Flames of the Chinar*, that he considered Kidwai as the man chosen by Nehru to topple him. But because of the confidence of being the master of the situation in the Valley, he believed in his own invincibility and the hopelessness of the Indian cause there without him. Therefore, it is only in retrospect that he claimed he could see the conspiracy being hatched when Nehru was seen holding discussions with Bakshi or in the appointment of Kidwai as the Kashmir in-charge. While reminiscing over the events, many years after they had happened, he forgot about the shabby treatment he meted out to senior Congress leaders like Maulana Azad and Rafi Ahmed Kidwai. He writes, 'Sickened by the double-dealings and changing loyalties of the Indian leaders, I informed Rafi Sahib that the situation had deteriorated to such an extent that it would defy all his efforts to improve it… The Jana Sangh and the Praja Parishad were demanding my arrest as the price for changing their hostile attitude to Jawaharlal Nehru. It was, therefore, agreed that I be made the scapegoat… In Delhi, preparations to overthrow my government and arrest me were now complete. Rafi Ahmed Kidwai and B.N. Malik [Mullik] were in charge of the coup d'état… On July 27, Karan Singh had received a secret message from Jawaharlal. Zero hour had been announced.'

However, the actual happenings belie Sheikh Abdullah's version. It is true that leaders in Delhi had agreed on the necessity of removing Sheikh Abdullah; it is also true that both Maulana Azad and Kidwai were not prepared to suffer Abdullah a minute longer. But ironically, the pace of the events or the 'predetermined' time, as alleged by Abdullah, was determined by him instead of Kidwai. The pro-Indian camp was apprehensive that Sheikh Abdullah was on the verge of assuming dictatorial powers since the new Constitution was still in the making and his office was governed by the old Constitution of 1939. They, therefore, wanted immediate punitive action against him. However, Sheikh Abdullah, confident of his power, still lumbered along, and on 7th August 1953, decided to peremptorily order Sham Lal Saraf to resign from the ministry. Saraf was the senior-most member of the National Conference and ranked second to Sheikh Abdullah in the Party. So, he refused to resign. Instead Saraf wrote to Sheikh Abdullah that 'the manner in which you have created a dangerous situation in the country by making highly inflammable speeches before the public, combined with your authoritarian attitude in the Cabinet, have convinced me that instead of helping the difficult situation my resignation will encourage you to pursue your policies unbridled. Such a course would be suicidal for the country.'[219] Meanwhile, Sheikh Abdullah had made at least three speeches at Mujahid Manzil, Khanyar and Ganderbal in July, making his intentions clear.

Technically, it was the Sadar-i-Riyasat who appointed and removed ministers on the advice of the Prime Minister. But to get this advice implemented, the Prime Minister had to approach the head of the State, who would then issue formal orders of dismissal or acceptance of the resignation, as the case may be.

This event was followed by the dissidents getting together, drafting a memorandum and sending it to Sheikh Abdullah. A copy signed by Deputy Prime Minister Bakshi, Finance Minister Girdhari Lal Dogra and Health Minister Sham Lal Saraf was also sent to the Sadar-i-Riyasat. It accused Sheikh Abdullah and Beg of blatantly flouting the agreed policies of the Cabinet. It said: 'After convening the Constituent Assembly, certain inescapable elaborations of the State's relationship with India were defined in the Delhi Agreement, of which you were the Chief architect on our behalf. Your stand was unanimously endorsed by the government, the National Conference, the Indian Parliament and the Constituent Assembly of the State. But you have not only deliberately delayed the implementation of the Agreement on these matters, which form the sheet-anchor of our policy, but have purposefully and openly denounced these in public. You have thus arbitrarily sought to precipitate a rupture in the relationship of the State with India… Mr M.A. Beg has persistently been following policies of narrow sectarianism and communalism, which have seriously undermined the oneness of the State. Unfortunately, you have been lending your support to his policies in the Cabinet and his activities in public. This has generated bitter feelings of suspicion and doubt in the minds of the people of the various constituent units of the State. You have connived at all these unfortunate happenings and thus strengthened and encouraged the forces of disruption. The result is that unity and secular character, the two fundamental aspects of our State, stand threatened today.'[220]

The memorandum concluded, 'We have been constantly urging upon you to put an end to these unhealthy tendencies and to undertake unitedly measures for restoring the morale of the people. In spite of our best intentions, we have failed in our efforts. It is, therefore, with great pain that we have to inform you of our conclusion that the Cabinet, constituted as it is at present and lacking as it does the unity of purpose and action, has lost the confidence of the people in its ability to give them a clean, efficient and healthy administration.'[221]

The State was still passing through a transitional period where laws overlapped and often, in the absence of any clarity, the interpretation of situations was made on the basis of the provisions of the Constitution of 1939. Undoubtedly the Constituent Assembly had convened and framed Articles relating to the office of the Head of the State, but the rest of the Constitution was still a long way away. As far as the Constitution of 1939 was concerned, the Sadar-i-Riyasat had to act on the advice of his Council of Ministers. The ball was therefore now in the court of the Sadar-i-Riyasat. When Saraf refused to resign, the alternative available for Sheikh Abdullah was to go to the Sadar-i-Riyasat and recommend his dismissal. Inexplicably, at that time, Sheikh Abdullah was not prepared to go to Yuvraj Karan Singh. Later accounts give an insight into the mind of Sheikh Abdullah, who had, by that time, come to take everything for granted and was offended even by the suggestion of Yuvraj Karan Singh holding any power over him.

No one knew better than the young Yuvraj that time was running out. For months he had observed the changes in the attitude and working of Sheikh Abdullah, and accordingly appraised and warned the Prime Minister of India. But now the ball was lobbed by Bakshi, Sadiq, Lal Dogra and Saraf in his court. He had to act in the best interests of the State and country, and also, in accordance with the law. The constitutional law and conventions suggest that the Head of the State acts only on the advice of his Council of Ministers. The Constitution of Jammu and Kashmir enjoins upon the Head that he must act on the advice of his ministers *and he must not act contrary to the Constitution.* But what is he to do if the advice given to him by his ministers is, in his opinion, 'repugnant to the Constitution? Since, the ministers hold office at his pleasure, he might possibly dismiss the ministers and save himself from acting in an unconstitutional manner and by appointing other ministers, who would give him such advice as he deems constitutionally right…'[222]

In this case, the question before the Sadar-i-Riyasat was whether he had the powers to intervene in the present situation, and he was convinced that since he was the appointing authority of the State's Prime Minister and other Ministers, no doubt on the advice rendered by the Prime Minister, he also had the power to dismiss him. But before doing that, he thought that it was only appropriate that he should talk to Sheikh Abdullah. 'I immediately invited him to come across to see me as soon as possible. He was going to Gulmarg that afternoon, and came to my residence around noon. When I enquired about the situation he narrated three long though petty incidents regarding Sham Lal Saraf, and disclosed that he had asked him to resign…I said that I was deeply distressed and concerned at the recent trend of events, particularly the complete absence of homogeneity in the Cabinet. I pointed out that it would be useful if he and his Cabinet colleagues were to come to my residence that evening so that the whole matter could be discussed in depth. He sidetracked the suggestion by launching into an angry tirade against the Indian Press which he accused of grossly misrepresenting and exaggerating the differences in the Cabinet. He made the astonishing claim that, although there was some difference of opinion, there were no basic political or administrative differences within his Cabinet. When I again stressed the necessity of doing something to rectify the situation he stated quite clearly that no internal solution was possible until there was some external solution acceptable to India as well as Pakistan.'[223]

In view of the developments of the past few months, it was clear that Sheikh Abdullah had come a long way from the person who had endorsed the Accession with utmost clarity as 'final and irrevocable'. A close analysis of the events would show that there was a method in all that he had done in the past. By endorsing the Accession to India, he prepared the people of Kashmir to rule out the possibility of Pakistan in their lives; but after doing that he had assiduously worked for the attainment of an autonomous, if not independent, State. It would be recalled that he had never entirely closed the issue of Accession. Even during his address to the Constituent Assembly, he had brazenly tried to appropriate the right to accede from the Maharaja to himself. By keeping that issue alive, he was able to extract one concession after another from the Government of India. Now he appeared to have reached a point where he thought he could force the Government of India to grant him the autonomy that he craved for. After much deliberation, he had secured the Delhi Agreement, but after that had deliberately refused to implement its terms. Was it possible that he bought the Delhi Agreement, only to bide time? Was he waiting for some assurance from the outside world to force India to grant him virtually independent status, and having now got that assurance, he had triggered this confrontation? He had let the cat out of the bag by mentioning the 'external solution'. This also gives lie to the accusation Sheikh Abdullah made in his autobiography about the 'zero hour' for his removal being fixed. As the events show, it was the act of demanding Saraf's resignation and the subsequent memorandum of the majority in the Cabinet that determined the course of action.

The Sadar-i-Riyasat knew that dismissing the Prime Minister of the State was no small matter. Sheikh Abdullah was still the most popular figure in the Valley, even if allegations of corruption and maladministration had taken some of the sheen off. After dismissal, if he decided to take the issue to the streets he would 'easily arouse acute communal and chauvinistic sentiments among the Kashmiri masses, which could in turn result in serious and violent disturbances. Anti-national elements and agents were active in the Valley and, if given the chance, would not hesitate to plunge the State into utter turmoil.'[224]

To deal with the situation, elaborate arrangements were made. The state government would have to rely on the police and militia in order to deal with the disturbances. To rule out the possibility of any mischief from sympathizers, the help of the army was sought. Brigadier B.M. Kaul was ostensibly on leave in the Valley, but he was entrusted with the task of sounding the Divisional Commander of Srinagar and Lieutenant General Atal, the Corps Commander at Udhampur. Two more officers were sent to the Valley, D.W. Mehra from the Intelligence Bureau and A.P. Jain, Kidwai's special envoy.

However, after all the arrangements had been made, the man who was number two in the government and was chosen to form the next government, developed cold feet. Bakshi Ghulam Mohammad absolutely refused to play his role if Sheikh Abdullah and Mirza Afzal Beg were not arrested and were allowed to freely roam the streets. He was right to a certain extent, for there was no knowing how Sheikh Abdullah would sway the emotional masses with his rhetoric. It was only after tying all the knots that the Sadar-i-Riyasat drafted the dismissal order as well as the covering letter. The documents read:

> You will recall that in the course of our meeting today I conveyed to you my deep concern at the serious differences which exist in your Cabinet. I impressed upon you the immediate necessity for restoring harmony and unity of purpose among the members of the Cabinet in the execution of its policies. You were, however, unable to assure me that these acute differences could be remedied.
>
> This conflict within the Cabinet has for a considerable time been causing great confusion and apprehension in the minds of the people of the State. The situation has reached an unprecedented crisis with the fact that three of your four Cabinet colleagues have in a Memorandum to you, a copy of which they have sent to me, expressed their complete dissatisfaction with your actions and policies, which have lost the present Cabinet the confidence of the people. The document clearly indicates that the divergence within your Cabinet has reached proportions in which the unity, prosperity and stability of the State are gravely jeopardized.
>
> When we met today I further suggested to you that an emergent meeting of the Cabinet should be held at my residence this evening so that we could jointly explore the possibilities of securing a stable, unified and efficient Government for the country. But to my regret you evaded the issue.

> Under these conditions I, as Head of the State, have been forced to the conclusion that the present Cabinet cannot continue in office any longer and hence I regret to inform you that I have dissolved the Council of Ministers headed by you. A copy of my order in this connection is attached herewith.
>
> I need hardly add how distressed I am at having to take this action, but the vital interests of the people of the State, which it is my duty to safeguard, leave me no alternative…

The order passed by the Sadar-i-Riyasat read:

> …And whereas, finally, functioning of the present Cabinet on the basis of joint responsibility has become impossible and the resultant conflicts have gravely jeopardized the unity, prosperity and stability of the State;
>
> I, Karan Singh, Sadar-i-Riyasat, functioning in the interests of the people of the State who have reposed the responsibility and authority of the Headship of the State in me, do hereby dismiss Sheikh Mohammad Abdullah, from the Prime Ministership of the State of Jammu and Kashmir, and consequently the Council of Ministers headed by him is dissolved forthwith.

The order had to be executed in utmost secrecy since any inkling might have alerted Sheikh Abdullah and there was no knowing how he would have galvanized people against the Sadar-i-Riyasat. But he was 'totally unaware of the developments, and so arrogant in the possession of power that he could never dream that anyone would dare to challenge him.' Not surprisingly, everyone waited for the news and hoped that no untoward incident would happen. Sheikh Abdullah had gone to sleep and when woken and informed of the development, flew into a rage and is said to have shouted, 'Who is the Sadar-i-Riyasat to dismiss me? I made that chit of a boy Sadar-i-Riyasat.'[225] That comment, more than anything, is indicative of the megalomaniac tendencies that began to be part of his personality. For years he had been told, even by Nehru, that he was Kashmir. Therefore, the dismissal at the hands of the scion of the same Dogra dynasty that he hated and had thought he had eliminated, was particularly devastating for his ego.

The next important task was to install the new government. With Bakshi refusing to take the oath till it was confirmed that

Sheikh Abdullah had been arrested, it was only in the early hours of 9th August 1953 that he was administered the oath of office of Prime Minister of Jammu and Kashmir. After that Karan Singh wrote a report to the President of India informing him of all the developments, and sent a copy with a covering letter to Prime Minister Nehru. It was only after doing this that he could sleep. It was almost dawn.

Some observant writers have found discrepancies in the narration of the events by Mullik and Karan Singh and tried to prove that Sheikh Abdullah's dismissal was a conspiracy. They particularly believe that the arrest of Sheikh Abdullah was hatched by a few in Srinagar, behind Prime Minister Nehru's back. Memoirs about momentous events that are emotionally draining, when written after the lapse of some time, are bound to be coloured with personal perceptions. It has been suggested that Prime Minister Nehru was furious at the arrest as if such a monumental decision had been taken against his authority. Such controversies are best settled by looking for some documentary evidence. The covering letter from the Sadar-i-Riyasat to Prime Minister Nehru was a matter of fact assessment and information but ended on a personal note with 'We are all acutely aware of the gravity of the steps that we have been forced to take… In this whole matter I attempted to act in a democratic and constitutional manner, keeping especially in mind what you said when we met last. On the whole, I feel that we have done the best that was possible under the circumstances…

'The last forty-eight hours have been a great strain, both mental and physical—and none of us have had a wink of sleep the whole night. I am keeping in close touch with the situation and will keep you informed of developments. I feel confident that with your blessings and guidance everything will turn out right.'[226] Nehru promptly replied on 10th August 1953 and sounded extremely sympathetic to Yuvraj Karan Singh, writing, 'I quite realize the great strain which you must have undergone during these few days. I think…you have acted with wisdom and dignity.'[227] These were not the sentiments of a person who has been outraged and angry, or whose authority had been misused.

Finally, was the dismissal of Sheikh Abdullah's government

by the Sadar-i-Riyasat constitutional? It is argued that the Sadar-i-Riyasat had no authority to dismiss a constitutionally elected government that had not lost the confidence of the House on its floor. The confidence of his colleagues was of no consequence if he had the support of the Assembly. But the Constitution of Jammu and Kashmir, as applicable at that time, vested the power of dismissal in the Head of the State. This power, normally in accordance with the practice and conventions of removing or dismissing a minister, is exercised on the advice of the Chief Minister. Normally, the entire Cabinet or an individual minister can only be removed after a vote of no-confidence on the floor of the House, but it may sometimes happen that, a minister is otherwise undesirable, even when he commands the support of the House. In such a case, the power of dismissal might be used. 'Although the Constitution does not specifically state that the council of ministers can be dissolved by the Sadar-i-Riyasat on grounds of inefficiency or misconduct…since [he] is obliged to ensure the stability of the administration, he may, if he thinks necessary, dismiss the cabinet as a whole,' according to Justice A.S. Anand.[228] He further elaborates on the subject: 'There had not been any vote of no-confidence against the ministry in the legislature, but a majority of the members of the Council of Ministers approached the Sadar-i-Riyasat and told him that they could not work collectively with the other two members of the Council, namely Sheikh Abdullah and Mirza Afzal Beg, the Prime Minister and Revenue Minister respectively. Apart from this the majority group consisting of M/s Bakshi, Saraf and Dogra submitted a memorandum to Sheikh of treasonable activities against the State. The Sadar-i-Riyasat had "other grounds" also to believe that Sheikh was engaged in activities against the security of the State, so, he dismissed Sheikh Abdullah and dissolved the Council of Ministers headed by him… In the Kashmir Conspiracy Case*, the defence has argued that the Sadar-i-Riyasat had no powers to dismiss. In

* The Kashmir Conspiracy Case was based on investigations by the Central Intelligence against Sheikh Abdulllah and his comrades for conspiring against the State and its secession from India. On the basis of evidence, the case went for trial in 1959 but was withdrawn in 1964 because of political reasons.

view of the above discussion, it is submitted that the action by the Sadar-i-Riyasat was not invalid and that it is difficult to see as the court will be able to look into the fact of the competency of the Sadar-i-Riyasat.'[229]

It must also be remembered that at that point in time the Constitution of the State was still a work in progress and the whole Constitution had not been drafted, debated or even passed. Later, informing the Prime Minister of India of the development, Karan Singh wrote: 'Yesterday matters came to a head when three out of Sheikh Abdullah's four Cabinet colleagues sent him a memorandum, a copy of which they sent to me, in which they openly denounced his policies and repudiated his leadership. They expressed that the policies he was pursuing were proving disastrous to the country and that the Cabinet, lacking as it did unity of policy and action, had forfeited the confidence of the people. This represented a complete breakdown of the cabinet system and the principle of joint responsibility, which is so vital to Parliamentary Democracy. I met Sheikh Abdullah, but he could not satisfy me regarding bringing the situation to a stable and speedy solution…I had no alternative but to dissolve the Ministry forthwith.'[230]

The immediate impact on the State was a mixed one. The Valley was in turmoil and required the strong will of the State government to restore normalcy. Jammu, on the other hand was ecstatic. Sheikh Abdullah's fall created near hysteria in Pakistan 'where there were public demonstrations in his support, notably in Karachi where Miss Fatima Jinnah [sister of the late M.A. Jinnah] addressed a vast crowd and called for the immediate liberation of Kashmir from Indian occupiers. As a symbol of solidarity, most of the celebrations scheduled for Pakistan Day, August 14, 1953, were cancelled. From this moment, Sheikh Abdullah became an official Pakistani public hero.'[231]

Telegrams and letters congratulating Yuvraj Karan Singh came pouring in from all over the country. The ones coming from West Bengal particularly referred to Dr Shyama Prasad Mukherjee. The unintended outcome was that the resentment of the Dogras against Yuvraj Karan Singh turned into adulation and all those who had led the protest against him when he accepted the office of the Sadar-i-

Riyasat came in droves to congratulate him. Jammu, they felt, had been avenged. Little did they know that the State, once again, had entered a period of uncertainty. So much depended on the manner in which the ship was captained.

Another wholly unintended result was that it marked the thawing of the relations between Yuvraj Karan Singh and his father! Maharaja Hari Singh immediately wrote a letter to the Yuvraj: 'All one can say and wish is that what has taken and is taking place may turn out to be for the good of the people and the State. That is also my prayer. You must be having a lot of strain in these exciting and busy days. Please take very good care of yourself.'[232] He was also apprehensive about the security of his son and asked him to tighten his security arrangements.

15

Period of Consolidation

The first task before the new government was to establish its authority in governance and create peace in the Valley. It was a challenge as protests had erupted in various places and the crowds were violent. As a result, the police had to open fire at many places in self-defence, killing 46 and injuring 148. It was then that Bakshi's administrative skills came to the fore. Within a short period, streets became quieter, making the celebrations of Independence Day pass off peacefully. The day began with the swearing-in ceremony of Sham Lal Saraf and Khwaja Mir Qasim as Cabinet ministers, after which the celebratory function began in the presence of senior government officials and judges of the High Court. More importantly, several pro-India processions were taken out in Srinagar with Bakshi and Sadiq addressing them. Before that, the Friday prayers too went off peacefully.[233]

On 9th August 1953, only Girdhari Lal Dogra had been administered the oath of office and secrecy along with Prime Minister Bakshi. A few days later, D.P. Dhar and Ghulam Rasool Renzu too were inducted as Deputy Ministers. The government was evidently preparing to undertake steps that would accelerate economic and administrative reforms. The Sadar-i-Riyasat informed Prime Minister Nehru on 16th August about his apprehension of the disruptive element gathering its wits after the initial shock, and for the struggle ahead. But he also commented, 'A very encouraging feature, however, is that a large number of the National Conference workers have rallied around Bakshi Sahib and are actively working to support and strengthen the new administration. The majority of [the] Government officials also seem to have adjusted themselves to the change. There was a move on the parts of hostile elements to try and get all the Muslim officials to resign, but that seems to have fallen through. There have been a few odd resignations but the administration has not been seriously affected.'[234]

But, even before the new found confidence had sunk in, the stability of the government was threatened by a crisis triggered by a development outside the State. When Prime Minister Nehru visited London to attend the Commonwealth Prime Ministers' Conference, he had also met and briefly discussed various issues, including Kashmir, with the newly appointed Prime Minister of Pakistan, Mohammad Ali Bogra. As a follow up, he made a trip to Karachi on 25th July 1953, just a few weeks before Sheikh Abdullah was dismissed. In Karachi, the people had accorded him a tumultuous welcome and he had fruitful talks with the Pakistani Prime Minister. It was decided then that the meetings between the two would continue to sort out the differences between the two countries, and that the next round would take place in New Delhi. However, the situation changed because of Sheikh Abdullah's dismissal and the resultant hue and cry in Pakistan.

Prime Minister Bogra insisted on holding the next meeting immediately because of the urgency and Nehru reluctantly advanced it. Consequently, the meeting was held on 16th August 1953. A joint communiqué was issued soon after, stating: 'Both the Prime Ministers were actuated by the firm resolve to settle these problems, as early as possible, peacefully and cooperatively to the mutual advantage of both the countries. The Kashmir issue was especially discussed at some length. It was their opinion that this should be settled in accordance with the wishes of the people of that State, with a view to promoting their wellbeing and causing the least disturbance to the life of the people of the State. The most feasible method of ascertaining the wishes of the people was by a fair and impartial plebiscite. Such a plebiscite had been proposed and agreed to some years ago. Progress, however, could not be made because of lack of agreement in regard to certain preliminary issues. The Prime Ministers agreed that these preliminary issues should be considered by them directly in order to arrive at agreements in regard to them. These agreements would have to be given effect to and the next step would be the appointment of a Plebiscite Administrator. In order to fix some kind of a provisional timetable, it was decided that the Plebiscite Administrator should be appointed by the end of April 1954. Previous to that date, the preliminary issues referred to above should be decided and action in implementation thereof should be taken.'[235]

No sooner had this news broadcast over the All India Radio than it evoked an emotional and strong reaction from Bakshi. In his letter dated 19th August 1953, Yuvraj Karan Singh informed Nehru, 'This came as a great shock to all, and Bakshi Sahib and his colleagues were stunned and bewildered. They are particularly upset that a decision so vital to the very existence of the people of the State is being taken without ascertaining the viewpoint of those who at this critical juncture accepted the responsibility of Government... The details of the proposed agreement came to Bakshi Sahib particularly as a grave blow...to him this represented complete reversal of the ideals, and position which, at considerable personal risk and sacrifice, he had fought for all these years.'[236]

Bakshi Ghulam Mohammad felt that he was not only betrayed but also undermined. He was really upset by the announcement of the deadline set for the declaration of the Plebiscite Administrator, for it put him in an awkward and risky position in relation to Sheikh Abdullah in Kashmir. To Bakshi, it amounted to negating the gains of the past few days and the futility of the dismissal of Sheikh Abdullah, as the declaration gave Abdullah a handle and strengthened his position. Bakshi was certain it would be impossible for him to stand up to Sheikh Abdullah and his supporters in the Valley. Consequently, he immediately sent his handwritten resignation to the Sadar-i-Riyasat. When informed of this development in Delhi, Prime Minister Nehru too flew into a rage at what he called 'ridiculous nonsense'. Thus the immediate challenge before the Sadar-i-Riyasat and A.P. Jain, who was still in Srinagar monitoring the developments of the State on behalf of Kidwai and the Centre, was to prevail upon Bakshi to be reasonable and pragmatic and not to rock the boat. Finally, he relented and issued a statement: 'This declaration was finalized on behalf of the Government of India with our concurrence and has our unqualified support.'[237]

By this time, new alignments had begun to take place in the world. The United States had displaced the UK as the pivot of the Western world and had thus come to view India and Pakistan from its new geopolitical point of view. Pakistan fitted in its scheme of things, and it was also more than willing to contribute to the interests of the West against the USSR and the newly awakened China. Similarly, a relationship with the US helped Pakistan in finding new and powerful friends against India. Consequently, military aid began to pour into Pakistan, making it belligerent and assertive. On the other hand, Prime Minister Nehru advanced his own logic for acting the way that he did, arguing, 'While it is perfectly true that Bakshi and others in Srinagar are in a better position to judge the situation there, there is always the danger of a limited and rather narrow viewpoint being taken and of other major facts being ignored. It is this balanced picture that is necessary; otherwise we shall get into hopeless trouble later… Recent events in Kashmir have had a very powerful reaction in other countries. This is completely against us.'[238] Nehru was, of course, referring to the extremely acerbic comments and severe criticism of India made in several Western countries. *The Daily Telegraph* said that the dismissal of Sheikh Abdullah had undone all the commendable work done by the Karachi Agreement (1953) between the Prime Ministers of India and Pakistan. *The New York Times* observed that no equitable solution of the Kashmir problem was possible without a free plebiscite. The *Daily Mirror* had gone as far as describing Nehru's attitude as 'that of an imperialistic conqueror not subject to the UN.' *The Egyptian Gazette*, edited by the British, was particularly caustic and wrote that although Nehru is proclaimed as a champion of democracy, '…he has a special brand reserved for Kashmir… labelled "incorporation in India"'.[239]

Nehru was, obviously, concerned about the image that he and India projected abroad. Luckily for India, Bakshi was prevailed upon to see the bigger picture that Nehru saw, and he relented. It, however, meant that the State administration was now under pressure to deliver on its promise of a better life, economically and administratively. As a first step, the Bakshi government made education free from primary class up to degree level. The State had continued to follow the old practice of *Mujawaza*—procuring food grains from the farmers at a fixed price. The continuance of this practice meant that the peasants were deprived of the benefits of the land reforms since their produce was procured at a cheaper rate and then they had to buy the same grains at a higher price for their consumption. Prime Minister Bakshi abolished this practice in its entirety to provide the much-needed relief to the farmers. This step alone went a long way in establishing Bakshi's authority and leadership. Emboldened by the response of the people, in September, he was confident enough to convene a convention of the National Conference, which was attended by many party leaders and cadres, except the hardliners and those who were in detention. It was a huge success and Bakshi became secure in the knowledge that a majority of the Kashmir population supported him in his effort to give up confrontational politics and work for the wellbeing of the people.

Buoyed by his success in the Valley, Bakshi received a shot in the arm when he visited Jammu where he was greeted with a grand ovation by the people. In a short span, he had earned their goodwill. In the process, the Dogras proved that they had been unfairly accused of communalism by Sheikh Abdullah and Prime Minister Nehru. Encouraged by the success, the Sadar-i-Riyasat wrote to Prime Minister Nehru, 'I feel at this stage a goodwill gesture to the people of Ladakh, who are bitter and resentful as a result of the treatment they received from the previous regime, will be of considerable value. I have discussed with Bakshi the idea of taking a Ladakhi as Deputy Minister for Ladakh Affairs, a gesture which will not only be much appreciated by the Ladakhis but will also make the task of the administration vis-à-vis Ladakh much easier and smoother.'[240]

When the Durbar moved to Jammu for the winter, on Yuvraj Karan Singh's suggestion, Bakshi ordered the flying of the Union Flag above the State Flag upon the Jammu Secretariat. This considerably mollified the Dogras. Bakshi was also adamant about not conceding ground to the Centre; he resisted all efforts to induct officers from outside the State, arguing that this would give the pro-Abdullah elements in the services a chance to indulge in avoidable propaganda. As the new Prime Minister, he held a series of conventions in the Valley to win over people, and to a large extent, he succeeded. The generous aid from the government of India also helped in improving the economic conditions; but, the administration was still a suspect. Yuvraj Karan Singh reported to Prime Minister Nehru, 'This is largely due to the fact that there is a considerable communal-minded section within the administration which has a very definite bias against India and against Bakshi.'[241] In the same letter, he also flagged the rampant corruption in the administration: 'Another factor is that there are officers who are known for their corruption. I feel it is a pity that there has as yet been no full enquiry into charges of corruption... Conventions and other political activities have their own undoubted value, but recent experience has shown that the integrity or otherwise of the administration is in the final analysis a decisive factor.' These elements were getting political and communal support too, and the Yuvraj informed Nehru, 'I may mention that a rather distressing feature of the communal activities that are still being carried on in the Valley is the fact that Sheikh Abdullah's family, his Begum, his two daughters and his eldest son Farooq, are playing a prominent role in these openly pro-Pakistan activities.'[242] Thus there was need for constant vigil against the corruption in administration and the nefarious activities of communalists who had political support from Sheikh Abdullah's disgruntled followers.

Another pleasant outcome of Sheikh Abdullah's ouster was that Yuvraj Karan Singh was given more room to play his public role. The former had expected the Yuvraj to be his constitutional captive and remain his rubber stamp. Now, for the first time, Karan Singh began to act as the Head of the State and a participant in the act of governance. He would invite secretaries of the departments in small groups over tea every week and discuss with them the nitty-gritty of administration. Thus, he not only kept himself abreast of the administrative and development problems facing the State, but also learned how they were to be sorted out. Unlike the time when Sheikh Abdullah had tried to bar him from visiting Kheer Bhawani, he was now free to visit various places unhindered by the insecurity of his Prime Minister. His visits in the Jammu region were particularly satisfying as this was the first time he could experience the love, affection and reverence that people had for the Dogra dynasty. In the process, he also got to know of the conditions in which the people lived and faced everyday challenges of existence.

The approach of the Constituent Assembly too changed after the dismissal of Sheikh Abdullah. Since he had resisted implementation of the Delhi Agreement, the functioning of the Constituent Assembly was also affected with no clarity regarding the status of the State in India. This ambiguity vanished with Bakshi announcing that the Delhi Agreement would be implemented in its entirety. The National Flag was now prominently flying and the mental barrier was lowered. On *Baisakhi* day, 13th April 1954, a major step was taken to integrate the State with the rest of the country. The custom duty on goods entering the State was abolished. This not only impacted in lowering the prices of the commodities but went a long way in removing an important psychological barrier between the two parts of the country.

The implementation of the Delhi Agreement though, was to have far-reaching political and constitutional consequences, notably relating to the State subjects or the Permanent Residents, as well as to citizenship. Prior to this, the State subjects enjoyed the rights of citizenship under the State laws and not the Constitution of India. This was the case in all the Princely States. In the rest of the country the State subjects were the 'protected subjects' of India. This was a leftover rule from the pre-independence era and was an unfinished task of merger of the State Constitution in the Constitution of India. Before the Indian Independence Act, 1947, the British-Indian Government directly ruled 'British India'; the Princely States were ruled and governed by the native princes who were subject to the 'paramountcy' of the British Crown. They were known as 'British-protected allies'. However, subject to British Paramountcy, they were not part of or governed by the laws of British India. They were not even 'British subjects', but since the foreign affairs of these States were controlled by the British-Indian Government, they were as much entitled to the protection of the British Government as the subjects of Her Majesty the Queen of England. This protection, however, was available to them only when they were abroad. In India, they were not British subjects, but State subjects or 'British-protected subjects'.

As far as citizenship was concerned, a person could acquire either the citizenship of India or the State, not both. As a result, a citizen of a State was an alien in another State or British India and vice versa. However, after the Indian Independence Act, 1947, while persons belonging to the Part 'A' States, which were earlier directly ruled by the British, became citizens of India, those belonging to the Princely States ceased to be British-protected subjects. All Princely States, barring Jammu and Kashmir, decided to merge with the Indian Union towards the end of 1949, when the Constitution of India was framed, and which was to come into effect on 26th January 1950. These States, falling in the 'B' category, also agreed that there should be a single citizenship for the whole of the country after the merger. As a consequence, their inhabitants became Indian citizens and lost their State citizenship after 26th January 1950.

However, in Jammu and Kashmir, a peculiar situation persisted. The State had decided not to merge in the Indian Union in the manner other States had, and had reserved the right to frame its own constitution. To accommodate the State, the Constitution of India made special provisions, and the citizenship laws of the country were not made applicable on the State subjects who continued to be governed by Maharaja Hari Singh's government under Notification No. 1-L/84, dated 20th April 1927, which defined a 'State Subject'. When this notification is read with Notification No. 13-L, dated 27th June 1932, the reader finds that they defined the 'Citizenship Laws' of the State. These laws had been drafted in response to the widespread presence of outsiders, mostly Punjabis, not only in government jobs but also trade, commerce and other businesses. Thus, to protect the less resourceful permanent inhabitants of the State from the onslaught of more resourceful outsiders, these laws were framed.

The relationship of the State with that of India was governed by Article 370 and its proviso. Accordingly, the President of India, in concurrence with the government of Jammu and Kashmir, issued 'The Constitution (Application to Jammu and Kashmir) Order, 1950' on 26th January 1950. By this, 'Entry 17 of the Union List, which empowers the Union Parliament on matters of "citizenship naturalization and aliens", was modified to read "naturalization and aliens" in its application to Jammu and Kashmir State. The Union Parliament had no power to make laws for the State on citizenship; the omission of "citizenship" from this entry to its application to Jammu and Kashmir, in fact, meant that in the State the old State Citizenship law prevailed. Thus, the people of Jammu and Kashmir State were "protected subjects" in the rest of India and not "Indian Citizens", even after India became Republic in 1950.'[243]

This incongruity was one of the subjects under discussion when the Delhi Agreement was concluded in 1952. It was agreed that even though there was need to protect the rights of the permanent residents, there was no reason to deny the Indian citizenship to the people of the State. The Government of India accepted the view that the State Legislature should retain the power to define and regulate the rights and privileges of the permanent residents, particularly regarding acquisition of immovable property, appointments to service in the State, etc. However, because of the ambiguous attitude of Sheikh Abdullah, the Agreement had remained in limbo. As a result, the citizenship and residency matters continued to be governed by the Notifications of 1927 and 1932. The citizens of the State continued to be 'protected citizens' of India outside the State, and the Indian citizens, aliens in the State till 1954 when the Constituent Assembly of Jammu and Kashmir ratified the accession to India. After prolonged discussions with Prime Minister Bakshi and his government, the government of India and the State finally agreed that the permanent residents could have special rights but they were to have common Indian citizenship. However, to avoid confusion, the term 'State Subject' was to be replaced by 'Permanent Resident'.

Once again, using the proviso of Article 370, the President of India, in consultation with the Government of the State, issued the 'Constitution (Application to Jammu and Kashmir) Order, 1954' on 14th May 1954, to come in force from the same date. By section

2(3) of the Order, Part III of the Constitution of India, dealing with Citizenship, was made applicable to the State. With this, the people of the State were to be regarded as citizens of India. However, the State Legislature retained the 'power to make special provisions for the "permanent residents"...[and] it was deemed necessary that some provisions be made in the Constitution [of India] to cover that case. Accordingly, Article 35-A was inserted by Section 2(4) of the Order, 1954.'[244] The constitutional application bestowed rights of a citizen on all the residents of the State, but it did not define the term 'Permanent Residents' of the State. Consequently, those who had been declared permanent residents earlier under the old laws, remained to be so under the existing laws of the State or any other future law that would be enacted by the State Legislature. Such laws 'may either confer special rights and privileges or impose restrictions upon the "permanent residents" with respect to any or all the matters enumerated in sub-section (b)'[245] of Article 35-A. Such legislation was deemed to be fit, notwithstanding the fact that it was inconsistent with the fundamental rights guaranteed by the Constitution, and was discriminatory in favour of 'permanent residents'. But looking at the fact that historically the State had been exploited by its well-to-do neighbours, it was necessary that special provisions were made to enable its residents to deal with the handicap they suffered in relation to other Indian citizens. Accordingly, the State Legislature inserted Section 5A to 5F in the Constitution Act, 1939, regarding the 'permanent residents' in 1954. Thus the 'permanent residents' continued to have the same privileges as before according to the old laws of the State, even when the State Legislature had the authority to modify the definition.

The year also saw a very important visit by Dr Rajendra Prasad, the President of India. The humble and self-effacing figure of the President created a very positive impression on the minds of the people. During this visit, he also inaugurated the Jammu and Kashmir War Memorial Hall in the Jammu Cantonment area. It ensured that the glorious history of the State Forces would never be forgotten even if at that point in time uncertainty hung over the fate of the Forces. Most of the State Forces in the country were disbanded, and in those States, where they were found valuable, they were inducted into the Indian Army after proper scrutiny, with many failing to make the grade. This led to considerable uncertainty and resentment. Earlier, Sheikh Abdullah had prevailed upon the Centre to disband about 3,000 State Forces soldiers. That had caused great economic distress among those whose sole support for livelihood was military service. Unlike many other State Forces, they were not part of a ceremonial force. These soldiers had a long record of serving in the most hostile terrain of the world to defend the borders, and they did it with minimum fuss and equipment. The exploits of the past battalions in conquering Ladakh and incorporating the Gilgit-Baltistan region into the State of Jammu and Kashmir were legendary and acknowledged by military historians.

Sheikh Abdullah, however, had adopted a hostile attitude towards the State Forces ever since he realized that the control of these Forces could not be handed over to him. He had made periodic attempts to either disband it in its entirety or secure its control. Though he never acknowledged it, the fate of these soldiers was a major issue and had added up to the movement against his rule. On the other hand, Yuvraj Karan Singh, in view of the record of these battalions, not only in the past but during the war with Pakistan, strongly advocated total integration of these soldiers in the Indian Army without scrutiny. This he did patiently and diligently by initially ensuring that no more battalions were disbanded and small matters were addressed. Thus, on 1st April 1953, he wrote to Prime Minister Nehru: 'In view of the peculiar political and strategic significance of the areas to which these men belong, it will be a great appreciation of their work and evoke a loyal response if the units and their personnel are maintained intact and these men, whose record of service has earned them fame and respect in various theatres and from reputed Commanders, are exempted from the process of screening. Their unique record of service over the last six years in which they have worked shoulder to shoulder in the defence of the nation as an integral part of the Indian Army singles them out for special treatment. Their case does not deserve to be treated on the analogy of other State troops.'[246]

While writing this letter, Yuvraj Karan Singh was also aware of the efforts made to the contrary, and, therefore, continued in the same letter: 'There will, I feel, be considerable opposition to their absorption and seniority in the cadres but it will be a pity if such considerations were allowed to create distress and dismay in the hearts of thousands of men and their dependents to whom loyalty to India is dearer than life.' The consistent requests and urgings of Yuvraj Karan Singh had not immediately yielded the desired results but they did have an impact. The inauguration of Jammu and Kashmir State Forces War Memorial in Jammu by the President and Supreme Commander-in-Chief of the Indian Army, Dr Rajendra Prasad, therefore, had a very positive impact not only on the grizzled and decorated ex-soldiers but also on those who were serving and living in a period of uncertainty about their future.

The integration of the State Forces in the Indian Army was still a distant hope. The technical obstacle of integrating them was removed in October 1956 when the State Constituent Assembly ratified the new Constitution, as well as the accession of the State to India. With this, the weight of moral obligation to make the reference of integration to the people of the State had been lifted. The normal procedure was of transferring certain selected units to the Indian Army for their absorption in the respective corps and services, while the rest were disbanded. Thus the integrated units lost their individual identity and assumed that of the Indian Army. The State Forces commissioned officers were put through screening tests and only the successful were given regular commissions in the Indian Army. The Jammu and Kashmir State Forces were subjected to a vicious onslaught by Sheikh Abdullah and only six Infantry battalions had survived the process to disband in 1951. Among the notable personalities, only Yuvraj Karan Singh consistently advocated the absorption of these battalions without screening. He argued that these soldiers had proved their mettle not only during the Second World War but also during the Pakistani invasion. But still another bloody battle was needed to reaffirm their courage, tenacity and soldierly qualities for the authorities to take action.

In March 1956, Fateh Shibji, the 4th Battalion—the same unit that had two Companies of Hindus and two of Muslims before 1947, and was tasked the defence of the Kohala bridge at Domel against any invasion from the Pakistan side, and had been betrayed by its Muslim soldiers—was in Ferozepur for training purposes. This battalion had carried the burden of guilt of having failed to defend the State borders, but fate ordained another chance to redeem itself and avenge the betrayed and fallen comrades of the Kohala debacle. While in Ferozepur, the 4th Battalion was ordered to move to Hussainiwala Headworks on river Sutlej for its protection. The Radcliffe Commission had, in its wisdom, allotted the Headworks, the area around it and the bund on the banks of the river to India, though they fell on the Pakistani side. Pakistan had challenged this allotment, particularly the bund since its control and command over the Pakistani side. Pending settlement, it was agreed that no troops would be located around the bund though its repair and maintenance would be India's responsibility.

In 1955, floods had ravaged the area and the bund required extensive repair work by the Indian engineers. But Pakistan objected to the lifting of earth from the 'Bela' area adjacent to the bund and resorted to military force. As the dispute escalated, the 4th Battalion of Jammu and Kashmir was ordered to take over the duty of protecting the Indian engineers. The battalion, under the command of Lieutenant Colonel Vakil Singh, moved in on 8th March 1956. The very next day, two Companies of the battalion, under Captains Ajit Singh and Hoshnak Singh respectively, occupied the 'Bela' area near the bund on the far side of the river to take the Pakistanis by surprise. 'Tactically it would have been advisable to occupy the Bund itself but the Battalion had strict instructions not to do so in view of the earlier agreement between the two Governments of keeping the Bund free of troops. For the same reason when [the] "D" and "A" Companies under Major Mahel Singh and Major Rashpal Singh respectively were pushed out to the far bank, they also took up positions in the low-lying areas between the bank of the river and the perimeter Bund to the left of the Headworks. Both these localities of the Battalion could not support each other mutually due to the lie of the ground and the intervening Headworks.'[247]

In 1947, the Commandant of the 4th Battalion played by the rules of the 'Paltan' loyalty and paid the price with his life; in the process he also suffered the odium of failure to defend the borders.

Now on the border,. the battalion again played by the rule book and once again treachery struck when on 18th March 1956, the Pakistani troops occupied the vantage point of the bund. After installing a light machine gun at that commanding place, they made an attempt to converge on the Indian positions in the Bela area. The Indians were awkwardly placed compared to the Pakistanis, with the bund in front and the fast flowing river behind. Tactically out-manoeuvred, the 4th Battalion was further hamstrung by the orders not to be the first to open fire. Major Brahma Singh describes the situation thus: 'As a result, the Pakistanis closed in without any hitch or hindrance to a distance from where they could hurl taunts and abuse on our troops. Ultimately taking the silence of the Jammu & Kashmir troops as a sign of weakness they went in for the assault. The Fateh Shibs were, on the other hand, waiting for a fight to be able to wreak revenge for what they had suffered at Domel in 1947. Within fifteen minutes of the bitter hand-to-hand fighting that followed the Pakistanis found things too hot and disengaging themselves made a hasty and somewhat undignified retreat, leaving behind eight dead bodies.'[248]

Not guilty of being the first to open fire, the 4th Battalion was now free to launch an offensive of its own in order to improve its tactical position. But this was not possible till the light machine gun of the enemy, situated on the bund, could be captured or neutralized. 'Consequently L/Nk Sunder Singh of [the] "C" Company, who was known for his bravery and courage, was selected to destroy the machine gun nest and pave the way for the attack on the Bund. Sunder Singh lived up to the trust reposed in him and in an astounding feat of individual stalking over the bullet swept area, he was not only able to silence the gun by killing all the crew with hand grenades, but was also able to pull it out of its nest and carry it back to his position, along with two bren magazine boxes containing fourteen bren-gun magazines... The Pakistanis launched a fierce counterattack but this was beaten back by the Fateh Shibs with equal ferocity, inflicting innumerable casualties on the attackers who fled in great disorder. Many Pakistani soldiers, including those not directly involved in this fighting, were burnt to death when the elephant grass on their side caught fire as a result of firing... The fighting at Hussaniwala lasted nearly 14 hours and the Pakistanis are estimated to have suffered about 500 casualties...over 90 dead bodies which lay near our forward positions were handed over to Pakistan after the cease-fire. Some revenge this! The price that the Battalion had to pay for this was 4 killed.'[249]

This heroic feat finally demolished the resistance to integrate the State Forces. The handsome praise lavished on the State Forces by General K.S. Thimayya, who had witnessed this performance as General Officer Commanding the 19 Indian Infantry Division, was at the helm of affairs as Chief of Army Staff, when the final integration took place. Thus the State Forces had the unique distinction of being integrated in the Indian Army without any scrutiny and screening. The officers and men, all merged seamlessly. This created immense goodwill in Jammu as most of the soldiers belonged from there. Apart from the honour that was involved, the fate of these soldiers affected the lives of thousands of their dependents.

Earlier, under the leadership of Bakshi Ghulam Mohammad, the process of the State's political and administrative integration was stepped up. 'On May 14, 1954 the President promulgated an order extending various articles of the Indian Constitution to the State as requested by the state government.'[250] Within the State, with the induction of Kushak Bakula in the Council of Ministers, the much-neglected Ladakh region was given representation, thus making them feel greatly integrated to the fate of the State. The same year, the Yuvraj struck a commercial deal with hotelier M.S. Oberoi to give the State its first five-star hotel and pioneer the process of converting large palaces as hotels in the country.

In his youthful exuberance, Yuvraj Karan Singh had, on an earlier occasion, toyed with the idea of donating the Gulab Mahal, which commanded the banks of Dal Lake, for housing the newly established Jammu and Kashmir University. However, Maharaja Hari Singh had rejected this proposal because he felt that it would be construed in public perception as another step by Sheikh Abdullah to strip the Dogra dynasty of power to manage its own property. Embarrassed, the Yuvraj donated his own orchard on the other side of Dal Lake to the University campus. Now, after he dismissed Sheikh Abdullah, the Maharaja too softened and gave the Yuvraj the liberty to manage properties the way he desired. Therefore, on 5th October 1953, he once again mentioned putting Gulab Mahal to good use in his letter to Prime Minister Nehru: 'As you know, I have a large palace here in Srinagar called Gulab Mahal, which is at present lying unused… I feel it would be a good thing if it could be put to some national use. Considering that the Government of India have so many responsibilities to discharge in the State, I feel this property might be of real utility to the Central Government for use of a National Laboratory, [or] a first rate government-run hotel… If so I would be very happy to place the use of this property at the disposal of the Government of India… I have also for some time been considering donating it to the University of Jammu and Kashmir, but have not done so yet for several reasons… I was a little hesitant because Gulab Mahal lies right in the middle of my private residential property, and a university being an expanding institution it is likely to lead to some friction and unpleasantness in future to both the donor and the donee, which would be most unfortunate.'[251]

Nehru, however, ruled out using the Mahal for an office of the Government of India in Srinagar as also the idea of a National Laboratory, which was not planned in the near future. He toyed with the idea of a State-run hotel and also suggested the names of the Tatas and the Oberois, who had considerable experience in running five-star hotels. The maintenance of the Mahal was an enormous challenge, making it imperative to either find a way of putting it to good use or spending substantial amounts of money for its repair and upkeep. It was then that Yuvraj Karan Singh struck a deal with the Oberois for converting it into a five-star hotel and making the Valley an attraction for upscale tourists from all over the world.

The Government of India too made every effort to have its ministries hold seminars in Srinagar so that both got acquainted with each other more intimately. Srinagar, indeed, was well on its way to becoming the hub of activity. This also gave Bakshi Ghulam Mohammad the opportunity to become the life and soul of all functions because of his increasing fame as a host. His '*goshtaba*'[252] hospitality was to soon assume legendary proportions with tales of his goading the unsuspecting vegetarian guest to partake a portion of '*goshtaba*'! Accounts of such encounters with guests became part of the political and social gossip everywhere.

In 1954, Yuvraj Karan Singh made a strong plea for constructing the Leh-Manali road via the Rohtang Pass so as to link it with the mainland. He pleaded that Ladakh had been part of the Jammu and Kashmir State for more than a century and during the past seven years it had been part of India. The people there had a great affection for India and were loyal to it, but in view of the developments in Tibet, it was important that these ties were strengthened. 'Uptil now the authorities in Tibet have not shown too much interest in Ladakh, but there is no guarantee that this attitude will continue indefinitely, and after consolidation in Tibet it will be too optimistic to believe that Ladakh will escape an undue share of attention. Our information, meagre as it is, shows that the Chinese are fast completing the road linking Lhasa with Peking thousands of miles away, and are also engaged in constructing a network of roads within Tibet.'[253]

The Prime Minister was attracted to the proposal but expressed constraints in taking it up. However, he promised to look into the matter further. Soon after this exchange of letters, the survey of the Leh-Manali road was taken up in right earnest but as later events proved, it was too late to be of any help during the Indo-Sino conflict.

The same year also saw the beginning of the ambitious digging of a tunnel through the Banihal Pass to give access to and from the Valley, even when snow had fallen. It would not only cut the distance between Jammu and Srinagar but also avoid the difficult climb to the top of the Pass. Another important decision taken during that year was extending the rail line from Pathankot to Madhopur so that it could ultimately reach Jammu. After the partition of Punjab, the State had lost its rail link with the rest of the country since the earlier link was from Sialkot to Jammu. Thus, the decision to link the State with the rest of the country was significant though this too took a long time to materialize.

Politically, a confident Bakshi began to emerge. Though Sheikh Abdullah was in detention, his confidant Mirza Afzal Beg and a few others were released, and they had the freedom to restart political activity in the Valley. They were mainly active in Srinagar and Anantnag—the home town of Beg, which became the hub of the newly formed Plebiscite Front. It also managed to secure the support of eleven members of the Constituent Assembly but overall, Bakshi not only retained a comfortable majority in the Assembly but also remained in control of the situation.

However, there was one problem that has remained intractable even today. Partition and the subsequent events brought in its train a large number of refugees from erstwhile west Punjab that had become part of Pakistan, and the Pakistan-occupied areas of Jammu and Kashmir. While those from west Punjab were given full compensation and also made part of the rehabilitation programme, those belonging to the Pakistan-occupied part of the State were denied on the ground that treating them as refugees would weaken India's case in the dispute as that would mean acceptance of the Pakistan-occupied part of the State as an integral part of Pakistan. Thus, for no fault of theirs, the PoJK refugees were discriminated and were reduced to an inferior status. Among these refugees, there were about 10,000 families of Harijans, who had come from Sialkot to avoid massacre. Although the refugees from the Pakistan-occupied region of Jammu and Kashmir were still State subjects and hence entitled to all the privileges that were granted to other State subjects, since they were from Sialkot, they had to suffer the ignominy of not being allowed to avail even those facilities. With democracy having been put on the rails, both these groups of refugees had found their voice and soon an agitation was launched. The Sadar-i-Riyasat made numerous efforts to intercede on their behalf and repeatedly wrote about the problem to the Government of India; but his best efforts were futile. The subject was so mired in the legal-cum-bureaucratic rigidity that he could not cut through it to do full justice to them.

However, the year 1955 turned out to be eventful for the State and India. After the visit of the Soviet leaders Nikita Khrushchev and Bulganin, the Secretary General of the Communist Party of USSR and the Head of the State respectively, new equations emerged at the international level and India found a steady and reliable friend in the Soviet Union. Earlier in the year, Prime Minister Nehru visited USSR and thus the bonds of an enduring friendship were tied. When Yuvraj Karan Singh read in a newspaper about the Prime Minister's visit, he wrote a letter to Nehru wondering if he could also be included in the official party accompanying him. But Nehru knew it was not feasible at that stage and replied, 'I do not think it will be feasible or desirable for you to go with me. I am going in response to a special invitation. I take a small staff with me to do my work. Otherwise, it will not be proper for me to add any important person to my party. Also, your going would have a certain political significance which might not be good for Kashmir at present.'

Yuvraj Karan Singh thus could not go on that trip to USSR because of Kashmir's disputed status and fear of causing embarrassment to the hosts. However, later that year, when the Soviet leaders came to India, Yuvraj Karan Singh impulsively invited them to Kashmir and they surprised everyone by accepting the invitation. The visit turned out to be a milestone. Relations between India and the Soviet Union had thawed after the death of Joseph Stalin and under Khrushchev. But strategically, the Soviet Union was being isolated, and with the United States taking the lead against communism, an alliance had developed to encircle the Soviets. Pakistan had seized this opportunity to become a party to one such treaty and alliance that gave it the support of the powerful West and also a free supply of the latest weapons. As a result, India found itself isolated and without the support of any major country. On the other hand, to counter the Western alliance, the Soviets too needed friends if not active alliance partners. India fitted the bill perfectly. India admired the free society of the West but also aspired for accelerated socio-economic transformation, and in this it found the Soviet planning, a useful tool. But pushed on the margins because of the geostrategic advantage of Pakistan, it welcomed the opportunity to come closer to the Soviet Union. Prime Minister Nehru's visit along with his daughter Indira Gandhi on an invitation to the USSR was hugely successful. The warmth thus generated had naturally led to inviting the Soviet leaders, and they came calling in November 1955. The wheels had turned. Not too long ago Stalin had derisively described Nehru as the 'running dog of Western imperialism'; now he was being wooed as a friend by his successors.

When the two Soviet leaders arrived in Delhi, the Yuvraj and the Yuvrani happened to be there, and when this came to Nehru's notice, he invited both for a dinner hosted in honour of the guests. 'In course of our conversation, I suggested that Khrushchev should pay a visit to Kashmir, and he turned to Jawaharlal with a smile.'[254] The matter rested there but no sooner had the Yuvraj returned to Jammu than he received a letter from the Prime Minister informing him that his suggestion to the Soviet leaders to visit Kashmir was accepted by them and they left the details of the date and schedule of the visit to him. They intended to spend two nights and the greater part of two days there, with one clear day set aside for Srinagar. The Yuvraj was also asked to immediately rush to Srinagar and be at hand for arrangements. He was specifically instructed to ensure that the rich Kashmiri cuisine did not upset the guests.

It was a long trip away from home, that included Burma (Myanmar), for the Soviet leaders and the schedule was packed and according to the understanding of Prime Minister Nehru they were on the verge of collapse; and yet they had agreed to a visit to Kashmir. It was obvious that it assumed diplomatic significance with international ramifications. It was all the more reason for the hosts to ensure that the guests did not feel burdened or too exhausted. Both the leaders were received with co-equal protocol and during the ride to the city from the airport, Khrushchev, on finding the Sadar-i-Riyasat squeezed into the back seat of the Chevrolet between the two big Russians, gave a glimpse of his humour and he recalled his earlier experience in Mysore, where they had to travel with the Maharaja of Mysore, the Rajpramukh, a person of some bulk and girth.

They stayed in the famed Gulab Mahal, already converted into the Oberoi Palace Hotel. The next day they attended a lunch hosted by the Yuvraj and the Yuvrani at Karan Mahal. They had brought with them ceramic figures of the King and Queen of Sea and when Yuvraj Karan Singh impishly commented that he thought the communists did not approve of kings and queens, Khrushchev once again demonstrated his witty and humorous side by laughing 'uproariously' and saying 'they were all right as long as they were ceramics!'[255]

The civic reception in the evening hosted at the Rajgadh Palace, under the *chinars* and on the banks of Jhelum, marked the beginning of an association that helped India through thick and thin. It was there that Khrushchev delivered 'the famous speech when, for the first time, the Soviet Union came out openly in support of Jammu and Kashmir being an integral part of India. Referring to the proximity of the Soviet Union he said, "If you are ever in difficulty all you have to do is to climb on top of those mountains and shout, and we will come to your aid."' This was no empty rhetoric as the sentiments were repeated the next day while responding to the farewell speech of the Sadar-i-Riyasat at the airport. India had found a powerful ally in a world that seemed to be ranging against it. Yuvraj Karan Singh, the Sadar-i-Riyasat, was a deeply contented young man. He noted with satisfaction in his letter to the Prime Minister after the conclusion of the visit: 'The Russians are the first great power to have definitely and clearly gone on record as accepting the accession of Kashmir to India as final'.[256] He was also pleased to have made a contribution during the epoch-making visit of the Soviet leaders.

16

The Clash of the Titans

Sheikh Abdullah's stature, his following and his ability to sway the masses was never in doubt; in erudition and ability to recite appropriate verses from the Holy Koran, there was no one in the Valley to match him. In contrast, Bakshi Ghulam Mohammad was a plebeian, but he had his fingers on the human pulse and events. He was an organizer of proven worth, even if lacking the intellectual flight of a political romantic. Leaders in Delhi, the Director of the Intelligence Bureau and the Sadar-i-Riyasat, all believed in his sincerity towards India. But he was not flattered by the attention and adulation, and kept his feet firmly planted on the earth. He recognized that his best chance at keeping the pro-Abdullah camp in the narrow confines of public perception depended on his ability to convince the people of his functioning within the framework of the Delhi Agreement. Anything less would give the impression of a sellout.

Being shrewd and a smart operator, he soon realized that unless he pitched himself against Sheikh Abdullah, he would never be able to put the issue of his legitimacy beyond debate. Thus, 1956 began with him toying with the idea of releasing the Sheikh from detention. Apparently, Bakshi was confident of dealing with the consequences if Sheikh Abdullah rallied people and Pakistan seized the opportunity to fan communal trouble. Yuvraj Karan Singh had reservations about the move and noted them in his long letter to Prime Minister Nehru on 11th January 1956: 'Despite all that has been done we cannot say that the political problem in the Valley has been solved. The reasons for this are primarily communal... In the light of the position now obtaining, the probable repercussions of the release of Sheikh Abdullah require careful consideration... There is little doubt that upon his emergence from detention, he will immediately become the rallying point for all the disruptionist forces and disgruntled factions. There emerges the distinct possibility of widespread lawlessness and violent clashes...[and] may expose us to severe criticism and distorted allegations in the sphere not only of local but wider public opinion.'[257]

The Yuvraj went on to warn Prime Minister Nehru of a more serious danger if a released Sheikh Abdullah was able to rally or browbeat the support of a majority of the members of the Constituent Assembly of which he too was a member. The Assembly was still in progress and was still to ratify the accession and draft a Constitution—tasks that it had set for itself. In that situation, the consequences would be disastrous for India. On the other hand, Bakshi recognized the demon lurking in the background, but probably also knew that sooner or later he had to face it. He was confident that Sheikh Abdullah would not succeed in weaning away a decent number of members of the Assembly. The Yuvraj did not share his optimism but at the end of the day, it had to be his decision. However, the Yuvraj brought to notice other factors, including the risk of the administrative services forming a nexus with the communalists to sabotage the government. He reiterated that 'I support the widely-held view that the proper time to release him...would be only after it is found possible to declare that the Kashmir dispute is finally closed, or at the very least until the State Constitution has been completely enacted and the Constituent Assembly dissolved... Until then, I venture to submit, releasing him would be taking formidable risk... Finally, I may submit that we cannot ignore the existence of powerful forces who would be eager to support financially and otherwise any disruptive movement within the State which would shatter its present stable and progressive association as an integral part of India.'[258]

No sooner did the letter reach Prime Minister Nehru than he explained to the Yuvraj in detail the reasons why delaying the release could prove counterproductive. He began on a personal note by stating, 'So far as I am concerned, my whole mind rebels against the long detention of any person without trial. I have objected to it so often in the past that naturally I do not like it. But I realize that sometimes circumstances compel one to take action which is normally undesirable. In the balance, therefore, I left it to the judgment of the Jammu and Kashmir Government to decide what they should do in the matter.'[259] Nehru also expressed disagreement with the view that Sheikh Abdullah be detained till the time the Kashmir issue was finally closed. On the contrary, he argued that as long as Sheikh Abdullah was in prison the Kashmir dispute would not be finally closed. 'It is only when he has been released and we have faced the consequences of the release and survived them, that it will be possible for the situation to develop towards a final end… There are the risks which you have mentioned. The question is whether the risks grow less or more by delay… I realize fully the risks involved. But one does not solve a problem or really avoid risks by running away from them… I would like to add that the visit of Soviet leaders to Kashmir and its effect on the internal and external situation, which has been all to the good and has influenced many people in the right direction, is a factor to be considered. The conditions in Pakistan and in "Azad Kashmir" are bad. Sheikh Abdullah may behave very foolishly but the effect of his behaviour is likely to be less now and can be dealt more easily.'[260]

During this period, subversive elements had made inroads into the political and administrative system. Bakshi, however, took calculated risks to handle them. In December 1954, he released Ghulam Mohammad Karra, the once-upon-a-time number two in the National Conference, from detention. He did so in the hope of winning him over but soon realized that a person who had at one point of time challenged the leadership of Sheikh Abdullah within the party would not accept a number two or inferior position under him. Moreover, by this time he was too deeply involved with his masters in Pakistan to accept the integration of the State with India. Intelligence reports suggested that soon after his release, he got in touch with Pakistan who supported and built him up for the next two years. But it soon dawned that during this period the world had moved on and he was rendered ineffective and therefore of no use to Pakistan. This is best explained by B.N. Mullik: 'Karra's eclipse was also partly due to the earlier release in November 1954, of Mirza Afzal Beg. This astute politician, who influenced the Sheikh to take a progressively strong anti-Indian attitude, had been suspected of holding strong pro-Pakistani leanings…Beg's aim was suspected to be [the] ultimate accession to Pakistan…'[261] Pakistan found him more relevant and useful to its designs and hence Karra was soon dropped from its scheme of things. Pakistan was, indeed, desperate to fan trouble in the Valley by supporting any group or individual which could destabilize the Bakshi government. But wily as he was, Bakshi remained a step ahead of them and managed most of the threats.

In 1956, a major shakeup took place in the country, with the Government of India announcing the acceptance of the recommendations of the States Reorganization Commission Report on 16th January 1956. Apart from redrawing the boundaries of the States, it was decided that the distinction between the Part 'A' and Part 'B' States should be removed. Significantly, it also got rid of the Rajpramukhs and replaced them with Governors, as in other states. In a republic, this was bound to happen. Prime Minister Nehru had forecast it to convince Yuvraj Karan Singh to accept being elected Sadar-i-Riyasat of the State, rather than insist on remaining a hereditary Head of the State. Therefore, with the new development, the Yuvraj felt vindicated. According to him, the Report failed to make efforts towards the greater integration of the State even as it was recommending steps for the States' increased cooperation. Yuvraj reacted to the Report by pointing out in his letter to the Prime Minister of 19th January 1956: 'It appears that Jammu and Kashmir was considered by the Commission to be outside their terms of reference, for they have made no recommendations for the State.' He conceded that because of the peculiar circumstances of the State, he knew that no territorial adjustments, as had been the case with many other states, could be made. But he pointed out that there were other issues, like the inclusion of the State in the North Zone, when the idea of Zonal Councils was mooted in the Report. 'The Zonal Councils as at present envisaged are advisory and deliberative bodies, and it is difficult to see why Kashmir should be left out of them. Its exclusion will deprive the State of the benefits of coordination with adjoining States forming the Northern Zone, with which we have many matters of common concern. What is more, the omission will be exploited and misinterpreted by interested parties, while inclusion will act as a stabilizing factor', he added.[262]

Yuvraj Karan Singh also raised the question of the linguistic minorities in the State—Dogras and the Ladakhis. He felt that it was an important issue that ought not to have been overlooked on the pretext that the recommendations of the Report did not pertain to these minorities. He noted that with the acceptance of the Report the disparity between the other Part 'A' and 'B' States had been removed, but since Jammu and Kashmir was governed by the Temporary Provision of Article 370, it continued to enjoy a separate status. While recognizing the compulsion to do so, he advocated steps that vested in the President of India, the authority to nominate the Head of the State instead of rubber-stamping the recommendation of the State Legislative Assembly as was the present provision. He also realized that this change could only be effected after a constitutional amendment, but argued that since this was the time when the country had already braced itself for large-scale changes, no delay should be made in this regard.

The same year, the Yuvraj and the Yuvrani, finally made their first visit to Europe and England. Soon after his return, the three-kilometres-long tunnel through the Banihal mountains was inaugurated, greatly increasing the connectivity of the Valley with the rest of the country. The UN Security Council continued to debate the Kashmir dispute and pass resolutions, reaffirming the earlier resolutions, and the Western world continued to support those resolutions. However, the visit of Soviet leaders to Kashmir in 1955 had changed the equations, as the Soviet Union steadfastly vetoed all of them. This stalemate was broken by the State itself when it moved towards adopting its Constitution according to the will of the people as expressed by its elected representatives. Towards the end of the year, the Constituent Assembly moved towards finalizing the Draft of the State Constitution.

On 3rd February 1954, Mir Qasim sought the permission of the

President of the Constituent Assembly, G.M. Sadiq, to present the report of the Basic Principles Committee before the House. Among other things, the Committee recommended defining the sphere of the Union's jurisdiction, modifications and necessary amendments, wherever necessary. However, Abdul Ghani Goni, a close follower of Sheikh Abdullah and one of the eleven who had mobilized themselves under the leadership of Mirza Afzal Beg, submitted a dissenting note:

> (1) I suggest that the right of secession should be provided. For this purpose the following sentence should be added at the end of the third paragraph of the report—"The State shall retain the right to secede from the Union of India."
>
> (2) I object to the application of the jurisdiction of the Supreme Court of India over the State, and suggest that the Judicial Board of the State should function as the highest court of the State...[263]

This, however, was rejected by the Assembly. On 15th February 1954, the Constituent Assembly gave its concurrence to the application of the Constitution of India in the manner indicated in the annexure of the Report.[264] There were other amendments that followed and then on 17th November 1956, Mir Qasim moved to the resolution that the Constituent Assembly be dissolved from 26th January 1957:

> Whereas the Constituent Assembly came into being for framing the constitution of the State;
>
> And whereas the Constituent Assembly has enacted and adopted the Constitution for the State;
>
> Now therefore, the Assembly resolves that it shall stand dissolved on 26th day of January, 1957, which is the date of the commencement of the Constitution.[265]

The Constituent Assembly met on night of 25th January 1957 for its concluding session and adopted the new Constitution. Mir Qasim aptly summed up the process of constitution making in his speech and focused on the issue of accession. He said: 'At the time when the National Conference decided to set up a Constituent Assembly the Government of India also stated that the proposed Assembly was to end the autocratic rule and set up a democratic regime in

Kashmir and besides this it will also ratify the accession of the State to India already entered into through the instrument of accession... The late Mr Gopala Swami Ayangar [*sic*] said in this connection that the Assembly was free if it chose to continue or not to continue the accession and could decide for Kashmir to secede from the Union... In view of the fact that this Assembly had the right not to confirm the accession, I wonder how one can have the face to say that this Assembly was incompetent to do the other. If it was competent to do one thing it was also competent to do the other. These things were manifest in our election manifesto.'[266]

The Constituent Assembly made an unequivocal affirmation of the State's accession to India and declared it to be an integral part of India. It also rendered the reference of the dispute to the UN Security Council as superfluous. The people had expressed their will, even if the UN Security Council had failed to persuade Pakistan to withdraw its army from the occupied part of the State so that conditions for holding a plebiscite could be created. A few days later, the Assembly passed the vote-on-account budget and other legislations including the Representation of People's Act that paved the way for dissolving the Constituent Assembly and holding elections for a new Legislative Assembly. But, the concluding remarks of Mir Qasim once again reiterated the insistence of the leaders from the Valley on manufacturing facts that were legally and constitutionally untenable. Following the example of Sheikh Abdullah, his successors in the government also tried to appropriate the right that had been vested in the Maharaja of the State on issues of accession. Mir Qasim too suffered from selective amnesia when he claimed credit for the promise of convening a Constituent Assembly and ignored the Proclamation of 5th March 1948 that had set before the new government the task of holding elections for the Assembly that was to frame a new Constitution. Contrary to his claim, no mention had been made of ending the 'autocratic' rule as the mandate of the Constituent Assembly. Democracy and constitutional monarchy were not considered mutually antagonistic. The fact was that these goals were injected in the system only when Sheikh Abdullah realized the power he had come to hold over Delhi and his appetite for vendetta had increased. The impulse to alter the facts and interpret them differently was most marked in Sheikh Abdullah, as demonstrated by him repeatedly during the negotiations with Delhi regarding the position of the Maharaja to the status of the State within the Union. The likes of Mir Qasim had inherited these traits after long years in the National Conference.

With or without Sheikh Abdullah, the leaders from the Valley were allowed to interpret history in a manner that suited their immediate needs. Delhi thought that with all the blemishes it suited its purpose of demonstrating to the world that an Assembly chosen for a purpose had spoken its mind in favour of India and there the matter ought to rest. Bakshi could now focus on the necessity to consolidate the political gains and work for the socio-economic development of the State. Politically, he had become more secure and confident enough to toy with the idea of releasing Sheikh Abdullah from detention. His immediate challenge, with the Constituent Assembly dissolved, was to win a mandate of the people on his own for the next Assembly. This he duly did in March 1957, but unfortunately, he could not overcome the temptation of using the same tactics in the Valley that were used by the National Conference in 1952 under the leadership of Sheikh Abdullah.

Of the forty-three seats, thirty-three went uncontested to the National Conference. The nomination papers of several candidates were rejected on flimsy grounds thereby silencing the voices of opponents and amputating the soul of democracy. The surprise, however, came from Jammu where the Praja Parishad had a sound following and was expected to win a number of seats. The Parishad could win only five seats, with the rest going to the National Conference. The message was clear. Earlier, the people of Jammu had rallied en masse behind the Praja Parishad when it was time to resist the politics of vendetta unleashed by Sheikh Abdullah. But now with the arch enemy gone and replaced by someone who was seen to be interested in the improvement of their daily lives, they had shaken off the tag of 'reactionaries' and 'communalists' and voted for the National Conference.

It was time for everyone to move forward, and the Government of Jammu and Kashmir, probably on the promptings of Prime Minister Nehru, decided to release Sheikh Abdullah on 8th January

1958. By then, everything had changed. The Constituent Assembly, consisting of handpicked men by Sheikh Abdullah, had decided on the issues that he had set before the Assembly. The Dogra dynasty stood abolished as he had wanted; the land reforms had been given legitimacy without providing for compensation; and the accession to India ratified as he had wanted and expressed in his opening address.

As long as he remained in office, Sheikh Abdullah had never shown any warmth to the idea of plebiscite, which was desired by the United Nations Security Council. In his arrogance and the fresh glow of his relationship with the Indian leadership that supported him, he had found the suggestion of plebiscite as an affront to his claims of absolute control over Kashmir. His word was enough for the people of the Valley, he believed. But those who had watched him over a period of time and had seen the transformation were not surprised to see him condemning the ratification of the State's accession. Now, soon after his release, Sheikh Abdullah became an ardent advocate of plebiscite. On 17th February 1958, in a press statement, he observed: '...One of the most important objects underlying the entire political movement in the State... [of Jammu and Kashmir]...has remained to secure the right of self-determination for the people of the State. Expression of the will of the people through a plebiscite is the one formula which has been agreed upon by the parties concerned, and in a mass of disagreements about details, this common denominator has held the field so far... The people of the State consider this formula of plebiscite as a clear interpretation of their long cherished aspirations and as a lasting solution of the complicated problem which is facing them.'[267]

Apart from this transformation there were other changes that took place. Sheikh Abdullah was now in touch with Pakistani handlers. Soon after his arrest, his followers established contact with a certain Major Asghar Ali and letters passed between the two sides specifying the terms under which the Pakistanis would be willing to assist Sheikh Abdullah's camp. As Abdullah's activities grew under the garb of the Plebiscite Front, the Intelligence Bureau too began to spread its network in the State, leading to unearthing evidence that these elements under Beg's leadership were hatching a conspiracy against India. This had led to the re-arrest of Beg in 1956. During the search, incriminating letters were recovered. B.N. Mullik has catalogued the events in considerable detail in his book *My Years With Nehru: Kashmir*, and he says, 'One of these letters showed that the Sheikh had sent instructions to equate Pakistan with India in future.' At another time, a copy of a letter was obtained in which the Plebiscite Front suggested that the letter that Sheikh Abdullah had purported to have addressed to the UN Security Council be simultaneously published in several languages and published on the same day in India and Pakistan, on the day it was submitted to the Council. A photostat copy of the letter appeared in January 1957, and had indeed appeared at the same time in Pakistani newspapers when it was presented to the Security Council.[268]

Some of the passages of the letter left little doubt in regard to their insidious nature and it was obvious even to the untrained eye that the conspiracy to raise an insurrection was being hatched. It read: 'A reliable man of Hyder Khan [Pakistan] came here last week. Long discussions were held with him and our position was explained to him in detail. They are prompting to come forward openly. I pointed out to him the harm which was occurring due to the indefinite postponement of the matter and it is possible, if it is delayed any further, irreparable damage may be done. Secondly, I pointed to him the necessity to prune branches in the garden. They had sent the scissors and other material but a gardener is not available. So, he was asked to send a good gardener from his village [Pakistan] itself. The rot that has set in can be remedied by immediate pruning of branches. He wanted to know your opinion as to their future programme. So, if you think proper send detailed instructions…'[269] This letter to Sheikh Abdullah leaves little to the imagination. Plans were drawn up, with the active support of Pakistan, to not only raise insurrection but also carry out selective 'pruning' of branches. Anyone reading this would understand that selective elimination of important pro-India personalities was also on the cards. It is clear that Sheikh Abdullah not only knew of this conspiracy but was actively involved since the final clearance was sought from him.

In another letter, Mirza Afzal Beg dictated to Pir Abdul Ghani, under the authority of Sheikh Abdullah, 'correspondence between Asad Saheb [Sheikh Abdullah] and Niazi [Pakistani officer in Rawalpindi]. In this it was also stressed that it would be very useful if Pakistan could get Sheikh Abdullah summoned before the Security Council in a regular way.' Mullik also claims that by 1956 'large sums of money in Indian currency started coming from Pakistan to the Sheikh's supporters and also other hostile groups.'[270]

Messages from Sheikh Abdullah, who was detained in Kud (Jammu), continued to flow to his supporters through couriers who visited him. In fact, Begum Abdullah, who visited him regularly, was even allowed to spend the nights there. The Bureau soon realized that she was one of the most important links between Sheikh Abdullah and the members of the Plebiscite Front. They also got the unwitting support of Mridula Sarabhai who believed that Sheikh Abdullah was basically pro-India but had not been properly handled. In later years when the Kashmir Conspiracy finally got under way, she was one of the main supporters of Sheikh Abdullah, providing considerable financial assistance.

Interception of these letters was made possible by the diligence of the Bureau, which quietly spread its network in the State from Ranbirsinghpura to Kargil. They had identified three points from where the Pakistani agents entered India. The Bureau could have made these nefarious efforts public but then it would have been deprived of the valuable evidence that was needed in a court of law. The then Home Minister, Gobind Vallabh Pant, also counselled caution and waited for an appropriate opportunity. By October 1957, the authorities were ready to move in and file a First Information Report against the leaders of the Plebiscite Front, including Mirza Afzal Beg, Pir Maqbool Gilani, Begum Abdullah, among others. In the absence of strong evidence, Sheikh Abdullah's name was not included in the FIR. Mullik claims, that by January 1958 'the entire range of conspiracy became apparent and we found that we had built a formidable case against all the accused mentioned in the FIR and also against Sheikh Abdullah and several others whose names had not been included in it.'[271]

Encouraged by its success in enlisting the support of the

Plebiscite Front, Pakistan believed that the ground had been prepared for a violent revolution. They sent a large group of infiltrators (code named *gardeners*) who actually carried out a series of explosions and sabotages, in which several lives were lost. After the invasion of 1947, this was the first of the many subsequent attempts made by Pakistan to send in armed and trained men to carry out subversive activities in the State. Many more attempts were foiled by interception but a few succeeded. However, the overall attempt to create anarchy through violence failed to get the public support that Pakistan and these subversive elements had hoped for. To a large extent credit needs to be given to the people of Kashmir for refusing to be hustled and also the people-friendly rule of Bakshi, who indeed, was popular.

By March 1958, the intelligence agencies pieced together considerable evidence to prove that Sheikh Abdullah was in fact the main conspirator and that if he was left out of the case, then it would be difficult to prove the culpability of others in it. They were prepared to submit a charge-sheet but it was pre-empted by the release of Sheikh Abdullah. The timing was most inopportune for pursuing the case against him for it was obvious that the defence would argue that if the case against him was so strong, then why was he was released at the time of filing the charge-sheet against him. Obviously, the Intelligence Bureau and all those who worked painstakingly on monitoring the anti-Indian activities were disappointed, but the Bureau Director's judgment about Sheikh Abdullah's responses was near perfect. He hoped that, 'intoxicated with his newly found liberty, which he must have ascribed to his strength in Kashmir Valley and which ultimately the government could not ignore, the Sheikh might stick his head out too much and in the process expose himself further, and bring to light more incriminating evidence against himself; and this is what happened.'[272]

Sheikh Abdullah returned to a tumultuous welcome in the Valley, and no sooner had he returned to Srinagar than he started holding public meetings in different parts of the city. He made a bitter and intemperate attack against the Bakshi government and the Government of India, calling the former a traitor and a usurper, and challenging the latter's right to be the arbiters of the fate of Kashmir. His effect on the people seemed to be electric and it appeared that the State was heading towards a violent uprising.

In one of his letters to Yuvraj Karan Singh, Prime Minister Nehru mentioned the fact that the Kashmir issue would never be closed till the State and the Government of India had faced the consequences of a free Sheikh Abdullah. The time to test the mettle appeared to have had arrived in a most dramatic fashion. His speeches were creating hysteria and it was feared that the presence of the Indian Army notwithstanding, the masses would just sweep aside the Bakshi government and install Sheikh Abdullah as the King, if he so wanted.

Having carefully measured the mood of the populace and testing his own ability to rouse the people, Abdullah gave a call for a mammoth meeting on Friday, 17th January 1958 at Pathar Masjid, located right opposite the Mujahid Manzil, the Headquarters of the National Conference. It was an obvious attempt to capture it and signal the people to occupy the government offices as well. Metaphorically, Mujahid Manzil controlled the keys of power and its capture by Abdullah's followers would have ended Bakshi's rule.

The area was heavily guarded by security forces and arrangements were made to thwart any attempt of the mob to seize Mujahid Manzil. But, with a crowd of 20,000 gathered there the thought of the consequences of confrontation was scary. These people had begun to gather since early morning and all through the day many more kept roaming the streets in anticipation, responding to the call of the leader. But as time passed, there was no sign of Sheikh Abdullah. The man who liked to be called 'Sher-e-Kashmir' (Lion of Kashmir) could not muster enough courage to meet the moment of reckoning. The situation is best described by Mullik: 'Everyone was anxiously waiting for the Sheikh's arrival. But the hero did not appear. At the last moment his courage [had] failed. He had never faced bullets and he was not going to do it now! What would happen to Kashmir if he died! So, whilst the crowd waited at Pathar Masjid and went on waiting for him, he went to Hazratbal where he gave vent to his anger and frustration by delivering one of the bitterest speeches...'[273]

It was an anti-climax; the man people thought was a lion turned out to be a timid creature. During the preceding week, he had gone about exhorting people to rise in the name of Prophet Muhammad, to face the bullets and drive away the oppressors. But now he had proved that he was a man with feet of clay. In contrast, his failure to muster courage proved to be a turning point for Bakshi Ghulam Mohammad. It was Bakshi's moment of glory in which he vindicated his decision to free Sheikh Abdullah. Thereafter, though Sheikh Abdullah continued to retain considerable influence to create mischief, he lost the moral authority to lead his followers to victory. Bakshi's success came at a time when a section of the National Conference, and an influential one at that, led by Sadiq, had broken away from Bakshi. Thus, Bakshi proved to the people and the world that he could not only stand up to Sheikh Abdullah but also worst him in any confrontation.

The struggle for supremacy, however, was not yet over. Less than a fortnight after the Pathar Masjid fiasco, Bakshi decided to strike back. He made elaborate plans to celebrate the Republic Day in a grand manner in the Valley to prove wrong all those people who claimed that he would not be able to hold his own when Sheikh Abdullah arrived on the scene. Picking up the gauntlet, Sheikh Abdullah issued a *firman* (religious notice) from the sacred precincts of Hazartbal, for a complete boycott of the function. Thus the stage was set once again for a trial of strength between Prime Minister Bakshi, who insisted on holding a grand celebration of the day and Abdullah, who called for a total boycott of the function by the people of Kashmir. The stage was set for the second and decisive round of confrontation, and this time it was clear that it was going to be bloody and painful.

Prime Minister Nehru too was concerned at the impending consequence and Mullik claims that Nehru asked him 'to go to Srinagar and ensure no violence took place to mar the day. He suggested that, rather than suffering the orgy of violence, it would be better to forego those parts of the celebrations which might encounter opposition from the Sheikh's supporters.'[274] Nehru was also wary of the adverse international publicity and hence, did not want any bloodshed on the country's Republic Day. But Bakshi was determined to go ahead with the planned march of about 50,000 National Conference volunteers over a five-mile route through the most congested part of Srinagar.

The narrow lanes were ideal for those wanting to create mischief. Therefore, those sent to Srinagar by Prime Minister Nehru to ensure that the situation remained under the boil, tried to convince Bakshi to avoid those tortuous lanes where the provocation could come from either side without anyone realizing what had happened. Bakshi insisted that his men had the upper hand along the route, but claimed that they were also instructed not to react to even the most provocative jeering. Mullik says that he was aware that it was not possible to have such a large crowd to remain calm in the face of provocation and hence, again pressed Bakshi to revise his plans for the route. 'But Bakshi would not agree. It was a question of life and death with him and if he had to bow down to the Sheikh's threat of boycott of the Republic Day, then he would not be able to face the people any longer and would rather bow out of the Government.'[275]

The weather on 25th January was one of the worst for any celebration. It rained and snowed all day and night. The town too had been cowed by the combination of weather and the tension of what was to happen the following day. Rain and snow continued to dog the dawn as it broke and it appeared that no large-scale gathering of any kind would take place. It was, therefore, a surprise to see a large gathering of invitees and ordinary people for the official function of the Republic Day. The trouble, though, was anticipated in the afternoon when the procession was supposed to be taken out. Mullik and Mehra, a brother officer from the Bureau, went out to inspect the route once again, even as the rain and icy winds lashed the city. They were surprised to see that all along the route, there was not a single black flag. They were told that a few of them were hoisted in the morning, but they had been taken down by the volunteers of the National Conference. The unending procession vended through those lanes as Sheikh Abdullah's followers confined themselves indoors. It finally gathered at the Civil Lines and was addressed by a jubilant Bakshi Ghulam Mohammad.

Once again, Sheikh Abdullah was worsted by Bakshi who proved that Sheikh Abdullah's writ no longer ran in Srinagar.

In no small measure, the success of the Republic Day procession was laid on 17th January, when everyone had seen that Sheikh Abdullah lacked the courage to face bullets even as he asked others to sacrifice their lives in the name of Prophet Muhammad. Twice in a fortnight, the two had clashed and on both occasions Bakshi had emerged victorious.

On his part, Sheikh Abdullah believed that he was not yet vanquished and hence continued his efforts to exhort people in the only manner that he knew. He used Hazratbal's sacred platform to rouse people against Bakshi and India after every Friday prayer, comparing them with the infidels who had to be destroyed by Prophet Muhammad and his followers to rid the world of them. Simultaneously, he held secret meetings at his home where elaborate plans for insurrection, plebiscite and merger with Pakistan were deliberated. Exorbitant amounts of money too began to pour in from the office of the Deputy High Commission of Pakistan in Chandigarh and Pakistan. Pakistan knew that their only horse to bet on was Sheikh Abdullah, and it redoubled its efforts. Sheikh Abdullah too tried hard to increase subversive activities. Pakistan found an excuse to intervene on the pretext of helping co-religionists. Finally, the Prime Minister lost his patience and agreed to the re-arrest of Sheikh Abdullah on 30th April 1958. Among the items recovered from his house, was a draft of the Plebiscite Front, corrected in the Sheikh's own hand at many places, essentially accepting accession to Pakistan.

Before the arrest, the Intelligence agencies prepared a 1,600-page type-written dossier, cataloguing the conspiracy. There was also incontrovertible evidence to prove the involvement of even Begum Abdullah, and there was considerable debate regarding her arrest. However, Bakshi put his foot down and bluntly declared that even if there was proof, he would not allow her arrest. He argued that it would go against the Kashmiri ethos and the people would never forgive him. By this time, the Begum was known in Kashmir as the '*Madr-e-Meherban*'—the kind mother. Prime Minister Nehru too agreed with him. Bakshi had reservations regarding two other conspirators—Pir Maqbool Gilani and Pir Maqbool Wigami—because of their religious status. But in their case, the Intelligence officers were able to prevail upon Bakshi. It was only then that a case was filed and the arrests made.

Prime Minister Bakshi Ghulam Mohammad now had a clear field. There was no looking over his shoulder for him and the State could now focus on the more important task of socio-economic growth.

17

The Chapter Closes

With Sheikh Abdullah back in prison after losing his battle for supremacy, life was more settled. For the government, it was a period of consolidation of gains, and the time to plan and execute socio-economic programmes. For Yuvraj Karan Singh, it was time to expand his horizon. After deciding to build a house in Delhi, he frequented the national capital more often. With the engagements that went beyond the frontiers of politics and administration, he got acquainted with the intellectual life of the city. As 1960 approached, it became obvious that the world was on the verge of entering an era of exciting discoveries, with changes and forays into unknown territories. In 1957, the Soviet Union heralded the space era by launching the first artificial satellite, Sputnik I, into space. Human life was never going to be the same again.

In 1960, the USA elected John F. Kennedy, the handsome and charismatic young leader with an aura that attracted the youth of the world, as its youngest President. The youth of the world believed that their time had arrived. Yuvraj Karan Singh was no exception. Like many other young men and women in India, he looked forward to public life so as to make some contribution to the process of transformation that everyone hoped would follow. The new home in Chanakyapuri was completed and therefore, he felt comfortable frequenting Delhi more often, and for longer periods. During his stay, he would not only meet the Prime Minister and the President but also other politicians, including the 'self-opinionated' Morarji Desai, the 'blunt and amusing' S.K. Patil, the 'wily and

Mephistophelian' Krishna Menon, the 'brilliant but cynical' T.T. Krishnamachari, Sardar Swarn Singh who was 'much shrewder than he appeared', among others. He also struck an easy rapport with Indira Gandhi, whom he had already come to know very well.[276]

He also began meeting members of the diplomatic corps and developed two extremely fruitful relationships. Soon after the election of John Kennedy, Prof. John Kenneth Galbraith was appointed the American Ambassador to India. A multidimensional personality, Galbraith was a Professor of Economics at the Harvard University and had been Kennedy's teacher and mentor at the University and his early years of public life. Before coming to India, he had authored two influential books—*The Great Crash* and *The Affluent Society*. He was also influenced by Jawaharlal Nehru and made no bones about his admiration for him. An exceptionally tall person, his height necessitated special arrangements for his bed whenever he had to spend the night away from his residence in Delhi. He was one of the earliest Westerners who took a keen interest in India's development story and became extremely popular wherever he went; and he went to almost all the nooks and corners of the country. He waded into the paddy-fields and joined the folk dancers whenever the opportunity arose.

In the early 1950s, liberal intellectuals, who were victims of the political witch-hunt launched by McCarthyism* in America, like Professor Daniel Thorner and Myron Weiner, had found refuge and meaningful work in India. After a decade, the USA shook off those extreme attitudes and once again embraced an enlightened and liberal era. Delhi reaped rich dividends from these winds of change. It was not difficult for the Yuvraj to establish a relationship with Professor Galbraith; one had an inquisitive mind and the other

---

* According to *The American Heritage Dictionary of the English Language*, McCarthyism is the 'practice of publicizing accusations of political disloyalty or subversion with insufficient regard to evidence'; and the 'use of unfair investigatory or accusatory methods in order to suppress opposition.' Senator Joseph McCarthy used this method to destroy many innocent lives, accusing them of having left-wing leanings. Even those who refused to 'name, names' of people accused of left-leaning were not spared by the Senate Subcommittee headed by him.

had so much to offer intellectually. Both the Yuvraj and the Yuvrani had no difficulty in developing a very informal relationship with Galbraith and his wife Kitty, who was equally keen to know India. This social and intellectual relationship was to become a subject of unwanted controversy when interested parties began to speculate about the 'hidden' motive of the Ambassador's visit to Jammu and Kashmir. The source of this speculation was a new newsmagazine, *Link*, with avowedly leftist leanings. It reported, 'Galbraith has been taking an active interest in the current series of Indo-Pak talks and is named as the author of the plan which provides a foot-hold to Pakistan in Kashmir Valley, lent credence to the view that he was on some "diplomatic" mission'. It added that, 'even the State Prime Minister lacked knowledge of the visit till newspapers reported on it made the argument suspect that it was a private visit.'

The 'news' was published by *Link* on 24th February 1963. On the 26th, the Yuvraj commented on the mischievous report in his letter to Prime Minister Nehru. In fact, the visit was arranged on a private level between the Sadar-i-Riyasat and Galbraith. A clarification too was issued by Ghulam Mohammad, the secretary to the Sadar-i-Riyasat, explaining that since Galbraith was an eminent economist, 'Dr Karan Singh arranged at his residence a small function at which the Professor gave a talk on Economic Development in the USA. The invitees were the staff and students of the university postgraduate departments, staff of other university postgraduate departments situated in Jammu, Principals and teachers of Economics of [the] Jammu Degree College and members of the small private book reviewing society known as the Wayfarers.'[277] This wholly unnecessary controversy once again underlined the fact that multiple forces were busy promoting their own narrow agendas in the State, and the need for caution by those at the helm of affairs. Even non-existent and innocuous events had the possibility of snowballing into controversies.

The Yuvraj also bonded with Alva Myrdal, the Swedish Ambassador in Delhi and her husband Gunnar Myrdal. They were one of the most gifted couples in the diplomatic corps. However, the most fruitful relationship struck by the Yuvraj was with Dr Clovis Maksoud, the Arab League Representative in Delhi and his first wife Rosemarie. It is ironical that it was through this foreigner, a Maronite Christian, that the Yuvraj came to know intellectuals of the country for Clovis had a very wide spectrum of friends from the intellectual world of India. It was in their house that Karan Singh first met Aruna Asaf Ali and Jayaprakash Narayan. During this period, the Yuvraj and the Yuvrani also came into contact with Raj and Romesh Thapar who launched the thought-provoking journal *Seminar*, and remained their lifelong friends. At that time, India was still under Nehru's spell but the fervent political and intellectual life was most palatable. A new generation of Indians was trying to find its way to the centre stage.

The year also saw some very significant development work in the State. Almost a decade after the Yuvraj, as a Regent, had brought into focus the problems and neglect that Ladakh faced, the road from Srinagar to Leh was opened. It was important not only because of the need of the army for its border outposts opposite China but also because it brought the people closer to the rest of the State and country. In another significant development, a road connecting Dhar, near Pathankot, to Udhampur was also opened. It was known as the Defence Road because it was laid to make the movement of the army easy in case of a threat from Pakistan to the main Pathankot-Jammu highway. But it also opened up those nearby accessible areas to the rest of the State in addition to being an alternate route to reach the important cantonment of Udhampur.

On the political front, it was decided that Sheikh Abdullah and his other associates under detention should be prosecuted for the Kashmir Conspiracy Case that had been put in abeyance after the decision to release Sheikh Abdullah was taken. Bakshi grew strong with the splinter group of the National Conference coming back and for the first time, a genuine communist party, the remainder of the splinter group that chose not to return to the parent party, was formed with Krishen Dev Sethi and Ram Piara Saraf as its leaders. The only cause of concern at that point in time was the inability of the policy planners to visualize the threat that was likely to emerge from the north.

Soon the Chinese moves in Ladakh became a matter of national concern. 'They flowed from the Tibet situation, and it was amazing that despite their move into the outlying areas of Ladakh, we were slow to react…a major weakness of our foreign and military policy was exposed, and the northern frontier became a sort of Achilles' heel. Early in 1961 there were a series of meetings between Indian and Chinese officials on the boundary question… Clearly the whole Indo-Chinese border had become a matter of dispute, not only in Ladakh but in the eastern sector too. Unfortunately, Jawaharlal fell between two stools; he was neither able to clinch a compromise give-and-take package, which would certainly have been attacked but which his immense prestige could have carried through, nor was he able to build up enough military strength on the northern borders to actually enforce our legal claim.'[278] Ladakh, by virtue of the fact that it was part of the State that was ruled by Maharaja Hari Singh, became an integral part of India after the Maharaja had signed the Instrument of Accession in favour of India. This, however, was contested by China on the basis of the history, long consigned to time. This problem was to develop into a major conflict with China and an occasion for Pakistan to forge very strong and reliable ties with it.

Life was settled and satisfactory by 1961 with all the fronts covered, except perhaps for the fact that Yuvraj Karan Singh's parents yearned for a grandson but had instead got a granddaughter. The Maharaja was probably keen on transferring much of his personal property to a male child and his plans seemed to have been thwarted by fate. The Yuvraj did not have an easy relationship with him. Among the Dogra Rajputs, this has rarely been normal. But in this case, which father would have a normal relationship after he had been ousted from kingship only to be replaced by his son? One could have reconciled with that because of the circumstances that were beyond the control of either the father or the son, but what had really disappointed and angered the Maharaja was that it was under his son's signature that the dynasty stood abolished, and then the son had allowed himself to be elected by the same people who had connived to first remove the Maharaja from the State and then abolish the dynasty. This to his mind had put Yuvraj Karan Singh at the mercy of those mean and vindictive enemies. He was bitter about the whole affair since the

Maharajas in other States had been allowed to remain as the Heads of their States. This bitterness was somewhat mitigated when the Yuvraj dismissed Sheikh Abdullah. Both father and son maintained a cordial relationship and wrote letters regularly, and in fact, the concern that Maharaja Hari Singh showed for the safety of his son when he was asked by Sardar Patel to appoint him as Regent and leave the State and then after Sheikh Abdullah's dismissal, speaks volumes about him as a father.

There was another factor that influenced the father-son relationship. The Maharaja and Maharani had a very unsatisfactory relationship. It is hard to say if this was solely because the Maharani chose not to accompany the Maharaja to Bombay owing to health reasons or, what he suspected to be undue influence of her brother in the affairs of the family, or the fact that their relationship had broken irretrievably much before that. But the fact remains that she had chosen not only to support any decision taken regarding the future by the Yuvraj but also to live in Alhilal in Kangra. This could not have gone down well with the Maharaja. Moreover, the Maharaja must also have resented the influence of Nehru on the Yuvraj and his dependence upon the Indian Prime Minister for guidance. He saw Nehru as the man who was instrumental and a mountain of support to those who wanted him humiliated and this must have been galling.

The last time the Maharani saw him was when she was to return to Kasauli after the marriage of Yuvraj Karan Singh. With all due reverence, she had touched his feet before leaving. Before the birth of their grandchild, the Maharani had expected to be asked to come to Bombay, but by then she was no longer a part of the Maharaja's life. Of course he was a difficult man, obstinate when he willed and not prone to forgiving emotional hurt. No one knew this better than Malka Pukhraj. Unable to handle the pressure of the latent communalism before Partition, she was among the first to betray the Maharaja and leave the State. Long after she was married, had children and settled with a very successful life in Lahore, she had, by her own admission, written numerous letters to him expressing her desire to come to Bombay and meet him. There was not a word of acknowledgement. No one would have known if these letters were ever written if Malka Pukhraj had not made the admission in her autobiography *A Song Sung True.*

Maharaja Hari Singh lived in Bombay much of the time after leaving the State, but was a regular visitor to the Poona and Bangalore (now Pune and Bengaluru respectively) turfs during the season. A prominent owner of race horses, he visited the stables regularly to keep himself updated of the horses even when he had to be taken there in a wheelchair. But the bitterness notwithstanding, he remained a very caring father who liked to oversee the planning of every detail when it came to the visit of the Yuvraj and the Yuvrani. Meticulous to a fault, he would get the luggage weighed in his presence to ensure no excess baggage was carried. He had a very special relationship with the Yuvrani and a lot of affection for her. Both the Yuvraj and the Yuvrani spent a fortnight a year with him, and as in the earlier days, the Yuvraj accompanied him to Mahalakshmi Race Course for the races.

By 1961, Maharaja Hari Singh had grown exceedingly thin in contrast to his slightly portly bearings. That was the year when the shortage of foreign exchange began to hurt foreign travel. The Yuvraj had wanted to visit South East Asia and accordingly everyone, including the President, was informed and the permission obtained. But owing to shortage of foreign exchange, the plans were changed. He wrote to Prime Minister Nehru on 31st March 1961: 'As you know, I had planned to visit South East Asia for two months… and had received permission from the President to remain out of the country for that period. Unfortunately, the foreign exchange situation turned out to be more difficult than I had expected, and the Finance Ministry did not find it possible to sanction a single rupee of exchange for this trip. As a result, I have had reluctantly to cancel the visit… I happen to have a few pounds in London, and as Asha [Yuvrani] and I were all prepared for a trip abroad we have decided to go on a short holiday to London instead.'[279] Both the Yuvraj and the Yuvrani spent five days with the Maharaja. His apparent weakness notwithstanding, he was cheerful during those five days and was excited about their visit. Looking forward to the future, he asked them to purchase a pair of Manchester terriers that were apparently bred in Scotland, and a pair of binoculars for the races.[280] He was fully engrossed in his passions and looking forward to life.

The couple had a very rewarding time in England, shopping and going to theatres. The Yuvraj duly purchased the Manchester terriers and binoculars, and made arrangements for the dogs to be brought to Bombay. Then they proceeded to Italy where their happy trip was rudely interrupted by the Indian Ambassador to Italy who brought with him the sad news of the Maharaja's death. The Ambassador had already booked two seats on the Delhi-bound flight and the Yuvraj and the Yuvrani left the same evening. 'That night on the plane I was unable to sleep and images crowded into my mind; my father, resplendent in uniform and medals, riding on a white horse at the head of his troops, inspecting the great Dussehra parade on the Batmaloo grounds in Srinagar; sitting in the Thricker fishing lodge after a successful day's fishing, sipping his whisky and laughing at the jokes made by his staff officers; cooking delicious recipes in the lovely lawns of Gulab Bhavan with my mother and a large entourage; sitting next to me at the Bombay races shouting encouragements to his horse as the animals crossed the finish line; beaming with pleasure when he won, angry and depressed when he lost… He was always a formidable, almost titanic figure in my consciousness.'[281]

Maharaja Hari Singh was taken ill on the morning of 26th April 1961 when a coughing bout developed into a heart attack. He knew that death had come knocking on the door and was ready. He remained meticulous even while preparing for his own death and left instructions in his will about his cremation. It was thus performed in accordance with the Arya Samaj rites without any delay after the death. The Yuvraj and the Yuvrani reached Bombay on 27th April and collected the bones and ashes the same day from the cremation ground. The bones were consigned to the sea in the Apollo Bunder. These instructions too were planned in the Maharaja's will: 'My *Asthis* should be thrown into the sea, but my ashes should be placed in a silver urn and taken up in a specially chartered plane and scattered over Jammu city, the place of my birth.'[282] The next day, 28th April, a chartered plane took them to Delhi where, after spending a fretful night, they left for Jammu as instructed by the late Maharaja.

Meanwhile, the Jammu province witnessed an unprecedented sight when the news broke. 'Shop after shop was hurriedly closed and within seconds all the bazaars and even isolated shops were closed. With their eyes full of tears and voices choked with emotions, the people passed on to each other the shocking news of the sad and sudden demise of their beloved former Maharaja... There was no body at the Palace to furnish details. Yuvraj Karan Singh had proceeded on a foreign trip a couple of days earlier and was then in Rome. The Maharani was at Alhilal in Kangra. Finally, a crowd gathered at the residence of Pandit Prem Nath Dogra, the Praja Parishad Chief, urging him to arrange for the body to be flown to Jammu for cremation with befitting honours. It was to be learnt, however, that the Maharaja's last will written more than a year earlier, did not permit this. Instead, it provided for his ashes to be flown over Jammu and sprinkled over the town... All roads then led to the Palace where thousands of people immediately assembled, and soon a sea of humanity flowed from the Palace through the main streets of the town, towards the Tawi, the like of which Jammu had not witnessed before. Women were beating their breasts and lamenting, and the men hung their heads in silence. The procession ended at the cremation ground at the Tawi and dispersed after a brief speech by a Praja Parishad leader Mr Ramnath Advocate.'[283]

It was, indeed, a strange sight—a funeral procession without the body of the deceased, no one from the family as the mourner-in-chief; a funeral appropriated by the people from all walks of life the commoners who believed they were safe and secure when the deceased was the king, and the nobles who had the privilege of becoming the tool of his governance and were the recipients of his munificence all came together to mourn the demise of a king who was treacherously used, betrayed and exiled by those who pretended to be his friends and well wishers. In death too he had demonstrated his popularity among the masses. The kitchen fires remained extinguished that day.

The plane that brought Yuvraj Karan Singh and the ashes, circled Jammu thrice, and the Yuvraj scattered the ashes out of a window over the soil below. 'All of Jammu had gathered for the last homage—endless crowds, crying and wailing for a man who had left them a dozen years earlier as their Maharaja. And I carried the urn in an open car through the milling crowds. Thirty years ago on the same route my father and mother had driven in an open carriage through cheering throngs in celebration of my birth. Twelve years ago my parents and I were taken out in a similar procession after my return from America. This time I was alone…'[284]

Huge crowds awaited the ashes at the airport with people from the villages also there to pay their homage. Bakshi Ghulam Mohammad, the Prime Minister made a brief appearance as the Yuvraj emerged from the plane with the urn and was greeted with the cries of '*Maharaja Bahadur Amar Rahe* (Long live the King)', renting the air. The large procession proceeded to the cremation *ghat* on the banks of Tawi where the necessary religious ceremonies were performed by the Yuvraj after which the people dispersed in silence. The religious ceremonies in accordance with the *Sanatani** tradition were followed despite the fact that the Maharaja had willed that no other religious ceremonies be performed. However, the Yuvraj felt it was his duty to follow the traditional of the thirteen-day period laid down by the *shastras*.

After the thirteen days ended, it was time to attend to the more mundane issues of life. Yuvraj Karan Singh wrote a letter to Prime Minister Nehru, with a copy to the Home Minister Lal Bahadur Shastri, reminding Nehru of the legal and constitutional requirement of issuing a notification of succession following the death of a former ruler as a result of the accession of a Princely State to the Indian Union. However, there were two problems. Prime Minister Nehru was not comfortable with the use of the princely titles in a Republic and thought it was time to bring about certain modifications. As it is, the princes were gradually eased out from their constitutional positions as Heads of the States, and with the reorganization of states, all of them ceased to hold those positions. In Yuvraj Karan Singh's case, there was an added problem. He was the elected Sadar-i-Riyasat of a State whose Constituent Assembly had abolished monarchy, making the use of the title Maharaja

* Duties and rituals—based on teachings of the Vedas, Upanishads, Puranas, and other ancient Hindu texts—that a follower is supposed to observe.

untenable in his case. But his recognition as the successor to his father was a constitutional requirement and a way out had to be found. Finally, Prime Minister Nehru conveyed to him a suggestion through Shastri, and on 7th July 1961, the Yuvraj wrote a letter addressed to Shastri:[285]

> My dear Shastriji,
>
> Although I have succeeded to the title of my late father His Highness Maharaja Hari Singh, I do not wish to use these titles so long as I hold the office of the Sadar-i-Riyasat of Jammu and Kashmir, and during this period I should like to be addressed as Shri Karan Singh.
>
> With kind regards,
> Yours sincerely,
> K. S.

On the 10th of the same month, the Government of India issued an official notification which read:

> Order
>
> In pursuance of clause 22 of Article 366 of the Constitution of India, the President is hereby pleased to recognize Yuvraj Karan Singh as successor to his late Highness Maharaja Hari Singh Indar Mahindar Bahadur with effect from April 26, 1961.

This order was accompanied by a press note that acknowledged the receipt of the request of Sadar-i-Riyasat that he did not wish to use the titles of 'His Highness' and 'Maharaja' and noted its appreciation of his desire. Upon being recognized as the successor of the late Maharaja, he became entitled to a privy purse of Rs ten lakhs per annum and hence he discontinued drawing the monthly salary of Rs 5,500, which he was entitled to as Sadar-i-Riyasat. This gesture was 'gratefully accepted' by the Council of Ministers of the State and greatly appreciated by the people. An era had thus come to an end, not very satisfactorily for the old order but a new dawn was clearly breaking on the horizon.

18

Holy Relic and its Aftermath

The educated classes in India have rarely concealed their contempt for those leaders who are not too well-versed in the English language and education in general. Unless exceptional, history too does not judge them too kindly. Bakshi Ghulam Mohammad falls in this category. A middle school drop-out, Bakshi was a street smart politician who learnt organizational skills from the school of life and rose to be the number two in the hierarchy of the National Conference because of his people-management skills and down-to-earth pragmatic attitude to problems. Not given to flights of ideological rhetoric, he instinctively knew what needed to be done; and more often than not, got it done. He had a clear practical mind, uncluttered by romanticism, and hence was among the early leaders of the National Conference to acknowledge the need for an attitudinal change after the Party was firmly entrenched in power, and have the shadows of the past removed.

Unlike Sheikh Abdullah, he did not pursue the politics of vendetta. With time, he evolved as a master in the art of neutralizing his opponents by persuasion, and hence by 1960, he was able to wean back Sadiq, Dhar, Lal Dogra, among others back to the National Conference and the government. They had broken away to form their Democratic National Conference but soon realized the futility of striking a lonely course. By now, Bakshi had been the Prime Minister for almost seven years and the exercise of power began to affect him. Thus, his six brothers and other relatives became satellite power centres around him without being accountable to anyone.

The acerbic humour of Kashmiris would refer to them as BBC—Bakshi Brothers' Corporation! Allegations of corruption, probably committed by his relatives, were attributed to him, giving occasion to the gossip mongers to spread stories of real and imagined acts of arbitrariness and corruption. Bakshi, in fact, represented the irony of presiding over a very popular and corrupt government. Stories abounded of him recommending jobs to the needy by writing on the inside of an empty cigarette pack. One story also stated that he had appointed a young man as Assistant Sub-Inspector of Police because he appeared to be '*hatta-katta*'—healthy and strong.

Apart from his inability to keep his relatives away from power and its misuse, in 1962, he made his first political mistake owing to a serious error of judgment. The consequence of the fallout was to reverberate for long in the history of the State and the country. It was the year when the acting Mirwaiz,[286] the highest religious functionary in the Valley and an institution that had become an integral part of Kashmiri Islam, died. The real Mirwaiz, Maulavi Yusuf Shah, a one-time comrade of Sheikh Abdullah when they were together in the Muslim Conference, opted for Pakistan and left the State in 1947. In his absence, the government proclaimed Maulavi Atiqullah as the Mirwaiz. On Atiqullah's death, Bakshi chose Maulavi Mohammad Farooq, a young man of twenty-three, as his successor. He was the nephew of Maulavi Yusuf Shah and much fanfare followed his appointment. The euphoria in official circles, however, was short-lived. In no time, Farooq became the rallying point for anti-India and pro-Pakistan forces in the Valley. The Valley was, indeed, preparing for another round of confrontation.

By this time, Mullik noted a change in Prime Minister Nehru's attitude towards Sheikh Abdullah. Till then, the prosecuting agencies were clearly told by the Home Minister Gobind Vallabh Pant, not to inject the element of politics in the Kashmir Conspiracy Case. He feared that if the prosecution brought up politics then the defence would have a field day and make rhetorical speeches for the galleries and the international press. But when this matter was brought to the Prime Minister's notice, he is believed to have said: 'This is all politics. How can we avoid politics? The accused committed all these outrages or planned to commit them due to political motivation. It would be incongruous to say that there was no politics in it.'[287]

Clearly Nehru had experienced a change of heart. Once the realization dawned that he was used by Sheikh Abdullah and that his faith in him had been so misplaced as to put the integrity and reputation of the country at stake, he recalled the events of the past with clarity and better understanding. If Mullik's version is truthful, then it was the only occasion when Prime Minister Nehru acknowledged that his friend had remained a communalist at heart. The Prime Minister recalled the events from 1930 onwards, when the Muslim Conference was formed, and because of the pressure on it because of the People's Movement in the rest of the country against the monarchical states, Sheikh Abdullah had to reinvent the Muslim Conference as the National Conference to seek the support of the wider world. But what surprised Mullik about this sudden and belated outburst against Sheikh Abdullah was a poser to him from the Prime Minister. Nehru wanted to know if, during his investigations, Mullik had found any evidence of British complicity in the turmoil that Maharaja Hari Singh faced in the 1930s. While, Mullik replied in the affirmative, the fact that all along Nehru knew of the imperial conspiracy to destabilize the Maharaja Hari Singh's rule, with Sheikh Abdullah as its tool, came as a surprise even to Mullik. Nehru further ruminated that it was the gruesome atrocities committed by the Pakistan-backed invaders in 1947 that mellowed Sheikh Abdullah for some time, but he returned to his communal politics soon after he became the Prime Minister of the State. As Prime Minister, Sheikh Abdullah was never tired of talking about the rights of the Muslims, completely ignoring the minorities that constituted more than 25 per cent of the population. He also candidly admitted that he had continued to support Sheikh Abdullah in the hope that he would see virtue in being part of a secular and progressive India; but the Sheikh refused to shed his communal cloak and narrow-minded approach. This admission vindicated what Sardar Patel had said in 1949, when he predicted that a time would come when Nehru would realize the error of backing a communalist like Sheikh Abdullah.[288] The Prime Minister's sudden and unexpected outburst against Sheikh Abdullah was also witnessed by Lal Bahadur Shastri, who commented that the former had let off a long and suppressed steam and anguish at being betrayed by a person who he had supported against the advice and judgment of his long-standing comrades.

Soon after, Nehru and the country suffered a humiliating defeat at the hands of China. Prime Minister Nehru once again failed the country by his inability to understand China and its motives. He did not see China as it was, but alluded to traits that he believed it ought to have. His failure and culpability notwithstanding, the country rallied behind him as one, after the democratic forums had been used to condemn him and his China policy. Nehru's former friend seemed to derive vicarious pleasure out of India's humiliation and the diminishing of Nehru's stature in the world. Using the occasion, Sheikh Abdullah wrote Nehru a letter, not of sorrow or to show solidarity in that hour of trial, but sermonizing the faulty Indian policy towards Kashmir and Pakistan. He stressed the need to work with Pakistan and Kashmir for peace in the subcontinent. The Prime Minister did not fail to notice that there was not a single word of condemnation of China in the letter, and that the solution suggested by Sheikh Abdullah was the same that was being advocated by the USA and Britain. Both had been pressing, in the wake of India's humiliation, to somehow come to terms with Pakistan, make adjustments on Kashmir and work in close cooperation to contain the rising threat from China.

Inexplicably, by 1963, the Prime Minister was again having second thoughts about Sheikh Abdullah. These were probably prompted by the fact that India was in dire need of help from the Western countries since it appeared that even though the Soviet Union stood solidly behind India against Pakistan over Kashmir, it could not do the same when a fellow communist country was involved. It appeared to have adopted a neutral stance. Helpless and without the support of a powerful friend, India looked Westwards. Taking advantage of the predicament, both USA and Britain pressed India to concede Kashmir to Pakistan so that the two neighbours could be brought together to aid the West in containing both the USSR and China. This was also candidly told to the then Finance Minister Morarji Desai who was equally straight forward in telling the West that aid or no aid, there could be no compromise on Kashmir.

Meanwhile the Kashmir Conspiracy Case dragged on in the Sessions Court. The defence used every conceivable trick to drag it interminably and it was apparent that with the prosecution case still not complete, and the defence and the arguments to follow, it would take a minimum of five years for its completion. The international pressure and the delay in the completion of the case were making Prime Minister Nehru reconsider the advisability of keeping Sheikh Abdullah in detention. Adding to the pressure was Mridula Sarabhai's persistent propaganda regarding the innocence of the accused. It convinced about fifty Members of Parliament, and adding weight to their voice was Jayapraksh Narayan. They all pressed Nehru for Sheikh Abdullah's release. The Sadar-i-Riyasat was vehemently opposed to it and argued that by doing so, not only would the effort of the preceding five years go waste, but it would also plunge the State back to the uncertainty of 1958 when instability began to threaten it. Mullik argued that withdrawal of the case at that stage would amount to expressing lack of confidence in the prosecution, and would permanently damage its reputation. But Prime Minister Nehru was assailed by self-doubts and insisted that because of the delay, the people had begun to lose faith in the government. Moreover, he argued that the people of Kashmir wanted Sheikh Abdullah to be free.

As a concession to the persistent arguments of Yuvraj Karan Singh and others, Mullik says that he was once again sent to Srinagar to make an on-the-spot assessment. He held talks with Sadiq, Qasim, Dhar, Bakshi Abdul Rashid, the Sadar-i-Riyasat, and of course Prime Minister Bakshi Ghulam Mohammad. The latter, in fact, was vehement in his assertion that no consideration should be shown to Sheikh Abdullah simply because of the contents of the letter that he wrote to the Prime Minister after the Chinese aggression and India's debacle. Moreover, he argued that the Kashmir Conspiracy Case had reached a critical stage after it was upheld by the lower court and that there was every possibility that the higher court too would uphold it. Thus, the collective urgings of all those who had a direct role in the State, which were near unanimous, finally prevailed upon Prime Minister Nehru and he allowed the case to continue.

In a different part of the country, a number of events radically changed the course of history. As it is, Prime Minister Nehru bore the anger of not only the members of the opposition party but also the people of the country in general. He was squarely blamed for the Chinese debacle and for promoting incompetent generals like Lieutenant General B.M. Kaul. When the war broke, Lieutenant General Kaul had not visited the forward areas. Instead, he reported sick, flew back to Delhi, and got himself admitted in the Military Hospital. He opened himself to charges of cowardice and none of his peers have credited him with competence. Nehru somehow managed to weather the storm in Parliament, but then came three bye-elections for the Lok Sabha. The constituencies at stake were Amroha, Farrukhabad and Rajkot. The opposition decided to field Acharya J.B. Kripalani from Amroha, Dr Ram Manohar Lohia from Farrukahbad and M.R. Masani from Rajkot—three of its stalwarts and known critics of Congress and Nehru. The Congress decided to field Union Minister of Irrigation and Power, Hafiz Mohammad Ibrahim from Amroha, former Union Minister, Keskar, from Farrukhabad and Jethalal Joshi, a member of the Rajya Sabha, from Rajkot. Thus the elections were turned into a prestige issue and much was at stake. 'The results of the three elections in each of which the Congress was defeated by a sweeping majority, created a sensation in the country. While the extent of the defeat surprised everyone, it nearly stupefied the Congress, and raised great jubilation in the ranks of the Opposition,'[289] wrote Rajni Kothari in *Economic and Political Weekly*.

The Congress was shaken and there was talk of its disintegration. To check the slide, its leaders chose the ingenuous 'Kamaraj Plan'. According to it, senior Congress leaders would quit their offices in the government and go to the country to work for people's participation in the democratic revolution, which seemed to have sweeped the whole country. The proposal was unanimously adopted by the Congress Working Committee on 10th August 1963.

On Gandhi Jayanti, 2nd October 1963, Kumaraswami Kamaraj resigned from the Madras Chief Minister's post. Six Union Ministers and six Chief Ministers, including Lal Bahadur Shastri, Jagjivan Ram, Morarji Desai, Biju Patnaik and S.K. Patil followed suit.

On the face of it, the Kamaraj Plan had the potential of shaking up public life and bring the people closer to the process of development and change. That's why senior Congress leaders were to quit their offices. How Bakshi Ghulam Mohammad came to be involved in it, is not clear. Various stories circulated without much credibility. But one can assess the events as they unfolded. Bakshi had reached a stage where there were no mountains left to climb in the State. He had served his State well after the turbulence of Sheikh Abdullah's rule and in doing so, proved that he was as much an Indian nationalist as anyone. He had held the State together, diminished Sheikh Abdullah and the Plebiscite Front, and more importantly managed to take the Dogras on board without compromising on the pre-eminence of the Kashmiris. He also began to play an important role in national affairs and was thus not only privy to the Kamaraj Plan but was one of the first state leaders, along with Biju Patnaik of Orissa, to offer his resignation.

He duly resigned and on 3rd October 1963, wrote a memorandum to Sadar-i-Riyasat Karan Singh and informed him that he had made two important political announcements during a debate at the Legislative Council of the State. Both the announcements were very close to the heart of the latter as he had favoured them for a long time. Bakshi wrote:

> As this was the last session of the Legislative Council to be attended by me as Prime Minister of the State, I made an announcement of the following policy directives for implementation by the successor Government:
>
> (a) that the designation of the Head of the State (Sadar-i-Riyasat) and that of the Head of the Government (Prime Minister) should be changed to 'Governor' and 'Chief Minister' respectively, as in other States of the country; and
>
> (b) that there should be direct elections to the Parliament instead of the present system of nominations—of course after the present Emergency is over.[290]

These directives, when implemented, would get rid of the two anomalies of the system, for it was very confusing to have two Prime

Ministers in the country. The manner in which representatives of the State were sent to the Parliament too was an absurdity in view of the fact that the remaining States had thrice-elected parliamentarians to represent them through direct elections. On a personal level, the directive to change the nomenclature of 'Sadar-i-Riyasat' was very satisfying for Yuvraj Karan Singh as that would give him the distinction of being the first and the last Sadar-i-Riyasat of the State![291] As Prime Minister, this act of paving the way for greater integration of the State was Bakshi's last gift to India. Soon after, the hounds of vendetta were let loose on him.

There is absolutely no doubt that whatever his role during the power-struggle with the Maharaja, once he became part of the government and realized the depth of the State's bonds with India, Bakshi Ghulam Mohammad was a true champion of nationalism in the State. He never wavered, though he jealously guarded the State's interests and the federalism that was inherent in the Indian constitution. He was also extremely loyal to Prime Minister Nehru and carried out his bidding without demurring. But over a period of time, he had made enemies too. As it is, because of his lack of education, the educated leaders held him in subtle contempt and the alleged corruption of his relatives did not help his cause. Therefore, many believed that he was one of those whom the Central leadership wanted removed from power in order to refurbish the image of the Congress. Bakshi was one of the many Chief Ministers who were considered to be symbols of all that had gone wrong with the party and hence, as a first step, they needed to be removed. The Kamaraj Plan gave a respectable exit to these chief ministers as well as the Central leadership. Many years later, Jagmohan, former Governor of the Jammu and Kashmir wrote: 'Bakshi Ghulam Mohammad, however, suffered from three disabilities. First, he was painted as a betrayer of the Kashmir cause; the Plebiscite Front carried out a virulent attack against him. Secondly, his political rivals within the National Conference continuously sniped at him and carried tales to New Delhi. Thirdly, the coterie around Bakshi Ghulam Mohammad built a system of personal and political patronage and indulged in gross nepotism and corruption.'[292]

Finding a successor to Bakshi was not easy. Sadiq would have made an ideal choice, but he could not muster enough support in the legislature party, even though everybody, including Sadar-i-Riyasat and the senior Congress leaders in Delhi, preferred him. But it appeared that Bakshi Abdul Rashid would defeat him to the post and Delhi did not want a poor imitation of Bakshi Ghulam Mohammad to succeed him. After quitting office, Bakshi too realized the enormity of his resignation and was averse to a life without power. He, therefore, pushed forward Shamsuddin's name as the Chief Ministerial candidate. He was successful in having Shamshuddin, his puppet, installed. Sadiq, Qasim and Dhar did not join the new Cabinet and soon it became obvious that the State had become a house divided. This was no different from what had happened in all those states where the Kamaraj Plan had been implemented. All those leaders who had been asked to resign were men of considerable substance, and once out of power, they had no choice but to work for the splinter groups that emerged in order to keep their followers in some kind of power structure. Mullik rightly summed up the impact of the Kamaraj Plan: 'To my mind the implementation of the Kamraj Plan [*sic*] really wrought havoc both in the political and administrative fields in India. It brought about serious disunity in the Congress practically in all States… Much of the political backsliding that took place in 1964 and 1965 could be traced to the Kamraj [Kamaraj] Plan… The final result of this was the complete debacle of the Congress in Kamraj's [*sic*] own State, Madras and in several other States of India during the general elections of 1967.'[293]

The challenge before the new Prime Minister of the State was to keep the disruptive forces at bay. For a decade, Bakshi had succeeded but many observers were not sure if Shamsuddin possessed the qualities needed to do that. It took only two months to find out. As for Bakshi, it must be said that the Congress leadership did not treat him fairly. After resigning, he came to Delhi ostensibly to be adjusted in some organizational role. Had the Congress done that, he would have been the first Kashmiri leader to have an all-India profile and that would have sent very positive signals in the Valley. His exit from power and the events that followed gave an opportunity to the anti-Indian forces to release their long suppressed resentment and fury. In the process, the State was to be overwhelmed by the events.

With Shamsuddin as the Prime Minister, the political parties suddenly found reason to be active. Bakshi had used all the tricks available to a person in power to keep these activities dormant. Now suddenly there was a spurt. The first major change was ushered by the Praja Parishad. Its proximity to the Bharatiya Jana Sangh, as that of the National Conference to Congress, was well known, but now Pandit Prem Nath Dogra gave the lead by merging it with the Bharatiya Jana Sangh. Thus a major step was taken with the entry of a mainland political party into the State. It was soon to be followed by the entry of the Praja Socialist Party with Balraj Puri[294] becoming the president of the State unit. Mohammad Shafi Qureshi[295] floated his own outfit called the Jammu and Kashmir National Congress.

Soon however, a crisis of unimagined magnitude rocked the State. In the early morning of 27th December 1963, Rahim Banday, the Senior Nishan Dez at the Hazratbal mosque, found that the side door of the passage leading to the room where Moe-e-Muqaddas (hair of the prophet) was housed, had been broken open. The locks on the inner door leading to the sanctuary too were broken. Also, the lock on the front door of the passage was forced open from inside. 'The wooden box containing the Moe-e-Muqaddas had been taken out from the small wooden shelf, in which it had been kept, after forcing open the shelf, and the small bag containing the tube with the Moe-e-Muqaddas inside had been removed leaving the velvet covering, the trappings and the wooden box behind in the shelf.'[296]

How the Moe-e-Muqaddas reached Kashmir and its resting place in Hazratbal, is a long history that has inspired reverence and faith in the Holy Relic and Prophet Muhammad. None of the narrations are absolutely correct but the one summarized by Mullik in his book is the one that the Kashmiris believe in.

In 1635 A.D., during the reign of Shahjahan, one Hazrat Syed Abdullah, claiming to be the Mutwali of the main shrine at Medina, arrived in Bijapur, then an independent State. He claimed that he was a direct descendant of Prophet Muhammad and had with him a strand of Prophet's holy hair, which came to be known as the

Moe-e-Muqaddas. The ruler of Bijapur, a fellow Shia, bestowed a *jagir*, which in due course passed on to Syed Abdullah's son, Syed Hamid. After the annexation of Bijapur into the Mughal Empire during Aurangzeb's Deccan campaign, Syed Hamid came into contact with a Kashmiri trader Noor-ud-din Ashwari, who had got to know of the Holy Relic and asked Syed Hamid to give it to him. It is said that though Syed Hamid refused at first, that same night he dreamt Prophet Muhammad asking him to hand over the Moe-e-Muqaddas to the Kashmiri trader. Ashwari too had a similar dream in which the Prophet asked him to take the Holy Relic to Kashmir and install it by a lakeside. On his way back to Kashmir, Ashwari gave *deedar* of the Relic to people and the news spread fast, reaching Aurangzeb who was in the Deccan. The emperor ordered that it be produced before him and Ashwari was put in prison. Medanish, Ashwari's servant, accompanied the Holy Relic for production before Aurangzeb who, after its veracity, ordered it to be sent to Dargah Sahib at Ajmer for preservation.

However, soon after its installation there, Aurangzeb had a dream in which Prophet Muhammad asked him to restore it to Ashwari so that it could be installed in Kashmir. In accordance with the orders, the Relic was given back to Medanish with some money and an escort to accompany it to Kashmir. In the meantime, Ashwari died in prison from an illness and the shock of the loss of the Moe-e-Muqaddas. Medanish had his body exhumed and then, escorted by guards and several holy men, proceeded to Kashmir where it was ordered by the Governor, Mir Fazil Khan, to be installed in the Khanqah Naqshband. However, because of the many devotees and the space constraint, it was installed outside the town in the Bagh-i-Sadiq built by Shahjahan on the banks of the Dal Lake. In due course, the place came to be known as Asar-e-Sharif or the Relic Shrine because of the presence of Moe-e-Muqaddas, and then later Hazratbal. After its installation, Ashwari's family kept control over it and were the only people entitled to exhibit it. With the passage of time these members came to be known as the Nishan Dez.

Mullik was deeply involved in the events after the theft of the Moe-e-Muqaddas. He was made in-charge of the operation to recover it, and there is no one better than him to describe all that went with the case. He also knew of the history, myth and faith involving it and knew that it was not the first time that it had been either stolen or removed, for there were instances of at least two previous occasions, when it was found missing. On both occasions, it had come back by a miracle. It reinforced the faith that it had travelled from Arabia to India to be installed at Hazratbal under its own grace and that it would not allow itself to be taken away from its resting place for long. In a year, there are ten days, all connected with the life of Prophet Muhammad, when it is displayed for the public. On the day it is to be displayed, the Nishan Dez on duty would bring the quartz tube containing the Relic on the balcony of the Hazratbal mosque and show it to the congregation in front. Except for those on the balcony none can actually see it but the mere sight of the container sends the pilgrims back satisfied. Apart from these ten days, the Nishan Dez was also known to hold a private display for selected people.

The Moe-e-Muqaddas was last displayed on 20th December 1963, the Friday following the *Miraj-e-Alam*, a holy day connected with the life and experience of Prophet Muhammad. After the display, it was put back in its place by the senior Nishan Dez, Rahim Bandey. On 26th December, the Relic was again taken out for a private exposition by the same Nishan Dez, after which he placed it in its resting place and went home. Only a few pilgrims remained in the mosque who prayed till midnight. By midnight, owing to the severe cold, all these pilgrims left the prayer hall and it was empty. On the morning of 27th December, Rahim Bandey noticed the theft.

The shocking news spread like wildfire and by afternoon thousands of people marched in the streets of Srinagar, protesting against the theft and demanding its immediate restoration and the punishment to the culprits. It was a spontaneous strike, with more and more people gathering around Hazratbal mosque and the streets of the city. At that moment another red rag was shown to the disturbed people when 'Bakshi Abdul Rashid, General Secretary of the National Conference [nephew of Bakshi Ghulam Mohammad] arrived there in an open jeep and, with good intentions but in his usual tactless and brusque manner, told the crowd to disperse and not to create any trouble and further added that, as on previous occasions, the Holy Relic was sure to come back, as there was nobody in the world who could remove the Relic permanently from its place of rest.'[297]

His presence and the people's disturbed state of mind, created an ugly situation. The general public's pent up anger against the Bakshis found a ruse in the event to express itself in the most violent terms. First, the crowd attacked Bakshi Abdul Rashid and it took the police a great effort to rescue him. By then the crowd had gone out of control and it marched towards the hotel and cinema house owned by Bakshi Abdul Majid, a brother of the former Prime Minister. They crowd set it on fire. The success of this violence whetted the crowd's appetite and it marched towards the Kothibagh Police Station and set fire to it too, whereupon the police opened fire, killing three. It is difficult to explain how anger at a sacrilege turned into an expression of deep anger against the Bakshi family and the government. There is little doubt that extraneous factors were involved in it for it is difficult to put Bakshi in the dock since everyone knew how much he had done for the improvement of the Hazratbal mosque. But now, the situation was that a matter of sacrilege had become an occasion to demonstrate anger against the government. For many days, the city and the Valley life remained paralyzed, with more and more people pouring into Srinagar from all over. In fact, the 'whole Valley went into mourning; peoplc wore black, and cars were allowed to ply only if they flew black flags. It was bitterly cold in Kashmir, but many people were so shocked that they stopped lighting their kitchen fires. Women came out onto to the streets in black gowns crying and wailing, though luckily there was no communal tension.'[298]

Sadar-i-Riyasat Karan Singh was in Varanasi to preside over the convocation of the Banaras Hindu University when he got the disturbing news. He immediately boarded the first train for Pathankot, then the railhead for Jammu. The first thing he did was to record a message for the radio, expressing his deep anguish at the theft. Meanwhile, Prime Minister Shamsuddin, who was in Jammu owing to the Durbar move, rushed to Srinagar but remained almost paralyzed, confined to his house since he dared not face the hostile crowds. The day the crisis began, Bakshi Ghulam Mohammad was in Delhi. No sooner did he hear the news, than he left for Srinagar. Only Sadiq and Mir Qasim were in Srinagar. Soon, it was evident that there were multiple forces trying to influence the course of events. So Yuvraj Karan Singh took an Indian Air Force plane to Delhi on 2nd January 1964, to consult with the centre. 'The Pakistan Radio, of course, was gloating over the incidents in Kashmir and was loudly accusing the Government of India for having engineered the theft of [the] Moe-e-Muqaddas in order to humiliate and completely suppress the Muslims of the Kashmir Valley.'[299]

While Mullik was sent from Delhi to take charge of the investigation and recovery of the Holy Relic, the Sadar-i-Riyasat was asked to be prepared to take charge of the administration, since it was becoming clear that the crisis was beyond the administrative and political capabilities of Shamsuddin. In Srinagar Mullik was assisted by Laksman Das Thakur, the Inspector General of Police, in what seemed like an impossible task in that charged atmosphere. There he found that apart from the general strike that brought life to a halt, an Action Committee had been formed under the chairmanship of Maulavi Mohammad Syed Masoodi and included Maulavi Mohammad Farooq, the same person who was appointed as the Mirwaiz and who had begun spewing venom against India, and Sheikh Abdullah's eldest son, Farooq Abdullah, then known as Sheikh Farooq. The city was taken over by the volunteers of the Action Committee and *langars* were organized at various places. 'Large crowds were coming from villages carrying food, bedding, and even fuel for warming their bodies. There was no end to the streams of people and all the main roads were blocked by thousands of people and the smallest procession was at least a mile long covering the entire width of the road including the footpaths… The people remained seated on the ice with the snow falling from the top, hearing the speeches of the Action Committee members for hours at a stretch… The Ministers were virtual prisoners confined to their houses with police guards protecting them. All public institutions and offices were guarded by armed police… It was the Action Committee which was ruling the city.'[300]

Before the day ended on 1st January 1964, Mullik recreated the theft in his mind. By his understanding, the 'locks had been broken open between midnight and 3 am on the night of December 26/27. Locks of both the front and the side door were broken. This was not necessary as the breaking of one lock was enough to allow entry and this could be the lock of the side door only which was locked from outside and not the lock of the front door which was locked from inside. The latter could be broken only after entry had been effected. Unless the culprit knew how and where exactly the Holy Relic was kept, it would have been difficult for an outside burglar to lay his hands on it… The culprit must have been one…whose presence in any part of the mosque including the passage in front of the sanctuary at any time of the night would not arouse suspicion.'[301]

The Director of the Intelligence Bureau clearly suspected the theft to be an inside job as there was no other way of stealing the Relic. But, why, and by whom, that remained unanswered. The Action Committee met him to seek assurance that not only would the Relic be recovered but the guilty, however powerful, would be booked and brought to justice. In fact, in no uncertain terms, they hinted at the complicity of the Bakshi family. Rumours were doing the round that an elderly member of that family was on death-bed and wished to have a *deedar* of the Relic before dying and hence it had been removed. Even as the state government went into stupor, the crowds became restive. In Delhi, it was finally settled that the Sadar-i-Riyasat, with a team of experienced and efficient officials, proceed to Srinagar and be ready to impose the Sadar-i-Riyasat's rule in accordance with the State-constitution. On 3rd January 1964, the whole party left for Srinagar by an Indian Air Force plane, but owing to the inclement weather it had to land in Jammu from where the party had to proceed by road.

On reaching Srinagar, Sadar-i-Riyasat Karan Singh played a master-stroke that greatly helped in keeping the people's rising frustration and anger under control and gave an insight into the kind of relationship that the ordinary Kashmiris, uninfluenced by the demagoguery of the politicians, had developed with the Dogra dynasty. 'It was bitterly cold, and instead of staying at Karan Mahal, I had decided that it would be more convenient to stay with my cousin Nasib Chand who managed my orchards and lived in a snug house called Cherry Grove inside our main orchard facing the Dal Lake.

'On the 4th morning my first action was to visit Hazratbal itself. I did not consult Shamsuddin, as I knew he would advise me against gong [going] on security and political considerations. However, I was quite clear on what I should do and, besides, I had genuine reverence for the shrine. I went in a private car without a flag, with only Nasib and a staff officer accompanying me. I did not allow either the pilot or the police escort to come, because any show of pomp and authority on that occasion would have been most inappropriate. As soon as we reached the shrine, I was immediately mobbed by thousands of people who had been virtually camping there since the relic had disappeared a week earlier. They seemed genuinely delighted to see me, and pressed around me. Some of the elderly people kissed my hands and embraced me saying, "*Hamara Badshah aa gaya*" ("Our king has come"). I was deeply moved to see that, despite three decades of anti-Dogra propaganda and brainwashing by Sheikh Abdullah and his party, the Kashmiris retained regard and deep affection for me even in their hour of anguish.'[302]

After proceeding to the shrine, Karan Singh offered prayers for the speedy return of the Relic and directed that special prayers on his behalf be conducted at the Muslim, Hindu and Sikh shrines in the Valley. Later, on his return, he prepared for the task of dealing with the situation and held discussions with political leaders across the board, and civil and military officials. Sadiq, Qasim and Dhar urged him to dismiss the Shamsuddin government and place the state under the Sadar-i-Riyasat's rule. An all-party delegation from Jammu, consisting of the Praja Parishad, the Praja Socialist Party and the Akali Dal favoured similar action. The city was taken over by the Action Committee and neither the government nor the National Conference was to be seen anywhere. So the Sadar-i-Riyasat decided to give twenty-four hours to the team working on the recovery of the Relic before he recommended to the Prime Minister that the Sadar-i-Riyasat's rule be imposed. Accordingly, he informed B.N. Mullik.

Anti-Indian forces actively supported by Pakistan, the so-called

'Azad Kashmir Radio', and a few Islamic countries began to raise the level of virulent propaganda. Mysteriously, posters appeared all over the city carrying a letter allegedly written by Sheikh Abdullah to Prime Minister Nehru. It alluded to the letter that he had written to him earlier after the Chinese aggression and repeated his demand of a triple alliance of India, Pakistan and Kashmir to bring about peace in the subcontinent. He also accused the Indian Prime Minister of lacking in wisdom and of allowing the State to be ruled by his stooges. Indirectly, the Sheikh also suggested that if Nehru wanted peace to return to the Valley, then he should be released. Effectively he warned that unless the administration was handed over to him, peace could not be restored. The theme of the posters was repeated in the public meetings that were held all over the State with the additional demand that the recovery of the Holy Relic be made under the supervision of Sheikh Abdullah else even if the recovery was made, it would remain a suspect.[303]

For the first time in its history, faith and politics joined on a common ground, forcing the authorities to subject the whole area around Hazratbal under security cover. By now, the investigators were certain of a Pakistan conspiracy through Pir Maqbool Gilani, who used his influence and contacts for the removal of the Relic. But they were certain that the Relic was still in Kashmir for it was unimaginable that anyone from Kashmir or the mosque would connive for its removal to be taken away from Kashmir or even Hazratbal. The importance of Hazratbal depended upon it, and so did the livelihood of all those who made money because of the numerous visitors there. But because of the delay in its recovery, a tricky situation began to emerge. The presence of the Sadar-i-Riyasat made people speculate about the impending dismissal of Shamsuddin. Once again people saw Bakshi's hand in it, for they thought that the theft and the uncertainty was created to set the stage for his comeback. Mullik is of the opinion that the demand that the Relic be recovered under the supervision of Sheikh Abdullah too was linked with the fact that the culprits knew that the noose was tightening and hence the conspirators wanted all the credit to go to Sheikh Abdullah.

It was in this context that, by the evening of 3rd January,

Mullik devised a brilliant strategy upon getting the Sadar-i-Riyasat's ultimatum to recover the Relic soon or have the government removed. Mullik decided that there was a possibility that the cornered culprits might throw the Relic away in the Dal Lake, making its recovery impossible. Hence, he wanted to give them the option of surreptitiously letting it return, as it had on earlier occasions. 'It was made public that for the next 24 hours all guards around Hazratbal would be withdrawn, so that whoever had taken the Relic could put it back without arousing suspicion.'[304]

The next day, 'At 5 pm…we recovered the Moe-e-Muqaddas! I cannot describe the process which led to its replacement at the place from which it had been removed on December 27. This was an intelligence operation, never to be disclosed. Thakur and I went to Hazratbal Mosque. We entered the holy shrine and the Moe-e-Muqaddas was resting in its old wooden box, broken though it was. We brought out the Moe-e-Muqadass [*sic*] with great reverence. I carried it on my head and told the waiting crowds that we had found their treasured Relic. They started jumping with pleasure and cried "*Mubarak*" to me,' wrote Mullik in his book.[305] Much of that night was spent in calling all the Nishan Dezs one by one so that they could authenticate the genuineness of the Relic. This was duly done and then it was placed in a big hall of the first floor of the Shergarhi Police Station, till the time it was formally identified and restored in its place. Besides the Nishan Dez, nearly a dozen other people who had had the private *deedar* of the Relic, saw it and also identified it.

Pakistan had been thwarted in its designs. But it was not yet done, and it began the propaganda, casting aspersions on the genuineness of the recovered Relic, provoking, the people in general and the Action Committee in particular, to restart the agitation. None of its objectives were achieved; Sheikh Abdullah remained in detention; the government was not changed; Bakshi was not arrested; there was no bloodshed except for the violence of the first day and importantly, India remained firm in its control. But Pakistani propaganda gave the Action Committee the idea to demand that its members be involved in the identification of the Moe-e-Muqaddas. That these members were puppets was beyond doubt, for while only a few days earlier they had congratulated Mullik for his role in the recovery of the Relic, now they were again casting doubts. Time was running out, since soon, on 6th February 1964, the next *deedar* was to take place. Thus, in a ceremonial procession, the Relic was taken to Hazratbal on a rainy, snowy and bitingly cold day and installed on 10th January 1964. Meanwhile Pakistan continued to fan disaffection by constantly harping on the subject of the fake Relic placed by the '*kafir*' Hindu officers. This began to have its effect and by 20th January aggressive demonstrations began in Srinagar. On the 25th, the situation took an ugly turn when people coming out of the mosques after prayers turned violent and attacked the Punjab Armed Police at many places, which in turn opened fire, killing six people. The Action Committee demanded that it have a special *deedar* but was refused, since 6th February, the appointed day for the *deedar*, was not too far away. It was obvious that the real target of the miscreants was the Republic Day.

The day passed amidst continued protests, but the persistence of the Action Committee to seek a special *deedar* gained strength. Finally, Prime Minister Nehru interceded to concede the demand, for it was feared that on the regular *deedar* day of 6th February, when thousands of people from all over the Valley would have gathered, there could be serious trouble if aspersions were cast on the genuineness of the Relic. Lal Bahadur Shastri was deputed from Delhi to be present there during this crisis. Much drama was to follow as a team of holy men was constituted by the Action Committee as identifiers. On the appointed day—3rd February—everyone including Shastri, Shamsuddin, Mullik and the members of the Action Committee along with the holy men gathered in the hall of Hazratbal. Syed Masoodi, an active member of the Action Committee and no friend of India, took charge of the proceedings and exhorted the holy men to be careful in judging the authenticity of the Relic and give their judgment. He gave copies of the Quran to each of the fourteen identifiers to swear by it, and to give only the correct verdict. Finally, the Relic was brought for identification. 'The first to give the verdict was Faqir Mirak Shah, the holiest of holy men in Kashmir, and the stir was caused when he uttered the single word "*Haq*" meaning right. All tenseness was broken. Everybody except the members of the Action Committee was jubilant.'[306]

Thus, a serious crisis that had gripped the Valley and which caused sleepless nights to the leaders in Delhi ended after thirty-seven days. The members of the Action Committee were crestfallen for they were sure that their plan would succeed. Pakistan had once again been worsted. Politically, a shakeup was in the offing. If the disappearance of the Holy Relic was linked to proving Bakshi's indispensability to the State, then this myth was to be exposed. With his aura of invincibility gone, there was no possibility of Bakshi staging a comeback. Powerful and credible voices spoke out against him, one such voice being Ghulam Mohammad Sadiq. On 15th January 1964, Sadiq wrote a long letter to Prime Minister Nehru. He too blamed Bakshi for trying to communalize the issue and inciting the people to violence, but of greater significance was the fact that he attacked some of the established beliefs that had taken root during the preceding decade. He wrote: 'One of the beliefs that has been commonly entertained in the past is that the influence of Pakistan on the Kashmir Muslims is fairly wide and firmly rooted. From this belief has stemmed a primordial fear of the people. Based on this fear, policies have developed and influenced every sphere of our life… The rule of law was thrown overboard and all executive agencies as well as the judiciary were bent to the service of the clique in the National Conference. Corruption in all branches of administration and political life was considered to be something inevitable in this situation… In this the Bakshi family held a place of significance, absolute prominence and power. From all this a myth was born that the National Conference is a sturdy organization of the people headed by two strong men, the twins of the Bakshi family. During the last ten fateful days the people of Kashmir, every man, woman and child irrespective of religion or party affiliations has given a lie to these assumptions. When the whole population of the State was on the move, these elements of the National Conference who had harmed the interests of the people for their personal benefits were hiding in their rat holes.'[307]

Sadiq went on to pay tribute to the people of all religions of the State who spared no effort to strengthen communal harmony in those trying times. He particularly singled out Pandit Prem Nath Dogra for special praise: 'The Hindus, Sikhs and Muslims mingled together and the blood of the common ancestors flowed in their veins, and tears came into my eyes when I heard their full throated cries of *Har Har Mahadev, Allah-o-Akbar* and *Sat-Siri-Akal*. This was the greatest moment of glory in their history. In this demonstration of civil behaviour who would not be proud to be a Kashmiri? In forging this unity between the people of Jammu and of Kashmir credit goes to the saner sections of the National Conference in Jammu and more prominently to Pandit P.N. Dogra. He along with others successfully combated the rumours of communal riots in Kashmir assiduously spread by the pro-Bakshi sections of the National Conference in Jammu.'[308]

It appeared that finally the narrative of the State was about to change. For the first time, a reputed Kashmiri politician had bluntly pointed out to the strength and the weakness of the State and told the Central leadership of how wrong it was in its assumptions.

19

A New Era

Life has an inscrutable way of compensating people. Soon after the Sadar-i-Riyasat Karan Singh had relinquished his right to the titles of 'His Highness' and 'Maharaja', he earned two new titles. The first was by virtue of the Delhi University accepting his thesis on the political thought of Sri Aurobindo and hence, rather than inheriting a title, he earned the right to be addressed as 'Dr Karan Singh'. This he realized was much more rewarding and satisfying. The second title was of the 'Honorary Major General' of the Indian Army, bestowed upon him by the new President Dr Radhakrishnan.[309] Amidst the Chinese crisis, he was also bestowed with the rare honour of being elected the Sadar-i-Riyasat for the third consecutive term.

Ironically, the Chinese debacle and the resultant re-ignition of patriotic and nationalistic fervour also triggered a transformation in the Dogra society that has not been fully appreciated by the sociologists. As a result of the vindictive policies of Sheikh Abdullah, a generation of youth in the rural areas, particularly among the Rajputs, had been lost to the agitation launched by the Praja Parishad. This generation had also suffered the psychological inability to adjust with the changes that took place in the society. The lost generation had been left behind in life because of the combination of disrupted studies and lack of focus. They were also denied the main avenue of employment, with the State Forces being the first to bear the brunt of changed policies. Thus, they could neither be commissioned with ease of the past as officers in the army, nor inducted as soldiers, as many of the battalions were subjected to disbanding. There was also no place for them in the administrative services of the State, since they lacked the essential qualification of being a member of the National Conference. However, with the Emergency having been declared in the wake of the Chinese aggression, recruitment to the Indian Army had opened up opportunities. The academically less qualified made a beeline to the recruitment centres. In addition, the work opportunities at the Emergency Commission too were offered and with academic standards lowered, a large number of Dogras were inducted as officers. It was this single blessing in disguise that began a transformation in the Dogra society as those inducted in the army were exposed to the wider Indian consciousness that gave them, and the succeeding generation, the wherewithal to avail of the opportunities of the emerging world. Jammu soon began to occupy its rightful place in the Indian Republic with ease and gratitude.

Another significant development that was going to impact the whole State was a fresh approach by the Kashmiri leaders towards the Dogras and Hindus who had an equal stake in the wellbeing of the State. The rule of Bakshi Ghulam Mohammad had greatly bridged the gap between the State and the rest of the country. But the arbitrary nature of the administration, however benign, had marred its reputation. The prevalent culture of nepotism and rampant corruption, real and perceived, at all levels had made the people cynical. This was manifested in the manner in which the shock of the people following the disappearance of the Moe-e-Muqaddas turned into an anti-Bakshi tirade. This also gave an opportunity to the anti-Indian forces to exploit the sentiments and the situation to their advantage. But there were also voices of sanity. They took a while in articulating themselves, but when they did they came as a whiff of fresh air. They dissipated the hatred and the anger; the suspicion and antagonism that had been brewing since the 1930s. One such voice was that of Ghulam Mohammad Sadiq. Politically placed among the left of the centre politicians, he was not only well educated but also liberal in thought and sensitive by nature. He had had his run-ins with Bakshi but had returned to the fold of the National Conference. Ideally, he should have succeeded Bakshi upon his resignation, but that was thwarted by the former

Prime Minister of the State. However, the Holy Relic episode had given considerable food for thought for all the politicians. The singular act of Yuvraj Karan Singh visiting the shrine in the midst of chaos and the scenes that followed signified the emotional ties of the Dogra rulers with the Muslim population and was an eye opener for many. But one of them who read the underlying message and chose to react was Sadiq.

In his long letter to Prime Minister Nehru, dated 15th January 1964, for the first time in recent history, a leading Muslim politician from the Valley had demolished the religious factor in the State politics by dismissing it as distorted by those who wished to exploit the people for their narrow political goals. With exceptional clarity of mind and 'intellectual integrity', Sadiq had written: 'We have been too often led to believe that anything that smacked of the Hindu world injured the sentiments of Muslims here. Therefore, we have been asked to prefer and tolerate the Muslim politician or a Muslim civil servant even though he be corrupt and tyrannous... Why is it that Dr Karan Singh, a scion of the Dogra Dynasty, was mentioned with the deepest affection and respect in the public meetings attended by lacs of people? Why is it that Sheikh Sahib's son and many other speakers from public platform demanded and continue to demand the rule of [the] Sadar-i-Riyasat in preference to the rule of 'Muslim' Bakshi? The people of Kashmir have torn to pieces shibboleths in which, alas, the Government of India has been led to place its faith by interested and self-seeking individuals for many years in the past.'[310] Sadiq was, in fact, pleading for the need to break out of these shackles and begin a new era.

On a political and constitutional plane, the nearly decade-long rule of Bakshi Ghulam Mohammad had brought the State closer to the Union and the Indian Constitution. It was not that he blindly followed the dictates of the Centre, but sweeping changes took place due to the goodwill that existed between the two. Voices were still raised for the abrogation of Article 370, as no doubt, they would be raised in the future, and it was left for the government to explain to the Parliament and the people at large, the necessity of the said Article.

By November 1963, this issue was once again raised in the

Parliament. By then, a number of changes had already been affected by the Presidential Order with the concurrence of the State government. The Constitution of India and Article 370 had specifically provided for this and Bakshi Ghulam Mohammad had recognized the need for such changes. This process was accelerated when Ghulam Mohammad Sadiq, who succeeded Shamsuddin as the Prime Minister of the State, decided to implement what Bakshi had promised the Legislative Council while announcing his resignation.

The issue came up for discussion in the Parliament while the erosion of Article 370 was being debated. The Minister of State in the Ministry of Home Affairs, Hajarnavis, informed the House of the applicability of a new entry 26 of the Concurrent List (List III) of the Seventh Schedule regarding legal and medical professions to the State of Jammu and Kashmir. He went on to inform that, among other things, '(3) It has been decided that the representatives of Jammu and Kashmir in the Lok Sabha should be chosen by direct election as in other States… (4) It has also been decided that the Sadar-i-Riyasat and Prime Minister of Jammu and Kashmir should be designated as Governor and Chief Minister respectively. Legislation to give effect to the proposal is expected to be taken up during the next session of the State Legislature… Since this Article [370] was incorporated in the Constitution, many changes have been made which bring the State of Jammu and Kashmir in line with rest of India. The State is fully integrated…the Government is of the opinion that they should not take any initiative now for the complete repeal of Article 370. This will, no doubt, be brought about by further changes in consultation with the Government and the Legislative Assembly of Jammu and Kashmir State.'[311]

Prime Minister Nehru too intervened in the debate and reminded the House that the said Article 'is a part of certain transitional provisional arrangements. It is not a permanent part of the Constitution. It is a part so long as it remains so.' He went on to add that '[the] Home Minister has pointed out, it has been eroded, if I may use the word, and many things have been done in the last few years which have made the relationship of Kashmir with the Union of India very close.'[312] Then he referred to certain provisions of the State that barred the citizens of the Union from buying land in the State and said that it was essential to safeguard the interests of the local population against the more resourceful outsiders just as it had been done in the North East Frontier Agency. Nehru asserted that this did not come in the way of full integration of the State. Finally, the Prime Minister added, '...we feel that this process of gradual erosion of article 370 is going on. Some fresh steps are being taken and in the next month or two [and] they will be completed. We should allow it to go on. We do not want to take the initiative in this matter and completely put an end to Article 370. The initiative, we feel, should come from the Kashmir State Government and people. We shall gradually agree to that. The process is continuing.'[313]

The critics of Article 370 were, however, not satisfied, and the next year the subject once again reared its head in the Lok Sabha when a Bill for omission of Article 370 was moved by Prakash Vir Shastri. After a lengthy debate, Home Minister Gulzarilal Nanda addressed the parliament on 4th December 1964. The Home Minister drew the attention of the mover of the Bill to the Article in its totality and weighed the pros and cons of its abrogation. During the course of his arguments he said, 'The power to amend the Constitution is derived from Article 368. If the hon. Member looks at the article, he will find that there is at the bottom a proviso which reads thus...

"In its application to the State of Jammu and Kashmir, to Article 368, the following proviso shall be added:-

"Provided further that no such amendment shall have effect in relation to the State of Jammu and Kashmir unless applied by order of the President under clause (1) of article 370."' Thus, if any constitutional change has to be brought, then one has to resort to the proviso of Article 370. The Home Minister reminded the House that every year some new constitutional provision is extended to the State under this proviso and if the Article is taken away, then the Union denies itself the route through which such changes can be made applicable to the State. He also warned that if 'it is imagined that by the repeal of Article 370 all the provisions of the Constitution will automatically apply to Jammu and Kashmir, it is

[a] very erroneous reading of the constitution. As things stand...the impediments in the way of achieving uniformity...are not created by Article 370. These impediments are strewn through the pages of the Constitution. In a hundred places, there are those provisions which take away the force of application of the Constitution to Jammu and Kashmir. What will happen to them? Remove Article 370. They remain... In the text of the articles of the Constitution also there are these qualifications and restrictions. You remove article 370. What happens to those articles? They still remain. This is a sizeable chunk of the Constitution. Article 308 and 152 make special reference to J&K. If we repeal article 370, these references still stand. There is the whole Part VI and Part XII relating to services.'[314]

Arguing for the retention of Article 370, Home Minister Gulzarilal Nanda also referred to a member calling it not just a wall between India and the State, but a mountain. Nanda replied that if it was so, then the provision under the Article was the tunnel through which the Union could reach out to the Valley. The provision under Article 370 to extend the provisions of the Constitution was a much more simple method for integration than taking the route of the Amendment, which is subject to various stringent conditions. At that stage of the debate, another member, N.C. Chatterjee referred to clause (3) of Article 370, which says: 'Notwithstanding anything in the forgoing provisions of this article, the President may, by public notification, declare that this article shall cease to be operative or shall be operative only with such exceptions and modifications and from such date as he may specify.' In making the statement the member omitted the proviso that said: 'Provided that the recommendation of the Constituent Assembly of the State referred to in clause (2) shall be necessary before the President issues such a notification.' But Chatterjee reminded the Lok Sabha that the fact was that the Assembly had been dissolved and, therefore, the proviso was 'otiose, and according to my submission when the Constituent Assembly is not functioning, the proviso does not operate any more, and the President has got unfettered powers to act under clause (3).'[315] Chatterjee was adamant that there was no impediment in extending the whole of the Constitution to the State and that it could be done by a simple executive order of the President. The Home Minister appeared to be taken aback by the force of the arguments and conceded that he was unable to say whether clause (3) was available or not, but he was certain that there 'is an easier path available to us, a more handy instrument for us to get the same thing done.' He posed the question, 'Why do we go about bringing in amendments to the Constitution itself with all the processes attendant on that, when article 370 itself enables—not through clause (3) but through clause (1) and (2)—the President to pass orders which will enable any entry in the Lists to be taken and applied to Jammu and Kashmir and any other provision of the Constitution?'[316]

The soul of Home Minister's argument remained that by taking away Article 370, there would be the challenge of dealing with the restrictions and qualifications to the various other articles in the Constitution where they are made applicable to the State. In the circumstances, the better route remained that of resorting to clause (2) and issuing a Presidential order to make the changes. Nanda also argued that Article 370 was not static and because of its dynamic nature, year after year, by the use of this clause, Jammu and Kashmir had been assimilated with the rest of the country and a general corrosion had taken place to the Article. Therefore, the policy pursued by the Government of India in this regard did not 'suffer from any kind of inherent limitation, because it can unfold itself completely. What happens is that only the shell is there. Article 370, whether you keep it or not, has been completely emptied of its contents. Nothing has been left in it. We can regulate it, we can do it in one day, in ten days, ten months. That is entirely for us to consider.'[317]

These were memorable words. The words that resonated in the Valley among the leaders and supporters of the Plebiscite Front in a manner that the debate continues unabated till this day. At this juncture of the debate, another member, Hem Barua from Gauhati (Guwahati), interjected and reminded the House of the harsh reality—that there were reports that the Plebiscite Front was planning demonstrations from the very next day against the policies of the Union and the State governments. The debate that day also brought out the deep-seated resentment that some members nursed regarding the benefits extended to Jammu and Kashmir. When Home Minister Nanda mentioned the beneficiary relations between the Centre and the State, parliamentarians N.G. Ranga and Kapur Singh made jealous comments, the former saying, 'They get so much more' and 'We have been subsidizing all the time.' The latter added, 'It is one-sided benefit.'

During the same debate, Home Minister Nanda informed the Lok Sabha that ever since Sadiq had become the Chief Minister of the State, the process of bringing the State closer to the Union by the use of the Presidential orders had been accelerated. Constitutional provisions regarding welfare of labour; legal, medical and other professions; trade and commerce; distribution of commodities; price control; gold control; enquiries and statistics regulation of labour and safety in mines; vital statistics including registration of births and deaths; vocational and technical training; and newspapers, books and printing presses had been extended to the State.

In the pipeline, at that point in time, was also the application of provisions regarding the election of Members of Parliament from Jammu and Kashmir. The application iterated how they too should be elected, like in the rest of the country, through direct elections. Till then, the Members of Parliament from Jammu and Kashmir were nominated by the State Assembly. In addition, the nomenclature of the Sadar-i-Riyasat and Prime Minister was also all set to be changed, so that the State had a Governor and Chief Minister like in all the other States of the Union. When the Home Minister was pressed to do more in removing the remaining hurdles in the total integration of the State, since so much ground had already been covered, he responded by telling the Lok Sabha that the doubters were guilty of giving too much importance to the said Article. By doing that, doubts had been planted about it with the message that there was some kind of deficiency in it. He reiterated, what the late Prime Minister Nehru and the then Prime Minister Lal Bahadur Shastri had said, that Article 370 did not make the integration of the State incomplete, and that by removing it, it will become more full. Nanda concluded the debate that day by referring to the proceedings of the UN Security Council where the Indian representative M.C. Chagla said, 'the accession of Kashmir to India is irrevocable and the present relationship between Kashmir and India must continue.' He added, 'I have said that there are certain facts of history which cannot be undone.'[318]

The parliamentary debates on Kashmir betrayed three different set of thoughts regarding the integration. While the government was convinced of the full-integration claim, there was a section that was not satisfied with the measures and Article 370, which they considered inadequate and an impediment. This section, though a small minority, was vocal, adamant and beyond reason. But, there was also a tiny section cutting across the party line, who were resentful of the concessions and were of the opinion that too much help was being granted to the State. This section argued that the Union was not getting commensurate returns to its investment. Meanwhile, the Valley too was not altogether quiet. The Plebiscite Front had not succeeded in garnering significant support but it had also not lost hope of turning the tide. After a lengthy debate in the Lok Sabha in 1963, and realizing that the issue of the integration of the State was questioned in some sections of the public opinion in India, the Front decided to write a White Paper in June 1964 in a bid to re-open the debate and put across its point of view. It invoked all the arguments that had been used by Sheikh Abdullah and the National Conference in the past to emphasize on the separate identity of the Valley and to be rid of the Dogra rule. But, like in the past, after arguing thus, it also staked claims to its right to rule the very State that had been created by the Dogras. Alternately, it used the terms from the Instrument of Accession to buttress its argument of keeping the State free of the 'encroachments' of the Indian Constitution, and simultaneously argue that the limited accession that took place was only because the National Conference agreed to it.

The White Paper also used the promises made by India in the UN Security Council regarding the plebiscite without referring to the fact that the conditions therein laid down by the Council had remained unfilled since Pakistan had stubbornly refused to implement them. It also ignored the fact that as a via media the Government of India had found the convening of the Constituent

Assembly as a tool of achieving the same goal, since one of the goals set before it was to settle the issue of accession once and for all. This was stated by Sheikh Abdullah in his opening address to the Constituent Assembly, of which Mirza Afzal Beg, the chairman of the Plebiscite Front, too was a key member. If the Constituent Assembly expressed the free will of the people of the State when Sheikh Abdullah was the Prime Minister and Beg was a key member of his Cabinet, then it was equally competent to do so when Bakshi Guhlam Mohammad was the Prime Minister. Even after removal from power, many of the Front members had remained MLAs, and, therefore a part of the voice of the House. But the collective voice of the Assembly, which included these Front members, endorsed the accession of the State to India. The best efforts of the Front had not been enough to canvass support and cast doubts on the legitimacy of the proceedings. The Constituent Assembly had unequivocally spoken its mind and settled the issue of accession. As far as the erosion of Article 370 was concerned, it had taken place under the provision of the said Article, which had been drafted after considerable debate and deliberations, with consultations with the National Conference under the leadership and guidance of Sheikh Abdullah and Beg. In fact, Beg was the key negotiator on behalf of the National Conference. The Plebiscite Front believed that Accession was temporary. But the Centre, rightly concluded that although Article 370 was temporary in nature, removing it would cause more complications. The Centre also pointed out that though temporary, nothing barred the Union or the State government from extending any or all features of the Indian Constitution to the State, since there was a clause in the Article for doing so in consultation and with the consent of the State Government and the Assembly.

It was natural that the activities of the Plebiscite Front found a counterpoint in the rest of the country and hence the demand to abrogate Article 370 would be made from time to time. This explains how and why the issue of Article 370 came to be discussed in the Lok Sabha in late November 1963, and then again in December 1964 after the first Prime Minister had passed away. During the first debate, Prime Minister Nehru had asserted that the Article had been considerably 'eroded', and in the second debate, Home

Minister Nanda categorically stated that it was an empty shell, the contents of which had been emptied by the Article itself. There is little doubt that the arguments of the Government of India were sound and suffering from no shortcoming, and its stand was legally and morally correct. But the political problems, the challenges, and the aspirations of the people are not necessarily based on logic or legal and moral correctness. The Plebiscite Front kept the embers of discontent warm. In this it drew hope from across the border. The propaganda against India and in favour of the Front had a powerful ally in the so-called 'Radio Azad Kashmir', which spewed venom and fanned emotions. It also drew strength from the fevered reaction in some sections of the population in Jammu and the rest of the country.

Regardless of the challenges, the new government under Ghulam Mohammad Sadiq went ahead using the proviso of Article 370 to forge stronger ties and pull down constitutional barriers. Of equal significance was the emergence of the Indian National Congress in the State, with the merger of the National Conference with it. With the political and governance structure created by Bakshi in shambles, different thought was needed to replace it. Luckily, the trio of Sadiq, Qasim and Dhar from the National Conference was waiting in the wings, chafing all this time under a system that challenged the moral correctness of governance. Sadiq addressed a letter to Prime Minister Nehru on 15th January 1964 in which he gave his frank and blunt opinion about the Kashmir of that time. He also wrote in the same letter: 'Another lesson which we must boldly draw from the situation is that the emergence of the Congress in the State as a prelude to closer political relations between Kashmir and the rest of the country is a matter of historical necessity. [The] National Conference no doubt was a powerful organization with a glowing past. It is the traditions fostered by this which are responsible for the sanity and goodness of our people. But that National Conference is dead. What we are trying to do now is to worship a stinking carcass.'[319]

With the Praja Parishad already merged with the Bharatiya Jana Sangh and the Praja Socialist Party unit organized in the State, the talk of the National Conference dissolving itself to merge with Congress was an important milestone in the integration story. Meanwhile, after the pitiable performance of the Shamsuddin government, there was demand for replacing it with someone who had a political stature of his own. This, however, was resisted by Bakshi, who had wisely remained absent during the Holy Relic crisis. It took the effort of Delhi to bring him around to finally propose the name of Sadiq as the leader of the National Conference legislature party. When Sadiq was administered oath of office and secrecy by the Sadar-i-Riyasat in the Hari Palace in Jammu, new ground was broken. A new breed of politicians, unshackled by the weight of the past and eager to explore new frontiers, had stepped forward to take charge of the State.

20

Renewed Battle for Control

The unfortunate events that followed the 'disappearance' of the Holy Relic raised doubts about the nature of peace that had existed in the State during the decade-long rule of Bakshi Ghulam Mohammad. The uncertainty, violence, the atmosphere of suspicion of the motives of those in power, and the vulnerability of the masses in the face of any—real or imagined—assault on their religious sentiments, proved that the Kashmiri society remained fundamentalist in nature. The ease with which anti-India elements succeeded in exploiting the distrust of authority, when the discovery of the Moe-e-Muqaddas was announced, was an eye opener. The hastily organized Action Committee, led by a pro-Pakistani lobby, had done their best to discredit and destroy the Indian credibility, and, but for the pious religious leaders of the Valley, Kashmir was all but lost. This forced a rethink of the Kashmir policy by New Delhi and Prime Minister Nehru, never comfortable with the idea of long incarceration of an individual due to lengthy process of law, once again began to have second thoughts about Sheikh Abdullah's detention.

Another disturbing aspect about the incident was the call by the leaders of Jammu to observe a general strike in the region to protest the theft of two idols from Hindu temples, and the general lack of trust in the government. Many suspected that this new development in the State was a result of Hindu reaction and was triggered by some vested interest to further vitiate the atmosphere. Luckily, the Sadar-i-Riyasat was able to convince the leaders from

Jammu to call off the strike. But the threat pointed to the fragile nature of communal peace in the State.[320] In the Valley, the Moe-e-Muqaddas incident had brought all the fringe forces opposed to India on a single platform. One wing of the Action Committee, formed under the chairmanship of Maulana Mohammad Sayed Masoodi, co-founder of the Muslim Conference along with Sheikh Abdullah, was represented by the followers of Sheikh Abdullah and the Plebiscite Front formed by Mirza Afzal Beg. Another wing was of the followers of the Mirwaiz-i-Kashmir, Maulavi Mohammad Farooq and the Action Committee, who were, and had been, vocal opponents of Sheikh Abdullah. Many among this group were fervent supporters of the demand for the merger of the State with Pakistan.[321] With the advent of Sadiq as Chief Minister, these elements had no option but to lie low and wait for an opportune time to strike again.

On the other side of the border, Pakistan too was smarting. Its carefully laid plan to exploit the situation had yielded nothing but disappointment. The religious ploy had been foiled by a few saintly men of Kashmir, who had refused to be part of deceit and lies. But when it came to Kashmir, Pakistan was nothing if not persistent. Kashmir had become its raison d'être. It bided its time and, the summer of 1964 had raised its hope for it. By then, Prime Minister Nehru was no longer in the best of his health. The long years in prison, the struggle for the country's independence and the deep disappointment at his failure to deal with the Chinese and the consequent humiliation of the defeat of 1962, took its toll on his health. It was then that he decided to resolve the Kashmir problem. It was a problem in the making, of which he had a fair share of blame. Thus, he concurred with the view to free Sheikh Abdullah. It was preceded by dramatic events in the State with the Sadiq government seen to be committed to the withdrawal of the Kashmir Conspiracy Case and the release of Sheikh Abdullah. Even Bakshi Ghulam Mohammad began to demand his release, and with the atmosphere vitiated by uncertainty, the prosecution witnesses began to waver.[322] On 5th April 1964, Chief Minister Sadiq announced the release of Sheikh Abdullah.

No sooner had this been announced than Nehru invited Sheikh

Abdullah to Delhi as his guest. By all accounts, the meeting between the two estranged stalwarts was an emotional affair. There is no denying that both loved Kashmir and wanted to possess it, and, in a way, were rivals in this pursuit. Not much is known of what actually transpired between the two in Delhi, except that they had long discussions. But it was soon announced that Sheikh Abdullah would be making a trip to Pakistan to meet President Mohammed Ayub Khan and achieve a breakthrough. Obviously, this was the Prime Minister's idea as he wanted Sheikh Abdullah to see for himself the conditions in Pakistan and then decide what he wanted from his association with India. There was an air of anticipation and excitement and both Delhi and Rawalpindi exuded confidence and optimism. Sheikh Abdullah was certain that a deal acceptable to all would be struck.

There are two different versions of what happened there. It has been suggested that there was a 'plan for a confederation between India and Pakistan, with Kashmir as an autonomous enclave between them on the model of Andorra, between France and Spain.'[323] In Rawalpindi, Sheikh Abdullah was received by Zulfikar Ali Bhutto as well as two prominent Kashmiri leaders, who had migrated to the other side after 1947 and were erstwhile colleagues of Sheikh Abdullah during the Muslim Conference days—Chaudhary Ghulam Abbas and former Mirwaiz of Kashmir, Maulavi Yusuf Shah. According to President Ayub Khan's autobiography *Friends Not Masters,* India did propose a confederation but was rejected by Pakistan since it believed that it was a plan devised by Nehru to extend Indian hegemony.[324] However, this claim was rejected by Sheikh Abdullah in his letter written to President Ayub Khan on 1st September1967: 'We had not taken with us any cut and dried proposal concerning Kashmir and, as a matter of fact, Jawaharlal Nehru had not asked us to put across any proposal. We are not made that way.'[325] It was in Muzaffarabad that the news of Nehru's death was broken to him and Sheikh Abdullah, in the presence of journalists, including the two Indians, Prem Bhatia and Inder Malhotra, broke down and wept. He immediately flew to New Delhi on the same plane that brought Pakistani Foreign Minister Bhutto.

However, once again, the version provided by B.N. Mullik is

probably closer to facts. 'He was apparently disillusioned with what he saw in Pakistan and was distressed at the pitiable conditions in which the Kashmiri refugees were living there.' Sheikh Abdullah also visited Muzaffarabad in the Pakistan occupied area of Kashmir, which was also the capital of the so-called 'Azad Kashmir'. There he was received by his separated countrymen with a tumultuous welcome that bordered on hysteria. Perhaps the people there could see the breakthrough and sensed the hope of meeting their loved and dear ones on the other side of the border. But when he 'met the Azad Kashmir leaders and learnt that Pakistan had given no scope for the establishment of [a] proper representative Government in Occupied Kashmir…[he was] disillusioned about the intention of Pakistan about Jammu and Kashmir and apparently he did not get any encouragement to his pet idea of an independent Kashmir.'[326] With Nehru's death, a road was closed.

Not surprisingly, soon after the death of Pandit Jawaharlal Nehru, Pakistan thought that a window of opportunity was opening up. Nehru was widely perceived to be a banyan tree, sheltering all those who came under it, but not allowing anything to grow. Thus, there was a lot of speculation, even during his lifetime, about not only who would succeed him but also the fate of the country and the ability of his successors to keep the country together. The debacle against the Chinese in 1962 had exposed the weaknesses, and the nuclear tests conducted by China in 1964 had further exacerbated the fears within the country. Meanwhile, Pakistan had developed a formidable leadership in President Ayub Khan and his charismatic Foreign Minister Zulfikar Ali Bhutto. Even when President John F. Kennedy was alive, Ayub Khan had struck a special relationship with the Americans in general and the First Lady, Jacqueline Kennedy, in particular, whom he gifted a fine black horse that caught the attention of the world when it accompanied President Kennedy's hearse. He also exploited the rift between India and China to Pakistan's advantage by ceding a large chunk of the territory in the northern region, to China, so that it could have a better link with its Xinjiang province. The ceded territory was legally part of the erstwhile State of Jammu and Kashmir and hence an integral part of India after the Accession. As a by-product of India's faulty China policy, India had failed to notice the changes taking place in the geostrategic relations in the region. Without even the political commentators noticing, the Indo-China relations had begun to be strained by the mid fifties of the last century. 'In their struggle for ideological leadership of the Third World, China and India had already been set at odds.'[327]

The Indian leaders refused to acknowledge the reality and, unnoticed by them and their diplomatic corps, at the first Afro-Asian Conference at Bandung, Indonesia in 1955, China is reported to have reached a 'strategic understanding with Pakistan founded on their convergent interests vis-à-vis India.'[328] Incongruously, Pakistan was also a member of the US-backed multilateral treaty organizations—the Southeast Asia Treaty Organization (SEATO) and the Central Treaty Organization (CENTO)—ostensibly to contain the reach of the communist USSR and China. These developments provided considerable international support as against the near isolation (barring support from USSR) to non-aligned India.[329] Pakistan was, at that point in time, flourishing economically, with a growth rate of 6.7 per cent per year, industrial production, 12 per cent and investment, 14 per cent a year.[330] The Pakistani rupee too stood higher than the Indian rupee for the first time in the world markets.[331]

On the other hand, India was heading towards a crisis of its own making. The myopic policies of the leaders who followed Nehru, not equipped to withstand the pressure of the ultra-nationalists from the Hindi belt, had announced their 'ill advised language policy. On 26 January 1965, Indian Republic Day, Hindi became the official language of the Union... The consequences were to be apparent almost immediately, for on 27 January serious rioting broke out in Madras State [Tamil Nadu] where Tamil speakers resented the linguistic policy of the Central Government.'[332] Additionally, the Indian economy in 1965 was arguably in difficulties. The industrial development was not matched by the corresponding increase in agricultural output. In fact, India was heading towards an agrarian crisis and soon its leaders were seen making a beeline for the Western world with a begging bowl to feed its teeming millions.

The mercurial Pakistani Foreign Minister Bhutto saw an

opportunity in the situation. As it was, he saw India sandwiched between China and Pakistan. China had conclusively demonstrated its military superiority over India and Bhutto felt that, 'Pakistan might in some more active way exploit the growing popular disenchantment with Indian control within "Indian-held" Kashmir. The affair of the disappearance of the *Moe-e-Muqaddas* had given rise to a great deal of Islamic protest in both Jammu and [the] Vale of Kashmir which some Pakistani observers, Z.A. Bhutto for one, interpreted as evidence that the State was ripe for rebellion. All it needed was to apply the right pressures and give the appropriate stimuli and Kashmiris would rise up *en masse* against the Indian overlords.'[333] India, in fact, had multiple reasons to feel insecure.[334]

It was in this atmosphere that India found itself facing the Rann of Kutch crisis. In hindsight, there is little doubt in the Indian mind that by triggering this crisis, Pakistan was testing the strength and preparedness of the Indian Army and the resolve of its political leadership. It was to be the dress rehearsal for something that Pakistan had contemplated for Kashmir. The Rann was most inappropriate for a sustained aggression since much of the land, barring few high grounds, were converted into sea with the advent of monsoon. Therefore, the hostilities came to an end by May when the monsoon was due. The British had, meanwhile, acted as mediators and on 30th June, an agreement was signed that required the maintaining of the status quo as of 1stJanuary 1965. In due course a tribunal, consisting of three members, was constituted, which by and large upheld the Indian position and as a kind of face saver, gave Pakistan 350 square miles of the disputed 3,500 square miles land.

That summer also saw Prime Minister Shastri and President Ayub travelling to London to attend the Commonwealth Prime Ministers' Conference. It was chaired by the British Prime Minister, Harold Wilson, who was confident of successfully mediating the wider issues between India and Pakistan after the success of the British in finding an amicable settlement in Rann of Kutch. While Prime Minister Wilson was working on both the parties, President 'Ayub did reiterate', according to a Pakistani academician, 'that negotiations needed to be continued and if they could not settle all the issues in London, then the talks could continue in Karachi or Delhi. And said he was even prepared to meet Shastri though he "disliked and despised" him.'[335] The fact was that President Ayub Khan was over six feet tall, a Pathan and a soldier to boot, and had utter contempt for the small-sized, dhoti-clad, non-martial Shastri. It is also believed that he had convinced himself, after meeting Shastri on the sidelines that it was the right time to grab Kashmir. There is little doubt that India was in deep trouble at that point in time and did not have a tall leadership, matching Nehru's stature to navigate through the political and economic challenges, but there was at least one crisis that had been dealt with firm resolve during this period.

The political developments in the Valley, meanwhile, began to take a disturbing turn. Maulavi Farooq, the traditional opponent of Sheikh Abdullah and the chosen President of the Action Committee after the Moe-e-Muqaddas crisis, was ousted from his position, forcing him to float a new political outfit, Awami Action Committee. Since he had a significant following in the Valley and his stand, supported by Pakistan, was anti-India, Sheikh Abdullah began to tour the Valley, rallying support for his own cause. He called upon all those pledged to secure self-determination to unite under the banner of the Plebiscite Front. 'With his amazing facility for shifting the political emphasis as and when the occasion demanded, he began reverting to his earlier, more strident, attitude on crucial political issues. The excuse his friends trotted out was that he had to do this in order to pre-empt Maulvi Farooq.'[336] Sadar-i-Riyasat Karan Singh was among those who had seen through Sheikh Abdullah and was not taken in by the defence offered by his friends. He wrote to the President that 'if he [Sheikh Abdullah] begins…to take a blatantly communal and extremist line the distinction between the two [Abdullah and Farooq] will hardly retain much significance.'[337]

It is true that when Articles 356 and 357 of the Indian Constitution* were extended to the State, forces inimical to India felt threatened. Their discontentment was fanned by Pakistan and

* The Articles provide for meeting a situation arising out of any failure of constitutional machinery within a State.

those who were acting on behalf of it. These Articles had brought the State on par with the rest of the States in the Union in the matter of failure of constitutional machinery. In such an eventuality, these Articles provided for the intervention of the Union. This gave Sheikh Abdullah another rallying point and he wasted no time to deliver an extremely hostile speech against India. He also used the Friday prayers platform at Hazratbal to come down heavily on the move to merge National Conference with the Indian National Congress. During his diatribe, he was at his eloquent best in raising the bogey of the Muslims losing their identity in the very near future because of the decisions of the 'weak' and 'suppliant' Sadiq government. He went to the extent of giving a call for the social boycott of those National Conference MLAs who had joined the Congress. The tirade firmed the opinion in Delhi of those who had been opposing granting Sheikh Abdullah permission to travel abroad on a Haj pilgrimage. He had made his intention clear that he proposed visiting other countries as well, and since the intelligence reports were categorical that he had told his followers of his intention to meet foreign leaders in order to muster support for self-determination, there was an opinion in Delhi that the permission should be declined. But ultimately, he was not only allowed to go, but also no restrictions were put on his movements abroad. Prime Minister Lal Bahadur Shastri had shrewdly judged that by misusing his freedom of movement he would only expose himself. On the contrary, if permission was not granted then it would give him a reason to make capital out of it.

Prime Minister Shastri had given a long rope to Sheikh Abdullah, Mirza Afzal Beg and the Plebiscite Front. His patience finally ran out when Sheikh Abdullah and Beg visited the Arab world, and the Haj pilgrimage soon turned out to be a trip to forge ties with forces inimical to India. Sheikh Abdullah had also visited Algiers, where he had a meeting with the Chinese Prime Minister Zhou Enlai. During the meeting, the Kashmir question was discussed and Sheikh Abdullah received an invitation to visit China. Ironically, the news about the invitation was broken by the Pakistani Foreign Minister Bhutto and not the Chinese Foreign Ministry. It was obvious that Sheikh Abdullah was attempting to make China a party to the Kashmir dispute and this could not have been acceptable to India. It was, in fact, a Pindi-Peking (now Beijing) conspiracy and promptly the passports of the two Kashmiri leaders were revoked. Sheikh Abdullah had the option of accepting the Pakistani offer of a passport but he chose to return to India, where he, along with Beg, was arrested and sent to Kodaikanal in south India. Expectedly, trouble broke out in the Valley, with the Plebiscite Front and the Awami Action Committee calling for protests.

In Pakistan, particularly by the combine of Ayub and Bhutto, these protests were interpreted as a popular upsurge against the pro-India Sadiq government and the Government of India. Therefore, Pakistan raised the tempo of its covert and overt activities in Kashmir. As a result, a serious clash between the two armies occurred along the ceasefire line on 19th May 1965, in which forty Pakistani soldiers were killed. Such clashes continued through the month of May and June. Pakistan claimed that the people of Jammu and Kashmir had revolted against the increasing control of the Government of India over the affairs of the State, and that the Kashmiris had taken up arms against India. When confronted with evidence about the presence of Pakistanis in the Valley with latest weaponry, it explained that in view of the struggle of the Kashmiri people 'freedom-fighters from Pakistan joined in their struggle' and that these 'freedom-fighters' or 'Mujahideen' were acting independently of Pakistan and on their own initiative.[338] Historian Alastair Lamb, normally a passionate advocate of the Pakistani case about the Kashmir dispute, also concedes that 'In 1965, however, we can definitely see *official* Pakistani policy at work, to a great extent inspired through President Ayub Khan and Z.A. Bhutto.'[339]

Pakistan had codenamed the aggression of 1965 as 'Operation Gibraltar'. It obviously had religious connotations.[340] Inspired by Bhutto, Pakistan was convinced that the State of Jammu and Kashmir was ripe for revolt and therefore, sent trained guerrillas of the Pakistan Army into Kashmir to provide inspiration and professional help to the people there. This part was to be followed by the support of an armed intervention of the Pakistan Army, which, Pakistan believed was more than a match for the Indian

Army that had been so roundly beaten by the Chinese in 1962. Pakistan hoped that this would force India to abandon the Valley or, at least, force it to a result-oriented discussions on the dispute. Pakistan had been planning for this operation ever since the Moe-e-Muqaddas crisis. A number of training camps had been established in Pakistan occupied Kashmir and volunteers were drawn, not only from among the Kashmiri residents of that region but also from the regular Pakistan Army. Estimates vary regarding the number of actual infiltrators who crossed over into the Valley during the summer months, with the climax reaching in August. The number was at least 1,000 and could be up to 3,000. But the operation was flawed right from the beginning, with the Pakistani strategists miserably failing to read the situation.

There is no doubt that a section of the Valley was unhappy with the developments that had taken place regarding the extension of the provisions of the Indian constitution to the State. They would have preferred an arrangement whereby the Union controlled only the Defence, Foreign Affairs and the Communications. But then, a larger segment of the population had begun to see the benefits accruing from greater integration. The people also had legitimate grouses regarding the administration that was marred by corruption and nepotism, and all this had burst forth in the wake of Moe-e-Muqaddas crisis, and which had been erroneously read by Pakistan as the sign of a population ready for rebellion. The scale on which the locals refused to cooperate with the infiltrators and their active help in locating and eliminating them was ample proof of the contentment of the people with the Union of India. But, most importantly, 1965 was not 1962; the Indian Armed Forces had greatly improved. Their strength, resilience and effectiveness were seriously underestimated by Pakistan. Another miscalculation was that Pakistan had assumed that just like in 1947-48, India would confine the hostilities to the State of Jammu and Kashmir. It had not bargained for another front that threatened to storm Lahore and Sialkot, two important cities of Pakistani Punjab. It had also not taken into account the possibility of Afghanistan collaborating with India in order to threaten Peshawar and fulfil the ambition of creating 'Pakhtunistan'. It never happened, but for the first time

Pakistan realized that it was possible. Finally, President Ayub, the burly Pathan, had grievously erred in judging the temperament of the small-sized, dhoti-clad Indian Prime Minister, Shastri. He demonstrated tremendous resolve and nerves when sanctioning the rolling of the Forces into Pakistani Punjab. This upset the plans of Ayub and Bhutto. Thus, the first open War, after the 1947-48 operations between India and Pakistan, unfolded itself. In the end, it was considered to be inconclusive and both sides reached an agreement at Tashkent, which was brokered by the USSR. India returned to the pre-hostilities position and there was considerable heartburn at having to give up the strategically important Haji Pir. But it adhered to the agreement even though it is believed that the harsh criticism of it by the Bharatiya Jana Sangh took its toll, and Prime Minister Shastri succumbed to a heart attack while still in Tashkent. The people of Kashmir were, however, to emerge as the winner out of those testing times as, after 1947, they once again rejected the overtures of Pakistan and sent a clear message that whatever their grouses against the Government of India be, they were an internal matter, to be sorted by the State, its people and the Union.

21

The Onward Journey

By 1964, the world of Sadar-i-Riyasat Karan Singh too had begun to change. Ever since he was appointed the Regent and then elected as the Head of the State, he had taken utmost care to be constitutionally correct in all his affairs. On a personal level, though, he was well on his way to a spiritual journey and discovering his self. He had been successful in both. The year also brought the news that after six years of the birth of his daughter, Jyoti, his wife was expecting another child. The birth of Vikramaditya brought great joy not only to the parents and the doting grandmother but also the people of Jammu who lined up from Pathankot to the palace in Jammu to felicitate the new born, when the proud family brought him to his ancestral city. The grateful Sadar-i-Riyasat had made three major offerings of Rs 11,000, each at the 'family temple Sri Raghunath Mandir at Jammu; to the Harmandir Sahib (Golden Temple) at Amritsar and to the Hazratbal shrine at Srinagar.'[341] All the three holy places were revered by the descendants of Maharaja Gulab Singh. The family had flourished due to the patronage and support of Maharaja Ranjit Singh therefore, that debt was acknowledged by a visit to the Golden Temple. They had successfully ruled Kashmir for a century and hence, veneration of the holiest shrine of the Valley came naturally. Raghunath Mandir was, of course, where the family deity resided. Individually, Karan Singh was a follower of the Vedanta philosophy which 'looks upon all religions as different paths leading to the same goal.'[342]

In another parallel development, over a period of time, as the challenges became complex, Karan Singh as the Sadar-i-Riyasat of the State, was drawn into the nitty-gritty of politics. Even during that period of family joy, he had to spare time for the political challenges. While in Delhi, on his way to Jammu, he was visited by Sheikh Abdullah to discuss the affairs of the State. He could not have been unaware of the fact that when darkness enveloped the Valley during the Moe-e-Muqaddas crisis, the only thing the Kashmiris agreed upon was for the scion of the Dogra dynasty to take control of the State. The long years of malicious propaganda against the Dogra rulers had done little to diminish their presence from the life of the Valley. During the long conversation, Sheikh Abdullah claimed that he was not committed to any particular solution to the problem of Kashmir, and that he was as anxious to find an acceptable solution. But, it was equally clear to the Sadar-i-Riyasat that the Sheikh favoured some kind of a semi-independence status that was guaranteed by India and Pakistan. This was known earlier too, but for the first time, during this particular meeting, Sheikh Abdullah appealed to the Sadar-i-Riyasat to play a 'positive' role in solving the problem.[343]

It was in this frame of mind that the Sadar-i-Riyasat returned to Srinagar in August 1964, where he discovered that the Plebiscite Front had commemorated 9th August—the day Sheikh Abdullah was arrested in 1953—as a 'Black Day'. A general strike had been called and a huge procession, in which Sheikh Abdullah participated, was taken out. Later it was addressed by their leaders, including Sheikh Abdullah. The tone of the speech was certainly not of a man who, only a few days earlier, had made a personal appeal to Karan Singh to play a 'positive' role in finding a solution to the problem. It was decidedly anti-India. He accused the Indian Government and Bakshi, Sadiq, Qasim and Dhar of conspiring to oust him in 1953. His hostility towards Sadiq too came out in the open and it was obvious that he was once again on a collision course with the Government of India. On the face of it, it appeared that Sadiq was well and truly in control of the situation. The Sadar-i-Riyasat was to soon discover that political appearances were often deceptive.

In September, a session of the Legislative Assembly was due. In the nick of time, the Sadar-i-Riyasat discovered that Chief Minister

Sadiq and his supporters were completely unaware of the silent coup that had been planned by Bakshi Ghulam Mohammad. He had a genuine grouse against the State leaders as well as the Government of India, which had failed to utilize his services in the organizational set up of the Congress. According to B.N. Mullik, he was one of the most enthusiastic supporters of the Kamaraj Plan, in the belief that it would strengthen the hands of Pandit Jawaharlal Nehru. Prime Minister Nehru was immensely satisfied by the role that Bakshi played in choosing his successor 'and he rang up Bakshi in my presence to congratulate on the agreed list…and suggested that the change should be effected immediately and Bakshi should come to Delhi to take up organizational work. He told me that Bakshi had responded enthusiastically.'[344] Obviously, something had happened between this point and the fact that Bakshi had been rendered jobless; ousted from power in his backyard and then unwanted in Delhi. Mullik is convinced that he was not treated fairly by the Government of India. In fact, what followed in Jammu and Kashmir was more or less the same that happened in all those States where the Kamaraj Plan had ousted strong leaders from seats of power, creating various coteries and increasing infighting within the Congress.

It was widely believed by Sadiq and his colleagues that having been refused the powers that his supposed martyrdom would have brought, Bakshi had lost his calm. But the fact was that he not only had die-hard supporters among the legislators but also a sizeable following outside the Assembly. More importantly, he had not lost any of his prowess as a strategist. He had, indeed, planned a bold bid to topple the Government on the floor of the House. There is little doubt that Bakshi had been very useful to the cause of India in the Valley and India owed a lot to him for bridging the gap between the State and the Union. But he had outlived his utility by immersing himself in systematic nepotism and corruption that was probably indulged in by his relatives and coteries of loyalists. Once out of power, and in the face of the crisis of the Moe-e-Muqaddas, the anger and resentment of the people had found full voice not only in Srinagar but also in the rest of the Valley. The Government of India could not have helped him in getting back to the seat of power on the premise that he had effectively dealt with Sheikh Abdullah and the Plebiscite Front in the past.

In a bid to neutralize him, the State Government had taken action against his supporters and Bakshi was personally threatened with extensive investigation of allegations of corruption against him. But instead of intimidating him, these threats had only pushed him to the wall where he was ready to strike back. He did not hide his intentions like a common-place conspirator and was bold enough to call upon the Sadar-i-Riyasat to inform him of his intention and also tell that he was prepared to face all the consequences of his actions. He claimed that he was 'victimized and vilified' by the Sadiq Government and that this campaign had crossed the threshold of tolerance. It is unfortunate that an objective assessment of Bakshi's contribution to the integration of Kashmir has never been made. But, away from the partisans, it need be said that it was immaterial if he was personally involved in the corruption, because after a while, people no longer feel indebted to the good deeds that a person does, if in the long run the moral fabric of the society grows thin because of his exertions.

Bakshi, the Sadar-i-Riyasat discovered, was in no mood to give Sadiq a free run. He was clearly angry, and beyond reason. Karan Singh also found that 'he had succeeded in getting the signatures of a majority of legislators for the no-confidence motion, which was not surprising considering the fact that nearly two-thirds of them had been returned unopposed, almost all handpicked by Bakshi and owing their political allegiance to him.'[345] This was nearly the same situation in which eleven years ago Sheikh Abdullah had found himself in. But the similarity ended there. In Sheikh Abdullah's case, only a handful of the legislators in 1953, from among all those handpicked by him, had remained loyal to him. The rest had shifted their allegiance to Bakshi. It was a commentary on the personality of both the leaders—one repelling legislators by his arrogant and dictatorial style and the other winning more friends by his ability to share power and influence. Both the situations were a tribute to the skills of Bakshi as an organizational leader. Then, he had consolidated his hold over power, and now, he was ready to wrest power from another incumbent.

Bakshi's frank admission of his plan to oust Sadiq caused worry to the Sadar-i-Riyasat. More so because Sheikh Abdullah was already on the warpath and the State could ill-afford instability if Sadiq was toppled at this juncture, since the return of Bakshi would have aggravated the situation. However, the period of his invincibility among the people was over since the anger of the Kashmiris had been openly expressed in the streets of the Valley during the Moe-e-Muqaddas crisis. 'If the no-confidence motion went through, there would be no alternative but to place the State under [the] Sadar-i-Riyasat's rule which, under the circumstances, would have been politically exploited to the hilt by Abdullah and the Plebiscite Front.'[346]

After prolonged discussions with the State leaders and the Government of India nominees in the office of the Sadar-i-Riyasat in Karan Mahal, it was decided that the lesser option before them was to arrest Bakshi and some of his main supporters and also prorogue the Assembly. It was clearly an undemocratic step, but not taking it would have meant handing over the State to confusion and chaos. In that case Pakistan would have made considerable capital and India would have to concede the ground that it had gained all these years. Accordingly, arrests were made under the Defence of India Rules and, ironically, Bakshi was taken to the same Tara House in Udhampur where eleven years ago Sheikh Abdullah was incarcerated. Sheikh Abhdullah condemned the arrests and the proroguing of the Assembly as being non-democratic. He also used the occasion to criticize the unrepresentative nature of the Assembly. His public utterances strengthened the view that somehow the move of Bakshi had found the blessings of his arch rival and that the purpose of the whole exercise was to pave the way for fresh elections to the Assembly. Sheikh Abdullah also made speeches at Hazratbal and Charar-e-Sharif, condemning the arrests and indirectly praising Bakshi, strengthening the suspicion of complicity between the two estranged former comrades.

In the midst of this new crisis, the Sadar-i-Riyasat found himself deeply involved in the process of dealing with it, and he did not shy away. He made several suggestions to the Government, that included expansion of the Cabinet so as to bring more elected representatives in the seats of responsibility and power, reconvening of the Assembly as soon as possible and pressing on with the inquiry into the theft of the Holy Relic. 'I found myself drawn increasingly into the political vortex. Far from being a detached and aloof constitutional head, I was rapidly becoming a major actor on the political stage. As it happened, I was by that time getting progressively more interested in politics and was beginning to strain at the leash which was the headship of the State inevitably constituted.'[347]

Most of the suggestions of the Sadar-i-Riyasat were implemented and Sadiq survived the crisis. Soon thereafter, during the Governors' Conference, the first after the death of Jawaharlal Nehru, Prime Minister Shastri came out strongly in support of Sadiq, though he acknowledged that the challenge mounted by Sheikh Abdullah was substantial and that his strength could not be underestimated. However, it was also clear that multiple forces in the country were trying to test the mettle of the new Prime Minister. Challenges had been mounted from various sources, including those who thought they had an opportunity to push their idea of India which, in Nehru's time had failed to take roots. The Sadar-i-Riyasat found that he was much more comfortable dealing with Prime Minister Shastri than with Nehru, who had straddled the mind space of most of his juniors. In addition, he had also struck a relationship with the President, Dr Radhakrishnan. Karan Singh had also become a frequent visitor to Delhi, having already built a house there, and had developed a very healthy and vigorous relationship with the intellectuals of the national capital. As a consequence, whenever he met the Prime Minister, the subject of conversation was not confined only to the State business and encompassed various aspects of the challenges facing the country. He also found himself outgrowing the State politics and straining to be part of the national scene.

It was in this context that on 1st March 1965, he finally wrote to Prime Minister Shastri:

> As you know, I have been Head of the State for almost sixteen years, having taken up my first appointment as Regent in June 1949 at the age of eighteen. I was elected Sadar-i-Riyasat in November 1952, and am now in my third term. During these

years I have sought to shoulder the responsibilities and fulfill the duties that devolved upon me to the best of my ability. In a few days I will be thirty-four, and for some time I have been feeling that it would be desirable for me to widen my field of experience. However, national interest being necessarily uppermost in my mind, I realized that until now my quitting the present post might have created avoidable complications. With the forthcoming amendment of the State Constitution the office of Sadar-i-Riyasat elected by the State Assembly will be replaced by a Governor appointed by the President, and in view of this development I do not think my personal presence here remains as important as it was previously. It is not desirable for anyone to remain too long in the same public office, and a change would now seem to be advantageous. With the advent of the office of Governor a wide choice of talent is now available, and I could offer my suggestions regarding a suitable person for this important appointment.

With regard to myself, I am seriously considering contesting the next general elections, especially as the people of this State will for the first time be electing their representatives to the Lok Sabha directly. Also, there is a general feeling that younger people should take a more active interest in politics, and it is possible that with such experience as I may have gained by being in public life since an early age I could if elected be of some service to the nation on the broader canvas.

The next elections are exactly two years away, and it is with special regard to the intervening period that I am writing this letter. I understand that the present High Commissioner in the United Kingdom Dr Jivraj Mehta is likely to be replaced soon. It is embarrassing for me to write this, but I do feel that perhaps I could fill that appointment successfully… It is with reluctance that I am inflicting upon you a letter concerning my own personal future, but as I do know your affectionate and understanding temperament I have written quite frankly and look forward to getting the benefit of your guidance and encouragement at your earliest convenience.[348]

The Prime Minister promptly replied but said that he would like to discuss the issue personally, which they did soon thereafter. During their conversation, Prime Minister Shastri pointed out the continued challenges in the State and the need of Dr Karan Singh to be there as the Sadar-i-Riyasat. But the very next year, his Principal Secretary L.K. Jha called upon Karan Singh to make the offer, but by that time other political developments had taken place, which made demands upon Dr Karan Singh. Who knows what the course would have been if the diplomatic offer had been made when he was keen on it and had volunteered for it!

The year 1965 was eventful for the State and the country with the Articles 356 and 357 of the Indian Constitution being extended to Jammu and Kashmir. The year also saw the important development of the merger of the National Conference with the Indian National Congress, thereby drawing the State one step closer to complete political integration. It was in this context that Sheikh Abdullah got the opportunity to raise the bogey of the survival of the Muslims in the State, and Prime Minister Shastri gave him a long rope till he had fully exposed himself during the supposed Haj pilgrimage. His call for the social boycott of those National Conference leaders and workers who had decided to merge with the Congress had had a pernicious effect, with instances when traditional burial ground was denied to the families thus affected. But it was what happened in South India that had more profound influence on the events that were to overtake the subcontinent.

The language issue had divided the country into pro and anti-Hindi camps with the opposition to Hindi, particularly in Tamil Nadu taking a violent and ugly turn. Dr Karan Singh expressed his deep concern at the turn of events and brought to attention the dangers of secessionist movements taking place in the deep south and up north. He pointed out that with Pakistan waiting in the wings to seize upon any opportunity, there was grave risk of the campaign of the Plebiscite Front assuming communal overtones. Thus the year unfolded bigger challenges to the country in which no small role was played by forces that wanted to test the ability of Prime Minister Lal Bahadur Shastri to withstand pressure and keep the country united. History records the successful manner in which he not only responded to these challenges but also his ability to rally the country behind him in meeting the aggression from across the border. What India would have been, had he survived his heart attack at Tashkent, is a matter of conjecture. But in the brief years, he had proved that even though he lacked charisma and could not match the dominating persona of Jawaharlal Nehru, he was, in his own quiet and unassuming way, effective and capable of holding on to his principles and stated goals.

In the year 1965, the constitutional amendments, changing the nomenclature of Sadar-i-Riyasat and Prime Minister to Governor and Chief Minister respectively, was implemented and the power was bestowed upon the President to appoint Governor to the State, as in other states of the Union. Thus, with the change, Dr Karan Singh became the first and the last Sadar-i-Riyasat of Jammu and Kashmir, and also, its first Governor. He was sworn-in on 10th April 1965. With this transition, the most compelling reason for having him appointed as the Regent was justified.

Satisfied that he had played his role to the best of his abilities to bring the State within the fold of the Union, Dr Karan Singh once again began to chafe within the confines of the State. He had seen and experienced all the fears and hopes, the highs and lows of every conceivable political challenge that the State could have faced.

It was in such an atmosphere that the impending war with Pakistan was building. Astonishingly, when it came, it took everyone by surprise and there is no rational explanation for the multiple levels of failure. After the Rann of Kutch, the country should have been better prepared, but the fact was that the large scale infiltration by Pakistani guerrillas was not detected either by the army that was spread all over the State or the Intelligence agencies of either the State or the Union. In hindsight, it can be said that it was complacency and failure of intelligence. After the Plebiscite Front had launched a civil disobedience movement and the Pakistan-inspired Awami Action Committee renewed its pledge to secure its right of self-determination, the Government and the intelligence agencies should have been more vigilant.

Dr Karan Singh first became aware of the possibility of war when he heard rumours during the party of the first birthday of his son Vikramaditya on 5th August. These rumours regarding infiltration were not taken seriously and life went on as if nothing was about to happen. A few days later, the news of a large-scale presence of guerillas in Kashmir broke. Not only had they entered undetected, but many of them had also reached the outskirts of Srinagar. Pakistan had carefully planned this attack and succeeded in implementing it without arousing the suspicion of the Intelligence agencies, even though it was known that Pakistan always banked on a situation where the Kashmiris had been sufficiently disgruntled against the Union and were led by a person who commanded following and credibility. It was Pakistan's belief that given the circumstances, if the Pakistanis reached the Kashmiris, the people of Kashmir would consider them as their liberators and rise against the Indian State.

The fact that Pakistan was given a befitting reply by the Indian Defence Forces does not mitigate the fact that a serious threat had been mounted on the integrity of the country and that there were a number of elements in the Valley who were willing to collaborate with the invaders. Luckily the Congress and the Jana Sangh sank their differences to come together to meet the challenge. But the truth was that on the political front the State had hardly made any progress since 1949 when Maharaja Hari Singh was virtually exiled and Yuvraj Karan Singh brought in as the Regent. The State, conceived by the genius of Maharaja Gulab Singh and the peculiar circumstances of the nineteenth century, was a challenge and evidently the new rulers did not know how to deal with it. If earlier Kashmir had felt discriminated against, now it was the turn of Jammu to feel the same. If earlier the Dogras ruled, then now their rule had been replaced with that of Kashmiris. The quiet of Jammu was deceptive. 'Jammu had clearly become a political colony of [the] Kashmir leadership.' Jammu in fact was, for the leaders and political parties in Delhi, the elephant in the room nobody wanted to see, even though, the fact that Yuvraj Karan Singh—the scion of the Dogra dynasty from Jammu—had been brought in as the Regent in 1949 and then made the Sadar-i-Riyasat and then the Governor of the State was a tacit acceptance of the Dogra factor in the State politics.

This problem had an unintended consequence when Dr Karan Singh spoke to Neville Maxwell, then a correspondent for *The London Times*, about the future of the State. His remarks were picked up by Kuldip Nayyar, then with the news agency, UNI. Nayyar sought an interview in which Karan Singh frankly spoke his mind about the need to bring the State under the provisions of the States Reorganization Commission so that if Punjab was reorganized, Jammu and Kashmir too could be reorganized on the basis of language. This was a subject that had been raised by him even in 1956. No sooner had he spoken this than all hell broke loose, with furious reactions coming from across the political spectrum. Obviously the country was not prepared to face reality and the issue and the problem has ever since only been addressed with band-aids from time to time. The unsavory controversy once again convinced Dr Karan Singh that he needed to get out of the State politics and play some more meaningful role at the national level. He was no longer prepared to be a ceremonial and constitutional head and yearned for greater space. The death of Lal Bahadur Shastri was to hasten this process.

Upon Shastri's death, Indira Gandhi was elected the Leader of the Congress Parliamentary Party and hence invited to form the Government. Dr Karan Singh, though not a member of the Congress because of his constitutional position, was of that post-Independence generation that was more comfortable with the younger Congress leadership under Indira Gandhi. When he went to congratulate her on her elevation, her first reaction was, 'I wish you were in Parliament now.' He himself was even more determined to leave the State for the bigger arena. It was 1966, and the general elections to the Lok Sabha were due the following year. With that in mind he wrote to the Prime Minister Indira Gandhi on 17th August 1966:

> You will recall that over the last few months I have mentioned several times my desire to relinquish the office of the Governor and seek a more active participation in national politics. I have been Head of the State for almost half my life since I first became Regent in 1949, and I do feel that it will now be desirable for me to change my field of public activity, even though it will be a wrench for me to dissociate myself from close contact with the affairs of the State to which I belong. In view of the fact that General Elections are approaching, I write to seek your approval

> to my requesting the President to accept my resignation from the post of Governor of Jammu and Kashmir sometime next month.[349]

The reply was prompt and she wrote:

> You have mentioned your desire to be relieved of your present office more than once in the past and ever since you did so, I have been giving anxious thought to your suggestion. I fully understand and appreciate that having served as Head of State in Jammu and Kashmir for nearly two decades now, you should wish to have a change and think of more active participation in national politics…However, as I have explained to you, we are passing through very critical times in economic and other fields. As the General Elections approach, our problems will increase. The threat to our borders also continues. In these circumstances and in this delicate situation I am worried at the thought of a new person taking up your important position. That is why I should like you to agree to stay on in your present office for the time being. I hope that you will find that possible.[350]

Once again a Prime Minister had invoked his indispensability to the State and asked to stay put. So, he once again focused on the State and did his best to influence the course of events. In view of the Lok Sabha elections, the Delimitation Commission was seized of the challenge to carve out constituencies that did justice to the people. D.P. Dhar had proposed that because of the meager population, Ladakh be made part of the Baramulla constituency and the Doda of the Anantnag in the Valley. Dr Karan Singh vehemently opposed this proposal on the ground that it would result in merging the identity and aspirations of Ladakh and Jammu with Kashmir and would also perpetuate the domination of Kashmir over these regions. This view was finally accepted. Unfortunately and regrettably, this divergence of views between him and Dhar caused a rupture in their relationship. In addition, Karan Singh also wanted a Commission to be set up to look into the regional disparities but this was not accepted though the very next year the State Government had to bow before the demand and set up the Gajendragadkar Commission to look into the matter. Interestingly, one of his recommendations was to rename the State as 'Jammu, Ladakh and Kashmir'!

In 1967, when the General Elections took place, the results were not what Prime Minister Indira Gandhi had anticipated. The Congress seemed to be overwhelmed by the economic and political challenges, and seemed to be succumbing to their pressure and handing the country over to chaos. The elections in the State were disappointing in the sense that the idealism of Sadiq, Qasim and Dhar notwithstanding, nothing had changed in the conduct of elections. Bakshi had revived the National Conference and had emerged as a leading challenger to the Congress in the Valley; in Jammu, the Jana Sangh, as ever, posed a serious challenge. In the Valley, when the nomination papers of the candidates were scrutinized, it was found that twenty-two Congress nominees for the Assembly and one for the Lok Sabha had been elected unopposed. As in earlier elections, the returning officers had rejected the papers of the opposition parties.

Dr Karan Singh reported to the President Dr Radhakrishnan: 'It was clear that the large-scale rejections had created a most unfavourable impression. On the one hand our foreign critics, and Pakistan in particular, fully exploited the episode to justify their contention that elections in Jammu and Kashmir have always been farcical, on the other indignation of the Opposition parties found considerable prominence and sympathy in the national press and there was widespread resentment within the State.'[351] It was in the light of this continued fraud on the people of the State that Dr Karan Singh persuaded Chief Minister Sadiq to initiate the legal process to amend the State Electoral Law so that the aggrieved candidates of the parliamentary constituencies of the State could file an election petition directly in the High Court as was the case in the rest of the country.

The results to the Lok Sabha were disappointing for Indira Gandhi and the conservative leader Morarji Desai had mounted a challenge to her leadership. In the end, she comfortably won the leadership battle but it was clear that with one-third of the Congress members supporting him, she would have to make concessions. In the State, Bakshi had staged a comeback by upsetting the Congress and winning the Lok Sabha seat.

In these circumstances, Dr Karan Singh was convinced that

Indira Gandhi needed all the support she could get and was no longer prepared to sit back and be a passive spectator. So he, accompanied by his wife, went to Delhi. Too embarrassed to directly talk to Indira Gandhi of the subject that was foremost in his mind, he met her Joint Secretary Sushital Banerji. It was through him that Dr Karan Singh conveyed that he was ready to resign and enter active politics if she so desired. It was on 12th March 1967 when Banerji called him to inform that the Prime Minister would like him to join her Cabinet as the Minister for Tourism and Civil Aviation. The very next day, he tendered his resignation as Governor. Accepting it, President, Dr Radhakrishnan wrote:

> I accept your resignation of the office of Governor of Jammu and Kashmir and am recognizing the Chief Justice, Shri J.N. Wazir, as Acting Governor until a successor is appointed. As he will not be able to assume charge until the morning of 15 March, your resignation may take effect from then.
>
> I know I voice the sentiments of the people of Jammu and Kashmir in particular and India as a whole in thanking you for your valuable services to the nation.

It was on 16th March that the oath taking ceremony took place. He was eighteen when he had been asked to take on the mantle of Regent in contentious circumstances. It was after eighteen years now that he was once again making a move. This time, it was he who had sought the change. The circumstances were not as contentious as in 1949, but the challenges were of no mean magnitude. A lot had changed in the intervening period. Jammu had come to terms with the abolition of the dynasty and had embraced republicanism. The demand for greater integration with the mainland was still very potent but it was supplemented by the more powerful voices that craved for equal opportunities for an all-round development of the region. These were vital issues that were raised by Dr Karan Singh from time to time. Not all of them had been addressed but they could no longer be brushed under the carpet. The Centre's gain was the State's loss of a voice that opposed any regional hegemony. But now, it was for the others to see how best the character of the State created by Maharaja Gulab Singh could be maintained.

Soon after his departure, upon his return to Srinagar in early July 1967, he found ominous signs of simmering dissent in Jammu, and the insensitivity of Kashmiri leaders towards it. He informed them to Prime Minister Indira Gandhi in a letter written on 10th July 1967. He recalled that before the general elections, when he was still the Governor of the State, he had held discussions with Sadiq, Mir Qasim and D.P. Dhar, and they had agreed that the problem of fulfilling regional aspirations existed and it needed to be urgently addressed. It had been agreed that the solution to the problem lay within the framework of the present State, rather than its reorganization on linguistic lines. They had also solemnly promised to consider the proposals made by him for redressing the issue. However, to his dismay, after being elected as Chief Minister following the general elections, Sadiq and the Pradesh Congress Committee President, Mir Qasim 'made public statements on several occasions reiterating their opposition to any such move. Recently, as...[I] mentioned to you, they have also launched a vicious campaign in Jammu, spearheaded by a Government body known as the Field Survey Organization in which they have tried to completely destroy the whole idea of regional autonomy and arouse caste and communal prejudices against it...On the 7th July, however, the Executive Committee of the J&K Pradesh Congress Committee passed a long resolution in which inter alia it openly condemned the idea of autonomy as "part of the same shop-soiled and oft-peddled solution of fragmenting the State and thus delivering it into the hands of Pakistan on the one hand and China on the other."...As a Congressman, I am deeply disturbed at the fact that the Congress Party in the State—in the Valley, in Jammu as well as in Ladakh—is getting dangerously isolated from the genuine aspirations of the people. If this present situation is allowed to continue, there is danger that under stress the whole structure may collapse, thus causing a grave setback to the national interest.'[352]

It took a little over fifty years for the warning to mature, but when it did, it wreaked such a havoc that no one can predict the ultimate end of the forces that have been unleashed, not only on the State but the country. Just as Karan Singh had warned.

Appendix 1

Jammu Agitation I[353]

New Delhi
January 7, 1953

My dear Yuvraj,

Thank you for your letter of the 4th January.[354]

I can quite understand your great concern over the developments in Jammu. I am naturally also very much concerned and I have followed them closely. I entirely agree with you that while police measures are of course necessary, that is only a negative way of dealing with the situation. A positive approach is always necessary. For your personal information, I might tell you that I have written at some length to Shaikh Saheb [Sheikh Abdullah] on this subject. I hope that he will come to Hyderabad for the Congress session and I shall certainly discuss these matters with him fully. And so with others. On my return from Hyderabad, I shall take such further action as might appear proper then. Perhaps I might come to Jammu myself.

I agree with you also that a negative and defeatist attitude is all wrong. To talk about the Jammu province, or part of it, breaking away from the rest of the State is folly. It is wrong for the Praja Parishad people as well as some of their supporters in India to talk of this. It is equally wrong for others to say that if Jammu wants to break away from Kashmir, it can do so. This defeatist tendency must not be encouraged.

...The situation in Jammu is serious enough to deserve our

fullest consideration and such positive action as may be considered necessary. At the same time, one has to view these matters, as all other matters, coolly and dispassionately.

I am terribly busy at present. That is my usual fate, but work and responsibility grow as India plays a more important role in the world. We have all kinds of conferences and seminars here drawing important people from other parts of the world.

With all good wishes,

Yours sincerely,
Jawaharlal Nehru

Appendix 2[355]

Jammu Agitation II[356]

The Committee have noted with deep regret that, in spite of condemnation in Parliament and all over the country, certain communal organizations have continued to carry on what is called the "Jammu Agitation". To describe this agitation as 'Satyagraha' is not only an utter misuse of that noble word and doctrine but an insult to the nation. The purpose of this agitation has become increasingly clear and it is evident that it has little to do with the Kashmir issue, which it seeks to exploit and in effect harms in many ways. The technique of the agitation has become increasingly violent. It represents an attempt on the part of the most reactionary, bigoted and communal elements in the country to obstruct the economic and social progress of the country and come in the way of India's integrity and advancement which are opposed by the reactionary vested interests represented by these communal organizations. These organizations have no programme of social and economic reform. From time to time, they try to raise agitations on such issues as the Jammu agitation, cow protection, refugee problems and Indo-Pakistan relations, thus seeking to exploit unthinking people for their wrong ends and divert their attention from the major problems of the country.

The Committee would like to warn all Congressmen as well as others against this functioning of reactionary forces, appearing under different guises and trying to delude the people. Reaction and communalism cannot be tolerated in any form and must be combated.

The Committee hope[s] that the Central and State Governments will take adequate steps to deal with this challenge to India's peace, integrity and progress.

Appendix 3[357]

Letter to Sheikh Abdullah

New Delhi
June 28, 1953

My dear Shaikh Sahib, [*sic*]

I sent you a telegram and brief letter this morning suggesting that you might come here about the 3rd July. I further suggested that you might bring with you some of your colleagues, as for instance Bakshi, Beg and Maulana Masoodi.[358] Of course, if others could also, such as Sadiq, I would be glad. In fact, I would welcome even more of your colleagues coming here. I am personally acquainted chiefly, apart from those mentioned above, with Dogra, D.P. Dhar and two or three others.

I should like to talk to all of you together, but more particularly to you. I wish I could come to Kashmir for this purpose, but I fear I cannot leave Delhi after my long absence.[359] Within a week I will have to go to Agra for the AICC meeting for about three days. Even after that it will be difficult to go away from Delhi. Apart from the heavy work here which has accumulated, the international situation is such that it requires constant attention. India, almost against her will, has been dragged into this international picture and we cannot escape our responsibilities. Some fate or circumstances have been pushing India forward in international matters even though we have tried to avoid pushing ourselves. The fact is that what India says or does counts today very greatly in [the] international affairs and especially in regard to Asia. Even in Europe our help is sought by Foreign Ministers and others. I am alarmed at this addition to our responsibilities because I want to devote myself to our internal problems. But I see no escape.

If possible, I can try to come to Kashmir late in this month. That is subject to developments here as well as internationally. But in any event, I should like you to come as early as possible here and before I go to Agra, so that we can have a full talk. Nothing is more depressing than confused thinking in any vital matter. One can face any problem however difficult, but there is no hope when there is confusion in one's mind. I have, thus far, kept my mind fairly clear on the Kashmir issue in spite of its difficulties. That did not mean that I had an easy solution up my sleeve, but that did mean that I was clear about the line of activity we should pursue. But lately I have not at all been clear as to what you have been thinking, and naturally that has a powerful effect on my own thinking. The long talk we had in Srinagar during my last visit in May brought to light to me from you and only led me to think that you are yourself not quite clear.[360] I requested you to keep any decision pending till my return.

As I have already written to you, my talks with Mohammad Ali [Bogra] were vague and general. Much of the time was taken up by subjects like canal waters, refugee problem and East and West Bengal issues. I referred to Kashmir and said that this was obviously a complicated matter and not particularly easy of solution suddenly. We shall have to approach it with care and caution and goodwill. The main thing was the goodwill. I added that of one thing I was quite clear that there should be no external interference and that this matter should be decided as between the Governments of India and Pakistan and Kashmir. I made it clear that I could not commit myself to anything without reference to the Kashmir Government, who would represent their people in this matter. Kashmir was not a piece of property to be bandied about between India and Pakistan. It was the chief concern of the people of Kashmir and they had to be consulted at every step. I also said that any decision should upset present conditions as little as possible. The more upset there was, the more it would bring unfortunate consequences in its train.

I then said that there were two main courses open to us: one was to follow the line which Graham and others had thus far followed and agree about the conditions for an armistice, number of forces, etc. This had not led us anywhere thus far. The second approach was to explore other avenues.

Mohammad Ali replied that he agreed with my general statement and would like me to take lead in the matter and put forward precise suggestions. He added that his own position in Pakistan was not too strong a one. He was a newcomer and had to function under some limitations. He was anxious, however, to find a way to a solution of our problems and he would do his utmost to that end. But he hoped that I would realize his position which was not as strong in his country as mine was in my country.

The question of our further meeting was mentioned. Maulana Azad had written to Mohammad Ali that it would be better for him to come to Delhi than for me to go to Karachi. Mohammad Ali said that he would gladly come to Delhi but it would help him greatly if I paid a previous visit, however short and even if it was for a day, to Karachi. He could later come to Delhi for longer talks. He stressed this as this would strengthen his position in Pakistan. I told him that I was perfectly prepared to go to Karachi on a short visit if that helped, but could not say when I would be able to do so as I would have plenty of work to do in Delhi on my return. So, the matter was left and no date has been fixed. I should like to go there some time towards the end of July. Our Parliament begins on the 3rd of August.

Of course, even when I go there, it does not mean that any decision will be arrived at then. That depends on many circumstances. I rather doubt if that meeting will be anything more than a further preliminary discussion of our main issues.

I had till recently a fairly clear idea of what you thought in this matter. I know that during the past three or four years doubts have arisen in your mind and we have discussed them. We did not agree about some things and, on one or two occasions, I even told you that I did not wish to come in your way if you differed from me in any vital manner. If so, we naturally have to think what our separate courses of action should be. However, we generally agreed about the policy that should be pursued and there the matter rested.

You will remember that when I went to Sonamarg last year, I wrote a note which I sent you analyzing the Kashmir problem in the hope that this might lead us to clear thinking. This note was discussed by us in Srinagar later and I gathered from you and your colleagues that you agreed with that analysis and conclusion. Recent developments have, however, led me to think that you have either changed your mind completely or are not clear about your thinking.[361] This necessitates our understanding, as clearly as possible, what we respectively think. If one cannot agree, one should at least know precisely what the difference is. The difference appeared to me considerable when we talked at Srinagar last. But it seems to me that I could not get a grip of what you had in your mind, except negatively. You told me that there were only two courses open for Kashmir: either full integration or full autonomy, whatever that autonomy might mean. I did not agree with you in this, nor do I agree with you even now, because there are many other middle courses. Nobody can guarantee the distant future.[362] We live in an age of revolutionary change. I am coming from Egypt where repeatedly changes have taken place in the course of last year, and I rather doubt if these changes have come to an end. So also in Pakistan where possibly further changes may be in store.

So no one can guarantee the distant future. One takes one step at a time and it seems to me that the step we should take now about Kashmir is definitely a step in between the two courses you had suggested. However, it is not my purpose to argue this matter in this letter or even later. We have argued enough and must accept each other's present conclusions and then discuss the future on that basis. If that future unhappily leads to divergence with all its consequences, we fashion our respective courses accordingly.

You know that the question of Kashmir has had not only a logical appeal for me but also a strong emotional one. But I can suppress my emotion, if necessary, if logic demands that. Thus far, I have proceeded on the basis of friendship and confidence in you and have been vain enough to expect the same approach from you. Whether that is justified now or not, it is for you to say. Individual relations should not count in national affairs and yet they do count and make a difference.[363]

To me it has been a major surprise that a settlement arrived at between us should be by-passed or repudiated, regardless of the merits. That strikes at the root of all confidence, personal or international. No treaty would be worth the paper it is written on, if it was to be repudiated soon after. So far as I am concerned, no power in this world could make me go back on the pledge that I gave in that Agreement. If my Parliament or my people in India repudiate that, they repudiate me. That was my approach. Of course, a new situation requires a new approach. But even that new approach would have been for me something following the implementation of that Agreement and something that upset it. My honour is bound up with my word.

It is because of this that I have been surprised at recent happenings in Kashmir, which seemed to imply that that agreement should not be acted upon and should be repudiated.[364] If that is so, then any other agreement could also be repudiated and there is no fixity or certainty about agreements. We are now facing a curious international situation in Korea where an armistice had almost been arrived when President Syngman Rhee upset the whole business. Syngman Rhee could at least say that he was personally no party to the agreement and yet world reactions have been powerfully against him.

The personal equation apart, I do not like the consequences in India, Kashmir or the world of an agreement being broken. Good can never result through wrong methods.

But quite apart from that Agreement, we have to consider the problem in its larger context. The Agreement did not put an end to the problem. It is about that larger context that I should like to talk to you, precisely and definitely, without too much argument on either side. We are intelligent men, you and I, and do not need repetition of what has been said.

Such information as I gathered during my visit to Kashmir in May and subsequently has distressed me greatly.[365] Whatever approach we might take to the solution of our problems, there are some basic considerations. Ultimately every solution of an international or national problem depends upon a balance of forces. Those forces need not necessarily be military. They are represented by disciplined organizations. In India, a major force has obviously been the National Congress which has held the country together. If this Congress had not been there, the country would have disintegrated, despite great leaders. Your strength in Kashmir was ultimately based on the great organization you built up, the National Conference. Of course, you had your personal popularity and appeal also which was considerable. But essentially it is the organization that gives strength and not the individual. Instead the individual acts through the organization if results are to be achieved.

What I have felt lately has been that your Government is very far from harmonious and in fact pulls in number of different directions, that your organization is also disintegrating in the same way.[366] If this process continues, I have little doubt that Kashmir would relapse in utter backwardness, so far as political life is concerned. It takes much time to build up organizations and discipline the people. Gandhiji for over a quarter of a century slowly built up our organization and taught it discipline, cooperative working and the capacity for sacrifice. He attached little value to public demonstrations but always laid stress on the discipline of an organization. The people of Kashmir have been trained, to some extent, by you and your organization but not nearly enough and a disruptive tendency is always dangerous. If these tendencies towards disruption and disintegration of the organization continue, then politically Kashmir will count for very little, regardless of other questions, and regardless of its relationship to India or its autonomous position or its relationship with Pakistan. It will then become a mere pawn for others to play with. That would be a tragedy.

In this world today, we are surrounded by the most difficult problems. Never before was so much maturity of thought and wisdom necessary as it is today. Much is said about democracy. But democracy can only function successfully with self discipline and some maturity of thought and action. Otherwise, it gives place either to totalitarianism or to subjection to somebody else.

I am therefore gravely disturbed, not so much about the political future of Kashmir but rather about the internal conditions that tend to disrupt Kashmir, both politically, and what is more important, organizationally and internally. This kind of thing used to lead to something in the nature of civil war. That will not happen in Kashmir because of various circumstances but a psychological civil war is as bad from the point of view of bringing about disintegration. No one wins in that and everyone loses.

My Government has stood, as you have so consistently stood, for a secular democracy.[367] I do not known what your feelings are on this subject now.[368] But I fear the tendency in Kashmir is away from it.[369] Unfortunately that will have its reaction in India as such tendencies in India have their reaction in Kashmir. On my part I am pledged to that ideal and I shall adhere to it to the bitter end, if necessary, and if my people throw me out. It will grieve me that anything is done in Kashmir which tarnishes that ideal and weakens those who stand for it. Whatever we might do, it is the least that we owe each other that we should try to understand each other and then decide on such courses of action as we might deem proper. It is always painful to part company after long years of comradeship, but if our conscience so tells us, or in our view, an overriding national interest so requires, then there is no help for it. Even so we must do it with full understanding and full explanation to each other and not casually.[370]

I have written rather a long letter to you. This was not meant to be argumentative for I think that the time for lengthy arguments is over. Such arguments only confuse the mind. The time for clear understanding has come. It is for this reason that I would beg of you to come here at an early date with as many of your colleagues as possible.

I am sending a copy of this letter to Bakshi, as the letter deals with problems and approaches in which he is obviously interested also.

Yours sincerely,
Jawaharlal Nehru

Acknowledgements

I would be failing in my duty if I did not acknowledge the debt of gratitude that I owe to so many people and institutions. On top of the list is the Nehru Memorial Museum and Library, New Delhi and Shri Radhe Shyam. I would also like to thank Shrimati Anju Gupta of T.S. Central Library, Chandigarh for assistance in the research; Shri R.S. Pathania of Amar Mahal Museum and Library, Jammu; Late Shri Shailendra Singh Jamwal of Jammu University, Jammu; my family for bearing with me these past few years; and Shri Ravi Singh and Speaking Tiger Books. I also thank Brigadier. (Retired) J.S. Rajput for extending all assistance whenever I needed it.

Notes

1. 24th November 1952

1 *Autobiography,* Oxford University Press India, 1994, pp. 79
2 Ibid, pp. 149
3 Ibid, pp. 88
4 Ibid, pp. 93
5 Ibid, pp. 100
6 Ibid, pp. 102

2. The Early Winds

7 *Kashmir: A Disputed Legacy, 1846-1990,* Oxford University Press, 1991, pp. 90
8 *Iqbal In Politics,* Sang-e-Meel Publishers, 2009, pp. 274 and Op cit, *Kashmir: A Disputed Legacy*, pp. 92
9 *Constitution of Jammu & Kashmir: Its Development & Comments,* Universal Book Traders, 1994, pp. 121
10 'Chapter 3', *Kashmir: Article 370*, Anmol Publishers, 1990
11 Op cit, *Kashmir: A Disputed Legacy*, pp. 123-124
12 'Memorandum of Maharaja Hari Singh', *Jammu and Kashmir 1949-64: Select Correspondence Between Jawaharlal Nehru and Karan Singh,* ed. Jawaid Alam, Penguin/Viking, 2006,pp. 315
13 Op cit, 'Chapter 3', *Kashmir: Article 370*
14 Ibid
15 Ibid
16 Nehru's Correspondence
17 Op cit, 'Chapter 3', *Kashmir: Article 370*
18 *Sardar Patel's Correspondence, 1945-50*, Navjivan Publishers, 1971
19 Ibid
20 Op cit, *Jammu and Kashmir 1949-64*, pp. 334

3. Prelude to Article 370

21 *Autobiography,* Oxford University Press India, 1994, pp. 67
22 Ibid, pp. 106
23 Kheer Bhawani, the most revered Holy Temple Shrine of the Kashmiri Brahmans. The Goddess Mata Ragnya Devi is symbolized as a sacred spring at Tula Mula village, 27 kms from Srinagar, Kashmir. The spring of Kheer Bhawani is quite large and has always been venerated by the Brahmin population of Srinagar. The Temple, dedicated to the Goddess Mata Kheer Bhawani (originally Bhawani Mata), has been constructed over a sacred spring. Within the spring is a marble Temple. The Temple spring complex is affectionately known as Kheer Bhawani as thousands of devotees offer milk and 'kheer' to the sacred spring.
24 Op cit, *Autobiography*, pp. 81-82
25 *Sardar Patel's Correspondence, 1945-50,* Navjivan Publishers, 1971
26 *Constituent Assembly of India Debates (Proceedings*), vol 8, 27 May 1949,
27 Ibid
28 Ibid
29 Ibid
30 Ibid
31 Ibid
32 Ibid
33 Ibid
34 Ibid, pp. 357

4. The Making of Article 370

35 *Jammu and Kashmir Constitution Act, 1939,* Section 18
36 *Jammu and Kashmir Constitution Act, 1939,* Section 15 (1)(b)
37 *Constitution of Jammu & Kashmir: Its Development & Comments,* Universal Book Traders, 1994,pp. 65-66
38 'Chapter 3', *Kashmir: Article 370,* Anmol Publishers, 1990
39 *Kashmir: A Disputed Legacy, 1846-1990,* Oxford University Press, 1991, pp. 166.
40 Op cit, *Constitution of Jammu & Kashmir*, pp. 93
41 This is also borne out by B.N. Mullik, who traces the genesis of this drift of thought to the visit of G.M. Ashai, Registrar, Kashmir University to India and reported to Sheikh Abdullah in June 1949

that the Muslims in India were treated as second class citizens, and that they had no future in India. See *My Years With Nehru: Kashmir*, Allied Publishers, 1971,pp. 11

42 *Constituent Assembly of India Debates (Proceedings)*, vol 8, 27 May 1949

43 *Autobiography*, Oxford University Press India, 1994,pp. 84

44 *Indian Constitutional Documents: Munshi Papers*, vol 2, Bharatiya Vidya Bhavan, 1967, pp. 519-520

45 'Ayyangar's letter to Sheikh Abdullah',*Sardar Patel's Correspondence, 1945-50*, Navjivan Publishers, 1971

46 'Ayyangar's letter to Sardar Patel on 15thOctober 1949', Op cit, *Sardar Patel's Correspondence, 1945-50*

47 Op cit, *Sardar Patel's Correspondence, 1945-50*

48 'Ayyangar's reply to Sheikh Abdullah'Op cit, *Sardar Patel's Correspondence, 1945-50*, pp. 308

49 Op cit, *Sardar Patel's Correspondence, 1945-50*, pp. 306

50 Ibid, pp. 308

51 Ibid, pp. 308

52 Ibid, pp. 308

53 Ibid, pp. 310

5. A Document of Change

54 *Song Sung True: A Memoir*, Kali for Women, 2003, pp. 200

55 *Autobiography*, Oxford University Press India, 1994, pp. 120

56 Ibid, pp. 120

57 Ibid, pp. 120-121

58 Before 1930, the young Muslims who took to modern education began to return to the Valley after graduating either from Punjab University, Lahore or Aligarh Muslim University, Aligarh. Having been initiated into the political processes then in vogue, they found the atmosphere in Srinagar oppressive. Young Sheikh Abdullah, Mirza Afzal Beg and Ghulam Mohammad Sadiq joined hands to regularly meet at what was known as Reading Room to divert attention from their political activities.

59 *Kashmir: A Disputed Legacy, 1846-1990*, Oxford University Press, 1991, pp. 87. Lamb noted that though the Kashmiri-Muslim community was introduced to the name of Mahatma Gandhi because of the *Khilafat* movement, it made no significant impact on the local Pandit community despite the role played in it in British India by Kashmiris like Sir Tej Bahadur Sapru and Motilal Nehru.

60 Born in Ajnala, Amritsar, Mohammad Din Taseer was the father of former Governor of Pakistani Punjab, Salman Taseer, who was assassinated by a Muslim fanatic for having espoused the cause of those suffering because of the blasphemy laws in Pakistan. Senior Taseer was one of the founding members of the Progressive Writers' Movement along with Faiz Ahmed Faiz and Sajjad Zaheer. For some time, he was also the Principal of Sri Pratap College, Srinagar.
61 'Naya Kashmir', *Wikipedia* (en.wikipedia.org/wiki/Naya_Kashmir, last accessed 20 March 2023)
62 Ibid
63 Ibid
64 Ibid
65 Ibid
66 Ibid
67 Ibid
68 *Tracts For The Times: Kashmir: Insurgency and After,* Orient BlackSwan, 2008, pp. 47
69 Op cit, 'Naya Kashmir'
70 'Memorandum to President of India' Op cit, *Autobiography*, pp. 310
71 Ibid, pp. 310

6. The Land Reforms

72 *Sardar Patel's Correspondence, 1945-50*, Navjivan Publishers, 1971
73 *Kashmir and Power Politics: From Lake Success to Tashkent,* Metropolitan Book Co, 1966, pp. 199
74 'The Kashmir Land Reforms: Some Personal Impressions', *The Economic Weekly*, 19 September 1953
75 Ibid
76 Op cit, *Kashmir and Power Politics*, pp. 201
77 Ibid
78 Ibid
79 *Tracts For The Times: Kashmir Towards Insurgency,* Orient Longman, 1993, pp. 120

7. The Regent Settles Down

80 *Autobiography*, Oxford University Press India, 1994, pp. 128-129
81 Ibid, pp. 129
82 *Political Conspiracies of Kashmir*, Light & Life Publishers, 1973, pp. 33

83 *Jammu and Kashmir 1949-64: Select Correspondence Between Jawaharlal Nehru and Karan Singh*, ed. Jawaid Alam, Penguin/Viking, 2006,pp. 25
84 Ibid, pp. 27
85 Op cit, *Autobiography*, pp. 129
86 Ibid, pp. 130
87 Op cit, *Jammu and Kashmir 1949-64*, pp. 4
88 Ibid, pp. 6
89 *Tracts For The Times: Kashmir Towards Insurgency*, Orient Longman, 1993,pp. 46-47
90 Ibid, pp. 47
91 Ibid, pp. 48
92 Op cit, *Autobiography*, pp. 122
93 Op cit, *Jammu and Kashmir 1949-64*, pp. 5.

8. The Response

94 *Tracts For The Times: Kashmir Towards Insurgency*, Orient Longman, 1993,pp. 47-48
95 *Autobiography*, Oxford University Press India, 1994, pp. 121
96 *The Shadow of the Great Game: The Untold Story of India's Partition*, HarperCollins Publishers India with India Today Group, 2005, pp. 318-322
97 *Introduction to the Constitution of India*, Prentice-Hall of India, 1982, pp. 18
98 Op cit, *Autobiography*, pp. 121
99 'Jammu and Kashmir: In the Shadow of Imperialism', *Studies in Inequality and Social Justice: Essays in Honor of Ved Prakash Vatuk*, Archana Publications, 2009
100 *Tracts For The Times: Kashmir Towards Insurgency*, Orient Longman, 1993, pp. 50
101 *My Years With Nehru: Kashmir*, Allied Publishers, 1971, pp. 19
102 Op cit, *Autobiography*, pp. 123
103 *Constituent Assembly of India Debates (Proceedings)*, vol 8, 27 May 1949. Gopalaswami Ayyangar said, 'No doubt, we have offered to have a plebiscite taken when the conditions are created for the holding of a proper, fair and impartial plebiscite. But that plebiscite is merely for the purpose of giving the people of the State the opportunity of expressing their will, and the expression of their will, will be only in the direction of whether they would ratify the accession that has

already taken place—not ratify in the sense that the act of ratification is necessary for the completion of the accession, but if the plebiscite produces a verdict which is against the continuance of accession to India of the Kashmir State, then what we are committed to is simply this, that we shall not stand in the way of Kashmir separating herself away from India.'

104 *Kashmir: Constitutional History and Documents*, Light & Life Publishers, 1977, pp. 548
105 Op cit, *Autobiography*, pp. 124
106 Ibid, pp. 96-97
107 Ibid, pp. 124-125
108 Ibid, pp. 125
109 *Jammu and Kashmir 1949-64: Select Correspondence Between Jawaharlal Nehru and Karan Singh,* ed. Jawaid Alam, Penguin/Viking, 2006, pp. 19
110 Ibid, pp. 19-20
111 Ibid, pp. 20.
112 Ibid, pp. 320.
113 Op cit, *Autobiography*, pp. 127
114 Op cit, *Jammu and Kashmir 1949-64*, pp. 24
115 Ibid, pp. 323
116 Ibid, pp. 323

9. Finally, The Constituent Assembly

117 htpp://www.jammu-kashmir.com/documents/abdullah51.html
118 Ibid.
119 Ibid.
120 *The Shadow of the Great Game: The Untold Story of India's Partition*, HarperCollins Publishers India with India Today Group, 2005, pp. 318.
121 'General Victor Scot's Report, OIC, British Library, London',qtd. in *The Shadow of the Great Game*, pp. 318
122 htpp://www.jammu-kashmir.com/documents/abdullah51.html
123 *Autobiography*, Oxford University Press India, 1994, pp. 131
124 *Constitution of Jammu & Kashmir: Its Development & Comments*, Universal Book Traders, 1994, pp. 98-99
125 htpp://www.jammu-kashmir.com/documents/abdullah51.html
126 'The Cabinet Mission Memorandum on Indian States, Treaties and Paramountcy', qtd. In *Article 370: A Constitutional History of Jammu and Kashmir*, Oxford University Press India, 2011, pp. 30-32.

127 htpp://www.jammu-kashmir.com/documents/abdullah51.html
128 Ibid.
129 Ibid.
130 Ibid.
131 Ibid.
132 Ibid.

10. Setting the Agenda

133 *The Shadow of the Great Game: The Untold Story of India's Partition*, HarperCollins Publishers India with India Today Group, 2005, pp. 316
134 'Memorandum' from *Jammu and Kashmir 1949-64: Select Correspondence Between Jawaharlal Nehru and Karan Singh*, ed. Jawaid Alam, Penguin/Viking, 2006,pp. 312. In his Memorandum to President Rajendra Prasad, Maharaja Hari Singh wrote: 'Lord Mounbatten stressed the dangerous situation in which Kashmir would find itself if it lacked the support of one of the two Dominions by the date of the transfer of power.' The advice came after the Viceroy had told the Maharaja that the newly created States Department of India was prepared to give an assurance that if Kashmir went to Pakistan, it could not be regarded as an unfriendly act by the Government of India.
135 *Constitution of Jammu & Kashmir: Its Development & Comments*, Universal Book Traders, 1994, pp. 98-99
136 Op cit, 'Memorandum' from *Jammu & Kashmir 1949-64*,pp. 312
137 *Jammu and Kashmir*, Martinus Nijhoff, 1968, pp. 196
138 *Kashmir and the Freedom Movement*, Sarup & Sons, 2004, pp. 78
139 *Party Politics in India: The Development of a Multi-Party System*, Princeton University Press, 1957, pp. 200
140 *My Years With Nehru: Kashmir*, Allied Publishers, 1971, pp. 11
141 Ibid, pp. 29
142 Ibid, pp. 30
143 Ibid, pp. 33
144 Ibid, pp. 33

11. The March of History

145 *Autobiography*, Oxford University Press India, 1994, pp. 102
146 Ibid, pp. 132
147 Ibid, pp. 133
148 Ibid, pp. 134

149 *Jammu and Kashmir 1949-64: Select Correspondence Between Jawaharlal Nehru and Karan Singh*, ed. Jawaid Alam, Penguin/Viking, 2006, pp. 33
150 Ibid, pp. 34
151 Ibid, pp. 34
152 Ibid, pp. 34
153 Ibid, pp. 35
154 Ibid, pp. 37
155 Op cit, *Autobiography*, pp. 137
156 Op cit, *Jammu and Kashmir 1949-64*, pp. 42-43
157 Ibid, pp. 44
158 Ibid, pp. 44
159 Ibid, pp. 49
160 Ibid, pp. 50
161 Ibid, pp. 51
162 Ibid, pp. 54
163 Op cit, *Autobiography*, pp. 145

12. The Crisis

164 *Autobiography*, Oxford University Press India, 1994, pp. 149
165 Ibid, pp. 150
166 *My Years With Nehru: Kashmir*, Allied Publishers, 1971, pp. 25
167 *Jammu and Kashmir Constituent Assembly Official Reports*, pp. 485-499
168 Ibid
169 *An Examined Life: Essays and Reflections by Karan Singh*, HarperCollins Publishers India, 2019, pp. 235
170 Op cit, *Autobiography*, pp. 140
171 Ibid, pp. 141
172 *Jammu and Kashmir 1949-64: Select Correspondence Between Jawaharlal Nehru and Karan Singh*, ed. Jawaid Alam, Penguin/Viking, 2006,pp. 59
173 Ibid, pp. 61
174 Op cit, *My Years With Nehru*, pp.26
175 Ibid, pp. 27
176 Ibid, pp. 28
177 Op cit, *Jammu and Kashmir 1949-64*, pp. 19. There were thousands of refugees from Pakistan-Occupied-Kashmir who were not even kept in the State and had to be housed in Yole Camp, near Dharamsala, Himachal Pradesh. This is referred to in a letter written by the Yuvraj to Prime Minister Nehru.

178 Ibid, pp. 47
179 Ibid, pp. 52
180 Ibid, pp. 52-53
181 Ibid, pp. 53
182 Ibid, pp. 56
183 Ibid, pp. 74-75
184 Ibid, pp. 85
185 Ibid, pp. 93
186 Ibid, pp. 95
187 Ibid, pp. 101
188 Op cit, *Autobiography*, pp. 154
189 Ibid
190 Ibid, pp. 155
191 Op cit, *An Examined Life*, pp. 229
192 Ibid, 155
193 Op cit, *My Years With Nehru*, pp. 30
194 Ibid, pp. 32

13. The Die is Cast

195 *Kashmir: A Disputed Legacy*, 1846-1990, Oxford University Press, 1991, pp. 195
196 Ibid, pp. 195-96
197 *Sheikh Mohammad Abdullah: Tragic Hero of Kashmir* by Ajit Bhattacharya, p. 160.
198 *Foreign Relations of the United States, 1948, Volume V: The Near East, South Asia, and Africa*, Part 1, Government Printing Office, Washington, 1975, p. 294
199 Ibid
200 *Jawaharlal Nehru: A Biography, Volume II (1947-1956)*, Oxford University Press, 1979, p.120
201 Op cit, *Kashmir:A Disputed Legacy*, p. 197
202 *Letters to Chief Ministers, Volume III (1952-54)*, Oxford University Press India, 1989, pp. 192 and 230
203 *Kashmir Politics: Problems and Prospects*, Ashish Publishing House, 1993, pp.57-58
204 *Bonfire of Kashmiriyat: Deconstructing the Accession*, Rupa and Company, 2006, pp. 177
205 Op cit, *Sheikh Mohammad Abdullah*, pp. 172-73
206 Op cit, *Bonfire of Kashmiriyat*, pp. 177

207 *My Years With Nehru: Kashmir*, Allied Publishers, 1971, pp. 35
208 Ibid, pp. 37
209 *Jammu and Kashmir 1949-64: Select Correspondence Between Jawaharlal Nehru and Karan Singh*, ed. Jawaid Alam, Penguin/Viking, 2006, pp. 116
210 Op cit, *My Years With Nehru*, pp. 39
211 Op cit, *Sheikh Mohammad Abdullah*, pp. 176-77
212 Op cit, *Bonfire of Kashmiriyat*, pp. 179-80
213 Ibid, pp. 181-84
214 Ibid, pp. 188

14. The Fall

215 *My Years With Nehru: Kashmir*, Allied Publishers, 1971, pp. 39
216 *Flames of the Chinar: An Autobiography*, trans. Khushwant Singh, Penguin/Viking, 1993, pp. 116-117
217 *Jammu and Kashmir 1949-64: Select Correspondence Between Jawaharlal Nehru and Karan Singh*, ed. Jawaid Alam, Penguin/Viking, 2006, pp.114-115
218 *Jawaharlal Nehru: A Biography, Volume II (1947-1956)*, Oxford University Press, 1979, pp. 133
219 *Autobiography*, Oxford University Press India, 1994, pp. 158-159
220 Ibid, pp. 159
221 Ibid, pp. 159
222 *Constitution of Jammu & Kashmir: Its Development & Comments*, Universal Book Traders, 1994, pp. 291
223 Op cit, *Autobiography*, pp. 160
224 Ibid, pp. 161
225 Ibid, pp. 164
226 Op cit, *Jammu and Kashmir 1949-64*, pp. 121
227 Ibid, pp. 122
228 Op cit, *The Constitution of Jammu & Kashmir*, pp. 301
229 Ibid, pp. 301-302
230 *An Examined Life: Essays and Reflections by Karan Singh*, HarperCollins Publishers India, 2019, pp. 231
231 *Kashmir: A Disputed Legacy*, 1846-1990, Oxford University Press, 1991, pp. 202
232 Op cit, *Autobiography*, pp. 169

15. The Period of Consolidation

233 *Jammu and Kashmir 1949-64: Select Correspondence Between Jawaharlal Nehru and Karan Singh,* ed. Jawaid Alam, Penguin/Viking, 2006, pp. 124
234 Ibid, pp. 125
235 *Autobiography*, Oxford University Press India, 1994, pp. 167
236 Op cit, *Jammu and Kashmir 1949-64*, pp. 128
237 Ibid, pp. 168
238 Ibid, pp. 129-130
239 Ibid, pp. 130
240 Ibid, pp. 132
241 Ibid, pp. 142
242 Ibid, pp. 138
243 *Constitution of Jammu & Kashmir: Its Development & Comments*, Universal Book Traders, 1994, pp. 259-60
244 Ibid, pp. 261-62
245 Ibid, pp. 262
246 Ibid, pp. 107
247 *History of Jammu and Kashmir Rifles, 1820-1956: The State Force Background*, Lancer International, 1990, pp. 287
248 Ibid, pp. 287
249 Ibid, pp. 287-288
250 Op cit, *Autobiography*, pp. 177
251 Op cit, *Jammu and Kashmir 1949-64*, pp. 138- 139
252 *Goshtaba* is a celebrated non-vegetarian Kashmiri dish of meat balls made out of ground mutton.
253 Op cit, *Jammu and Kashmir 1949-64*, pp. 166- 167
254 Op cit, *Autobiography*, pp. 182
255 Ibid, pp. 184
256 Op cit, *Jammu and Kashmir 1949-64*, pp. 183

16. The Clash of the Titans

257 *Jammu and Kashmir 1949-64: Select Correspondence Between Jawaharlal Nehru and Karan Singh,* ed. Jawaid Alam, Penguin/Viking, 2006, pp. 185
258 Ibid, pp. 186
259 Ibid, pp. 187
260 Ibid, pp. 187-188
261 *My Years With Nehru: Kashmir*, Allied Publishers, 1971, pp. 51-52

262 Op cit, *Jammu and Kashmir 1949-64*, pp. 190

263 *Jammu and Kashmir Constituent Assembly Debates, Official Report Part I,* Volume 1, P 726.

264 Ibid, pp. 873-874

265 Ibid, pp. 1249-50

266 Ibid, pp. 1265

267 *Kashmir: A Disputed Legacy*, 1846-1990, Oxford University Press, 1991, pp. 203

268 Op cit, *My Years With Nehru*, pp. 65-66

269 Ibid, pp. 66

270 Ibid, pp. 67

271 Ibid, pp. 71

272 Ibid, pp. 77

273 Ibid, pp. 79

274 Ibid, pp. 80

275 Ibid, pp. 81

17. The Chapter Closes

276 *Autobiography*, Oxford University Press India, 1994,pp. 224

277 *Jammu and Kashmir 1949-64: Select Correspondence Between Jawaharlal Nehru and Karan Singh,* ed. Jawaid Alam, Penguin/Viking, 2006, pp. 294

278 Ibid, pp. 226-27

279 Op cit, *Jammu and Kashmir 1949-64*,pp. 282

280 Op cit, *Autobiography*, pp. 229

281 Ibid, pp. 230

282 Op cit, *Autobiography*, pp. 230-31

283 *Political Conspiracies of Kashmir*, Light & Life Publishers, 1973, pp. 10-11

284 Op cit, *Autobiography*, pp. 231

285 Ibid, pp. 232

18. Holy Relic and its Aftermath

286 In Kashmir, 'Mirwaiz of Jama Masjid' is not only a religious leader, but also holds a prominent position in society with considerable political clout. It is normally hereditary but has to be validated by the government. The Mirwaiz of Jama Masjid follows Hanifite Islam, while the followers of the other shrine dedicated to Shah Hamdan are Shafiai. They do not always agree on matters religious and political.

287 *My Years With Nehru: Kashmir*, Allied Publishers, 1971, pp. 101
288 Ibid, pp. 101-102.
289 www.epw.in/system/files/pdf/1965/three_byeelections
290 *Autobiography*, Oxford University Press India, 1994,pp. 257
291 Ibid, pp. 257
292 *My Frozen Turbulence* by Jagmohan, P. 100.
293 Op cit,*My Years With Nehru*, pp. 111
294 *Tracts For The Times: Kashmir: Insurgency and After*, Orient BlackSwan, 2008
295 Mohammad Shafi Qureshi was a one-time supporter and confidant of Sheikh Abdullah. The party survived only for a short time and soon became irrelevant.
296 Op cit, *My Years With Nehru*, pp. 120
297 Ibid, pp. 120
298 Op cit, *Autobiography*, pp. 263
299 Op cit, *My Years With Nehru*, pp. 123
300 Ibid, pp. 128
301 Ibid, pp. 130-131
302 Op cit, *Autobiography*, pp. 264
303 Op cit, *My Years With Nehru*, pp. 139
304 Op cit, *Autobiography*, pp. 265
305 Op cit, *My Years With Nehru*, pp. 144
306 Ibid, pp. 162
307 Op cit, *Autobiography*,pp. 267
308 Ibid, pp. 268

19. A New Era

309 *Autobiography*, Oxford University Press India, 1994, pp. 237
310 Ibid, pp. 268
311 *Lok Sabha Debates,* 27 November1963, Volume XXII, cols 1631-32 (https://eparlib.nic.in/bitstream/123456789/2997/1/lsd_03_06_27-11-1963.pdf, last accessed 13 April 2023)
312 Ibid
313 Ibid
314 *Lok Sabha Debates,* December 4, 1964, Volume XXXIII, cols 3449-65.
315 Ibid
316 Ibid
317 Ibid
318 Ibid
319 Op cit, *Autobiography*, pp. 269

20. Renewed Battle for Control

320 *Autobiography*, Oxford University Press India, 1994, pp. 270 and *Kashmir: A Disputed Legacy, 1846-1990*, Oxford University Press, 1991, pp. 205
321 Op cit, *Kashmir: A Disputed Legacy*, pp. 206
322 *My Years With Nehru: Kashmir*, Allied Publishers, 1971, pp. 170-71
323 *Sheikh Mohammad Abdullah: Tragic Hero of Kashmir*, Roli Books, 2008, pp. 219
324 Ibid, pp. 221
325 Op cit, *Sheikh Mohammad Abdullah*, pp. 221
326 Ibid, pp. 175-76
327 *Does the Elephant Dance?: Contemporary Indian Foreign Policy*, Oxford University Press, 2011, pp. 132-33
328 *Protracted Contest: Sino-Rivalry in the Twentieth Century*, University of Washington Press, 2001, pp. 5
329 *Defeat is an Orphan: How Pakistan Lost The Great South Asian War*, Random House Publishers, 2017, pp. 33
330 *Between Dreams and Realities: Some Milestones in Pakistan's History*, Oxford University Press, 2009, pp. 36
331 Op cit, *Kashmir: A Disputed Legacy*, pp. 253
332 Ibid, pp. 253
333 Ibid, pp. 253
334 Op cit, *Defeat is an Orphan*, pp. 33
335 *From Kutch to Tashkent: The Indo-Pakistan War of 1965*, Hurst & Company, 2013, pp. 90. (The author quoted from the declassified papers of 16/6/1965, Downing Street Notes, PREM 13-190 PRO).
336 Op cit, *Autobiography*, pp. 281
337 Ibid, pp. 281-82
338 Op cit, *Kashmir: A Disputed Legacy*, pp. 258
339 Ibid, pp. 258
340 Historically, Gibraltar was first foothold of Islam in Europe.Tariq Ibn Ziyad, a Moor military leader anchored there 711 A.D. The place was named after him as 'Jabal-al-Tariq' or 'Hill of Tariq'.It was later anglisized to Gibraltar.

21. The Onward Journey

341 *Autobiography*, Oxford University Press India, 1994, pp. 284
342 Ibid, pp. 284
343 Ibid, pp. 284

344 *My Years With Nehru: Kashmir*, Allied Publishers, 1971, pp. 113
345 Op cit, *Autobiography*, pp. 286
346 Ibid, pp. 286
347 Ibid, pp. 287
348 Ibid, pp. 291-92
349 Ibid, pp. 316-17
350 Ibid, pp. 317
351 Ibid, pp. 324-25
352 *An Examined Life: Essays and Reflections by Karan Singh*, HarperCollins Publishers India, 2019, pp. 358-360

APPENDIX 1: Jammu Agitation I

353 *Selected Works of Jawaharlal Nehru (1 January 1953-31 March 1953)*, series 2, vol 21, S. Gopal (ed.), Jawaharlal Nehru Memorial Fund, 1997,pp. 177
354 Karan Singh urged the Government of India's intervention in the Jammu situation so that the State Government dealt with the agitation there not only with police measures but with concrete political, economic and administrative measures.

APPENDIX 2: Jammu Agitation II

355 *Selected Works of Jawaharlal Nehru (1 January 1953-31 March 1953)*, series 2, vol 21, S. Gopal (ed.), Jawaharlal Nehru Memorial Fund, 1997, pp. 186
356 Resolution drafted by Nehru for the Congress Working Committee, New Delhi, 16thMay 1953. From the *Jawaharlal Nehru Collection*. This resolution was adopted on 17thMay 1953.

APPENDIX 3: Letter to Sheikh Abdullah

357 *Selected Works of Jawaharlal Nehru (1 April 1953-30 June1953)*, series 2, vol 22, S. Gopal (ed.), Jawaharlal Nehru Memorial Fund, 1997, pp. 193
358 Shaikh Abdullah did not come to Delhi for the 3rd July meeting but sent Bakshi Ghulam Mohammad and Mirza Afzal Beg. He replied on 4th July: 'I would have certainly come down myself to Delhi but Bakshi and Beg will explain to you why it is not desirable for me to leave Srinagar at present.' By the time this letter was written, it was obvious that the two stalwarts had drifted apart, as the response of

Abdullah's letter shows. Both determined to do what they believed was the right thing to do.

359 Jawaharlal Nehru had just returned from a month-long tour to Europe and England but had kept himself abreast of the developments in Kashmir.

360 Abdullah was quick to rebut this. He replied that he did not understand how Nehru had got the impression that he lacked clarity about his objective, as he had 'now been in intimate touch with Kashmir and its people for the last 22 years' and had never therefore been hazy in regard to the objective and there was, therefore, no question of confusion in his mind.

361 It was widely reported in the press that Abdullah was championing the cause of an independent Kashmir at the behest of the Americans and thus was reluctant to implement the Delhi Agreement in full. His public declarations promising autonomy to each cultural unit in Kashmir and his insistence on the rights of Kashmiri Muslims in services gave rise to a measure of uncertainty about his intentions.

362 To this Abdullah replied: 'You have spoken about guarantees. We certainly believed that the terms of the Indian Constitution provided adequate guarantee…But I would point out to you the discrepancies that we come to notice from time to time in the attitude of the Government of India in regard to this position. When Article 370 was devised, we felt assured by Sardar Patel that the Instrument of Accession would be the final basis of the Indo-Kashmir relationship. Subsequently, when the Delhi Agreement came up before the Council of States on August 5, 1952. Shri Gopalaswami Ayyangar stated that Article 370 was not a permanent feature of the Indian Constitution and "when the time was ripe" the provision could be wiped off the Constitution. This clearly shows that even though assurances were given to us…such assurances came with good deal of mental reservation.'

363 To this, Abdullah replied: 'I agree that personal relationship between individuals should not be a consideration when larger national interests are involved. Friendship and sentiments are worthy of respect but they should not come in the way of dispassionate appraisals of one another's difficulties.'

364 On 12th and 15th April 1953 at Jammu and 18th April at Srinagar, Shaikh Abdullah hinted that he was being forced to reassess the Delhi Agreement due to the growing incidents of communal activities in Jammu and India. He openly criticized the Central government for

not being able to quell the spread of communal activities and insisted that the State had acceded on only three subjects and had complete autonomy in all other matters.

365 It was widely rumoured that in early May Adlai Stevenson and Chester Bowles met Abdullah and encouraged him for an independent Kashmir. Further, in a Working Committee meeting of the National Conference, on 18th May 1953, Abdullah put forward his views about an independent Valley, which was opposed vehemently by G.M. Sadiq and G.L. Dogra.

366 Abdullah replied: 'I have not been able to understand your reference to disruptive tendencies both in the administration and in the organization. All I can say is that it is baseless and probably the result of incorrect information given to you. I may, however, assure you that so far as the basic principles are concerned, there is no difference of opinion among us in Kashmir.

367 Abdullah wrote: 'Muslims may rightly feel that in spite of you and many others, the ideals of secular democracy are not much in evidence in so far treatment to Kashmiri Muslims is concerned. I derived my strength from what I supposed was an assurance that the State's accession with India would result in a fair deal to all sections of the people. But unfortunately that goal has not been achieved.'

368 Abdullah retorted: 'May I say, this is an unkind cut. Time alone will prove my faith in the principle for which I have consistently fought all these years. My idea about secular democracy is not cramped or narrow-minded. I believe in justice for all sections of the people and my attitude is conditioned by realities and not by wishful thinking.'

369 During the period of November 1952 to June 1953, Abdullah was continuously accused by a certain section of the press of communalism, of intentionally breaking up Hindu majority districts for electoral purposes, of making Urdu a compulsory subject for all, of filling up key posts with Muslims, and of promoting Muslim interests at the expense of Hindu minority through sweeping land reforms etc. It further charged the Shaikh of planning to establish an independent Kashmir, evidenced by his insistence on a separate flag, constitution, Head of the State and his reluctance to comply with the Delhi Agreement fully.

370 Abdullah replied: 'I may, however, assure you that whatever lot may be in store for us, never can you expect me to abandon my respect and affection for you.'

Bibliography

Abdullah, Sheikh Mohammad. *Flames of the Chinar: An Autobiography*, trans. Khushwant Singh, Penguin/Viking, 1993

Anand, Justice Adarsh Sein. *Constitution of Jammu & Kashmir: Its Development & Comments*, Universal Book Traders, 1994

Aziz, Sartaj. *Between Dreams and Realities: Some Milestones in Pakistan's History*, Oxford University Press, 2009

Bajwa, Farooq Naseem. *From Kutch to Tashkent: The Indo-Pakistan War of 1965*, Hurst & Company, 2013

Bamzai, Prithivi Nath Kaul. *Kashmir and Power Politics: From Lake Success to Tashkent*, Metropolitan Book Co, 1966

Bamzai, Sandeep. *Bonfire of Kashmiriyat: Deconstructing the Accession*, Rupa and Company, 2006

Basu, Durga Das. *Introduction to the Constitution of India*, Prentice-Hall of India, 1982

Bhattacharjea, Ajit. *Sheikh Mohammad Abdullah: Tragic Hero of Kashmir*, Roli Books, 2008

Constituent Assembly of India Debates (Proceedings), vol 8, 27 May 1949

Crocker, Walter. *Nehru: A Contemporary's Estimate*, Penguin Random House India, 2009

Foreign Relations of the United States, 1948, Volume V: The Near East, South Asia, and Africa, Part 1, Government Printing Office, Washington, 1975

Gopal, Sarvepalli. *Jawaharlal Nehru: A Biography, Volume II (1947-1956)*, Oxford University Press, 1979

Graver, John W. *Protracted Contest: Sino-Rivalry in the Twentieth Century*, University of Washington Press, 2001

Gupta, Jyoti Bhusan Das. *Jammu and Kashmir*, Martinus Nijhoff, 1968

Hall, Kira (ed.) *Studies in Inequality and Social Justice: Essays in Honor of Ved Prakash Vatuk*, Archana Publications, 2009

Kapur, Ashok Dr. *India's Strategic Problems*, Lancer Publishers, 2015

Khan, Mohammad Ayub. *Friends Not Masters: A Political Autobiography*, Oxford University Press, 1967

Lamb, Alastair. *Kashmir: A Disputed Legacy, 1846-1990*, Oxford University Press, 1991

Macdonald, Myra. *Defeat is an Orphan: How Pakistan Lost The Great South Asian War*, Random House Publishers, 2017

Malik, Hafeez. *Iqbal In Politics*, Sang-e-Meel Publishers, 2009

Malone, David M. *Does the Elephant Dance?: Contemporary Indian Foreign Policy*, Oxford University Press, 2011

Mullik, B.N. *My Years With Nehru: Kashmir*, Allied Publishers, 1971

Munshi, Dr K.M. *Indian Constitutional Documents: Munshi Papers*, vol 2, Bharatiya Vidya Bhavan, 1967

Nehru, Jawaharlal. *Letters to Chief Ministers, Volume III (1952-54)*, Oxford University Press India, 1989

_______. *Selected Works of Jawaharlal Nehru(1 January 1953-31 March 1953)*, series 2, vol 21, S. Gopal (ed.), Jawaharlal Nehru Memorial Fund, 1997

_______. *Selected Works of Jawaharlal Nehru(1 April 1953-30 June 1953)*, series 2, vol 22, S. Gopal (ed.), Jawaharlal Nehru Memorial Fund, 1997

Noorani. A.G. *Article 370: A Constitutional History of Jammu and Kashmir*, Oxford University Press India, 2011

Parashar, Parmanand. *Kashmir and the Freedom Movement*, Sarup & Sons, 2004

Patel Sardar Vallabhbhai. *Sardar Patel's Correspondence, 1945-50*, Navjivan Publishers, 1971

Phukraj, Malka. *Song Sung True: A Memoir*, Kali for Women, 2003

Puri, Balraj. *Tracts For The Times: Kashmir: Insurgency and After*, Orient BlackSwan, 2008

Sarila, Narendra Singh. *The Shadow of the Great Game: The Untold Story of India's Partition*, HarperCollins Publishers India with India Today Group, 2005

Singh, Lieutenant Colonel Bhagwan. *Political Conspiracies of Kashmir*, Light & Life Publishers, 1973

Singh, Karan. *Autobiography*, Oxford University Press India, 1994

_______. *Jammu and Kashmir 1949-64: Select Correspondence Between Jawaharlal Nehru and Karan Singh*, ed. Jawaid Alam, Penguin/ Viking, 2006

Singh, K. Brahma. *History of Jammu and Kashmir Rifles, 1820-1956: The State Force Background*, Lancer International, 1990

Teng, Mohan Krishen. *Kashmir: Article 370*, Anmol Publishers, 1990

———, Ram Krishnen Kaul Bhatt and Santosh Kaul. *Kashmir: Constitutional History and Documents*, Light & Life Publishers, 1977

Thorner, Daniel. 'The Kashmir Land Reforms: Some Personal Impressions', *The Economic Weekly*, 19 September 1953. (epw.in/system/files/pdf/1953_5/37/the_kashmir_land_reforms.pdf, last accessed 20 March 2023)

Verma, Raghav (ed.) *An Examined Life: Essays and Reflections by Karan Singh*, HarperCollins Publishers India, 2019

Wani, Gull Mohd. *Kashmir Politics: Problems and Prospects*, Ashish Publishing House, 1993

Weiner, Myron. *Party Politics in India: The Development of a Multi-Party System*, Princeton University Press, 1957

Index

A Song Sung True (Malka Pukhraj), 244
Abbas, Chaudhary Ghulam, 58–59, 285
Abdullah, Begum, 232
Abdullah, Farooq, 206, 263
Abdullah, Hazrat Syed, 259
Abdullah, Sheikh Mohammad, 2, 5–8, 13–17, 19–21, 23–25, 27–33, 35–38, 41–47, 49–61, 64–71, 73–75, 79–81, 85–102, 106–114, 116–117, 119–132, 134–135, 137, 139, 140–153, 155, 158–199, 202–207, 209, 211–212, 215, 217, 222–224, 227–237, 239, 242–243, 250–256, 259, 263, 265–267, 271, 279–280, 283–286, 289–291, 295, 297–299, 301, 309, 313
Accession, 3–6, 8, 10, 12–13, 15–17, 22–23, 25–27, 31–32, 35–43, 46–47, 51, 56–57, 68, 71, 80, 84, 89, 93–94, 103, 108, 111–112, 114, 117, 119, 120–123, 126, 135, 143, 147, 157, 167–168, 171, 178, 183–184, 194, 209, 212, 221, 223, 225, 227–228, 230, 237, 243, 248, 279, 280, 286
Act of 1935, 9
Advocate, Ramnath, 247
Ahamadiyas, 9
Akali Dal, 154, 265
Alhilal, 244, 247
Ali, Aruna Asaf, 241
Ali, Major Asghar, 230
All India Kashmir Committee, 9
All India Radio, 203
All Jammu and Kashmir Rajya Hindu Sabha, 123
alliance, 97, 219, 266
Amar Singh Bagh, 83
Amritsar, 56, 294
Amroha, 255
Anand, Girdharilal, 142
Anand, Justice A.S., 34, 37, 198
Anantnag, 218, 305
Arce, Dr Jose, 168
Article 306-A, 40–49, 51
Article 370, 19, 33, 45, 51–53, 56, 80, 94, 120, 173, 183, 209, 226, 273–281
Asad Saheb. *See* Abdullah, Sheikh Mohammad
Ashai, G.M., 126
Ashraf, K.M., 60
Ashwari, Noor-ud-din, 260
Atal, Lieutenant General, 195
Atiqullah, Maulavi, 251
Aurangzeb, 260
Austin, Warren, 169
Awami Action Committee, 289, 291, 302
Ayyangar, Gopalaswami, 14, 16–17, 25–26, 32–33, 40–50, 52, 82–83, 87, 94, 103–104, 125, 133, 139, 141, 147, 156, 183
Azad Kashmir, 36, 224, 286

Azad Kashmir Radio, 265, 281
Azad, Maulana, 14, 48, 50, 141, 180, 188–190, 315

Badami Bagh, 4
Bagda, Moti Ram, 28
Bagh-i-Sadiq, 260
Bakshi Brothers' Corporation, 251
Bakula, Kushak, 149–150, 215
balkanization, 57, 169
Baltistan, 4, 56, 64, 66–67, 82, 121, 179, 211
Bamzai, K.N., 177
Bamzai, Prithvi Nath Kaul, 74, 78
Bamzai, Sandeep, 176–178
Banaras Hindu University, 82
Bandung, 287
Banerji, Sushital, 307
Banihal Pass, 7, 217
Baramulla, 46, 305
Barua, Hem, 277
Batmaloo, 246
BBC. *See* Bakshi Brothers' Corporation
Bedi, B.P.L, 60
Bedi, Freda, 60
Beg, Mirza Mohammad Afzal, 28, 38, 42, 47, 78, 128, 140, 147, 163, 189, 195, 198, 217, 225, 227, 232, 280, 284, 290
Bengal, 9, 164, 168, 181, 199, 314
Bhadarwah, 178
Bharatiya Jana Sangh, 101, 259, 281, 293
Bhatia, Prem, 285
Bhave, Vinoba, 73
Bhoodan, 73
Bhopal, 27, 89
Bhutto, Zulfikar Ali, 285–291, 293
Bidar, 27
Bijapur, 259
Board of Judicial Advisors, 34, 72, 97, 162
Bonfire of Kashmiriyat (Sandeep Bamzai), 177, 185
Brahmins, 158
Britain, 15, 59, 60, 138, 253
British Paramountcy, 57, 207
Buddhist, 44, 150
Buddhists, 10, 168, 172
Bulganin, 218

Cabinet, 20, 26, 28–29, 31, 57, 92, 112, 121, 147, 163, 191–196, 198–199, 201, 258, 280, 298, 307
Central Treaty Organization (CENTO), 287
Chagla, M.C., 279
Chamber of Princes, 21, 119
Chanakyapuri, 239
Chancellor, 84
Chand, Nasib, 264
Chandgraon, 74
Charar-e-Sharif, 298
Chatterjee, N.C., 159, 160, 276
China, 204, 242–243, 253, 286–288, 290, 308
Chinani (Chenani), 60
Cochin, 34
Communist Party of USSR, 218
communists, 59–60, 67, 71, 86, 92, 220
Comptroller General of India, 147
Constituent Assembly, 5, 12, 14–15, 23–25, 27–28, 32–33, 35, 38–42, 47–50, 52, 55–57, 64, 69–70, 80, 88–91, 93–96, 98–99, 103–109, 111, 113, 115, 117–118, 120–121, 124, 131, 133, 135, 138–139,142, 145–146, 147–148, 165, 191, 192, 194, 207, 209, 212, 218, 223, 226–230, 248, 276, 280
Constitution Hall, 32
Constitution of the State, 14, 39, 188, 199
Constitutional History of Jammu & Kashmir (Justice A.S. Anand), 37
Crocker, Walter, 170

Dalits, 22
Dalmia, R.K., 22
Danish, Ehsan, 60
Davidson, Michael, 15, 16
deedar, 260, 264, 267, 268
Defence of India Rules, 298
Delhi, 7, 13–15, 19, 21–22, 27–32, 35, 38, 41, 54–55, 68–69, 74, 80, 87, 89, 91, 93–95, 98, 102–103, 110, 119, 120, 127, 136–137, 141–142, 145, 148–149, 151, 153–155, 157, 161–163, 167–177, 179–180, 183–185, 189, 190–191, 194, 202–203, 207, 209, 220, 222, 228–229, 239, 240–241, 245–246, 257–258, 262–264, 268–269, 271, 282–283, 285, 289, 290, 295–296, 299, 303, 307, 309, 313, 315
Delhi Agreement, 1952, 30, 136, 148, 157, 162–163, 167–168, 172–177, 183, 191, 194, 207, 209, 222
Desai, Morarji, 239, 253, 255, 306
Devi, Maharani Tara, 5–6, 12, 99, 158, 244, 247
Dewan, 23, 28, 29, 31
Dhar, D.P., 140–141, 147–148, 151–152, 179, 189, 201, 242, 250, 254, 258, 265, 281, 295, 305–306, 308, 313
Dharmarth Trust, 100
Directive Principles of State Policy, 42, 45, 46
Dixon, Sir Owen, 111
Doda, 86, 128, 178, 305
Dogra, 1–2, 5, 7–9, 11–14, 19–21, 27, 30, 37, 53, 55, 58, 61, 66–68, 70, 74–75, 79, 82, 85, 91, 95, 99–102, 111, 117, 123, 125, 128–129, 131–132, 134–135, 140, 145–149, 153–154, 156, 161, 171–172, 174, 176, 178–179, 188–189, 191–192, 197–201, 205–207, 215, 226, 230, 243, 250, 256, 264–265, 271–273, 279, 295, 303, 313
Dogra, Pandit Prem Nath, 106, 123, 125, 143, 154–155, 247, 259, 270
Domel, 212, 214

Eastern Switzerland, 115
Economic and Political Weekly, 255
Elizabeth II, Queen, 163, 180
Emergency Administration, 5, 29, 86
Enlai, Zhou, 290

Farooq, Maulavi Mohammad, 251, 263, 284, 289
Farrukhabad, 255
Fateh Shibji, 212
First World War, 59
Flames of the Chinar (Sheikh Abdullah), 60, 190
Food Control Department, 78
French Revolution, 111
Frontier Regions, 60
Fundamental Rights, 35, 39, 41–43, 45–46, 51, 135, 136, 210

Gajendragadkar Commission, 305
Galbraith, John Kenneth, 240, 241
Ganderbal, 191
Gandhi, Indira, 84, 219, 240, 304–308
Gandhi, Mahatma, 22, 58–59, 90, 121
Germany, 28
Ghani, Pir Abdul, 227, 232
Gilani, Pir Maqbool, 232, 237, 266
Gilgit, 3, 4, 56, 64, 66, 82, 121, 179, 211
goshtaba, 216, 217
Government Gandhi Memorial College, 125
Government of India, 10, 12, 24, 31–32, 51, 54, 88, 96, 103–104,

113, 119, 120, 134–135, 147–148, 151, 194, 216, 218, 279, 291, 293, 295, 296
Governor-General, 25–26, 32, 103
Gulab Bhavan, 82, 84, 246
Gulab Mahal, 82, 215–216, 220
Gurais, 178, 179

Hajarnavis, Ramchandra Martand, 274
Haji Pir Pass, 293
Hamid, Syed, 259, 260
Harijans, 63, 218
Harmandir Sahib (Golden Temple), 294
Hazaratbal, 83
Hazratbal, 85, 179, 234, 237, 259–262, 264, 266–268, 290, 294, 298
Henderson, Loy, 93, 169, 170
Hindu, 10–11, 13, 34–37, 41, 53, 67, 90, 94, 100, 113, 126–128, 140, 150, 153, 159, 165, 168, 171, 174–175, 178, 188, 265, 268, 273, 283
Hindu Mahasabha, 126, 159, 174
Hitler, Adolf, 28
Hunza, 66
Hussainiwala Headworks, 213
Hyderabad, 21, 27, 34, 309

Ibrahim, Hafiz Mohammad, 255
Imperial War Cabinet, 59
India, 3–16, 18–26, 28–29, 31–32, 34–48, 50–59, 61, 63, 65–66, 71, 75, 77–78, 80, 84, 87–90, 92–98, 101–104, 108–122, 126–130, 132–137, 139–143, 148, 150–152, 154–155, 157–159, 161–172, 174–185, 187–188, 191–194, 197, 199, 201, 204, 206–210, 212–213, 216–219, 221–234, 237, 239, 240–241, 243, 249–254, 257–258, 261, 263, 266–268, 273–274, 276–277, 279, 281, 283–293, 295–296, 298–299, 301, 307, 309–314, 317–319
Indian Constitution, 10, 12, 19, 34, 39, 41–42, 51, 53, 57, 69, 108, 113, 118, 135–136, 139, 147, 171, 178, 183, 207, 208, 215, 273, 279, 280, 289, 301
Indian Dominion, 4, 10, 40, 56
India's Strategic Problems (Dr Ashok Kapur), 93
Indian Army, 3–4, 8, 12, 24–25, 46, 66, 89, 132, 210–212, 215, 234, 271–272, 288, 291
Indian Independence Act, 25, 207, 208
Indian National Congress, 9, 18, 22, 59, 73, 75, 90, 112, 114, 121, 128, 130, 168, 171, 173, 176, 190, 255–259, 281–282, 290, 296, 301, 303–304, 306, 308, 309, 318
Indian National Flag, 157
Interim Government, 10–13, 29, 38, 46–48
Iqbal, Allama, 9
Ismail, Sir Mirza Mohammad, 177
Iyer, C.P. Ramaswamy, 22, 23

Jagirdari, 54, 70
Jaipur, 34
James, Michael, 93
Jammu, 1–2, 5–8, 10–11, 13, 16, 18, 21–27, 30–41, 48–49, 52–53, 55–58, 60, 62–69, 71–75, 79, 83–84, 86, 88–91, 93–95, 97, 99–111, 117–118, 120–138, 140–144, 146–149, 151, 153–159, 161, 163–165, 167–168, 170–178, 180, 188, 193, 196–199, 205, 207–209, 211–218, 220–221, 224–226, 229–230, 240–242, 246–248, 257, 259, 262, 264–265, 270, 272, 274–278, 281–284,

286, 288, 291–292, 294–296, 301–309, 311
Jammu and Kashmir Agrarian Reform Act,
1972, 74
1976, 74
Jammu and Kashmir Big Landed Estates Abolition Act (1950), 71–73, 157
Jammu and Kashmir Constitution Act, 1939, 33, 38, 71–72, 120
Jammu and Kashmir State Army, 3–4, 12, 24, 30, 39, 61, 63, 99, 110, 158, 184, 210–212, 215, 271
Jammu and Kashmir State Forces War Memorial, 212
Jammu and Kashmir University, 82, 84, 215
Jana Sangh, 126–129, 154, 159, 161, 165, 168, 174, 180, 190, 259, 303, 306
Jehlum, 59
Jha, L.K., 301
Jhelum, 7, 145, 221
Jinnah, Fatima, 199
Jinnah, Mohammad Ali, 58–59, 97, 199
Joshi, Jethalal, 255
Jullundhri, Hafeez, 60
Junagarh, 21

Kachru, Dwarka Nath, 16, 17
Kamaraj Plan, 255–258, 296
Kamath, H.V., 27
Kangra, 7, 158, 244, 247
Karan Mahal, 19, 220, 264, 298
Karapatri, Swami, 126
Kargil, 150, 179, 232
Karra, Ghulam Mohiuddin, 92–93, 147, 224–225
Kasauli, 7, 244
Kashmir, 4–5, 7–11, 13, 15–16, 21–27, 30–34, 36, 38–40, 42–44, 48–68, 71–75, 79, 82–85, 88–90, 92–97, 100, 103–105, 107–109, 111–114, 116–118, 120, 124, 126–130, 135–139, 141–143, 147–148, 151, 154–155, 158, 163, 165, 168–185, 187, 189–190, 193–194, 196–199, 202–205, 208–209, 211–221, 223–235, 237, 240–242, 248, 253–254, 257, 259–260, 262–263, 266, 268–270, 273–279, 281, 283–286, 288–297, 301–307, 309, 311, 313, 314, 316–319
Valley, 7–9, 13, 30–31, 33, 35, 56, 58, 64, 75, 78–79, 84–87, 91, 106, 123–124, 127, 152, 157, 159, 165, 167–168, 170, 176–178, 187, 189, 190, 194–195, 199, 201, 203, 205–206, 216–218, 222, 225–226, 228–230, 233, 235, 241, 251, 258, 262–263, 265–266, 268–269, 273, 276–277, 279, 283–284, 289, 291–292, 294–296, 298, 303, 305–306, 308
Committee, 9
Kashmir Conspiracy Case, 198, 242, 251, 254, 284
Kashmir Delegation, 44, 141, 148
Kashmir Political Conference, 93
Kashmir University, 126
Kashmiri Pandits, 20, 63
Kathua, 74
Katju, Kailash Nath, 87, 156, 176
Kaul, B.M., 195, 255
Kennedy, Jacqueline, 286
Kennedy, John F., 239–240, 286
Keskar, 255
Khan, Abdul Ghaffar, 58
Khan, Mohammad Ayub, 285–286, 289, 291
Khan, Zafrullah, 4
Khanqah Naqshband, 260

Khanyar, 191
Kheer Bhawani, 20, 81, 207
Khidmat, 92
Khrushchev, Nikita, 218
Kidwai, Rafi Ahmed, 185, 187, 189, 190, 195, 203
Kilam, Pandit Jia Lal, 60
King Farouk of Egypt, 138
Kishtwar, 86, 128, 178
Kodaikanal, 291
Kohala, 46, 212–213
Kohala bridge, 46
Kothari, Rajni, 255
Kripalani, J.B., 121, 255
Krishnamachari, T.T., 240
Kud, 232

Ladakh, 56, 60, 64, 66, 86, 107, 149, 150–152, 167–168, 172, 177–178, 205, 211, 215, 217, 242–243, 305, 308
Lahore, 9, 59, 244, 292
Lake Success, 11, 17, 92–93, 103, 125
Lakshmi, Yuvrani Yasho Rajya, 81
Lal Dogra, Girdhari, 11, 35, 147
Lamb, Alastair, 36, 167–168, 291
Lateefi, Danyal, 60
Legislative Assembly, 33–34, 226, 228, 274, 295
Leh, 149, 150–151, 217, 242
Lhasa, 217
Link, 240, 241
Lohia, Ram Manohar, 255
Lok Sabha, 160, 255, 274–276, 278–280, 300, 304–306

Madhok, Balraj, 123, 154
Madhopur, 163, 217
Madras, 22, 171, 255, 258, 287
Mahajan, Mehr Chand, 12, 28
Majid, Bakshi Abdul, 262
Maksoud, Dr Clovis, 241
Malhotra, Inder, 285
Malviya, Pandit Madan Mohan, 82
Marshall, George, 169
Martyrs' Day, 53–54, 69, 74, 100
Masani, M.R., 255
Masoodi, Maulana Mohammad Syed, 28, 38, 189, 263, 268, 284, 313
Maxwell, Neville, 303
McCarthyism, 240
Medanish, 260
Medina, 259
Mehra, D.W., 195, 236
Mehta, Dr Jivraj, 300
Memorandum to the President of India, 66
Menon, K.P.S., 118
Menon, Krishna, 240
Menon, V.P., 103, 119
Ministry of States, 98, 119
Miraj-e-Alam, 261
Mirpur, 10, 58, 127
Mirwaiz, 251, 263, 284, 285
Moe-e-Muqaddas, 259–261, 263, 266–267, 272, 283–284, 288–289, 295–296, 298
Mohammad, Bakshi Ghulam, 1–2, 20, 92, 147–149, 151–152, 155, 163, 181, 184, 188–192, 195, 197–198, 201, 203–207, 209, 215–218, 222–225, 229, 233–238, 242, 247, 250–251, 254, 256–259, 261–262, 264, 266–267, 269, 270, 272–274, 280–284, 295–298, 306, 313, 319
Mohammad, Ghulam, 1–2, 20, 92, 147, 151, 155, 163, 184, 188, 195, 203, 215–216, 222, 224, 235–236, 238, 241, 250, 254, 256–258, 261–262, 269, 272–274, 281, 283–284, 296
Mohani, Maulana Hasrat, 25
Mountbatten, Lord Louis, 22–23, 26, 32, 37, 89, 103, 119, 121
Mujahid Manzil, 59, 191, 234
Mujawaza, 78, 205

Mukherjee, Dr Shyama Prasad, 126–127, 154, 159, 160–161, 163–164, 176, 180, 199
Mullik, B.N., 93, 129, 151–152, 165, 179–180, 187, 190, 197, 225, 231–232, 234–236, 251–252, 254, 258–259, 260, 263, 265–268, 285, 296
Muslim, 3, 8, 10, 20, 34–37, 41, 54, 58–59, 66, 82, 85, 90, 100, 115, 122, 123, 127–128, 135, 173, 175, 178, 184, 202, 213, 251–252, 265, 273, 284, 285
  Kashmiri-Muslim, 9
Muslim Conference, 8, 10, 20, 58, 66, 100, 123, 128, 135, 184, 251–252, 284, 285
Muzaffarabad, 66, 127, 285–286
Muzzafarabad, 10
Myrdal, Alva, 241
Myrdal, Gunnar, 241
Mysore, 23, 31, 118, 220

Nanda, Gulzarilal, 275–278, 281
Narayan, Jayaprakash, 180, 241
Nath, Wazir Janki, 145
National Conference, 1–2, 8–14, 17, 20–21, 28, 33, 35–50, 53, 56–61, 64, 65–71, 74–79, 85–86, 88, 92, 94–95, 99–100, 102, 106–107, 110, 121, 123–125, 128–129, 132–133, 135, 138, 140, 145, 147, 149, 153, 163, 170, 173, 180, 182–184, 190–191, 201, 205, 224, 227, 229, 234–236, 242, 250, 252, 257, 259, 261, 265, 269, 270, 272, 279, 280–282, 290, 301, 306, 318
  Working Committee, 40–42, 163, 189, 255
National Constituent Assembly, 24–27, 29, 33–35, 38, 47, 90–91, 126
Naya Kashmir, 58–60, 65–66, 85
Nayyar, Kuldip, 303–304
Nehru, Pandit Jawaharlal, 4–6, 13–16, 18–20, 22–24, 26–27, 30, 32, 35–37, 43–46, 48, 51–52, 58, 69, 80, 82–84, 86–87, 92, 96–97, 100–104, 121–122, 125, 128–130, 134, 136–145, 150–156, 158–163, 165, 167–168, 170–182, 184–185, 187–188, 190, 196–197, 201–206, 211, 216, 218–220, 222–225, 229, 231, 234–237, 240–242, 244–245, 248, 251–255, 257, 265–266, 268–269, 273–275, 278, 280–281, 283–287, 289, 296, 299, 302, 310, 319
Niazi, 232
Nishan Dez, 259–261, 267
Nizam of Hyderabad, 6, 89, 118, 132
Nowshera, 4

Oberoi, M.S., 215, 220
Operation Gibraltar, 291

Pakistan, 9–13, 15–16, 21, 23, 28, 34, 36–38, 46, 66, 89, 90, 92–95, 100, 109–112, 114–115, 121–123, 127, 144, 152, 155, 165, 169, 170, 173–175, 177, 178, 182, 187, 188, 193–194, 199, 202, 204, 206, 211–213, 215, 218–219, 222, 224–225, 228, 231–233, 237, 241–243, 251–253, 265–269, 279, 284–295, 298, 301–303, 306, 308, 311, 314–316, 318
Pakistani occupation, 31, 170
Pakistan Radio, 263
Palestine, 9
Panjab University, Shimla, 82
Pant, Gobind Vallabh, 232, 251
Panthal, 99
Partition, 9, 34, 90, 113, 154, 218, 244

Patel, Sardar Vallabhbhai, 3–7, 10–11, 13–18, 22–24, 28, 30, 35, 43, 45–46, 51–52, 57, 68, 80, 87, 89, 96–98, 101, 110, 117–119, 123, 131, 183, 243, 252
Pathankot, 161, 217, 242, 262, 294
Pathar Masjid, 234–235
Patil, S.K., 239, 255
Patnaik, Biju, 255–256
Peking, 217, 290
People's Courts, 63
People's Panchayats, 62–64
Permanent Residents, 207, 210
Plebiscite, 11, 18–19, 21, 25–26, 28, 32, 36–37, 88, 93–94, 120, 127, 144, 172, 178, 202, 204, 228, 230, 237, 279
Plebiscite Administrator, 203
Plebiscite Front, 218, 230–233, 237, 256–257, 277, 279, 280–281, 284, 289–291, 295, 297–298, 301, 302
Poonch, 11, 58, 60, 64, 107, 127, 178
Praja Parishad, 1, 33, 74, 101–102, 106, 122, 123–127, 129, 130, 140, 142–143, 146, 152–153–156, 158, 160–162, 164–168, 174, 180, 188, 190, 229, 247, 259, 265, 271, 281, 309
Praja Sabha, 33–34, 71
Praja Socialist Party, 259, 265, 281
Prasad, Dr Rajendra, 27, 87, 102, 144, 171, 210, 212
President of India, 47, 136, 167
Price, Ward, 15
Prime Minister of the State, 1, 21, 33, 38, 42, 87, 98, 158, 194, 252, 256, 258, 273, 274
Princely States, 8, 21, 23, 25, 31, 59, 89, 117–119, 121, 207, 208
Princes, 23, 89, 117, 119, 121, 207, 248
Privy Council of the King of England, 72
privy purse, 118, 249
Proclamation of 5th March 1948, 5, 8, 27–29, 31, 38, 48, 50–52, 54–55, 64, 67–73, 88, 95–96, 98–99, 103–106, 133, 228
Progressive Writers' Movement, 58
Prophet Muhammad, 235, 237, 259, 260–261, 266
Pukhraj, Malka, 244
Punjab, 9, 15, 58, 74, 123, 128, 152, 155, 160, 163, 168, 217–218, 268, 292–293, 304
Punjab University, Lahore, 82
Puri, Balraj, 35, 65, 67, 79, 85–86, 92

Qasim, Khwaja Mir, 201
Qasim, Mir, 189, 226–229, 262, 308
Quit India Movement, 59
Quran, 268
Qureshi, Mohammad Shafi, 189, 259

Radcliffe Commission, 213
Radcliffe Line, 179
Radhakrishnan, Dr, 271, 299, 306, 307
Raghunath Temple, 2, 82, 294
Rajgarh Palace, 145
Rajkot, 255
Rajouri, 178
Rajpramukh, 23, 118, 132, 157, 220
Rajputs, 61, 158, 243, 271
Rajya Sabha, 255
Ram Rajya Parishad, 126, 159, 174
Ram, Bhagat Chhajju, 67
Ram, Jagjivan, 255
Ramban, 178
Ranbirsinghpura, 74, 128, 147, 171, 173, 232
Ranga, N.G., 278
Rann of Kutch, 288, 302
Rashid, Bakshi Abdul, 254, 258, 261, 262
Rashtriya Swayamsevak Sangh, 123, 129
Rawalpindi, 232, 285
Razakar, 21
Reading Room, 58, 168
Reasi, 178

Renzu, Ghulam Rasool, 201
Representation of People's Act, 228
Republic Day, 177, 235–237, 268, 287
Reserved list, 28
Reserved subjects, 23, 30
Rishis, 173
River Ravi, 163
River Sutlej, 213
Robespierre, 111
Rohtang Pass, 217
Rondu, 66
Roy, Dr B.C., 164, 180
RSS. *See* Rashtriya Swayamsevak Sangh
Russian Revolution, 58

Sadiq, Ghulam Mohammad, 147–148, 152, 163, 188–189, 192, 201, 227, 235, 250, 254, 257–258, 262, 265, 269, 272–274, 278, 281–282, 284, 290, 291, 295–299, 306, 308, 313
Sahay, Vishnu, 54, 96, 97
Samba, 158
Sarabhai, Mridula, 185, 232, 254
Saraf, Ram Piara, 35, 67, 242
Saraf, Sham Lal, 11, 35, 147, 188, 190–191, 193, 201
Sarila, Narinder Singh, 22
Scindia of Gwalior, 34
Second World War, 59, 88, 212
Security Council, 3–4, 17, 19, 23, 30, 43, 80, 88, 91, 93–94, 120, 154, 165, 168, 226, 228, 230–232, 278, 279
Seminar, 241
Sethi, Krishen Dev, 16, 242
Shah, Faqir Mirak, 268
Shah, Ibrahim, 150
Shah, K.T., 25–26, 32, 285
Shah, Maulavi Yusuf, 251
Shahjahan, 259, 260
Shahmiri. M.A., 140
Shamsuddin, 258, 262–266, 268, 274, 282
Shastri, Lal Bahadur, 248, 253, 255, 268, 278, 288–290, 292, 293, 299–301, 304
Shastri, Prakash Vir, 275
Sheikh Farooq. *See* Abdullah, Farooq
Shergarhi Police Station, 267
Sialkot, 217–218, 292
Sikh, 35, 41, 153, 265
Singh, Captain Ajit, 213
Singh, Captain Hoshnak, 213
Singh, General Zorawar, 149
Singh, Jyoti, 124, 294
Singh, Kapur, 278
Singh, L/Nk Sunder, 214
Singh, Lieutenant Colonel Vakil, 213
Singh, Maharaja Gulab, 82, 84, 132, 134, 149, 168, 178, 294, 303, 307
Singh, Maharaja Hari, 2–8, 10–35, 37–38, 40, 42–44, 47–48, 50–52, 55–62, 65–74, 80, 83, 85, 88–91, 95–96, 99–104, 109–114, 118–123, 127, 129, 131–134, 137, 143, 144, 146, 152–153, 156, 161, 168, 175, 194, 200, 208, 215, 220, 228–229, 243–249, 252, 257, 271, 303
Singh, Maharaja Ranbir, 132
Singh, Maharaja Ranjit, 294
Singh, Major Brahma, 214
Singh, Major Mahel, 213
Singh, Major Rashpal, 213
Singh, Masha Nahar, 67, 133, 145
Singh, Master Tara, 154
Singh, Sardar Swarn, 240
Singh, Vikramaditya, 294, 302
Singh, Yuvraj Karan, 1–2, 5–8, 14, 19–21, 23–24, 30, 51–52, 54–55, 71–72, 81–85, 87, 91, 95–106, 111, 130–147, 149, 150–152, 154, 156–164, 168, 170, 174, 176–177, 179, 188, 190, 192, 196–197, 199, 200, 203, 205, 206, 211–212, 215–217, 219, 220–226, 234, 239, 240–249, 254, 256–257,

262, 264–265, 271, 273, 289, 294–295, 297, 299, 301–309
Regent, 6–8, 19–21, 23–24, 27–29, 51–52, 54, 69, 71–73, 81, 83, 85, 87, 89, 96, 98, 104, 106, 111, 120, 131–133, 242–243, 294, 299, 302–304, 307
Sadar-i-Riyasat, 2, 132, 145 146, 149, 160, 163–164, 174, 179, 188, 191–201, 203, 205, 218, 220–222, 225, 241, 248, 249, 254, 256–257, 262–267, 271, 273–274, 278, 282–283, 289, 294–295, 297–303
Skardu, 3–4
Southeast Asia Treaty Organization (SEATO), 287
Spear, Dr Percival, 168
Srinagar, 1, 4, 7, 16, 20, 43, 53, 58, 76, 84, 85, 107, 121, 128, 142, 150–152, 157, 163, 164, 170, 173, 175, 179, 180, 185–186, 188–189, 195, 197, 201, 203–204, 216–218, 220, 233, 235–236, 242, 246, 254, 261–264, 268, 294–296, 303, 308, 314, 316
Standstill Agreement, 16, 118, 119
State Flag, 136, 146–149, 157, 161
State Museum, Srinagar, 82
State Subjects, 207–208, 218
States Ministry, 13
States Reorganization Commission, 225, 304
Stephens, Ian, 175
Stevenson II, Adlai, 170
Sunderbani, 158

Tamil Nadu, 287, 301
Tandon, Purshottam Das, 180
Tara House, 298
Taragabal, 178
Taseer, Mohammad Din, 60
Tashkent, 293, 302
Tawi, 247–248
Thakur, Laksman Das, 263
Thapar, Raj, 241
Thapar, Romesh, 241
The Affluent Society (John Kenneth Galbraith), 240
The Daily Telegraph, 93, 204
The Great Crash (John Kenneth Galbraith), 240
The Guardian, 93
The London Times, 303
The New York Times, 93, 204
The Observer, 15
The Scotsman, 15, 16
The Statesman, 175
The Washington Post, 93
Thimayya, General K.S., 215
Thorner, Daniel, 75–79, 240
Titwal, 178
Travancore, 21–23

Udhampur, 128–129, 178, 195, 242, 298
United Nations, 3–4, 15, 19, 30–31, 35, 81, 87–88, 93–94, 112, 116, 167, 187, 230
United Nations Commission, 87
Uri, 178
USA, 1, 15, 43, 93, 116, 204, 219, 239, 240, 241, 253

Vaid, Guru Dutt, 180
Vedanta philosophy, 294

Wazir Wazarat, 86
Wazir, J.K., 86, 145, 307
Weiner, Myron, 126, 240
Wigami, Pir Maqbool, 237
Wilson, Harold, 288

Xinjiang, 9, 286

Zamindari, 75
Zanskar, 150–151
Zoji La Pass, 4, 17

ALSO FROM SPEAKING TIGER

A MODERN HISTORY OF JAMMU AND KASHMIR, VOLUME ONE

THE TROUBLED YEARS OF MAHARAJA HARI SINGH (1925-1949)

Harbans Singh

The modern history of Jammu and Kashmir is often focused mainly on the Kashmir valley, leaving out the other regions that make up the bulk of the erstwhile Princely State. A similar limitation marks most discussions of the rule of the fourth-generation Dogra ruler of Jammu and Kashmir, Maharaja Hari Singh. After his inheritance of the throne in 1925, Hari Singh introduced a number of progressive reforms—among them, programmes for girl education, opening temple doors for Dalits and abolishing the exploitative *begar* system of labour. However, contemporary historians look past these reforms and focus only on the issue of the accession of the State to India.

At a time when the entire subcontinent was reeling from the shock and violence of Partition, the Maharaja had to decide which dominion—India or Pakistan—the State would join. How was he to choose where to put his trust, especially after Pakistan-backed Pashtun tribals invaded the State and India refused to offer military help? Was any decision possible that would appease all—the Muslim majority of Kashmir, the Hindu majority of Jammu and the Buddhist majority of Ladakh?

Those tumultuous times took a toll on Hari Singh during the final years of his reign. Accession to India was not as easy as he had hoped, and pressurised by Nehru and Sardar Patel, the Maharaja was forced to choose exile in 1949 and spent the rest of his days in Bombay. Harbans Singh's *A Modern History of Jammu and Kashmir, Volume One: The Troubled Years of Maharaja Hari Singh (1925-1949)* offers a more rounded history of the State than most available scholarship. The first volume in a trilogy, this book offers a strong and nuanced defence of the last ruler of Jammu and Kashmir and is a valuable document in understanding its evolving history.